NEW LIGHT ON GEORGE FOX AND EARLY QUAKERISM

The Making and Unmaking of a God

NEW LIGHT ON GEORGE FOX
AND EARLY QUAKERISM
The Making and Unmaking of a God

Richard Bailey

Mellen Research University Press
San Francisco

Library of Congress Cataloging-in-Publication Data

Bailey, Richard (Richard George)
    New light on George Fox and early Quakerism / Richard Bailey.
        p. cm.
    Includes bibliographical references and index.
    ISBN 0-7734-9829-X
    1. Fox, George, 1624-1691. 2. Quakers--England--History--17th
century. 3. England--Church history--17th century. I. Title.
BX7676.2.B25   1992
289.6'09'032--dc20   92-27477
                                                                          CIP

Editorial Inquiries:

Mellen Research University Press
534 Pacific Avenue
San Francisco
CA 94133

Order Fulfillment:

The Edwin Mellen Press
P.O. Box 450
Lewiston, NY 14092
USA

Printed in the United States of America

To John F. H. New

Si veritatem quaerimus,

scientiam invenimus

TABLE OF CONTENTS

COMMENDATORY FOREWORD

FOREWORD (I)

In his preface to *The History of Pendinnis*, William Makepeace Thackeray wrote, "If truth is not always pleasant; at any rate truth is best, from whatever chair." This book's author is sensitive that his picture of George Fox as a theological radical might distress historians who like to belittle the power of religious convictions in a world where everyone (except Pascal's hypothetical atheist) assumed that all creation and earth's Destiny were divinely ordained and everyday reality was sustained by Divine power. His portrait, however disturbing, carries the shock of recognition. Suddenly those elements of Fox's story that have been set aside, ignored, even ridiculed, take on new purpose. And what is true of Fox holds true for the early Quakers. The self-affirmation of poor unenfranchised Quakers takes on integrity and grandeur. They are transfigured.

The root of this is what Dr. Bailey believes to have been the original sense of the inner light, which was the pan-historical, pre-existent Christ – The Spirit, conceived as substantial, was conflated with this Christ – who inhabited the believer in the form of celestial flesh and bone. Flesh and bone, not metaphysical body and blood! The idea is of the heavenly, eternal body of Christ the light becoming physically manifest in the saint in some palpable fashion. To be honest, given the limitations of our time and circumstance, our imaginations fail us. Can we grasp what it must have meant to harbour such a conviction? The volatile behaviour of Fox and early Quakers who believed Christ was embodied in them in this way is suddenly comprehensible. At least we can touch the surface texture of the belief, and feel some *frisson* of excitement, though a deeper empathy eludes us. One can see why they quaked when they were "in the power of the Scriptures," for that power of scriptures, the celestial Christ, was literally in them.

The author has suffered the pangs of originality, the isolation and the doubt. There have been so many exemplary scholars of Quakerism, yet none has seen what he has seen. It is a truism that what we don't know is perceived through the prisms of what we do. Fortunately, before turning to Fox, Dr. Bailey was thoroughly schooled in radical Anabaptist thought where hints of the doctrine of celestial flesh can be found in some Anabaptists' notions of the Incarnation and the Supper. Fox moved a giant step further than these foreshadowers. What was earlier a doctrine about Christ was extended to a doctrine about true believers.

It is not odd, then, that Fox (or Nayler or Howgill) should have been regarded as blasphemous by the orthodox. Since the grounds for this judgement were (and still are) so very sectarian, the fair historian must abandon the reckoning of theological "truth" to seek the deeper truth of why such charges were levelled and what lay behind them. Dr. Bailey has done this with remarkable calm. The reader might well think that the discussion of Fox's Lancaster trial is the most perceptive and judicious to have appeared. Who can say without bias that Fox's sense of the inner light is less sensible and less weighty a key to the meaning of the New Testament than Milton's doctrine of Christian liberty, or Tyndale's Covenant theology, or Luther's Justification by faith alone?

Fox lies outside the circle of Calvinist or Armenian theologies alike. They were pre-occupied by atonement, while Fox's is a theology of fulfillment. Fox's view, it should be added, was not a disembodied Spirit theology. In showing us the sources of this charismatic revival, Dr. Bailey is giving us something fresh. He implies that charismatic movements vary; they feed on ideas; and ideas have histories. His discussion of the process of retreat from the original ecstasies is equally well done, showing Fox clinging bravely, if forlornly, to a theme others were abandoning.

A gracious English scholar of the social history of Quakerism has called the argument brilliant, challenging and profound. Clearly nobody in English seventeenth century studies can afford to miss it. In future its thesis may be questioned, qualified, expanded, refined. But it remains the most interesting thing to appear on Quaker origins in a long, long time.

As for Fox, whose body contained the Celestial Flesh, he takes on intellectual flesh as never before. His doings make sense as never before. If this Fox is flawed, he is vastly intriguing, vastly audacious.

John F.H. New
Trumpington, Cambridge

FOREWORD (II)

In this monograph, Richard G. Bailey has produced one of the most challenging and remarkable historical reinterpretations of George Fox, the early leader of the Society of Friends, to appear in many years. From the time of the Restoration of the Stuart monarchy in 1600 onward, the second generation of Quakers – especially those with higher social standing and education – began to modify the theology and religious practices of their forebearers to better fit into the new context of always open and sometimes vicious persecution. "Enthusiasm" lost its positive meaning and "respectability" became the watchword for survival. Dr. Bailey's book shows how Fox himself, although remaining a figure of veneration and retaining more of the original theology than his successors, participated in these changes. After his death, the process accelerated and deepened to the point of deliberate suppression of evidence which might mislead the faithful; for example, the "official" edition of Fox's *Journal*, edited by Thomas Ellwood, first appeared in 1694 with many references to the "miracles" which he had performed and other manifestations of ecstatic behavior which no longer seemed respectable deleted from the text. Enough of the original material remained in this edition the *Journal*, however, to give the reader a strong impression of the zeal and spirit driven strength of George Fox. During the early part of present century, Quakers scholars began to redress the balance by reinterpreting their early history and sources of their fellowship, for example, with Norman Penney editing the text of the Spence manuscript as The *Journal of George Fox*, 2 vol. (Cambridge, 1911) and of experiences dictated by Fox 1664 as *The Short Journal of George Fox* (Cambridge, 1925), William Braithwaite publishing his magisterial, *The Beginnings of Quakerism* (London, 1912), Henry J. Cadbury recreating and publishing *George Fox's Book of Miracles* (Cambridge, 1948).

The present monograph carries that task forward by drawing deeply upon the manuscript and printed sources produced by George Fox and his contemporaries to argue that the early Quakers followed a Christocentric, immanent theology which stressed ecstatic experience, interpreted as the possession of the inner person by the pre-existent spirit of God, as normative. Although all of the early Friends, experienced what Bailey calls "celestial inhabitation", this was especially true of Fox, who was seen by some of his followers as possessing an equally divine spirit as Jesus, and, for some early Friends, of the man who many have seen as his rival, James Nayler. While historians have long agreed upon the importance of the spirt of God for Fox and the early Quakers, Bailey redefines the meaning of this spirit on the basis of Fox's letters, writings, and actions. This redefinition, in terms of celestial inhabitation by a God whose being is spirit, throws a good deal of light on many of the actions and words of Fox, his enemies, and his supporters. It narrows the distance between Fox and Nayler in the 1650's and provides theological reasons for their disputes. It helps us better to understand the female Quaker prophets currently being studied by Phyllis Mack and their role in the early gatherings of the Friends. It provides a reason for some of the shifts in Quaker theology which took place even before the Restoration and sheds light on the further changes which took place later. As Bailey shows, the passing away of the theology of "celestial inhabitation" necessitated changes in early texts, deletions in letters, for example, which he credits to Fox, so that he traces the first major reinterpretation of the theology of the Friends back to the first generation of witnesses. Much recent writing on the early Quakers, especially in such books as Richard T. Vann, *The Social Development of English Quakerism, 1655-1700* (Cambridge, Mass., 1969), Christopher Hill, *The World Turned Upside Down: Radical Ideas during the English Revolution* (London, 1972), J. F.. McGregor and Barry Reay, ed., *Radical Religion in the English Revolution* (Oxford, 1984) and Barry Reay, *The Quakers and the English Revolution* (New York, 1985), the stress upon social history had almost displaced theological considerations. So strong had this focus become that in Reay's history, George Fox, James Nayler, and the other early leaders of the Society of Friends almost disappeared from view! For this reader, the focus provided by Richard G. Bailey will provide a welcome shift in emphasis back to the personal and theological concerns which impacted so strongly upon those who experienced the English Revolution.

Paul Christianson
Queen's University

PREFACE

Very little adverse historiography has been done on George Fox. The sources do turn up awkward facts about his life but they are often pushed to the fringes or reinterpreted in the interests of respectability and orthodoxy. By piecing together bowdlerized fragments and re-emphasizing Fox's electrifying doctrine of celestial inhabitation (the notion that the saints became flesh and bone of Christ) an unusual picture of Fox and early Quakerism begins to emerge: a picture which makes sense of a whole spectrum of embarrassing indecorous activity and exalted language, as well as the rage of opponents.

To get under and behind the exalted language is to rediscover a power in early Quakerism that emanated from a centre best defined as a christopresent (not simply christocentric) inner light. Fox's christopresentism divinized the saints and gave Quaker theology its principle of social compensation, as Professor New calls it, first in an interior psychological sense and then externally. The knowledge that Christ's flesh and bone permanently possessed the saint, literally, created perfervid behaviour: continuous ecstasy and exalted language. What was involved in the early stages of Quakerism was a recrudescence of early Christian charismata; a recrudescence, too, of one aspect of Gnosticism - that of the divine in the person.

Celestial inhabitation simply strikes the twentieth century reader as 'otherness' and incomprehensible 'strangeness'. But it was not naive, immature, or inadequate theology. Rather, a serious effort needs to be made to sympathetically understand it and the high language it fostered. This is all the more important because there is a direct link between Fox's notion of celestial inhabitation, the exalted language, the Nayler incident and the Quaker deportment of bravado in society. The eccentric aspects about Fox and early Quakerism reveal a conception about the process of history quite different from the expectations of orthodox religion and they are made central here not to be trivial but because they help to explain the plight of the early Quaker who was braced by an extraordinary conviction that has not been fully appreciated.

A work of this length and scope cannot be completed without the support and guidance of many helpful persons. Parts of the manuscript have already been read at the Friends' Historical Society Meeting, London, England (June, 1990); the International Conference on George Fox held at Lancaster University, England (March, 1991) and the Humanities Lecture Series at Bishop's University, Quebec (January, 1992). Bishop's University also provided generous financial resources necessary to complete this project.

Professor Kenneth Davis, Professor James Stayer and Professor Walter Klaassen deserve mention for their interest in my earlier enquiries. As members of my dissertation committee Professor Paul Christianson, Professor Stanley Johannessen and Professor E. Palmer Patterson have made useful suggestions, many of which are incorporated in the following pages. Professor Michael Mullett has been a constant source of encouragement and advise.

Thanks must go to Malcolm Thomas and the staff at Friends Reference Library (London) who have been very patient and helpful. The staffs at Dr. Williams Library, the University of London library, the British Library, the Bodleian library, Christ Church library (Oxford), Fisher Rare Book Library (University of Toronto), Swarthmore College, Haverford College and Friends' House (Toronto) have also been helpful and generous in granting me use of library and archival facilities. Jane Zavitz, archivist at Pickering College, was always willing to answer my many questions about Friends past and present.

Very special thanks go to my *Doktorvater*, Professor John New, who rekindled my excitement in historical research and writing and above all taught me the importance of getting under and behind prevailing views of things with an ever-searching, ever-critical hermeneutics of benign doubt. From him I learned to look for what is not written in the traditional historiography and to look ever closer at the period's literature. I learned to let the sources speak as much as they can for themselves without falling prey to artificial intellectual constructs (which albeit are somewhat necessary to write history) either because they are respectable, comfortable or fashionable. I thank him for his friendship and the great care he took to advise me and encourage me, especially at times when I desperately wanted to flee from contention and controversy and remain safe within the house of respectability.

Last but not least, I wish to express my special gratitude to my friend and wife, Skye G. McFadden. She has been a constant support and inspiration. She introduced me to Henri Ellenberger's magisterial commentary, *The Discovery of the Unconscious*, which provided new insights at a critical juncture in the writing. Her classical French lycée education, her keen intellect, her language skills, and her broad reading have, over the years, been the bulwark against my own shortcomings. It was Skye who kindly consented to proofread the manuscript. The errors and omissions that remain are my own.

ABBREVIATIONS

Ann. Cat.	*Annual Catalogue of George Fox's Papers.* (Compiled 1694-1697). Ed. by H. Cadbury.
BFHS	*Bulletin of the Friends' Historical Society*
BIHR	*Bulletin of the Institute of Historical Research*
BL	British Library
Bodl.	Bodleian Library
BQ	*Baptist Quarterly*
CH	*Church History*
DNB	*Dictionary of National Biography*
FRL	Friends Reference Library (London)
JEH	*Journal of Ecclesiastical History*
JFHS	*Journal of the Friends' Historical Society*
JIH	*Journal of Interdisciplinary History*
JR	*Journal of Religion*
JRH	*Journal of Religious History*
ORS	*Original Records of Sufferings*, FRL (London)
P&P	*Past and Present*
QH	*Quaker History*
SC	*The Seventeenth Century Journal*
SCJ	*Sixteenth Century Journal*
Swarth Mss	*Swarthmore Manuscripts*, FRL (London)

They that saw his glory were ministers of the word, the only begotten Son of the Father, full of grace and truth; which same word is now manifest that ever was, Christ the same today, yesterday and forever: and saith Christ, 'If they call them gods to whom the word of God came, the scripture cannot be broken'; and saith Christ, 'As it is written in your law, I say you are gods'.

George Fox
Works, 4, p. 93

INTRODUCTION

Early Quakerism is a field well harvested. I am a gleaner at the harvest after the reapers have passed; a prospector searching for tailings after the mining has been done. And yet, there has been some grain to find and nuggets to discover. I acknowledge the reapers and miners who passed before me not only for the massive work they did but for the little work they left undone.

This study, the centrepiece of a trilogy on early Quakerism, pursues the theme that George Fox was a charismatic prophet, a magus and, above all, an avatar. These terms may sound anachronistic. In the seventeenth century and earlier the term "magus" was tainted by association with necromancy. Indeed, Fox wrote a tract against Simon Magus and he would have called anyone who called him a magus an "evil spirit". But essentially magus and wonder-worker are the same thing and Fox was indisputably a wonder-worker, a worker of miracles and more: he was thought to appear and disappear at will. Enough people in seventeenth century England thought of Fox as a magus to warrant use of the term. Nor would Fox have appreciated comparison with the Hindu "avatar". But avatar, precisely, is the "descent of deity" and again, Fox was indisputably a manifestation of deity and he was exalted as such. The term is not used here in association with the original mythic appearances of Vishnu. Both terms express the importance of the argument and suggest that Fox's characteristics need not be bound to the Christian tradition alone. There are wider associations with other global religions. The terms are not a distortion and need not create barriers because they remove the discussion from the Christian language used by Fox.

The magus, like a shaman, was an instrument connecting unearthly and earthly spheres. He could summon the eternal 'spirit' realm and its powers to the temporal. By special preparations and knowledge he could perform the inexplicable, make specific prophecies, and do miracles of all sorts ranging from healings to teleportations. He had a revolutionary influence on human behavior, especially among the ordinary people who were sometimes promised a new world of justice and equality - a new world where the oppressed would rule.

An avatar would also command magus powers. His authenticity was often confirmed by long periods of trial and suffering, followed by visionary breakthroughs and the working of signs and wonders. He unlocked the physical and spiritual secrets of the universe and personified a cosmic drama in which humans were wedded to gods or God.

The life and work of the avatar, who commanded magus powers, is best defined as revelatory and prophetic, not in the sense he foretold the future although that kind of prophecy may have been involved, but in the sense he made remarkable declarations disclosing divine purpose - the divine was momentarily immanent and the divine plan was made known. The traditional chasm between heaven and earth was closed. Humans were touched by divinity. Jewish-Christian messiahs are our familiar example.

Like some ancient Gnostics Fox was devoted to a notion that stressed unity and identity with the divine rather than distinctiveness. Fox could not have read the Gnostics since their works lay buried from the fourth century to the very recent past but the genealogy was not completely unbroken. Some Cathars and Anabaptists did revive Gnostic notions, as did the Elizabethan natural philosopher and magus John Dee. Quite unconsciously of Gnosticism, this idea cropped up in Fox as it did from time to time like spring water bubbling beneath the surface of human experience. The emphasis on unity with the divine terrified the orthodox because it led to an anarchy of ideas - "notionism". They feared a loss of uniformity; they feared chaos from a lack of obedience and discipline. Had Gnosticism become orthodoxy, had Valentinus become Bishop of Rome, then things might have been very different. As it was, Gnosticism became a subterranean religion of those on the margins - buried for centuries to erupt here and there, in one form or another - surfacing to fill a need to know for those who wanted direct knowledge because they did not have the education or sophistication for indirect knowledge, fancy exegesis and doctrinal indoctrinations.[1]

George Fox and the religion he founded was but a short chapter in the recurring history of the magus. The appearance of such a person had been prefigured in sacred writings for over a century. Sebastian Franck, Henry Barrowe, the Collegiants and the English Seekers all waited for one who would re-establish the true Gospel Order and attest to God's presence with signs and miracles.[2] And then in the mid-1640's George Fox appeared preaching and working signs and wonders throughout the English Midlands - a fulfillment some thought of Margaret Fell's vision of the coming of a 'teacher of righteousness' and Jacob Boehme's prophecy that the 'Lily' (signifying the dawning of the new age) would come from the 'north'.[3] Curiously, at the same time in Smyrna a young Sabbatai Zevi had gathered a small following and proclaimed himself the 'Messiah' in fulfillment of a view prevalent among Jews of the time that the Messiah would appear in 1648 and his coming would be accompanied by miracles and a new age of redemption.[4]

---

[1]The most recent work on Dee is N.H. Clulee, *John Dee's Natural Philosophy: Between Science and Religion* (Routledge, 1988). John Owen spoke of Gnostic tendencies in Quakerism with reference to their replacing the historic Christ with the inner light [John Owen, *Collected Works*, ed. by W.H. Goold, 1 (1850), p. 38 and vol. 4, p. 331].

[2]Henry J. Cadbury, ed., *George Fox's Book of Miracles'* (Cambridge: Cambridge University Press, 1948), pp. x-xi. Seekers believed one's true 'calling' as a minister of the gospel was confirmed through miracles. One Seeker, Clement Wrighter, expected Fox to confirm his call by miracles.

[3]The prophetic symbolism of the 'lily' was ancient. It was used in the *Prophecy of Thomas Becket*, a prophecy of obscure origin and published in England in 1645 by William Lilly [*see* Keith Thomas, *Religion and the Decline of Magic* (Penguin University Books, 1973), p. 468]. Margaret Fell's vision of a "man who would come and confound the priests" is recorded in the *Spence MS.* of Fox's *Journal* [Norman Penney, ed., *The Journal of George Fox*, 1 (London: Cambridge University Press, 1911), p. 52. Hereafter cited as the *Cambridge Journal*].

[4]Described in L. Festinger, *When Prophecy Fails* (University of Minnesota Press, 1956), p. 8.

Fox was the son of a Leicestershire weaver. He was a shoemaker's apprentice when in 1643, at the age of nineteen, he left home "at the command of God" as he tells us in the opening pages of his *Journal*.[5] He was seeking answers to an undefined youthful identity crisis.[6] His quest initially proved fruitless and he grew increasingly discouraged. He questioned and disputed with numerous "professors" (Puritans) but none was able to satisfy his unsettled state. He found no bard, no answers and no religious fellowship. He became skeptical of any human solution to what we may interpret as a profound personal problem.

He began to spend more and more time alone. He wandered through the Midlands, traversing fields and orchards, sitting in hollow trees reading his Bible and sleeping in haystacks. He said he came under great temptations and overcame them through fasting. He adhered to no religion, travelling instead "up and down as a stranger in the earth."[7] Around him the Royal and Parliamentary armies were locked in an epic struggle. Fox's peers were rushing to battle in the name of the Good Old Cause. But Fox was locked in his own epic struggle that would eventually give birth not to a worldly commonwealth but to what he believed was the very Kingdom of God.

During this time he had several major 'openings': God did not dwell in temples made of hands; being bred at Oxford or Cambridge did not fit one to be a minister of Christ and the knowledge of God did not come by history or books, leading Jones to identify Fox as the "genuine apostolic successor of

---

[5]J.L. Nickalls. ed., *The Journal of George Fox* (London: Religious Society of Friends, 1952), p. 3. Hereafter cited as Nickalls, *Journal*.

[6]We know very little about Fox's youth or what prompted him to leave home. Maybe he was resisting pressure to join in the civil war. Michael Watts thinks that his crisis was "associated with the awakening of sexual desires" [*The Dissenters From the Reformation to the French Revolution* (Oxford: Clarendon, 1985), p. 187]. *See also* Lawrence Stone, *The Family, Sex and Marriage in England, 1500-1800* (New York: Harper and Row, 1977), p. 615. Stone says the repression of sexual desires "was undoubtedly aided by the moral pressures of Puritanism".

[7]Nickalls, *Journal*, p. 10.

Wyclif's 'Evangelical Men'".[8] These revelations lead Jones to identify Fox as the "genuine apostolic successor to Wyclif's 'Evangelical Men'. Also during this time of long solitude there were mystical and visionary experiences and other times when God spoke audibly to him. He discovered that knowledge of God did not come from any external source but from inward revelation.[9]

Slowly Fox came into a sense of God's purpose for his life and it was a prophetic one - the universal proclamation of the 'everlasting gospel' or the power of God to restore all things to Paradise.[10] But he was more than a mere prophet. He became known as a man who had been taken up to Paradise and had seen things "not fit to declare".[11] Among these great revelations was the fact that Christ, the 'first-speaker' to Adam and Eve in Paradise was once again 'first-speaker' to the world. And Fox was the one chosen to declare and complete God's work of restoration. Confirmation of Fox's special powers and divine status came through a multitude of wonders that included visions, prophecies, healings and the casting out of demons.[12]

---

[8]Rufus Jones, *Studies in Mystical Religion* (New York: Russell and Russell, 1909), p. 366.

[9]Nickalls, *Journal*, p. 11.

[10]In 1674/75 Fox dated the beginning of his ministry back to 1644 when he says he was divinely commissioned to declare the everlasting gospel [*A Collection of Many Select and Christian Epistles* (1698), in *The Works of George Fox*, 7-8 (Philadelphia: Marcus Goold, 1831), 8, pp. 61. Hereafter cited as *Epistles*].

[11]Nickalls, *Journal*, p. 10.

[12]*Ibid.*, pp. 21, 43. Henry Cadbury, ed., *Narrative Papers of George Fox* (Richmond, Indiana: Friends United Press, 1973), p. 12. Fox eventually documented over 150 miracles and gathered them into a now lost lost *Book of Miracles*, meticulously reconstructed by Henry Cadbury from annotations in the *Annual Catalogue of George Fox's Papers* [Henry Cadbury, ed., *Annual Catalogue of George Fox's Papers* (London: Religious Society of Friends, 1939)]. The *Annual Catalogue* was compiled between 1694 and 1697 and was an attempt to annotate all of George Fox's extant papers and epistles. It is the most complete catalogue of Fox's works in existence. Unfortunately a very large number of sources used and annotated are now lost. From this catalogue and its extensive index Cadbury was not only able to piece together the *Book of Miracles* but bring to light numerous lost documents in the hope they would be found in extant *MSS.* collections, private collections and larger printed works.

When, as Fox put it, the "Lord's power" first began to "brake forth" it was 1644 and Fox was twenty years old.[13]

What has been described here are the stock features of the avatar/magus type, adapted from E.M. Butler's *The Myth of the Magus*: portents before birth, supernatural initiation, far distant wanderings, trials, and tribulations all followed by visionary openings and miracles.[14] Much of this dimension of Fox's life and work was edited out of the sources shortly after his death, under the supervision of the Second Day's Morning Meeting which censored Quaker publications in the interests of curbing the 'enthusiasm' of the early years. Over forty-five years ago, in a debate published in the *Journal of Religion* (1944) Winthrop Hudson charged that Quaker sources had been bowdlerized in the interests of both respectability and hagiography. Henry Cadbury ably responded to Hudson's charges but one undisputed fact remained - Quaker sources had been selectively edited. Hudson said that it involved matters of substance. Cadbury said that it involved matters of indifference, of adiaphora. He argued that highly sensitive material was considered damaging to the movement and by bowdlerizing the sources Quakers were able to get some respite from heavy persecution. The intentions were noble.[15]

---

[13]*Epistles*, 7, p. 10. This Epistle was written in 1676.

[14]E.M. Butler, *The Myth of the Magus* (London: Cambridge University Press, 1948). *See also* P. Grant, "Imagination in the Renaissance," in *Religious Imagination*, ed. by J.P. Mackey (Edinburgh: Edinburgh University Press, 1986), p. 86.

[15]Most recently H. Larry Ingle has raised similar charges, using lively language to accuse Quakers of "whoring after the goddess Respectability". Ingle does not generally advance on Hudson's earlier charges. But he has brought to light a relatively unknown thesis by Aimo Seppänen. Ingle calls Seppänen's work "the best, most balanced, theological analysis of Fox I have ever read". Seppänen's careful assessment of Fox's theological language reaffirms the conclusions reached by leading Quaker interpreters of this century, many of whom helped to create the theological mould which Ingle seems to be trying to belittle: W.C. Braithwaite, Rachel King, Neave Brayshaw, Hugh Barbour and Lewis Benson [H. Larry Ingle, "On the Folly of Seeking the Quaker Holy Grail," *Quaker Religious Thought*, 25 (No. 1, 1991), pp. 17-29]. Ingle's article is followed by comments from Douglas Gwyn and Hugh Barbour. Seppänen's L.Phil. dissertation, done at the University of Helsinki in 1965, is entitled "The Inner Light in the Journals of George Fox: A Semantic Study". It was later published by the Department of English Philology, University of Tampere.

For over two centuries certain things deemed 'unseemly' were hidden from public view. That began to change earlier this century with the publication of the original *MSS.* containing the *Short Journal* and the *Journal* of George Fox. This enabled a critical comparison of the bowdlerized features of Fox's *Journal* to begin. The most thorough comparative work was done by Henry Cadbury.[16] The majority of the hundreds of changes were found to be no more than cosmetic in nature, a stylizing of the text, but some changes were substantive and suggested a deliberate attempt to minimize Fox's early status as an avatar and diminish but not totally cut out the signs and wonders aspect of his ministry. This dimension of Fox's life and message is documented but it continues to occupy a hidden position in Quaker historiography.

The purpose of this study is to draw out the charismatic part of Fox's life and message and go beyond what Ibn Khaldun called "tradition-bound" history, to offer a new and hopefully more convincing explanation for the rapid change in early Quakerism. It is not a sophisticated theological study following the example of Maurice Creasey on Isaac Penington or Melvin Endy on William Penn. Rather theology is used to explain early Quaker behaviour. A new interpretation is put forth of Fox as an avatar and the argument is developed in stages. In the first section, entitled "The Making of a 'God'", Fox's early role as an undisputed prophet, wonder-worker and thaumaturge is discussed. His life and work were interpreted by him and others as the consummation of God's dealings with human history. This period of Fox's life lasted roughly from the mid-1640's to the mid-1650's. The central issue here is Fox as an avatar. Fox was devoted to a doctrine of the inner light that divinized the saints, and gave him exalted status among his followers.

Then came the great embarrassment of the messianic claims (rooted in Fox's own notions of celestial flesh) and celebrated blasphemy trial of the other leading Quaker avatar and magus James Nayler. There was a rapid retreat immediately following the Nayler dispute and this was followed by a

---

[16]Henry Cadbury, "The Editio Princeps of Fox's Journal," *JFHS.*, 53 (1974), pp. 198-218.

radical readjustment of values and a reordering of theology. The evidence for this early and decisive entropic event is assessed in the section "The Unmaking of a 'God'". It is argued that the Nayler case was Fox's undoing as a 'god'. His self-dethronement saved his movement but cost him something of his charismatic leadership. Younger Quaker theologians de-divinized the movement by redefining the concept of the 'inner Christ' and Fox was forced to adjust to leading a movement that was no longer theologically his.

1

HISTORICAL CONTEXT, HISTORIOGRAPHY, NEW DIRECTIONS

Quakerism was born in a profoundly disturbed time in Europe and England. The Thirty Years War (1618-48) had generated impassioned religious views and, when it ended with the *Treaty of Westphalia* in 1648, religious sectarianism was entrenched in European life and thought. In England a civil war that lasted nearly a decade ended with the unprecedented act of regicide. These events were immediately followed by the Irish and Scots campaigns. The psychological effects of the plague of 1651-52, which carried off one-fifth of the English population and has either been underestimated or ignored in the histories of the period, added further anxiety to this age of tremendous upheaval. It was also a time of social and intellectual uprootedness. There were major demographic shifts from rural to urban settings. Scientific rationalism was on the rise[1] among the educated elite and the clergy of the day while the 'magical' and traditionally superstitious explanations for the natural order of life were on the decline. Major institutional changes were sustained by attitudinal changes and effected further changes of attitude. There is a lovely little Jacobean poem

---

[1]Documented by K. Thomas, *Religion and the Decline of Magic* and M. MacDonald, *Mystical Bedlam: Madness, Anxiety and Healing in Seventeenth Century England* (Cambridge University Press, 1981), p. 213.

by Richard Corbet (1582-1655) decrying the "disappearance" of fairies: *The Faeries Farewell.* He links their loss to the loss of Catholicism.

The founding of the Republic in 1649 also helped to create a climate conducive to the spread of political and religious radicalism. Liberty of conscience was established and later enshrined as law in the *Instrument of Government.*[2] Censorship was lifted and a limited form of toleration was established. In the wake of these developments religious invention ran riot and a plethora of sects and heresies emerged in a manner unparalleled in western history since the founding of Christianity. In *Gangraena* Thomas Edwards identified sixteen new sects and in excess of one hundred and seventy-six heresies that emerged during this time.[3] Religious radicalism emerged out of this revolutionary context and the socio-economic ferment that followed in its wake contributed to the meteoric rise of groups like the Quakers.[4]

Social historians of Quakerism maintain that this disturbed revolutionary setting contributed to a radicalism that has been muted by generations of Quaker hagiography. 'The Quakers of the 50's were the Roundheads of the 40's' - 'Roundhead' being a derisive term for political

---

[2]The *Instrument of Government* was a new written constitution drawn up by the officers of the Army in December, 1653. Article 37 provided for significant religious liberty [*See* W.L. Sachse, *English History in the Making: Readings From the Sources, to 1689*, vol. 1 (New York: John Wiley, 1967), pp. 276-79].

[3]Thomas Edwards, *Gangraena* (London, 1646, Revised Edition), volume 1, pp. 13, 15-32. Another fifty-three heresies were listed in volume 2, pp. 2-17.

[4]H. Barbour set the number of Quakers in 1657 at 20,000 [*The Quakers in Puritan England* (Philadelphia: Friends United Press, 1985), p. 182. First published in 1964]. M. Watts set the size of groups between 1660 and 1700 at the following: Presbyterians (185,430); Congregationalists (67,580); Baptists (39,510) and Quakers (39,510 excluding Wales) [M. Watts, *The Dissenters: From the Reformation to the French Revolution* (Oxford: Clarendon, 1978), pp. 267-89]. W.C. Braithwaite had 30,000 - 40,000 Quakers in 1661 out of a population of 5,000,000. He cited *The Travels of Cosmo through England in 1669* which gave an estimate of 60,000 Quakers at the time of the Restoration [W.C. Braithwaite, *The Beginnings of Quakerism to 1660* (2nd ed.; York: William Sessions, 1981), p. 512. Hereafter cited as *Beginnings*, 2nd ed.]. Barry Reay also put the totals as high as 60,000 in the 1660's making Quakers as numerous as Catholics and more numerous than Baptists [Barry Reay, *The Quakers and the English Revolution* (New York: St. Martin's, 1985), pp. 26-27].

radical.[5] When the dreams of many in the New Model Army were dashed by Cromwell's betrayal of the 'Good Old Cause' many soldiers (like the future Quaker James Nayler) left the army and turned to Quakerism in the hope of keeping the 'Godly Commonwealth' alive.[6] The exact social demography of the movement has not yet been fixed with certainty.[7] The median age of the 'First Publishers of Truth' (the so-called 'Valiant Sixty')[8] at conversion was twenty-three. This may explain the strong antinomic spirit of early Quakerism as well as Richard Baxter's claim

---

[5]J.F. Maclear, "Quakerism at the End of the Interregnum: A Chapter in the Domestication of Radical Puritanism," *CH*, 19 (Dec., 1950), p. 243. "Roundhead" was a term for a religious and purportedly social radical, originally for a separatist, but from 1642 onward was applied to all parliamentarians by royalists as a term of abuse. During the 1640's it encompassed Presbyterians and Congregationalists, as well as members of sects.

[6]Quakers, including Fox, were not fully pacifist from the beginning. They looked for an external agent to enact God's work of judgment on earth. Burrough supported Cromwell's bloody crusade in Ireland. Fox called upon Parliament to use force to obliterate the Inquisition and "sack Rome" while Nayler, a former soldier, praised the losses of life in the Parliamentary cause (*See* C. Hill, "Quakers and the English Revolution," *Quaker Monthly*, (1984), p. 78.

[7]E.E. Taylor, "The First Publishers of Truth," *JFHS*, 19 (1922), pp. 66-81 and A. Lloyd, *Quaker Social History, 1669-1738* (London: Longmans, 1950) provide a good introduction to this part of the discussion. In 1957 Alan Cole stated that Quakers were drawn mainly from the "urban and rural petite bourgeoisie" [Cole, "The Social Origins of Early Friends," *JFHS*, 48 (1957), pp. 99-118]. Over a decade later Richard Vann revised that picture so that the "middle to upper bourgeoisie ... was strikingly more prominent among the early Quakers" [Vann, "Quakerism and the Social Structure in the Interrregnum," *P&P*, 43 (1969), pp. 71-91]. Quaker support was drawn largely from Yeomen and wholesale traders. Barry Reay, who has done the most recent work in this respect, tended to agree with the findings of Alan Cole. Early Quakerism was mainly petite-bourgeoisie. They were high in the agricultural sector (especially yeomen) and had strong representation from traders and artisans. Reay found less gentry in the movement than Vann and he concluded that Quakerism was more plebeian than Vann's results suggested. It was predominantly a movement of the 'middling order' [Reay, "The Social Origins of Early Quakerism," *JIH*, XI (1980), pp. 56-72]. Apart from these differences Cole, Vann and Reay each successfully demonstrate that Quakerism built on a rural base and achieved its initial success in the penetration of the rural counties.

[8]The 'Valiant Sixty' were the first Quaker missionaries to take Fox's message from the North-West of England into the South and thence to other lands between 1652 and 1654 [*See* E.E. Taylor, *The Valiant Sixty* (York, U.K.: Sessions Book Trust, 1988), p. 9. First published in 1947]. For a complete list of the names, gender, occupations and places of origin of the original sixty-six *see Ibid.*, pp. 40-41. Fifty-four were men; twelve were women; the majority were involved in agriculture; two were soldiers.

4

that Quaker's were a "wild ... generation" and a "young, unsettled sort."[9] Quaker strength lay particularly in the rural north and east of England - areas which had traditionally suffered from ecclesiastical neglect. Parishes were large. Clergy were scarce. Churches were run-down. In Tudor times little was given, said Hugh Barbour, "to replace the broken remnants of medieval popular Catholicism".[10] By Fox's time most of the major towns had Puritan preachers but much of the outlying area remained untouched. What became obvious, continued Barbour, was that Quaker anticlericalism and antisacramentalism "must have arisen from the debased form in which these had been familiar for generations in the Northwest."[11] Quakerism took root in the areas where the church and the economy had given the least. These regions were also the centre of older traditions of radical dissent such as the Familists and Grindletonians.[12]

There were, it would appear, few things that Fox attributed to 'openings' or 'direct revelation' that were novel. Christopher Hill found no theological novelty in Fox's *Journal* or his works, nor did Fox say anything that would be "unacceptable to any Puritans".[13] Even his actions of interrupting church services and denouncing were not without precedent.

---

[9]Richard Baxter, *The Quakers Catechism* (London, 1655), in his *Preface To the Reader* and B3a.

[10]Barbour, *The Quakers in Puritan England*, p. 80.

[11]*Ibid.*, p. 83.

[12]The infamous town of Grindleton was close to Pendle Hill, the site of Fox's greatest visionary 'opening' and the place from whence he set out to gather a people to his cause. T.J. Pickvance's superb study of the radical Puritan milieu in which Fox grew up is one of the best such studies on Fox's early life that we currently have. The Purefoy family were the "territorial aristocracy" of the Fenny Drayton area for over three hundred years. By the time of Cromwell they had become a dominant Puritan force in the area. Certain features of Purefoy Puritanism suggested a radical, lay non-conformist Puritanism that was all around Fox as he grew up. He was raised in a community that was riddled with lay-nonconformity. His parents were Puritans with radical tendencies as well [T.J. Pickvance, *George Fox and the Purefoys: A Study in the Puritan Background in Fenny Drayton in the 16th and 17th Centuries* (London: Friends Historical Society, 1970)].

[13]C. Hill, *The World Turned Upside Down: Radical Ideas During the English Revolution* (Penguin, 1975), p. 232.

Fox left behind a library that contained the writings of Sebastian Franck and Hendrick Niclaes.[14] The idea of searching the 'light within' was already found in the writings of Denck, Franck, Schwenckfeld, Boehme, Niclaes, and latterly in the Grindletonians, Seekers, Ranters and Cambridge Platonists. The rejection of all sacramental forms had been articulated by the Seekers William Dell and William Erbury; the priority of the Spirit over the Letter by Denck and the doctrine of perfectability by Niclaes. Fox's teaching that every person is born with the 'light of Christ' was a salve on the wounds of calvinistic predestinarian theology which had driven many, including Bunyan, to periodic bouts of despair. But even here the General Baptists had anticipated Fox by rejecting all predestinarian theology and teaching universalism well before Fox's time.[15] The peculiar Quaker use of 'thee' and

[14]J.L. Nickalls, "George Fox's Library," *JFHS*, 28 (1931), pp. 3-21; H. Cadbury, "George Fox's Library: Further Identifications," *JFHS*, 29 (1932), pp. 63-71; H. Cadbury, "George Fox's Library Again," JFHS, 30 (1933), pp. 9-19.

[15]For Quaker interconnectedness with Baptist movements on the Continent *see* R. Barclay, *The Inner Life of the Religious Societies of the Commonwealth* (London: Hodder and Stoughton, 1876), pp. 247-48, 352. G.M. Trevelyan agreed with those interpreters who saw Quakerism as a product of the transmigration of Anabaptist ideas from Holland and Germany. But he also observed that the doctrine of the 'inner light' "was at once the outcome and the counter-check of the Puritan Bible worship" [G.M. Trevelyan, *England Under the Stuarts* (London: Methuen, 1949), p. 260]. Trevelyan had also adopted a favourable sectarian view of Quakerism that emerged out of the work of Max Weber and Ernst Troeltsch. Quakerism grew out of a sectarian ethos of social oppression. This ethos was traced back through the Anabaptists and medieval heretics to the Primitive Church. The unifying 'ideal' was the Sermon on the Mount and *praxis*. Troeltsch considered Quakerism to be "the final expression in its purest form of the Anabaptist movement," especially in its incarnation of the Baptist ideals of a pure and voluntary community [Ernst Troeltsch, *The Social Teaching of the Christian Churches* (University of Chicago Press, 1981), vol.1: pp. 331-43; vol.2: pp. 780-84]. While others categorically deny any Baptist influence on Quakers [W.I. Hull, "The Mennonites and Quakers in Holland," in *Children of the Light*, edited by H. Brinton (New York: Macmillan, 1938), pp. 191-201] the recent research of Michael J. Sheeran has reopened the question by considering a number of individuals and groups as conveyors of Anabaptist ideas to Quakers. These would include Jacob Boehme and the Familists who "represent a transitional stage between Evangelical Anabaptism and the completely nonsacramental spiritualism of the Quakers." Sheeran also points out that what may be termed the earliest Quaker congregation developed out of the "broken Baptist community of Nottinghamshire, which Fox encountered in 1647-48," something already brought to our attention by William C. Braithwaite. It is from these General Baptists, surmises Sheeran, that Fox may have assumed Smyth's earlier practice of meeting without totalling votes or seeking pluralities [M.J. Sheeran, *Beyond Majority Rule: Voteless Decisions in the Religious Society of Friends* (Philadelphia: Philadelphia Yearly Meeting, 1983), pp. 124, 125, 127, 128]. Braithwaite's discussion of the

6

'thou' was common in the rural North and the refusal to acknowledge the traditional custom of hat honour preceded Quakers by over a century. The Anabaptist Kraut said in his execution speech "Some men insisted on being addressed as lords and required [others] to remove their hats. But such honours belonged to God alone and not to men."[16] A similar stand was taken by the Marian martyrs and in Fox's time by Lilburne, Winstanley, Everard and the Ranters. It would later appear as a form of social protest in the French Revolution. Refusal to take oaths had precedent as well. The Bogomils, Cathars, Lollards, Taborites and Anabaptists all refused to take oaths as a symbol of the denial of state authority. Even going naked was a sign used by the Ranters.[17] Leveller and Digger ideas appeared in Quaker literature and both Lilburne and Winstanley became Quakers in later life. It would appear there was little that was new in Fox. "The Quaker position," said Barry Reay, "was reached, or nearly reached, before the arrival of the Quakers."[18]

Hill and Reay argued that it was not theological novelty but the political tone of Fox's writings and Quaker activities that explained the extreme popular hostility directed against Quakers.[19] Quakers threatened

---

"broken" Baptist community in Nottinghamshire is in *Beginnings*, pp. 44-45. Fox had numerous ties to the Baptists. His uncle Pickering was a Baptist. He healed a Baptist woman. And a whole Baptist church followed him. Craig Horle dealt with the controversialist side of Quaker-Baptist relations in "Quakers and Baptists 1647-1660," *BQ*, 26 (1976), pp. 344-62. Remaining fragments of Oliver Hooten's *History of Quakers* (the first such history ever written) in which he discusses the origin of Quakers, how they were first called 'Children of the Light', and Rice Jones' broken Baptist community may be found in the *Children of the Light Papers*, a manuscript collection relating to the origin of Quakerism located at *FRL*, Box A "George Fox and Stephen Crisp MSS." as well as Portfolio 10, No. 42.

[16]P. Wappler, *Täuferbewegung in Thüringen von 1526-1584* (Jena: Gustav Fisher, 1913), pp. 429-30, 432.

[17]See C. Hill, *Society and Puritanism in Pre-Revolutionary England* (London: Seeker and Warburg, 1964), pp. 383, 418 and "Quakers and the English Revolution," p. 78. All these things were a "long-standing gesture of popular social protest in a social environment that was riddled with class and status distinctions" (Kent, "Psychological and Mystical Interpretations of Early Quakerism," p. 264).

[18]Quoted in Reay, *Quakers and the English Revolution*, p. 17.

[19]Hill, *World Turned Upside Down*, pp. 233-58. Especially pp. 233 and 243.

social conventions and stirred fears of anarchy. Women were allowed to preach. The clerical institution was attacked. A strong anti-tithe campaign, which threatened the old economic order and reflected deep hostility toward class exploitation, became the heart of the Quaker campaign against the national church system. Tithes were the support of Satanic external religion which included the whole church structure: its worship, its buildings, its doctrines, its personnel and all its institutions. As we shall see later, the totality of external religion was at issue. Quaker ranks burgeoned as many who had already been involved in anti-tithe activity during the Revolution joined the movement in the 1650's.[20] The spectre of another Münster was ever-present and the fear of radical sects infiltrating the army and destroying the last vestiges of peace and order may have contributed to a conservation reaction that led to the Stuart Restoration.[21]

The restored monarchy caused Quakers to despair for the 'Good Old Cause' and a political solution to their calls for a new order. This "experience of defeat", as Christopher Hill called it, this shattering of millenial hopes, forced Quakers to adjust to political realities. A formal pacifist position was adopted (a product of the realistic need for survival) and the absolute authority of the inner light which had generated anarchical tendencies was subjected to stricter organizational controls.[22]

[20]M. Mullett, *Radical Religious Movements in Early Modern Europe* (London: George, Allen and Unwin, 1980), p. 53; B. Reay, "Quaker Opposition to Tithes," *P&P*, 86 (1980), pp. 98-118.

[21]B. Reay, "Quakerism and Society," in *Radical Religion in the English Revolution*, ed. by J.F. McGregor and B. Reay (London: Oxford University Press, 1984), p. 163 and Reay, *Quakers and the English Revolution*, pp. 84-107. On the Quakers and Münster *see* Reay, *Quakers and the English Revolution*, pp. 92, 96, 98 and "The Quakers, 1659, and the Restoration," *History*, 63 (1978), p. 211.

[22]C. Hill, *The Experience of Defeat: Milton and Some Contemporaries* (New York: Penguin, 1985), pp. 129-69. Monarchists were hoping for a general purge of religious radicals in order to bring peace and order back to the land. This was a serious enough threat that Quakers felt compelled to adopt an official pacifist position in an effort to reassure the King that they were not party to any seditious or treasonous plots. Pacifism, said Alan Cole, "was forced upon them by the hostility of the outside world" ("Quakers and the English Revolution," p. 42). In May, 1660 Edward Burrough wrote that they would continue the fight against oppression "but not in the way of outward warring and fighting with carnal weapons and swords" [Burrough, *A Visitation and Presentation* (London, 1660), pp. 10-11]. Another Quaker

There have been other explanations, outside the socio-economic sphere, for the rise and progress of Quakerism. In the early Quaker view God supernaturally intervened in history to revive the spirit of Christ after a long night of apostasy. The church had lost its power to speak to man's condition shortly after the death of Christ and the Apostles. In seventeenth century England God had restored his church through his chosen instrument, George Fox.[23]

Not all seventeenth century writers adhered to this partisan view. Many saw Quakerism as a recurrent disease that had afflicted the church for centuries. The New England Puritan patriot, Cotton Mather, wrote of the Quakers as the worst kind of heretics: "For in Quakerism ... the "sink of heresies", we see the vomit cast out in the by-past ages, by the whole kennels of seducers, lick'd up again for new digestion."[24] Gerard Croese tended to accept this diagnosis uncritically when, shortly before the death of Fox, he began work on the first comprehensive history of Quakerism. He was inclined to portray Quakers as 'enthusiasts' of the type that had plagued the church since the time of Corinth. This view persisted through the centuries

---

wrote that if the King, "shall require of us, which for conscience we cannot do, we shall rather choose to patiently suffer, than sin against the God of our life. Nor can we, or shall we, rise up with carnal weapons to work our own deliverance" [N. Penney, ed., *Extracts From State Papers Relating to Friends, 1654-1672* (London: Headley Bros., 1913), pp. 122-3]. It should be emphasized that not all Restoration Quakers adopted a pacifist position.

[23]This was the view of Fox himself as well as Edward Burrough, Robert Barclay, William Penn and many other leading Quaker theologians. Penn set this view forth most clearly in his short work entitled *The Rise and Progress of the People Called Quakers*. Shortly after the death of the Apostles the false church arose, full of human inventions in doctrine and worship. The true church was forced to flee into the wilderness. Over the centuries it made many attempts to return but it was repressed and persecuted. The Protestant Reformation then took a step toward full realization of a 'spiritualized' church but the reformers 'apostasized' by building a new church of externals on the same corrupt foundation. Quakerism appeared as the culmination of a movement of spiritual seeking that began on the Continent and crossed to England. In Fox the "rise of truth" reached its historical climax [William Penn, *The Rise and Progress of the People Called Quakers* (Richmond, Indiana: Friends United Press, 1980), pp. 9-21].

[24]Cotton Mather, *Magnalia Christi Americana; or The Ecclesiastical History of New England* (Cambridge, Mass.: Belknap Press, 1977), p. 174.

and was still in recent circulation in R.A. Knox's wide-ranging study of religious enthusiasm.[25]

Anti-Quaker polemicists in the seventeenth century interpreted Quakers as being everything from disguised Jesuits to militant Anabaptists.[26] On the eve of the Restoration, when Quakers were among those who were suspected of plotting against the government, alarmists even expected an English Münster.[27] Thus, while early Friends were interpreting their movement as a restitution of the true church, anti-Quaker apologists were maintaining that it represented the true tendency of all heretics - the devolution to anarchy.

As F.B. Tolles has so clearly demonstrated these two opposing lines of interpretation continued into the eighteenth and nineteenth centuries.[28] By the mid-nineteenth century the idealized caricature of Quakerism as a

---

[25]R.A. Knox, *Enthusiasm: A Chapter in the History of Enthusiasm* (Oxford University Press, 1950).

[26]Thomas Underhill linked them to Anabaptists in Germany [*Hell Broke Loose* (London, 1660)] while William Prynne linked them to Romish emissaries, Franciscan friars and Jesuits. He also accused them of using witchcraft [*The Quakers Unmasked* (London, 1655), p. 37]. *See also* John Faldo, *A Vindication of Quakerism No Christianity* (London, 1678), p. 47. George Whitehead denied that Quakers were of Popish origin or Franciscan stock [*Truth Prevalent* (London, 1701), p. 83].

[27]One minister in Oxford reported to his congregation, during the turmoil just preceding the Restoration, that God might "suffer England to be transformed into a Münster" (Reay, *Quakers and the English Revolution*, p. 92).

[28]I am indebted to F.B. Tolles and Melvin Endy for many of the ideas used in the following pages [Tolles, "1652 in History: Changing Perspectives on the Founding of Quakerism," *BFHA*, 41 (1952), pp. 12-27; Endy, "The Interpretation of Quakerism: Rufus Jones and His Critics," *QH*, 70 (1981), pp. 3-21]. David Hume, *The History of England* (Philadelphia: Porter and Coates, 1776), 5, pp. 520-24, continued to pillory Quakers, characterizing them as fanatics and violent 'enthusiasts' who disturbed the public peace and seduced the New Model Army zealots, William Sewel's *The History of the Rise, Increase and Progress of the Christian People Called Quakers* (London: Darton and Harvey, 1834), was destined to become the standard history of the movement until William C. Braithwaite's two volume general history appeared earlier this century. Sewel's history was dedicated to George I of England in an effort to convince the King that Quakers were peaceful and loyal citizens. Earlier this century Henry Cadbury pointed out the need for a critical comparison of Croese and Sewel. Sewel considered Croese's work to be "imperfect and defective". Croese, he said, "presumed to relate things of which he had no true knowledge" (*Ibid.*, I, p. xi).

pillar of the Modern Era and its counterpoint in anti-Quaker polemic[29] was beginning to yield to new and critical interpretations. Forms of future historiography were beginning to take shape in the work of partisan historians like W. Wagstaff and non-partisan historians like S.R. Gardiner. Wagstaff became an important forerunner to Rufus Jones by interpreting Quakerism as the synthesis of an inner dialectic between the extremes of 'spirituality' and 'formalism' that had been at work throughout the history of the Christian Church.[30] Gardiner anticipated the work of Geoffrey Nuttall and other twentieth century interpreters of Quakers as radical Puritans by tracing Quaker origins to their immediate spiritual environment. They were part of a larger movement recoiling from the "intellectual rigidities of Calvinism."[31] In his *History of the Commonwealth and Protectorate* Gardiner wrote of Fox's doctrine of the 'inner light' as the "quintessence of Puritan

---

[29]Carlyle portrayed Fox as "the greatest of the Moderns, and greater than Diogenes himself: for he too stands on the adamantine basis of his Manhood, casting aside all props and shoars; yet not, in half-savage Pride, undervaluing the earth" [*The Works of Thomas Carlyle* (New York: Charles Scribners Sons, 1903), 1, p. 168]. Carlyle was reshaping Fox under the influence of German Romantic philosophy and he was specifically referring to the epic symbolic significance of Fox making himself a suit of leather. This clothes philosophy is overdrawn as the act was of a purely practical value for the itinerant Fox. Carlyle's interpretation influenced the American liberal idealist historian George Bancroft who interpreted Quakerism as a moral revolution that established absolute freedom of conscience. The common man was liberated from feudal strictures and was given the potential to rise to new heights of freedom and power. This was the time when "the freedom of Bacon, the enthusiasm of Wickliffe, and the politics of Wat Tyler, were to gain the highest unity in a sect" [*History of the United States of America*, vol. 1 (Port Washington, New York: Kennikat Press, 1967), p. 529]. Bancroft was proposing a type of romantic secularization of Fox's bold concept of the divinization of man. T.B. Macauley, on the other hand, saw Fox as a fit companion for Joanna Southcote and Lodowick Muggleton. Quaker 'enthusiasm' was clearly distasteful to the aristocratic Macauley. Fox's only redeeming feature was his association with men like Penn and Barclay - men of class, poise and education - who polished his "rude doctrines" [*The History of England*, in *The Works of Lord Macauley*, (Philadelphia: The University Library Association), 7, p. 163].

[30]W. Wagstaff, *A History of the Society of Friends* (New York, 1845), pp. viii-lvi; 1-3.

[31]S.R. Gardiner, *History of the Commonwealth and Protectorate, 1649-1656* (New York: A.M.S. Press, 1965), 2, p. 91.

protest against external formality, though he carried his opinions into practice with greater consistency than other Puritans."[32]

The roots of Jones' fresh 'metaphysical' approach lay in a meeting he had with J.W. Rountree in Switzerland in 1892.[33] There, Rountree set before Jones his goal of revitalizing the Society of Friends through the recovery of Quaker history. He was responsible for pointing out to Jones that one of Fox's most important contributions was the "escape" he offered "from the terrible shadow of predestination."[34] Jones recognized this when he defined Quakers as "mystics in type and disposition"[35] and set Quakerism over against Puritanism which he called "forensic". What he meant was that the essence of Quakerism was 'first-hand' experience as opposed to rigid 'biblicism' or an external source of spiritual authority.[36] Fox revolted against forensic theology as he heard it preached from the Puritan pulpit in his birthplace Drayton-in-the-Clay (now Fenny Drayton). In time he came to

---

[32]*Ibid.*, p. 91.

[33]D. Hinshaw, *Rufus Jones: Master Quaker* (New York: G.P. Putnam's Sons, 1951), pp. 123-24. William James influenced both Rountree and Jones. The latter was particularly drawn to James' conclusion that there were links between Jacob Boehme's mystical experiences and those of Fox - especially the mystical insights into the nature of creation [*See* S. Kent, "Psychological and Mystical Interpretations of Early Quakerism: William James and Rufus Jones," *Religion*, 17 (1987), pp. 251-74].

[34]T.C. Kennedy, "History and Quaker Renaissance: The Vision of John Wilhelm Rountree," *JFHS*, 55 (1986), p. 447.

[35]R. Jones, *The Church's Debt to the Heretics* (London: James Clark and Co., 1924), p. 247.

[36]Quakers lived in this mystical world of thought and shared with all "devoted humanists" the belief that "deep in the central nature of man - an inalienable part of Reason - there was a Light, a Word, an image of God, something permanent, reliable, universal, and unsundered from God himself" [R. Jones, *Spiritual Reformers in the Sixteenth and Seventeenth Centuries* (Boston: Beacon Press, 1959) p. xxx]. This brought Quakers into conflict with the Puritan who lived in another world of thought completely. The Puritan arrived at his view of God not through transforming experience but "by logical and argumentative interpretation of the great texts of Scripture, which were for him the literal words of God, once for all naturally revealed to man. He didn't look inward for his basic truths; he turned to his sacred book and took it as settled beyond controversy that God's covenant as expressed in that Book was the pattern for the saints of all time" [R. Jones, *Mysticism and Democracy in the English Commonwealth* (Oxford University Press, 1946), p. 19].

preach a Christianity of inward life and experience in which the work of Christ was not forensic but was an operative power in the innermost being. This theology of 'first-hand' experience evolved into a highly developed form of mysticism, defined by Jones as "life itself at the highest inward unity and its most consummate attainment of reality."[37] This was not the way of the *via negativa* - sheer abandon; a sinking into pain, silence and darkness of nothingness by baring one's mind of all thoughts, notions, symbols and images of God and thus making contact with the dark, deeper, mysterious side of God. Rather, it was what Jones called 'positive mysticism', described by Melvin Endy as "a personal consciousness of fellowship and relationship between man and God, a consciousness that brought an immense transformation of life."[38]

This was also the type of mysticism that Jones believed was revived by the spiritual reformers of the sixteenth and seventeenth centuries, eventually culminating in Quakerism. In Jones' panoramic view, it was adopted by Denck, Bunderlin, Entfelder, Franck, Schwenckfeld, Castellio, Coornhert, Weigel and Boehme before crossing the Channel to Everard, Randall, Rous, Sterry, Vane, the Cambridge Platonists, the Spiritual Poets (Traherne, Milton, Donne), the Familists, Seekers, Ranters and finally the Quakers. They all tended to share a direct knowledge of God through the inner light.[39] They all believed the world was entering a new dispensation of the Spirit.

---

[37]R. Jones, *Introduction*, in W.C. Braithwaite, *The Beginnings of Quakerism to 1660* (1st ed.; London: Macmillan, 1912), p. xxxiv.

[38]M.B. Endy, "The Interpretation of Quakerism", p. 6; R. Jones, ed., *George Fox: An Autobiography* (Philadelphia: Ferris and Leach, 1903), p. 31.

[39]The Quaker printers Giles Calvert and Thomas and Matthew Simmonds began as early as 1648 to print the works of the Continental mystics Hendrik Niclaes and Jacob Boehme. Most of Boehme's works were available in England, in translation, by the mid-1650's (*See* Wing, *Short Title Catalogue*, B3397-B3427ff.). One of the specific links between Quakers, Cambridge Platonists and the Continental Reformers was Francis Mercury Van Helmont. Van Helmont "had been associated with the leaders and disciples of many of the contemporary sects [on the continent] all of whom laid their chief emphasis in religion upon the light within" [Marjorie Nicolson, "George Keith and the Cambridge Platonists," *Philosophical Review*, 39 (1930), pp. 49-50]. Van Helmont spent eight years (1670-78) at Ragley Hall as Lady Conway's personal medical adviser. Both were Quakers. While there Van Helmont met many of her Quaker guests including George Fox, Robert Barclay and George Keith. Another guest who

When the reformers moved toward a strictly forensic theology the spiritual reformers were prompted to redefine their view of God and man in more mystical terms:

> By a shift of view, as revolutionary as that from Ptolemaic astronomy to the verifiable insights of Copernicus, they passed over from the dogma of Christ who came to appease an angry God ... to the living apprehension of a Christ - verifiable in experience - who revealed to them, in terms of his own nature, an eternally tender, loving, suffering, self-giving God, and who made them see, with the enlightened eyes of their heart, the divine possibilities of human life. Through this insight they were the beginners of a new type of Christianity ... a type that finds the supreme significance of Christ's life in his double revelation of the inherent nature of God, and the immense value and potentiality of man, and that changes the emphasis from schemes of salvation to interpretation of life, from the magic significance of doctrine to the incalculable worth of the moral will.[40]

The spiritual reformers broke with the main course of the Protestant Reformation and Protestant theology in their basic view of God and the person of Christ. The focus of salvation shifted from the imputation of Christ's righteousness to a life of moral rectitude lived in unity with God. A new basis for religious authority was erected wherein the Spirit was victorious over form and letter. Fox was the culmination of a great shift that had been occurring toward inward 'personal' religion for over a century. Placing Quakerism in a type of *successio apostolica* was not new. Penn and Sewel had already done it. But Jones' metaphysical constructs were unprecedented. By positing mysticism as the epicentre of Quakerism Jones was able to provide a unified and intelligible interpretation for the origins and rise of Quakerism.[41]

---

visited the group at Ragley Hall was the Cambridge Platonist Henry More. These links came well after early Quaker theology was in decline and in transformation [On Van Helmont *see* W.I. Hull, *Benjamin Furly and Quakerism in Rotterdam* (Swarthmore College Monograph, No. 5, 1941), pp. 105-23. Fox and Van Helmont were together at least once, at James Claypole's house in Jan., 1683 (*Ibid.*, p. 117).

[40]Jones, *Spiritual Reformers*, p. xl.

[41]In addition to mysticism Jones found two other dominant features in early Quakerism - propheticism and moralism. Quakers borrowed from the common stock of

Jones' view that a huge tradition of mystical religion was the forebearer of Quakerism has been critiqued in the other massive groundshift in Quaker historiography this century. The revival in Puritan studies earlier this century generated a renewed interest in Puritan personal religion and the doctrine of the Holy Spirit. What followed was a broadening of the definition of Puritanism which allowed Commonwealth Quakerism and other radical groups and individuals to be incorporated within its scope. Rather than being a 'revolt' or a 'reaction' against Puritanism it was a 'fulfillment'. Quakerism was not an alien phenomenon but was a native plant which could not be properly understood outside the context of Puritan England. Scholarship was seen to take an antithetical stand to the interpretation of Rufus Jones.

It was the broadened definition of Puritanism that was responsible for changing the focus on Quaker origins. Accordingly, English Puritanism produced a radical wing of famous Separatists, notably Williams, Milton, Vane, Saltmarsh and Fox. One of this new generation of Puritan scholars, Alan Simpson, described what it was that united these Puritan radicals:

> all recoil from the external discipline which orthodox Puritanism tries to insert between the regenerate conscience and God; ... all combine an acute sense of the uncertainty of human judgment in the past with an abounding confidence in the revelation that is going on around them; most of them are pronounced rationalists or pronounced mystics.[42]

Rationalism and mysticism were presented as two sides of the same phenomena - the move towards an inward religion. On the one hand Reason

---

prophetic literature of their time. This, combined with mysticism, helped to produce the mental and emotional climate of the movement. Early Quakers saw themselves as prophets to their age and saw the apocalyptic language of the Old and New Testaments as fulfilled in their own experience. Quaker moralism was a corrective to other extremist tendencies of the time, which were "dreamy, visionary and seething with ill-directed enthusiasm." Fox's moral concern was "that society here on earth might take on the likeness to the Kingdom of Heaven." He called for the removal of oppression and injustice and was particularly concerned to "break down the slavery of superficial fashions and cramping customs, and to restore individual responsibility, spiritual initiative and personal autonomy." These ideas were all fused with moral earnestness and *praxis* (Jones, *Introduction*, in *Beginnings*, 1st ed., pp. xxxvii-xxxix).

[42]A. Simpson, *Puritanism in Old and New England* (Chicago: University of Chicago Press, 1955), p. 43.

(of the regenerate soul) was the faculty through which one related to God and his fellow man. The regenerate life was one of free moral choice and self-determination. Spiritual life was not bondage to external laws and outward forms. On the other hand, and very much a part of this, God's Spirit was immediate and indwelling. It was the right to spiritual authority and free expression. The Puritan radicals were types of mystics[43] who located spiritual authority within the person, although Milton did tie the movement of the Spirit to Scripture in an effort to guard against anarchy.

Geoffrey Nuttall has been the most influential interpreter of the links between Puritanism and Quakerism. According to Nuttall, Quakerism was not the product of imported ideas but of seventeenth century English calvinism. Quakers were indicators of "the *direction* of the Puritan movement as a whole."[44] Nuttall took a number of radical Puritan themes and demonstrated how they logically flowed into the thought-world of Quakerism. He concluded that the Quakers "repeat, extend, and fuse so much of what is held by the radical, separatist party within Puritanism, that they cannot be denied the name."[45] Quakerism emerged from within the *Zeitgeist* of Reformation Protestantism.

According to this 'Protestant view' the movement of independent lay searching and the calls for the reform of the Church of England came from within the Puritan *Zeitgeist*, not from the *Spiritualisten* on the Continent. The 'middle' and 'conservative' (Presbyterian) Puritan parties (which Nuttall distinguished from the radical Puritan) tied the movement of the Spirit to the Bible. Many questioned this external basis for spiritual authority, believing that the Spirit acting in the individual as the Word was the ultimate source of spiritual authority. The question put forward by the radical Puritans, of how God's Spirit was to be discerned and where spiritual authority was located, formed the context out of which Quakerism emerged. Like other radical

---

[43]This case has been most recently made by J. Brauer, "Types of Puritan Piety," *CH*, (Mar., 1987), pp. 39-58.

[44]G.F. Nuttall, *The Holy Spirit in Puritan Faith and Experience* (Oxford: Basil Blackwell, 1947), pp. 13-14.

[45]*Ibid.*, p. 13.

Puritans, they disassociated the Spirit in the external Word and the Spirit in themselves, giving the latter primacy.[46] This, according to Nuttall, was true Puritanism.

The radical Puritans preceded Fox in other areas of spiritual and liturgical emphasis as well. The famous Seeker William Erbury believed in continuing revelation. John Saltmarsh disliked read prayers since the Holy Spirit worked immediately in people's hearts. Quakers developed the practice of 'prophesying' (this being a form of biblical exegesis plus personal exhortation by gifted brethren) from the Independents and Separatists who developed the centrality of the sermon in Puritan preaching.[47] William Dell, Saltmarsh and Erbury were also part of a tendency to weaken the importance of the sacraments by viewing them as symbolic and not necessary to the *esse* of the church. The culmination of this tendency was Fox, who disposed of the sacraments altogether. Most radical Puritans believed they were living on the threshold of the new age of the Spirit and they contributed to an atmosphere of heightened eschatological awareness which again culminated with the Quakers viewing themselves as the saints of the new age of the Spirit.[48]

[46]*Ibid.*, p. 30.

[47]Since all Quaker preaching was spontaneous prophesying they did not write down and deliver their sermons. No Quaker sermons survive in written form prior to 1660 [N. Smith, *Perfection Proclaimed: Language and Literature in English Radical Religion, 1640-1666* (Oxford: Clarendon, 1989), p. 334].

[48]Nuttall, *The Holy Spirit in Puritan Faith and Experience*, pp. 66, 76, 90, 111, 148-49. There is one point of agreement between Jones and the Protestant interpreters. Both identify the same people as the forerunners of Quakerism. Jones calls them mystics and Nuttall calls them radical Puritans. The same phenomenon (a strong 'spiritualizing' tendency) is organized under different interpretive paradigms. Hugh Barbour's socio-historical study of Quakerism built on Nuttall's work. He, too, found the origins of Quakerism in radical Puritanism where daily life and worship were increasingly subjected to the Spirit's leading. Quakerism was a frontier 'Great Awakening' in the untouched territories of northern England - a type of Puritan revival movement (Barbour, *Quakers in Puritan England*, p. 83 for the analogy). This theology of inward experience, argued Barbour, was developed within the radical Puritan milieu. The radical Puritans were interpreted as laying the foundation for Quakerism, both in matters of theology and ethics. Quakerism was the outcome of a large movement, native to England, which "stressed the Spirit as a practical guide" (*Ibid.*, p. 71). This broad movement of reform that emanated from within the radical Puritan milieu broke the tension between imputed righteousness and the overwhelming sense of sin by turning to inward religion. God's

Rufus Jones had an oversimplified view of Puritanism and Quakerism. He dealt with them as "ideal types" and this prevented him from seeing the "spiritualizing thrust" in left-wing Puritanism. His typology forced him to look elsewhere for Quaker roots - namely to spiritualizing tendencies on the Continent.[49] However, Jones was correct on other leading points of interpretation. Quakerism was a rejection of forensic Christianity. And a monocausal Puritan origin is inadequate given the complex revolutionary milieu out of which Quakerism emerged although the search for historical precedents can be a red herring. Illuminist religions do not require, of necessity, historical, intellectual precedent. They are most often born out of personalized, independent Bible study.

The Protestant interpretation successfully balanced Jones' over-emphasis on Continental origins by refocusing on the radical Puritan *Zeitgeist* out of which Quakerism emerged. But the shortcomings of this interpretation remain formidable as well. The major problem remains the accuracy of placing Quakerism within the Puritan fabric. Puritanism is a difficult term to define but it may accurately be identified with a general thought world that was in substantive conflict with the thought world of Quakerism. Quakers, like their Puritan counterparts, did experience intense conviction of sin, judgment and self-denial but they had opposing views of man's role and man's capacities in the salvific process. In addition, Puritanism was predestinarian in outlook. Although Nuttall, and more recently Jerald Brauer, would argue that predestination was not the defining feature of Puritan piety this was precisely the outlook that caused so many spiritually sensitive people to recoil from Puritanism and seek solace in a purely spiritualized religion. Quakers also held the Puritans to be their chief opponents. The feeling was mutual as the Quakers were abhorred by those whose theology was calvinist. Thomas Hodgkin believed that the 'high professors' with whom Fox had so many sharp encounters were, without

---

grace was primarily a moral power (an inner experience of fiery judgment and the complete rooting out of all sin in the present tense) rather than imputed forgiveness.

[49]Endy, "The Interpretation of Quakerism," pp. 11-13, 17.

18

exception, Puritans. They used the term in derision long after the Stuart Restoration.[50]

Nuttall interpreted the Quakers as the logical terminus of radical Puritanism, yet he admitted that at times the Quakers went beyond the bounds of Puritanism by minimizing the authority of the Bible and rejecting all external forms and ceremonies. By his definition the radical Puritans themselves embraced some of these "occasional exclusions" to the point where they fell outside the purvue of Puritanism.[51] Jones was more accurate by making a sharp distinction between the Puritan and Quaker world of thought. Quakerism, as Lewis Benson pointed out, did not follow Puritanism in all its chief features - the Scriptures, ecclesiology, the sacraments, moral perfectability and the relation of the Christian and the state.[52] However, all views converge at one point - the spiritual and psychological dilemmas posed by Puritanism contributed to the rise of spiritualized religion in seventeenth century England. Calvinistic theology created a spiritual crisis that was only resolved on the battleground of the location of religious authority. This became the watershed that marked the parting of ways between the Puritans and the Quakers.

There was, however, much more to the Lamb's War than any of these interpretations has revealed. All the spiritual reformers of the sixteenth and seventeenth centuries (and Joachim before them) anticipated a new age of the Spirit (when immediate revelation would be universally normative in accordance with Joel 2:28 and Acts 2) but they were no more than prophets, foretelling its coming. There was nothing 'superhuman' or thaumaturgical about them or their works. Their theology was strictly pneumatic. The Holy Spirit was working in and through them, preparing the way for the return of Christ.

---

[50]T. Hodgkin, "Introduction", *The First Publishers of Truth, ed. by N. Penney* (London: Headley Bros., 1904), p. 9.

[51]A point made by Endy, "The Interpretation of Quakerism," p. 13.

[52]Benson, *Catholic Quakerism* (Gloucester, U.K.: The Author, 1966), p. 9.

This all changed with the coming of Fox who pronounced something that had rarely been heard or seen since Apostolic times, or at least since the days of the high heresies of the first and second centuries. The new message had to do with Fox's radical christology and his claim to be the 'Son of God' and it logically led to the claim that Nayler was the Messiah. Due to the selective editing of the early Quaker manuscripts Quaker historiography has failed to discern the true nature and full implications of Fox's christology. Fox believed that the inward dwelling Christ literally transformed and perfected the saints so that they became flesh of His flesh and bone of His bone.[53] We may call this Fox's doctrine of celestial inhabitation.

When early Quakerism is cast in the mystical, Puritan, contemporary evangelical or universalist mould the true force and radicalness of Fox's message is lost or greatly distorted. His theology was neither exactly mystical nor pneumatic. It was a christopresent theology - traditionally far more dangerous in Christian history. It was just this theme - Fox casting himself not only as an eschatological prophet but as a magus, avatar, even the very 'Son of God', a new incarnation of Christ representative of the culmination of God's dealings with human history - that was the quintessence of early Quakerism. Fox as a self-styled Son of God was perceived by opponents to be the most radical and disturbing part of his message. It was his claim to divinity, above all else, that prompted the charges of heresy and blasphemy.

---

[53]Maurice Creasey, Lewis Benson and more recently Douglas Gwyn saw the christocentrism in Fox but they failed to draw out the most radical implications of his celestial adoption theology [M. Creasey, "Early Quaker Christology: With Special Reference to the Teaching and Significance of Isaac Penington, 1616-1679," D.Phil. Thesis, University of Leeds, 1956; L. Benson, *Catholic Quakerism*; and D. Gwyn, *Apocalypse of the Word: The Life and Message of George Fox* (Richmond, Indiana: Friends United Press, 1984)]. Gwyn followed Benson's lead in rejecting Jones' mystical reading and Nuttall's Protestant reading of early Quakerism. And with Benson he interpreted the central feature of Fox's message as the apocalyptic appearance of Christ among his people. But each retained the fundamental and orthodox distinction between God and man, which was adopted by the second generation of Quaker divines who transformed Fox's Christology. Gwyn, especially, argued that a close reading of Fox revealed a belief "in a universal spiritual experience that may remain unnamed," but the light itself definitely had a name - Jesus Christ. And that light was both inward and fundamentally alien to human experience (*Apocalypse of the Word*, p. xv). This study takes issue with the spiritualist, mystical and evangelical readings of Fox, an interpretation that belongs to later developments in the story.

20

Fox's theology of celestial adoption or celestial inhabitation[54] led ultimately to the regaining of Paradise in the present. This was his most radical and creative contribution to the strange era in which he lived. Others opposed tithes and oaths. Others used plain speech and refused to doff the hat to social superiors. Yet others used sign enactments in public. None proposed the regaining of Paradise by becoming 'gods' again. This was the part of Fox's message that was selectively edited from the record.

There was a broad historical context, well beyond our scope here, for the appearance of the *Eigenkirchen* (literally personal church) of Fox, an understanding of which must be sought in a sect-spawning context that is much broader than strictly mid-seventeenth century Quaker or even English social and institutional terms; in a setting that is broader than strictly biographical, personal, or controversial terms. The following chapters find in the appearance of the *Eigenkirchen* of Fox a cult life that had generally been emerging in the West since the late Middle Ages. It contained the germs of a 'radicalism' (in this case a Christological radicalism)[55] that posed an even greater threat to many authorities than did the political and economic radicalism that was its by-product.

The findings of the social historians into the socio-economic roots of anti-clericalism and anti-liturgical protest against tithes and social oppression are not refuted here. Indeed they are accepted as of considerable help. The shift in the following study back into the field of intellectual history is, however, not to be construed as a reengaging of past partisan or denominational disputes. It is best described as the kind of "social study of

[54]Adoption sometimes has a specific theological meaning about the process by which Christ became flesh at the incarnation, and the repercussions of this on the meaning of the Lord's Supper. The term celestial inhabitation is therefore used to avoid any misinterpretation.

[55]Technically christology is defined as the study of the person and work of Christ. It involves notions about His saving work. It includes the *corpus* of answers past and present to Jesus' profound question to his followers - "But who do you say that I am?" Over the centuries that question has evoked a mountain of differing answers and even yet there is no consensus on just who Jesus Christ was. Traditionally the dialogue centred upon his supposed two natures - how could he be both God and man at the same time? More recently attention has been focused on what Schweitzer concluded was the futile quest for the historical Jesus. The best introduction to the subject is Cullen Murphy's article "Who Do Men Say That I Am?" in *The Atlantic Monthly* (December, 1986), pp. 37-58.

religion" already foreshadowed in the work of Patrick Collinson.[56] The writings of the dissenters alone tell us a great deal about societal interrelationships. From them we learn about the "society of the godly" and about the "human affection" and "fervent love" that bonded it together. "Friendships so demanding and exclusive," said Collinson, "must have upset all kinds of other, pre-existent relationships."[57] The exclusive godly society of Quakers, for example, renounced altogether any intercourse with the world and its institutions and instead fashioned a new model, a religious model, for complete transformation of the world - religious, social and psychological.

Christopher Hill finds nothing theologically novel about early Quakerism. Nothing in Fox's *Journal* or his writings convince Hill about a 'radicalism' in Fox that was capable of provoking the kind of hostility Quakers experienced in the 1650's. Instead both Hill and Reay look elsewhere, to socio-political explanations.[58] And they do accurately demonstrate how Quaker anti-clericalism and anti-tithe agitation provoked popular fears of a crumbling social order - fears that eventually contributed to the Stuart Restoration. But the record shows that three of Fox's earliest imprisonments were on blasphemy charges. So also was Nayler's imprisonment and celebrated trial in Parliament. In addition many other Quakers were charged with blasphemy, especially in the years preceding the Nayler case. A fresh look at what was suppressed in the sources suggests that there was a radicalism of a theological nature in early Quakerism that was considered as dangerous or more dangerous than the socio-political radicalism to which it gave rise. So many movements - Quakers, Fifth

---

[56]P. Collinson, *Godly People: Essays on English Protestantism and Puritanism* (London: Hambledon, 1983).

[57]*Ibid.*, pp. 546-47.

[58]The predominant view today is that the religious ideas of Quakers cannot be studied apart from their "social environment in which they were performed and in which they acquired their meaning" [S. Kent, "Psychological and Mystical Interpretations of Early Quakerism," pp. 264-65 and L. Ingle, "From Mysticism to Radicalism: Recent Historiography of Quaker Beginnings," *QH*, 76 (1987), pp. 79-94]. The interplay between ideas and the socio-cultural environment is important in any study of this nature although recent historiography has tended to over-emphasize the socio-cultural side in reaction to the dominant and pervasive views of Rufus Jones.

Monarchists, Baptists, Levellers and Diggers - drew their strength from prevailing conditions in the social, political, religious and cultural order, that the general background explanation is insufficient to explain the peculiarity of any one movement. By concentrating on tithes the social explanation does not go far enough even in secular terms, for the attack on tithes was part of something much larger. Tithes were a means and not an end. The social explanation does not go nearly far enough toward helping us to understand the idiosyncrasy of Quakerism. Here one must look to leadership and ideas. There was a truly social relevance to Quaker theology. The conviction of the inner Christ overturned the world order in an interior, psychological sense and this was the Quakers' principle of social compensation. Quakers were divinized and they became part of God's nobility, the gentry of heaven. The dispossessed of this world were spiritually ennobled and they became sons and daughters of God - the Kings and Queens of the emergent new order while the worldly Kings and nobles were the damned. For this very reason the importance of Quaker theology (especially Fox's celestial flesh theology) should not be minimized. It liberated the oppressed and ennobled the dispossessed who became gods and goddesses in their own right and heirs of the Kingdom that had come and was in the process of overturning the worldly order. This theological radicalism was considered serious and detrimental enough to the movement to warrant expunging it from the sources, even while Fox was still alive.

Quakerism did not appear *de novo*. It appeared in a revolutionary context that helped to shape it and give it its character. But there were other aspects to the movement that were truly unusual and added a rationale, motivation and colour to the Lamb's War. The following chapters propose to draw out the fundamental importance and illustrate the radical implications of Fox's theology of celestial inhabitation.

PART 1

THE MAKING OF A GOD

2

PROPHET

Interpreters of early Quaker eschatology have generally remarked on its crusading rhetoric or its 'realized' characteristics.[1] This chapter, which deals with Fox as a prophet, moves beyond these approaches. The literal identification of Quaker with Christ was the prophetic edifice upon which Fox built his new religion. Outside of this context none of his life and work can be understood.

In addition to Fox's christopresentism there was an originality to Fox's prophetic view of history that overshadowed its similarities with other ideologies adhered to by his contemporaries.[2] It can be briefly summarized

---

[1]Eschatology: From the Greek *eschatos* or 'last' - being the doctrine of the last times. By 'realized' I mean that Fox did not believe in a future coming of Christ or a future Kingdom. His Christ had already come and was coming, within - it was not an external event but an ongoing process in the present. As a result of this 'realized' eschatology Christ's Kingdom had also already come and was in the process of being universally established. On Quaker eschatology *see* T.L. Underwood, "Early Quaker Eschatology," in *Puritans, the Millenium and the Future of Israel: Puritan Eschatology 1600 to 1660*, ed. by P. Toon (London: James Clark and Co., 1970), pp. 91-105; B. Ball, *A Great Expectation: Eschatological Thought in English Protestantism to 1660* (Leiden: E.J. Brill, 1975), pp. 195-210; D. Gwyn, *Apocalypse of the Word: The Life and Message of George Fox* (Richmond, Indiana: Friends United Press, 1986).

[2]Several writers in this century have acknowledged the similarity between Quakerism and the Hermetic tradition or the "belief that man has fallen out with creation but in the state of perfection (of restoration) unity can once more be achieved and nature's secrets revealed" [Reay, *Quakers and the English Revolution*, p. 37; Thomas, *Religion and the Decline of Magic*, p. 352; G. Nuttall, "Unity With Creation: George Fox and the Hermetic Philosophy," *Friends Quarterly*, 1 (1947), pp. 139-143; H. Cadbury, "Early Quakerism and Uncanonical Lore,"

in the following manner. In Paradise God was the 'first-speaker' to Adam and Eve. When they forsook God they lost their divine union. At that time God made a promise to restore the lost communion and he did that when Christ came, as Fox said, 'over 1600 years ago' in human flesh. Christ began to reestablish the one true 'inward' religion, but his work of restoration was aborted when the Beast led all nations, peoples and tongues back into external religion. Christ reappeared in a new mode in mid-seventeenth century England. Through his oracle and avatar, George Fox, He publicly exposed the work of the Beast, and once and for all was finally poised to complete the work of restoration.[3] Put succinctly, Fox's reading of history and all events leading up to his own time was the history of this divine work of restoration and his prophetic role in bringing that process to completion.[4]

Harvard Theological Review, 40 (1947), pp. 191-195]. Hermeticism, however, lacked the fiery apocalyptic of early Quakerism and this is a fundamental distinction. Fox's proclamation of the everlasting gospel also linked him to a host of medieval, Reformation and early modern English prototypes of Joachim who anticipated a new age of the Spirit wherein a type of democratic mysticism would prevail in the 'inner' and 'outer' orders (Hill discusses the "myth of the everlasting gospel" and its effect on contemporaries of Fox in *World Turned Upside Down*, pp. 147-148). Early Quakerism is the last significant manifestation of the basic postulates of the Joachite everlasting gospel. Joachites tended to read in the events of their own day all the signs of the imminent change of the ages. For example, two proponents of Joachim's ideas, Salimbene of Parma and Gerard of Borgo San Donino, both preached the arrival of the everlasting gospel in their own day, providing specific dates commensurate with biblical prophecy and current events. Other leading lights among the Fransciscan Spirituals, like Pierre Jean d'Olivi and Ubertino of Casale, made similar predictions based on Joachite ideas. There are echoes of this in Fox although there is no evidence he ever read Joachite literature. Quakers too, tended to read in the English Revolution, the victory of the 'Good Old Cause' and the Restoration, signs of the imminent change of the ages. Where Fox differed from many militant, crusading Joachites, like the German Reformer Thomas Müntzer, was his claim to be a theophany, his aversion to armed insurrection of any kind (although the call to take up arms was not wholly absent from other quarters of the Quaker movement even after the Restoration) and his view that the new age of the Spirit was not imminent but immanent in the present.

[3]This summary, in one form or another appears frequently in Fox's writings. *See Cambridge Journal*, 1, p. 124 and H. Cadbury, (ed.), *Narrative Papers of George Fox* (Richmond, Indiana: Friends United Press, 1972), pp. 35-36.

[4]One of the driving forces in Christianity has been the striving for perfection and Fox was not the first to proclaim a total reversal of the effects of the Fall in this life. The Marcionites and Montanists did so before him, as did the Cathars. Arius not only reaffirmed man's capacity for perfection but wrote "indeed we can become Sons of God like Christ" [Quoted in R. Lane Fox, *Pagans and Christians in the Mediterranean World from the second century A.D. to the conversion of Constantine* (Penguin, 1988), p. 602]. This belief, at least

There were several important features about Fox's conception of Paradise that enable us to understand what it was that he believed was being restored in his own day. In the beginning God had created man and woman in his image. What this meant to Fox was that they were in a pre-Fall, pre-carnal state which made them equal to God and put them in direct communion with him. This direct communion was possible because the eternal, pre-existent, unchanging creator Christ ('seed') dwelt in them.[5] It was this direct, inward, immanent communion that Fox was referring to when he called God, and more specifically, Christ, the 'first-speaker' in Paradise.

In their state of pre-Fall glory Adam and Eve lived as yet untouched by the sin that would eventually destroy their union with God. This occurred when they chose to follow the 'second-speaker' who was defined by Fox as Satan.[6] The result of this cleavage was catastrophic. There was a loss of the divine image, power, perfection, dominion and a silencing of the divine voice within.[7]

Adam and Eve were subsequently driven out of Paradise and into the earth (not so much a physical place as a spiritual state) where death passed over all things. A flaming sword (a biblical symbol for the return to Paradise) was placed before the entrance to Eden to guard against any

---

among those who proclaimed it, has had a pronounced effect on views of the equality between men and women as well as on views of sexuality. Because the effects of the Fall had been reversed women as well as men could teach, preach, exorcize and hold office. Celibacy too, was a sign of the recovery of Paradise and a return to 'a childlike simplicity of heart'. In early Christianity virginity "makes itself equal to the angels: it excels the angels, because it must struggle against the flesh to master a nature which the angels do not possess," so wrote Novatian (Quoted in Lane Fox, *Pagans and Christians*, 366). Celibacy and virginity were linked to the reversal of the Fall. Fox considered himself to be transfigured and of an 'altered human nature' such as was possessed before the Fall. After his marriage to Margaret Fell, Fox bluntly inferred to a Puritan that because he was in a glorified state even sex was "below him." (Nickalls, *Journal*, p. 557). Celibacy was a sign of the return to pre-Fall glory.

[5]George Fox, *Gospel Truth Demonstrated in a Collection of Doctrinal Books*, in *The Works of George Fox*, 4-6, (Philadelphia: Marcus T. Gould, 1831), 4, p. 367; 5, p. 300; 6, p. 357. Hereafter cited as *Gospel Truth Demonstrated*.

[6]*Ibid.*, 6, p. 31.

[7]*Ibid.*, 5, p. 307; 6, pp. 31-32.

possible return.[8] At the same time God made a promise to restore all things to their pre-Fall state of perfection and glory. This promise, Fox believed, was not made to woman but to the pre-existent 'seed' (Christ) who dwelt in woman.[9] This 'seed' (not 'seeds') would 'bruise the serpent's head' or deal a death blow to the power of Satan and thus restore the broken unity between God and man,[10] a promise, said Fox, that was believed by all the ancient Fathers and Prophets.[11] Because the promise was made to the Christ within woman (and all humankind) Fox was able to believe in the potential of a total and irreversible[12] restoration of all people to Paradise as opposed to the calvinist particularism predominant in his day.

The final and complete restoration of the breach between God and man, the return to Paradise and the divinization of the saints was the everlasting gospel that was given to Adam and Eve (the "seed of woman") and to Abraham ("in thy seed") four hundred and thirty years, by Fox's calculation, before Moses and the giving of the Law.[13] It was then given to Moses, all the prophets, the Apostles and now to Fox. Although all Quakers proclaimed one or another version of this everlasting gospel Fox believed that he was its first proclaimer after 1600 years of darkness. It was a powerful and fresh proclamation of a message that had not been heard in quite the same way since the days of Jesus and it even contained elements

---

[8]Genesis 3:24. This was a common symbol in Fox's writings. It also appeared in one of his great visions and on one of his three seals Fox had imprinted "GF and the Flaming Sword". In his will Fox left the seal to Nathaniel Meade (*The Last Will of George Fox*, in *The Harleian Miscellany*, p. 639; *Cambridge Journal*, 2, p. 355).

[9]*Epistles*, 8, p. 146; *GMGW*, 3, p. 508.

[10]*Epistles*, 7, pp. 75, 155, 210, 218, 264. This reconciliation was ultimately the uniting of "heaven and earth into one" again (*Epistles*, 8, p.273).

[11]*Gospel Truth Demonstrated*, 6, pp. 30-31.

[12]*Epistles*, 7, pp. 225, 228, 254, 325; 8, pp. 139, 243. *See also* H.L. Doncaster, "Early Quaker Thought on "That State in Which Adam was before he Fell"," *JFHS*, 41 (1949), pp. 13-24.

[13]*Gospel Truth Demonstrated*, 4, p. 32; 6, pp. 390-391; Cadbury, *Narrative Papers*, p. 36.

that superseded the message of Jesus, for Fox was not a reincarnate Jesus in the flesh but a new and final revelation of the pre-existent Christ.

Christ's first appearance in the flesh of this world was a crucial event in Fox's prophetic view of history.[14] With the physical appearance of Christ Daniel's vision (7:13) of the Kingdom of God and the Son of Man came to pass. Daniel's 'little stone' (2:40) crushed the four monarchies (Babylon, Persia, Greece and Rome) and in their place he became a mountain that began to fill the whole earth.[15] What people everywhere saw was not a physical phenomenon. It was the inward revelation of the everlasting gospel, the rising of the Christ within. People everywhere were enabled to see because the Spirit of understanding and power had been poured out upon all flesh in accordance with Joel 2:28.[16]

However, in the days of the Apostles an event occurred that aborted the universal growth of the one true worship. The Devil appeared and made war against the "man-child" (Jesus Christ) and his seed. The man-child was caught up to heaven and the seed was persecuted and scattered. In Fox's view of things external religion once again became predominant. Christianity was planted by men and women who were out of the spirit and power of the Apostles. It was planted by men's will and not God's will. It was planted by those who rebelled against the Spirit of God by teaching that prophecy, visions and immediate revelation had ceased.[17] This was the spirit of the

---

[14]Fox and other early Quaker writers, including Margaret Fell, expended much energy writing and directing pamphlets to the Jews (especially in Holland) both in order to convince them that the Messiah had come and because Quakers believed that the Jews had an important role in the apocalyptic events of the last days. For a description of Quaker relations with the Jews in Holland *see* H. Cadbury, "Hebraica and the Jews in Early Quaker Interest," in *Children of the Light*, pp. 135-163; W.I. Hull, *The Rise of Quakerism in Amsterdam, 1655-1665* (Swarthmore College Monograph, No. 4, 1938) and *Benjamin Furly and Quakerism in Rotterdam*; R.H. Popkin, "Spinoza's Relations With the Quakers in Amsterdam," *QH*, 73 (1984), pp. 14-28.

[15]*Gospel Truth Demonstrated*, 5, p. 413; *Epistles*, 8, pp. 155, 310 and Burrough, *A Measure of the Times*, p. 4.

[16]*Gospel Truth Demonstrated*, 5, pp. 314, 321, 344-45, 414; 6, p. 334.

[17]*Gospel Truth Demonstrated*, 6, p. 394; Burrough, *A Measure of the Times*, pp. 5-6. If all Christendom had remained in the life and power of Christ and the apostles then the work

false church (Beast)[18] that arose in the days of the Apostles. It professed the saints' words but was out of their life. It had the 'notion' but not the 'possession', the 'profession' but not the 'substance'.[19] External religion was rebuilt and it was taught, said Fox, that there could be no restoration to Paradise and pre-Fall glory in this life.[20] Christ was encased in heaven, far away from man, and the separation between God and man was entrenched as a pillar of Christian orthodoxy.

The true church that continued in the spirit and power of the Apostles was forced to flee into the 'wilderness'. This was the beginning of the latter three and one half days or years (forty-two months) recorded in Daniel 9 and it applied to the whole period of time between the appearance of the Beast and the great apostasy and the present time when Fox's apocalyptic appearance and proclamation of the everlasting gospel exposed and brought to an end the rule of the Beast.[21] During the time, and times and a half time (the time between the apostasy and Fox) the building of the New Jerusalem ceased.[22] However Christ returned inwardly and continued to reign in his

---

of universal restoration would have been completed before Fox's day (*Gospel Truth Demonstrated*, 5, p. 336).

[18]The coming of Antichrist or 'man of sin' was not a future event for Fox. He said that in John's *Apocalypse* all nations had already drunk of the whore's cup and followed the Beast. Had not Christ said that false prophets would come and had John not seen them in his own day (I John 2 and 4)? And "Paul saw the man of sin before his decease, the coming of sin before his decease, the coming of him with lying signs and wonders" [*The Great Mystery of the Great Whore Unfolded; and Antichrist's Kingdom Revealed Unto Destruction*, in *The Works of George Fox*, 3, (Philadelphia: Marcus T. Gould, 1831), 3, p. 184. Hereafter cited as *The Great Mystery of the Great Whore*. *See also Gospel Truth Demonstrated*, 4, pp. 169-70, 227, 235; 5, pp. 86-87].

[19]*Epistles*, 7, pp. 165-66, 326; 8, p. 138.

[20]*Ibid.*, 7, pp. 327-28.

[21]Underhill, "Early Quaker Eschatolgy," p. 97 confirms the interpretation from Daniel 9. Fox never used prophecy to forecast the future, probably because the future was already present for him. Rather, he used prophecy to explain what had already come to pass - the historical appearance of the Messiah, his subsequent 'cutting-off', the dark night of apostasy that had since arisen and now the present return of Christ from the wilderness.

[22]The New Jerusalem was a subject of special interest to Fox. It had both spiritual and physical dimensions. In 1671 Fox and two friends made a calculation about the physical size of the New Jerusalem based on Revelation 21:16. They found it to be 216,000 miles or

persecuted followers. This was in fact Christ's promised second coming and it was on ongoing event. For the past 1600 years, said Fox, Christ was present but hidden in the earth (people's hearts).[23]

The loss of immediacy and the reversion to external religion brought with it a loss of immediate revelation. With the loss of immediacy came the loss of power. This allowed confusion, disunity, injustice and inequity to re-entrench in the world.[24] One of the certain marks of the false church was its

---

1,728,000 furlongs (*Cambridge Journal*, 2, p. 170). Fox later discussed this calculation in a 1677 pamphlet entitled *A Testimony of What We Believe of Christ* where he used a Greek copy of Arius Montanus' interlinear translation of the Bible to confirm the earlier calculation of 216,000 miles (*Gospel Truth Demonstrated*, 5, p. 139). He also had, in his library, a copy of a Dutch commentary on the Book of Revelation, written by Jan Stevensz. In this commentary, *Apocalypsis*, [now located in the Mennonite Library (Bibliotheek der Vereenigde Doopsgezinde Gemeente) in Amsterdam], Stevensz calculated the size of the New Jerusalem to be only 1,500 miles. Concerned Dutch Friends probably passed this commentary on to Fox who was sufficiently disturbed by its calculations of the New Jerusalem to send a correction back to Holland [H. Cadbury, "George Fox's Library Again," *JFHS*, 30 (1933), p. 11]. Fox's concerns about the correct literal dimension of the New Jerusalem appear to reflect his belief about the literal universal scope of the Kingdom of God. When the imminent victory over the Beast was complete the whole earth would be transformed into the New Jerusalem. To suggest any dimension less than the size of the earth was to confess to a less than complete victory in the Lamb's War.

[23]*Gospel Truth Demonstrated*, 5, p. 150; *Epistles*, 7, p. 291. Christ was not taken up out of the earth and made spiritually remote from people. He was taken to the right hand of God in heaven which was within. There the saints sat and reigned with him in heavenly places, also within. And from here, within the saints, he continued his work of restoration. As for Fox's belief in a remnant of the true church continuing to exist through the ages this is confirmed in his *Itinerary Journal* where he writes of those saints who were living 300 years after Jesus Christ [George Fox, *Short and Itinerary Journals of George Fox*, ed. by N. Penney (Cambridge University Press, 1925), p. 203]. Edward Burrough also followed this line of interpretation. The true church of Christ, the Lamb's spouse, had been forced to flee into the wilderness for 1,260 days or 42 months. There the true church was subjected to severe persecution and suffering "though she hath not been prevailed against nor overcome, so as to be extinguished from having a being" [*A Visitation and Warning Proclaimed* (London, 1659), p. 21].

[24]*Gospel Truth Demonstrated*, 4, p. 410; *Epistles*, 8, p. 57; Burrough, *A Measure of the Times*, pp. 10-12. Thus the devastating impact of the early schisms in Quakerism. Public and spiritual unity among Friends "was part of the doctrinal bedrock of Quakerism - a corollary of the Inward Light ... If Friends disagreed irreconcilably about spiritual matters and split into factions, the foundation of the doctrine of spiritual unity was undermined and the credibility of Truth compromised" [R. Bauman, *Let Your Words Be Few: Symbolism of Speaking and Silence Among Seventeenth Century Quakers* (London: Cambridge University Press, 1983), p. 142]. The purity of the Church was another major theme in early Quaker writing and preaching. A church without spot or wrinkle was another product of their perfectionism and their realized

declaration that all prophecy had ceased. Fox identified all this with the spirit of "Judas" - an inward state of sin that arose at the time of the apostasy and openly attacked all those who upheld the spirit of prophecy and immediate revelation.[25]

The attack on immediate revelation was central to Fox's counter-attack on external religion. Immediacy was an essential part of the everlasting gospel preached by Christ as the new covenant under which there was no further need for one person to teach another about the things of God.[26] The great assault against immediacy (the attack on inward, spiritual religion) was the very heart of the religion of the Beast. Instead of external religion falling away as Christ had intended, external religion was reconstituted by the very ones who, in outward profession, claimed to follow Christ. The tithe system, professional clergy and the national or state church (all things Fox criticized the Reformation for failing to change) became pillars in the religion of the Beast which succeeded in deceiving all peoples, nations and tongues save for the persecuted few who continued to constitute the true church in the wilderness.[27]

The prophetic appearance of Fox was not only a new proclamation of the everlasting gospel after 1600 years of darkness but it was the final proclamation. What distinguished Fox from Jesus was that the assault against external religion begun by Jesus would be completed by Fox. Daniel's 'stone' was growing again, having commenced with the appearance of Fox, and this time the Beast would be overthrown and the New Jerusalem

---

eschatology [Fox, *Epistles*, 8, pp. 148, 275-277; James Parnell, *A Shield of Truth* (London, 1655), pp. 29-33].

[25]*Gospel Truth Demonstrated*, 6, pp. 432-453. "Judas" was a metaphor for spiritual disobedience, but it was much more as well. Because Christ was present in Quakers as he had been in the prophets and apostles, when Fox *named* one as 'Judas' he was making more than a simple analogy. The accused "experience is Judas' experience, just as the Christ within makes Fox able to say so bluntly of his own prophecy, 'it was the word of the Lord and of Christ to him'" (Cope, "Seventeenth Century Quaker Style," p. 223).

[26]*Ibid.*, 6, p. 396.

[27]Margaret Fell made the same criticism: "O how dare you profess reformation when cruelty and tyranny rules in the land" (*See* Margaret Fell's public letter concerning Fox's trial at Carlisle, *Cambridge Journal*, 1, p. 118).

would reach universal proportions.[28]   What remained in this apocalyptic drama, then, was the final overthrow of the Beast and the completion of the promised work of restoration.

Fox had a unique prophetic role in this final apocalyptic drama. William Penn considered him to be "the pre-eminent prophetic figure of the times."   He called Fox "God's angel and special messenger".[29]   Fox was considered to be the first to rediscover the lost inner Christ after over 1600 years of apostasy.   This alone would have given him a position of pre-eminence.   His youthful revelatory "openings" described in his *Journal* tell us something of the development of a prophet with a unique mission: "I was commanded to turn the people to that inward light", "I was to bring them off from Jewish ceremonies ... heathenish fables ... men's inventions and windy

---

[28]*See* Francis Ellington, *Christian Information Concerning These Last Times* (London, 1664) as an example of a Quaker author, other than Fox, who makes extensive and accurate use of Fox's eschatology. Ellington, a Quaker from Wellingborough, was twice imprisoned for his beliefs. In addition to writing two pamphlets he wrote rhymes, as did his fellow Quaker John Swinton. In an unpublished paper I argue that Keith Thomas' linking of Ellington's use of Boehme to the *Prophecy of Thomas Becket* is a misnomer (Thomas, *Religion and the Decline of Magic*, p. 468). After an internal analysis and comparison of the *Prophecy of Thomas Becket* [which dates as far back as 1338 according to P.A. Brown, *The Development of the Legend of Thomas Becket* (Philadelphia, 1930), p. 230] in Royal 12.C.XII (BL) and in J.P. Migne, *Patrologiae Cursus Completus*, CXC (1854), p. 354 with Boehme's prophecies contained in *Mercurius Teutonicus, or; a Christian Information Concerning the Last Times* (London, 1656; BL) I concluded that the parts of Boehme's prophecies which Ellington used approximated the symbols in Becket's *Prophecy* but too much dissimilarity remained in the particulars for the two to be specifically equated. Boehme showed none of the consistency of *Becket's Prophecy*. Boehme's major theme was different - it was purely religious and involved the tribulation of the lily (God's elect) and the final destruction of Babylon through God's agent of divine judgment, the Turks. Becket's *Prophecy* was a political prophecy that implied an apocalyptic style victory of the English over the lily or French crown. The imagery was drawn from a common source (Jeremiah, Ezekiel and Isaiah) and many prophets through the ages used it, including Nostradamus. We must, therefore, call into question the view that Quakers attributed the *Prophecy of Thomas Becket* to Jacob Boehme. The prophecy used by Ellington and attributed to Boehme was a separate prophecy, a Behemist prophecy that used similar symbolism and was much better adapted to Quaker purposes. Boehme's 'lily', as opposed to the lily in Becket's Prophecy could easily be interpreted as Quakerism. By using Boehme's prophecy Quakers were also able to overcome their disappointment in eschatological delays by turning to ancient and modern prophecies which spoke of their imminent deliverance from the Beast.

[29]M. Endy, *William Penn and Early Quakerism* (Princeton University Press, 1973), p. 335.

doctrines ... images and crosses ... sprinkling of infants ... holy days ... vain traditions."[30] He was to sound the Day of the Lord and in the power of the everlasting gospel call people back from their long apostasy, into the true church that was returning from the wilderness. This was no small claim and Fox backed it up with signs and claims of power - miracles, visions, altered states and ultimately claims to be equal with God. His perceived unique place in his age and movement was confirmed and re-confirmed throughout his life and especially whenever his pre-eminence was threatened or, in the 1670's when he used a powerful vision of the inner Christ (to be discussed in a later chapter) to compel his followers to recognize him as a specially empowered prophet. This vision, too, was selectively edited from the sources.

Soon after his famous vision at Pendle Hill in 1652 (where the twenty-eight year old Fox came to believe that he was divinely called to gather a great people for his cause)[31] Fox stood atop a rock at rugged Firbank Fell (not unlike Paul on Mars Hill) and for three hours spoke prophetically to a very large gathering of local people, many of whom belonged to a Seeker group led by Francis Howgill and John Audland. What he told them was that God had sent him to declare the everlasting gospel and reveal to the world things that had not been known since the days of Jesus:

> And so I opened the prophets and the figures and shadows and turned them to Christ the substance, and then opened the parables of Christ and the things that had been hid from the beginning, and showed them the estate of the Epistles how they were written to the elect; and the state of the apostasy that has been since the apostles' days, and how the priests have got the Scriptures and are not in that spirit which gave them forth; who make a trade of their words and have put them into chapter and verse; and how that the teachers and priests now are found in the steps of the false prophets, chief priests, scribes, and Pharisees.[32]

---

[30]Nickalls, *Journal*, pp. 35-36.

[31]*Ibid.*, p. 104.

[32]*Ibid.*, p. 109.

Fox perceived his mission to be a uniquely prophetic one, that was, to expose and judge external religion and everything associated with it and complete the repairing of the breach between God and man. In Fox's words he had been called to "reap out" the everlasting gospel from among apostates. What he 'saw' by divine revelation and then prophetically conveyed to his hearers was that Christ had returned (ie. Christ and his saints were coming up out of the wilderness) and through the words of his avatar was proclaiming the final judgment of the Beast and the completion of the restoration of all things to their pre-Fall paradisiacal state.[33]

Fox never sought prophetic precedent for his declaration that Christ had returned to complete his work of restoration nor did he make any calculations that brought him to the year 1648 or 1652.[34] He simply declared

---

[33]*Ibid.*, p. 27.

[34]He did date the time between Adam and the giving of the Law at roughly 1600 years. He may have drawn a parallel between the beginning of apostasy and the rise of the 'man of sin' in Apostolic times and the roughly 1600 years to the return of Christ in his own day (*Short and Itinerary Journals*, p. 204). He once commented on the vision in Daniel 7:13 and then asked his adversaries to calculate the time (in days or years) "and see what time yourselves be in" (*Gospel Truth Demonstrated*, 5, p. 62). At another time he made a reference to *Esdras* 7:26ff. followed by some unusual calculations which are vague (*Ibid.*, 5, 84). The only two times I found a Quaker reference to other prophecies (apart from the direct revelations within their group) were a reference to Jacob Boehme in Francis Ellington's *Christian Information Concerning These Last Times* which prophecied of a great people of God coming from the North and the Quaker Thomas Killam reported to the learned Quaker Thomas Lawson that his wife had uncovered an apocryphal book entitled *The Testament of the Patriarchs* (published in English translation since 1581). Killam discovered therein reference to a prophecy known as the *Book of Enoch*, another apocryphal work that contained a strident anti-clericalism. This work was not yet discovered and therefore unavailable to Killam apart from brief references to its anti-clerical nature in the *Testament of the Twelve Patriarchs*. Nevertheless, Enoch's prophecy did capture the attention of some Quakers, not specifically for what it foretold but because it seemed in its purposes and insights to be aligned with the Quakers purposes (*See* "Thomas Lawson to Margaret Fell," *Swarthmore MSS.* 1, No. 243; H.J. Cadbury, "Hebraica and Jews in Early Quaker Interest," pp. 160-61). Fox frowned on prophetic speculation because, in his mind, Christ had already come and no further physical coming was expected. The only purpose of ancient prophecy was to show what had happened, not what was to happen in the future. All that was expected for the future was the capitulation of Babylon as the Stone (Christ) grew. This was where a tension arose between an inward and present and a yet-to-come Kingdom in Fox's eschatology. This ambiguity as we will see, led Quakers into troubled times especially when some Quaker prophets, like James Milner and James Nayler proclaimed themselves to be the returned Messiah. This was not in keeping with Fox's spiritualized and realized eschatology and he denounced this kind of speculation as the folly of an "airy" spirit (ie. of the Prince of the air or Devil) that was not the true Spirit of

this fact through visionary insight and direct revelation. Prophetic precedence was not necessary. The message was new. An avatar does not base his claims on prophetic precedence or the written word. He is a unique manifestation of the divine.

The old and the new were contained in this prophetic declaration. The return of Christ was but a continuation of his inward return to his own generation and his continued dwelling in the saints in the wilderness. What was new in this proclamation was that Christ was speaking in a new way through a new avatar (not through the historic Jesus) and the work of restoration was to be completed universally, once and for all time, through the proclamation of this prophet, magus and avatar.

The penultimate stage in Fox's prophetic view of history, and in fact the most publicized aspect of Quaker eschatology, was the actual overthrow of the Beast along with his institution of external religion.[35] Mystery Babylon was being confounded and though it rose up against the Lamb and the saints, this time it was being revealed, judged, defeated and cast into the lake of fire.[36] The day had dawned and the Kingdom of God was emerging from its long hiatus in the wilderness.[37] The everlasting gospel was being preached

God which renewed the mind. Presumably, says Braithwaite, Fox was able to distinguish these spirits (*Beginnings*, p. 147).

[35]The identification of the Beast of Revelation with external religion was prefigured in Thomas Edwards' catalogue of heresies (*Gangraena*, first edition), p. 32.

[36]*Great Mystery of the Great Whore*, 3, pp. 249, 489-90; *Gospel Truth Demonstrated*, 4, pp. 100, 229, 238; 6, pp. 124-25. The mere presence of a place of eternal torment in Fox's writings is a challenge to any notion that Fox was a universalist. It is not coincidence, then, that most works on Quaker universalism by-pass the first generation of Quakers (with their crusading apocalyptic and belief in eternal damnation for those who extinguished the light of Christ within) and begin with Penn and Barclay. Arthur Roberts would tend to agree with this view, although for other reasons articulated in his recent article "The Universalism of Christ in Early Quaker Understanding," *Quaker Religious Thought*, 24 (1989), pp. 2-17.

[37]Descriptive imagery that described the breaking of the dark night of apocalyptic history was frequently used by Fox and other Quakers. The 'day was breaking', 'light was springing', 'life was rising', 'glory was reappearing', the 'night was over', the 'darkness past', the 'Day-Star' that rose in the apostles' days had returned, the 'morning-star was rising', the sun was rising, the 'morning had broken', the 'day was dawning', the 'winter past', 'summer had come', the 'singing of birds was heard in the land', the pearl that had been hidden in the earth was found, the 'Lamb's voice was known', the 'wedding-day was appearing', the 'true church was appearing', the everlasting gospel was going forth into the whole world again (*Great*

(prophetically proclaimed) "over the heads of the beast and false prophet".[38] The 'stone' (Christ) had already fallen upon the reprobate and the gospel's growth to universal proportions was unstoppable, even if the priests, learned scholars, government and King rose up against it.[39] The growth of the 'stone' could not be restrained by the Beast. The victory denied the Lamb and the saints over '1600 years ago' was now assured. This act of 'overthrowing' was the act of revealing mystery Babylon, not by taking up the physical sword, although some early Quakers saw that as a possibility, but by proclaiming the everlasting gospel. The new commission had been given. Fox had announced it. Burrough set the date of the giving of this new commission at 1652 and located the springing up of the 'seed' in the north of England where Fox first began his preaching,[40] (although Fox had begun his preaching well before this time) - a strange fulfillment of Jacob Boehme's prophecy that "the

---

Mystery of the Great Whore, 3, pp. 170, 294 and 1659 edition, Hh1r; *Gospel Truth Demonstrated*, 4, p. 166; *Epistles*, 7, pp. 157, 268; 8, p. 33; Burrough, *A Measure of the Times*, pp. 23, 25). This was all in contrast to the medieval eschatological outlook in which the present was still the winter of apocalyptic history.

[38]*Great Mystery of the Great Whore*, 3, pp. 354-56.

[39]*Ibid.*, 3, p. 100; Ellington, *Christian Information Concerning These Last Times*, pp. 3-5.

[40]*Great Mystery of the Great Whore*, 3, p. 11. Burrough's dating is in line with what is generally considered the formal origin of Quakerism - Fox's vision at Pendle Hill and his first visit to Swarthmoor. Fox was at work preaching, proclaiming the everlasting gospel and performing all manner of signs and wonders between 1644 and 1652, long before Burrough, Dewsbury or any of the 'valiant sixty' knew him. Not all Quakers set the date of origin at 1652. John Whitehead, set the time of beginnings at 1648: "... in the year 1648 God ... did cause a Branch to spring forth of the root of David ... and he spread and shot forth many branches ... and the weary came to rest under his branches." Whitehead then cited 1652 as the year of his conversion when "I being a branch of this tree, the life of its root caused me to bud forth" [*A Small Treatise* (London, 1661), p. 4]. Whitehead may have been referring to the broken Baptist congregation following Fox in 1648 while Burrough was referring to Fox's vision at Pendle Hill and his appearance at Swarthmoor Hall. The influx of new blood into Fox's fledgling movement may generally be associated with the end of the civil war when many young and idealistic soldiers left the army and returned to their homes, still prepared to continue the fight for the 'Good Old Cause' at every turn. These early years of the *Interregnum* coincided with the meteoric rise of Quakerism. This was when Quakerism gathered many of the young antinomic personalities that had developed throughout the turbulent 1640's (a time that may be socially and psychologically compared to the 1930's or 1960's of our present era).

lily would bloom in the North."[41] The sign of the new commission was the preaching of the everlasting gospel with all its commensurate revelations, signs and wonders.

The declaration of this new order was not only through preaching in the early years. Proof that the Kingdom of God was once again present and growing also lay in Quaker prophecies, visions, healings, the casting out of demons, raising people from the dead, innumerable varieties of sign enactments like running naked through public places, refusal to pay tithes, take oaths, doff the hat to superiors or address superiors with the customary "you". This was all part of the act of 'overthrowing' the Kingdom of Antichrist and making room for the Kingdom of God to reach universal proportions.[42]

With this goal in mind the Quakers uttered the judgments of the Lord upon all ministers and priests and teachers and churches and practices that

---

[41]Hill, *World Turned Upside Down*, p. 176. The idea of a chosen people coming down from the north may be located in Jeremiah 6:22. In Psalms 42:8 the inhabitation of Zion is in the far north. While the entire Boehme corpus was translated into English between 1647 and 1661 by John Sparrow and John Ellistone his actual influence on Fox and Quakers is still uncertain. Jones, influenced by William James in this matter, exaggerated the ties to Boehme in the interest of proving continental mystical influences on Fox [Jones, *Mysticism and Democracy in the English Revolution*, p. 140. Nuttall is more cautious, *Holy Spirit in Puritan Faith and Experience*, p. 140]. For an excellent discussion of the impact of Boehme on sectarian discourse *see* Nigel Smith, *Perfection Proclaimed*, pp. 185-225. According to Smith, Boehme only "had a significant influence upon a handful of important sectarians," who in turn disseminated Boehme's ideas and thus made them "part of a wider knowledge" (*Ibid.* pp. 185-86). While the "finer points" of Boehme's thinking escaped most sectarians some of his more popular phrases, like "Day-Spring" (which is biblical: Job 38:1 and Luke 1:78) did work their way into sectarian vocabulary (*Ibid.*, p. 225).

[42]This also included treating women as equals. All people were restored to the pre-Fall image of God and their pre-Fall equality. Man no longer ruled over woman. The removal of the 'curse' and the restoration to Paradise was absolute in the present and all people and nations that experienced the rising of the Christ within were to reorder their lives accordingly. According to Fox Joel 2:28 was a present reality for male and female equally. To prophesy was a sign of the presence and power of God among His people. Christ was in male and female alike and where Christ was there was also freedom from the law and full equality. See *Great Mystery of the Great Whore*, pp. 106, 453; *Epistles*, 8, pp. 39, 69; *Concerning Sons and Daughters, and Prophetesses, Speaking and Prophesying, in the Law and in the Gospel* (London, No Date). The idea that it was "lawful for women to preach ... and ... [have] gifts as well as men" was prefigured in Thomas Edwards' catalogue of heresies (*Gangraena*, first edition), p. 30.

were perceived to be a part of Babylon or the Kingdom of Anti-Christ. "The day of vengeance of our God is come," said Margaret Fell while Fox wrote: "Reap out, reap out, reap out, (with the power of God) ye reapers unto the Lord, for here is the day of harvest."[43] This work of 'threshing' (going forth to reap the earth) was intimately linked to the work of restoration.[44] When Fox encouraged his followers to follow Christ into battle and take up the "sword of the Almighty, to hew down Baal's priests, corrupt judges, corrupt justices, corrupt lawyers, fruitless trees which encumber the ground"[45] and oppress tender consciences he was affirming the preaching of the everlasting gospel as a propaedeutic leading to the Kingdom of God.

The Kingdom grew from the inside out.[46] Personal transformation within the context of immediate revelation had to find its twin in the radical

---

[43]Margaret Fell, *A Testimony of the Touchstone* (London, 1656), p. 13 and Fox, *Epistles*, 7, p. 262.

[44]Threshing was a term Quakers drew from Revelation 14:14-20 where Christ was depicted as returning to earth with a sickle in his hand. One distinctive characteristic of early Quakerism was what they termed the 'threshing meeting'. These were great meetings held in large places or 'threshing floors'. Their specific purpose was the separation of the 'convinced' from the world. This separation was achieved by 'threshing' or bold and charismatic preaching, a very apocalyptic task given the days in which they were living. These meetings were held regularly (especially in London) and could attract up to thousands of people at a time. They were quite different from Quaker 'Retired Meetings' which were smaller meetings for worship where only the convinced attended. In 1652 Fox was already instructing his followers that only the strong in Truth were to undertake the arduous task of leading threshing meetings: "When there are any meetings in unbroken places, ye that go to minister to the world, take not the whole meeting of Friends with you ... but let Friends keep together, and wait in their own meeting place ... And let three, or four, or six, that are grown up strong, and are in the truth, go to such unbroken places, and thresh the heathenish nature" (*Epistles*, 7, p. 23). This policy was followed, for in 1655 Edward Burrough and Francis Howgill wrote: "We get Friends on the first days to meet together in several places out of the rude multitude ... and we go to the great meeting place which we have, which will hold a thousand people, which is nearly always filled, to thresh among the world" ["Edward Burrough and Francis Howgill to Margaret Fell" (January 27, 1655), in A.R. Barclay, (ed.), *Letters of Early Friends* (London: Darton and Harvey, 1841), p. 27]. Some Quakers were 'threshermen' (the angels were the reapers) - surely an exalted place and even a place of pride in early Quakerism.

[45]*Gospel Truth Demonstrated*, 4, p. 19; Ellwood, *Journal*, p. 187.

[46]Quaker writers acknowledged that Babylon was an inner, spiritual condition that had external consequenses [*see* William Dewsbury, *The Discovery of Man's Return to his First Estate* (London, 1654), p. 20].

38

transformation, or overthrowing of society. The latter could not precede the former. When Fox and early Quakers set out to overturn the world they were doing no more than proclaiming something they had personally and inwardly experienced. Even the dramatic act of Daniel's 'stone' striking the image was personalized. Before Christ the hills moved, mountains melted and the rocks broke apart.[47] As the terrible Day of the Lord drew near there would be great earthquakes and the Beast and false prophets would meet their end. It was an inward and outward phenomenon: "As thou hearest the thunder without thee, so thou must hear the thunder within thee; the voice without thee, so the voice within thee; these are figures: as the earthquake without thee, so earthquake within thee." Fox continued: "As there is a kingdom without, so there is a kingdom of heaven within; and the axe is laid to the tree root without, to hew down the tree without, so the axe is laid to the tree within."[48] Fox read scripture rather literally. When the earth was shaken and moved it was a sign that Christ was rising, both within and without. Fox said that the earth was shaking in his day and it was shaking in a way in which it had never shaken before, because the work of restoration was finally being brought to completion in the sense that there would never be another appearance of the 'man of sin' and there would never be another falling away: "and an earthquake is coming upon you that hath not been since the foundation of the world, out of which earthquake we are come, into that which cannot be shaken."[49] This earthquake was the denouement of history. It was the complete displacement of mystery Babylon and all external religion by the Kingdom of God. Fox described this inner apocalyptic drama in a 1648 vision:

> I saw there was a great crack throughout the earth, and a great smoke to go as the crack went; and that after the crack there should be a great shaking. This was the earth in people's hearts, which was to be shaken before the seal of God was to be raised up out of the earth. And it was so; for the Lord's

[47]*Gospel Truth Demonstrated*, 4, p. 19.

[48]Fox and Nayler, *A Word From the Lord to all the World, and all Professors in the World* (London, 1654), pp. 4, 6.

[49]*Great Mystery of the Great Whore*, 3, p. 99.

power began to shake them, and great meetings we began to have.[50]

The shaking of the kingdom of Babylon within created a crack which released the victorious inner Christ. This shaking was a fulfillment of the breaking of the sixth seal in Revelation 6:12ff. in which there was a great earthquake that displaced and darkened the natural order. There was no concept of a future external judgment here. It was inward and personally experienced in the present.

The exposing and judging of external religion and the linking of judgment to an inward disposition was a variation on an English apocalyptic interpretation of the history of Christianity that was widespread in mid-seventeenth century England. It was a view that did not need a theology of celestial inhabitation to spring forth. However Fox's christopresentism informed, shaped and enriched Quaker apocalyptic thinking. The literal incarnation of the flesh and bone of the glorified Christ (indeed of the whole Godhead) within the believer made the notion of realized eschatology intensely personal. The fact that Quakers were not distinct from Christ was not only a variation on English apocalyptic thought, it was a novel addition. Think, for example, how a proponent of celestial inhabitation would interpret Fox's statement: "Christ is come to reign ... who will rule the nations with a rod of iron, whose dread and power is to be sounded over all nations."[51] The Christ who had come was *in* the saints and from within them he rode conquering and to conquer, slaying all apostasy with the sword which was the "words of his mouth".[52] We will discuss celestial inhabitation in greater detail in chapter four but one brief statement from Fox will serve to illustrate the point here: "God's Christ is not distinct from his saints, nor their bodies, for he is within them; nor distinct from their spirits, for their spirits witness him ... he is in the saints, and they eat his flesh, and sit with him in heavenly places."[53] Fox was not speaking of a disembodied Christ here. Quakers were

---

[50]Nickalls, *Journal*, p. 22.

[51]*Gospel Truth Demonstrated*, 4, p. 225.

[52]*Great Mystery of the Great Whore*, 3, p. 288.

[53]*Ibid.*, 3, p. 340.

Christ, in some sense, and they were the instrument through which the final universal apocalyptic drama was enacted. When Fox repeatedly declared "Christ is come" he understood Christ to have been revealed *bodily* in the saints and that bodily appearance was a highly charged apocalyptic event that had meaning and significance for the early Quaker. It explains their powerful prophetic deportment in mid-seventeenth century English society.

Quaker conversion testimonies illustrate the apocalyptic meaning and significance of the experience of the inner Christ.[54] The subsequent outward experience of literal shaking, the great earthquake, was symbolic of that experience.[55] Quakers not only quaked, they even fell down under this power. Buildings were literally thought to shake when it was proclaimed, especially in the presence of Fox.[56] Once Fox caused a tumult in the city of Carlisle when he entered a steeplehouse and began to speak after the priest had finished the devotion. At that time, he wrote, "a mighty power of the Lord God ... made people to quiver and tremble ... that some thought the very steeplehouse had shaken."[57] The people perceived that a divine creature was in their midst. Trembling and certainly fear which caused it was

---

[54]Francis Howgill, *The Inheritance of Jacob Discovered After his Return out of Egypt* (London, 1656), pp. 11-13. This is the classic testimony that encapsulates events from Genesis to Revelation in a magnificent allegory of the fall of spiritual Babylon and the birth of the Kingdom of God within [*See also* William Dewsbury, *The Discovery of the Great Enmity* (London, 1655), pp. 17-19]. It was in the heart that these dramatic apocalyptic events were enacted. Fox pointed out that this great inner tribulation where the sun was darkened and the moon turned to blood and the stars fell and the grass withered had to occur first within before Christ could arise without (*Epistles*, 8, p. 59). Fox was still using this apocalyptic imagery of the moon turning to blood in 1690, shortly before his death (*Ann. Cat.*, #39H, p. 202). Owen Watkins concurred on the topic of Quaker use of biblical metaphor: "All the historical events of the Bible - the fall of man, the rule of sin and death until Moses, the giving of the Law, the hope of a redeemer given by the prophets, the preparation by John the Baptist who washed with water, the death and resurrection of our Lord, the spread of the knowledge of the gospel and the final cleansing of all things - all these events found their truest significance as they happened in turn to the individual believer". Watkins concluded, "Thus while not denying the historical truth of Scriptures the Friends were able to interpret their own lives as an actual re-living of the Bible, and so found in its pages the language of their written confessions" [O. Watkins, "Some Early Quaker Autobiographies," *JFHS*, 45 (1953), p. 73].

[55]The liberation of the soul from the body of sin that was its prison (*Great Mystery of the Great Whore*, p. 140).

[56]Nickalls, *Journal*, p. 122.

[57]*Short and Itinerary Journals*, p. 62; Nickalls, *Journal*, p. 23.

a general response to the appearance of biblical theophanies. Moses, David, Daniel, Habakuk, Isaiah and Paul trembled at the word of the Lord. In Joel the earth trembled. When Jesus spoke his voice shook the heavens and the earth.[58] This was occurring again in Fox's day when, "the trumpet is blown in Zion, and the alarm is sounded in his holy mountain, which makes the earth to tremble, and it doth tremble at the Word of the Lord, (and is by the dark world called Quakers), which power and voice now is known among us, which doth not only shake the earth but the heavens."[59] There was a blurring of the distinction between metaphoric and literal experience. Their conception of language was that it was borne out of the power of personal experience. When they opened their mouths God spoke and the earth trembled,[60] especially in the presence of an avatar like Fox who proclaimed that the glorified Christ actually inhabited them - a notion, if it can be grasped, that would make any believer tremble!

The experience of trembling ultimately defies analysis of reason. In fairness to those early Quakers they were neither epileptics as Casaubon said, nor insane as their Anglican opponents charged. Critics simply did not experience the immanence of God the way Quakers did. Opponents of early Quakers also accused them of confusing the spiritual judgment at the time of conversion with the great judgment at the end of time. Fox replied that this was no more than a ploy to avoid judgment in the present. It only hindered the raising of the Kingdom of God. By procrastinating on the judgment the Kingdom of God would never be realized in the present but would always be

---

[58]*Gospel Truth Demonstrated*, 4, pp. 255-58; *Epistles*, 7, p. 173; George Fox and James Nayler, *Saul's Errand to Damascus* (London, 1653). The copy used for this study is located in Fox, *Works*, vol. 3. *See* p. 590. Also Exodus 33:18-23, 19:16ff., Psalms 119:120, Job 4:14ff., Augustine, *Confessions*, Book 7, chap. 10 and St. John of the Cross, *Spiritual Canticle*, Stanza xii: 3, first recession.

[59]*Gospel Truth Demonstrated*, 4, p. 72.

[60]"The Quaker understanding of how one reaches the spiritual truths locked in the magic of words ... demands an ever closer attention to the words "syllabatim" until one is drawn physically into the special literalness in which alone words can give up their secrets" (Cope, "Seventeenth Century Quaker Style," p. 214). When the Quakers waited in silence during their worship they were never waiting for the "voice of human piety" like the Puritans, they were waiting for the voice of God. "When the answer came, it came as an immediate grasp of spiritual reality; when it was spoken out to the meeting, it was the voice of God which sounded the deeps of divine significance in the words" (*Ibid.*, pp. 216-17).

42

a future event. This was the most common complaint that early Quakers laid against their critics - they put Christ too far off. They also complained that their critics were fighting the enemy in the wrong place. Fox roundly condemned the Fifth Monarchists for seeking to kill the whore without when in fact they should have been, he said, looking within. "I told them the whore was alive in them",[61] and it was not purged with the carnal sword but with the power and spirit the Apostles were in. Those who were looking strictly for an outward kingdom were misguided as were those who put the judgment in the future and looked for an external appearance of Christ in the future.

However, once the Kingdom of God was established within it would not be without external consequences that would involve the complete reordering of all orders. Out of this personal apocalypse emerged an all out war against external injustice and the Quaker doctrine of immanence gave added authority to this war. When Fox called down woes upon the 'Bloody city of Lichfield' (which he knew had been the scene of past bloody martyrdoms)[62] and attacked greed, dishonesty and inhumanity he did so as the 'Son of God' who had come to proclaim the day of harvest and judgment, just as Jesus had done in his day. Fox spoke with divine authority when he said, "Arm yourselves like men of war that ye may know what to stand against ... set up truth and confound deceit which stains the earth ... the dead stinks upon the earth ... therefore bury it."[63] Fox sounded the battle cry after over 1600 years of apostasy. In 1653 he wrote: "The battle is begun and the sword drawn which must not be put up until he has made a separation in hewing down... The glittering sword is drawn to hew down you fruitless trees."[64]

---

[61]*Cambridge Journal*, 2, p. 12.

[62]*See* Braithwaite, *Beginnings*, p. 56 and Beatrice Saxon, "Woe to the Bloody City of Lichfield," *JFHS*, 41 (1949), pp. 86-87. Fox's mother may have been the descendant of one Mrs. Joyce Lewis who was burnt at Lichfield in 1557 (Braithwaite, *Beginnings*, p. 29).

[63]*Epistles*, 7, p. 70.

[64]*Gospel Truth Demonstrated*, 4, pp. 29-30. Even Margaret Fell used such rhetoric. In 1653 she wrote a public letter in support of the imprisoned Fox at Carlisle. She charged that God would "dash to pieces all his enemies" with a rod of iron. "They shall find the Lord of the vineyard is coming to look for fruits and will reward every man according to the deeds ..." (*Cambridge Journal*, 1, pp. 118, 120). *See also* William Dewsbury, *A True Prophecy of the Mighty Day of the Lord* (London, 1655), p. 6.

Such rhetoric found inspiration in the context of revolutionary England. The English Revolution itself was laden with apocalyptic meaning and the apocalyptic language often reached a fervent revolutionary pitch. Nonconformists of all shades marched forth under the banner of the 'Good Old Cause' and participated in the great 'triumph of the saints'.[65] The more astute opponents of Quakerism in Parliament, and in city magistracies like Bristol, recognized that it was but a short step from spiritualized crusading apocalyptic language to the externalizing of that violence as had happened a century earlier in the German Peasants' Revolt and Münster. It was a disconcerting element in early Quaker rhetoric that eventually contributed to General Monck's decision to purge Quakers from the army.[66]

---

[65]*See* M. Tolmie, *The Triumph of the Saints* (Cambridge University Press, 1977).

[66]There was ambiguity in early Quakerism about how the victory of the Lamb and the saints would be accomplished. In 1653 Nayler said "mind the promise of the Father, at the coming of Christ to his Kingdom. I will overturn, overturn, overturn, till it come into his hand whose right it is, and upon his shoulders shall the government be established" [*The Power and Glory of the Lord* (London, 1653), p. 14]. Edward Burrough used the phrase "overturn, overturn, overturn" (*A Standard Lifted Up*, p. 9) as did the Ranter, Abiezer Cope (Hill, *World Turned Upside Down*, p. 210). Repetition was "a means of maintaining the emotional power of particular exclamations" (Smith, *Perfection Proclaimed*, p. 334). As time progressed and as the persecution of Quakers increased Quakers found it necessary to explain that the sword that threshed was a spiritual sword (Fox, *Gospel Truth Demonstrated*, 6, p. 165). Fox portrayed Christ as returning riding on a white horse and slaying with his sword, "which are the words of his mouth" (*Great Mystery of the Great Whore*, 3, pp. 171, 214). And Nayler wrote of Quakers: "And as they war not against men's persons, so their weapons are not carnal, nor hurtful to any of the creation: for the Lamb comes not to destroy men's lives, nor the work of God, and therefore at his appearance in his subjects, he puts spiritual weapons into their hearts and hands" [*The Lamb's War Against the Man of Sin* (London, 1657), p. 4]. This statement came after the Nayler incident in 1656 when Friends generally were carefully measuring their radical language and muting their crusading rhetoric. Burrough also said that the victory would not be achieved by carnal weapons or "by the multitude of an host of men" (*Measure of the Times*, p. 34) and that attitude was shared by most early Quakers. The spirit of their writing, even with its violent invective, suggested that they believed the imminent, universal transformation would be a wholly supernatural event accomplished by the returned Son of God "without the help of another" (*Ibid.*, p. 35). The event, it seems, was to be precipitated by the preaching of the everlasting gospel and the transformation was to occur quickly "for in one hour shall she [Babylon] be made desolate," said Burrough (*Ibid.*, p. 24). Even if the one hour was figurative it represented a general attitude among early Quakers that the transformation was imminent and would occur quickly and supernaturally. Nonetheless, the help of an external godly agent wasn't ruled out and this explains the constant ambivalence among early Quakers about supporting diverse political causes and even armed campaigns. Fox's eschatology contained immanent and imminent elements and this lead to tension and confusion in the Quaker camp

Fox and his followers personified the very Kingdom that was proclaimed. In them the great apocalyptic struggle against the Beast had already been completed. God was again the 'first speaker' in them as He had been to Adam and Eve and the apostles. From there it was a logical step for Fox and his fellow Quakers to advocate social and economic justice and equality. For this reason Quakers could be found throughout England setting up trade apprenticeships, building hospitals for the mentally handicapped or ceaselessly petitioning Parliament to equalize wealth and thus act on behalf of the poor and oppressed.[67] And it was a logical step for the sick to be healed and demons to be cast out in their presence, for the presence of Quakers was the very presence of God on earth. Signs and wonders were proof that Christ had come. It was so in Jesus' earthly ministry and it was so in Fox's ministry.[68] Among themselves they were divine, as 'gods', and it was Fox's theology of celestial inhabitation that produced this kind of thinking. To understand early Quakerism is to imagine being part of a group of people who truly believed the celestial body of Christ inhabited them, to imagine being part of a group of people who had been restored to the pre-Fall paradisiacal state. In them the restoration of the image of God was absolute and signs and wonders were a natural by-product of that belief.

This kind of thinking (of being divinized) had radical social consequences beyond Quaker reformist acitivity. Their deportment in society was one of 'bravado'. As they perceived Christ and the Kingdom so they were. And in this Kingdom they were Kings and Queens. They were God's nobility. The whole social hierarchy was overturned. Their Kingdom refashioned everything along the lines of peace, justice, equality and perfection. They were products of their perception of Christ and the

---

as the 1650's wore on and expectations of an imminent transformation led to disillusionment and finally abandonnment of eschatological hope.

[67]Burrough wrote that the Lord was coming to reign with his saints and together they would defeat the Beast who had "long reigned over the earth." He added, "And this is a warning to all nations ... laws must be changed among you, governments and orders must be changed, unjustice and oppression shall be removed and every yoke and burden shall be taken off the neck of the poor, true judgment, and justice, mercy, and truth, peace and righteousness shall be exalted' (*A Measure of the Times*, pp. 33-34).

[68]*Gospel Truth Demonstrated*, 5, p. 87.

Kingdom of God. When the Kingdom didn't appear as quickly as expected some Quakers became anxious and confused. The festering tension between the immanent and the imminent, between the inward and present and the yet-to-come Kingdom broke out in open conflict when some Quakers, like James Milner, Martha Simmonds and James Nayler, tried to bring in the delayed Kingdom by proclaiming themselves, or others, new Messiahs.

Fox's doctrine of immanence was the key that explained the apocalyptic drama enacted by all early Quakers. The possibility of being restored up into the divine image again in the present and the idea of an apocalyptic transformation of the earth that would make Quakers the Kings and Queens of the new external order was itself a revolutionary leaven that lead to the peculiar Quaker deportment - the flouting of decorum and all manner of signs and wonders. At the beginning this was no abstract concept of future glory. The message of early Quakerism is more intelligible when interpreted in the context of the apocalyptic incarnation of Christ in humanity - Fox's theology of celestial inhabitation. Christ was being revealed universally but he was revealed in Fox in a special way as we will see in the following chapters.[69]

---

[69]Fox was not the only mid-seventeenth century Englishman to preach the everlasting gospel, formulate a realized eschatology of Christ's second coming or even suggest that people could become sons and daughters of God (*See* Hill, *World Turned Upside Down*, p. 148). However, Fox's inward Christ was more than the Seekers' inner light or Winstanley's spiritualized "inner Christ". No one else at that time formulated the celestial inhabitation theology of Fox.

Figure 1
An Older George Fox. Painted by Sir Peter Lely

3

MAGUS

The seventeenth century English sectarian context, when broadly viewed and against the context of biblical Christianity in the West after the Middle Ages, was part of a larger displacement of biblical narrative into social forms. Miracles were produced at new centres of production, so to speak - the monarchy in France, *Eigenkirchen* in Germany and cult life in England. Specifically, one of the by-products of Fox's notion of the immanence of Christ's celestial flesh was signs and wonders. Fox made a fundamental distinction between the healing of the medical profession of his day and even the healings enacted by the Royal Touch and the miracles he and other magus Quakers performed through the vehicle of the ever-present inner Christ.

In 1672, while in America, Fox was asked about the healing of a woman in Cumberland. He replied that "many things had been done by the power of Christ." Thomas Ellwood, who tended to minimize the role of miracles in Fox's ministry prefaced this remark with "I told him we did not glory in such things but ..."[1] In fact, Ellwood tampered with each one of the twelve miracle accounts he allowed to remain in his 1694 edition of Fox's *Journal*. In each case he changed the context so as to minimize the miracle and detract any glory away from Fox. It was this type of editorial tampering

---

[1] Compare *Cambridge Journal*, 2, p. 234 with Ellwood, *Journal*, 2, p. 120.

that resulted in a lingering hagiographic tradition that causes us to puzzle at Keith Thomas' observation that "the early days of Quakerism had been marked by healing miracles on a scale comparable to those of the early Church."[2] Dr. Thomas is quite right. For over three hundred years Quaker historiography has portrayed Quakerism as spiritualist, mystical, radical and even evangelical but rarely as a restitution of the New Testament *kerygma* - the proclamation that the Kingdom of God has come and is witnessed by an outpouring of attendant signs and wonders.

The hagiographic caricature is no longer adequate. Both Cadbury and Thomas have brought material forward that proves that Quakers were the greatest of the revolutionary sects to work miracles. Reports of miracles occurred with greater frequency in Quaker writings than any other contemporary documents including those associated with the 'Royal Touch' (or 'Royal Evil' as Quakers called it) and Valentine Greatrakes, the Irish 'touch doctor'.[3] Fox's own *Book of Miracles* contained at least 150 cures and these were only a few representative samples chosen randomly by Fox to illustrate how the power of God broke forth among early Quakers. To minimize the role of the miraculous in early Quakerism only distorts our picture not only of the charismatic nature of early Quakerism but of Fox's magus role in the movement.

The receptivity of people to signs and wonders, especially on the level of popular culture, may be attributed to the fact that the world of seventeenth century Europe was still alive with supernatural forces and unseen beings. The age of skepticism was dawning and the gap between the educated elite (those who represented orthodox religion) and popular belief was widening, but among the ordinary people belief in the magical power of

---

[2]K. Thomas, *Religion and the Decline of Magic*, p. 150.

[3]During the reign of Charles II (1660-1682) his surgeon, John Browne, wrote a treatise on the subject in which he reported that Charles touched 90,000 persons out of which there were 50 documented cures, including two Quakers (Cadbury, *George Fox's 'Book of Miracles'*, p. 76). On Greatrakes *see* Thomas, *Religion and the Decline of Magic*, pp. 240-42.

astrologers, village wizards, witches and spirits remained widespread.[4] As Michael MacDonald has said, "Seventeenth century villagers believed whatever cunning made their misery, pain, and squalor easier to bear."[5] The whole social, physical and religious world of the ordinary person was still associated with good and evil spirits, even though the emerging rational world view was beginning to assail religious enthusiasm and belief in direct inspiration as insane delusion.

Fox's interest in healing was not scientifically motivated and did not reflect the thinking of the educated elite of his time. His attitude was best defined in some 'queries' he and some Friends drew up after a confrontation with a group of mountebanks at Lyme Regis in 1657. Physicians were out of the wisdom of God and they had no knowledge of the true virtues of things, especially as they had been revealed to Fox. Since Christ had come all things were restored to the pre-Fall paradisiacal state in which there was no sickness or disease.[6] Miracles and healing were a major ingredient in Fox's proclamation of the everlasting gospel. They were prophetic signs of the presence of the Kingdom of God. Those who denied immediate revelation, prophecy and the gifts were out of the life and power of the apostles.[7] The outpouring of miraculous phenomena in accordance with Joel 2:28 was as normative among mid-seventeenth century Quakers as it was among the Apostles. It is curious, then, that Hanna Darlington Monaghan, who wrote a 'revised' biography of Fox, minimized Fox's role as a faith healer. And yet another of Fox's twentieth century biographers, A.N. Brayshaw, claimed that

---

[4]It was not just at the level of popular culture that superstitious beliefs remained widespread. Revisions of this concept which suggest that people of all social levels consulted astrologers and cunning folk in mid-seventeenth century England are presented in the work of Keith Thomas, Margaret Jacob and for France, Robert Darnton.

[5]M. MacDonald, *Mystical Bedlam: Madness, Anxiety and Healing in Seventeenth Century England* (Cambridge University Press, 1981), p. 213.

[6]Nickalls, *Journal*, pp. 287-88. *See also* pp. 27-28.

[7]*Epistles*, 7, pp. 114, 321ff; *Gospel Truth Demonstrated*, 5, pp. 228-53. The idea that miracles had not ceased and that they and visions should attend the ministry as a sign of the last days was prefigured in Thomas Edwards' catalogue of heresies (*Gangraena*, first edition), pp. 27, 32, 66.

50

"miracles were not generally regarded as characteristic of Quakerism."[8] They, and other contemporary interpreters recognize the presence of the miraculous in early Quakerism but minimize its importance. They do not see it as normative.[9]

Fox's miracle-working began in the mid-1640's. This is, unfortunately, also the period for which there is virtually no source material and what existed has been lost. In his testimony on Elizabeth Hooten, Fox's first convert, he said that she was convinced in 1646 and shortly thereafter (probably in 1647) began to hold meetings at her house where many miracles occurred.[10] Miracles continued to abound through the ensuing years for in 1649 Fox recorded:

> Many great and wonderful things were wrought by the heavenly power in those days, for the Lord ... manifested his power to the astonishment of many, by the healing virtue whereof many have been delivered from great infirmities, and the devils were made subject through his name, of which

---

[8]H.D. Monaghan, "Dear George": George Fox, Man and Prophet (Philadelphia: Franklin, 1970), p. 265; A.N. Brayshaw, The Personality of George Fox (London: Allenson, 1933), p. 173. For further discussion of Fox's miracles by Quakers see K.L. Carroll, "Quaker Attitudes Towards Signs and Wonders," JFHS, 54 (1977), pp. 70-84 and E. Grubb, "George Fox and Spiritual Healing," The Friend, (July 11, 1924), pp. 600-1.

[9]The important role of miracle-working in Fox's early ministry has generally been left in the shade of Quaker historiography. The great oversight that needs to be redressed is that this topic does not belong on the fringes of early Quakerism but at its very centre. In 1836 Edward Smith published his Life of William Dewsbury in which he said that neither Fox nor "his companions, nor his successors in belief, have ever laid great stress on such occurrences however true; and have avoided insisting upon them as proof of their ministry." They occurred, they were consistent with Scripture and they were collateral assurances [E. Smith, The Life of William Dewsbury (London, 1826), p. 132]. Smith was following a line of reasoning established by Penn, Barclay and George Whitehead. To read this view back into the earliest attitudes in the movement leads to historical inaccuracies.

[10]Cadbury, Narrative Papers, p. 177. Fox recollected these early meetings: "She had many meetings in her house where the Lord by his power wrought many miracles to the astonishing of the world and confirming people of the Truth." (Cadbury, George Fox's 'Book of Miracles', p. 60). According to a remaining fragment from the now lost earliest history of the Quaker movement by Hooten's son Oliver, these meetings began in 1647 when Quakers were known as "Children of the Light", after George Fox who was known as a preacher of the Light (Children of the Light Papers, FRL, Box A, Portfolio 10, No. 42).

particular instances might be given beyond what this unbelieving age is able to receive or bear.[11]

The earliest documented miracle was a case of exorcism. Fox encountered a 'possessed' woman while in prison in Nottingham in 1649. The people about her claimed she had been possessed for thirty-two years. The 'priests' had tried unsuccessfully to exorcize her though they had fasted days over her. When Fox was released from prison the woman apparently followed him to his Meetings for he reported: "The poor woman would make such a noise in roaring, and sometimes lying along upon her belly upon the ground with her spirit and roaring and voice, that it would set all Friends in a heat and sweat. And I said, 'All Friends, keep to your own, lest that which is in her get into you'".[12] So wild was this woman, and others as well, that the 'priests' and the 'world' were frightened to attend Quaker meetings and accused them of being 'false prophets', 'deceivers' and even witches.[13] Fox then called a

---

[11]Nickalls, *Journal*, p. 44.

[12]*Ibid.*, p. 42.

[13]Even though Fox spoke against witchcraft (*Gospel Truth Demonstrated*, 4, p. 30.) the charge of witchcraft was not uncommonly applied to Quakers [*see* William Prynne, *The Quakers Unmasked* (London, 1655), p. 37 and Nayler, *Answer to the Fanatick History*, p. 7] and was often associated with their miraculous powers and evident charismatic activity. In 1652, for example, Fox was specifically accused of witchcraft. Others accused him of practicing the black arts by tying ribbons onto people's arms so they would follow him - a kind of bewitching of people (*Cambridge Journal*, 1, pp. 104, 169). The accuracy of the charges is not as important here as the fact that something in Fox's ministry provoked such charges. The charge of witchcraft was also frequently applied to a curious group known as the 'singing' or 'dancing' Quakers. Increase Mather referred to them in his *Essay for the Recording of Illustrious Providences*. He recounts incidences both from England and New England where they were accused of various improprieties (like dancing naked together), of being witches, under the control of Satan or demon possessed. Benjamin Bullivant encountered them in Newport, Rhode Island in 1697 and described them as "an ancient sort of Quakers" who would suddenly fall into rapturous singing. Because of their disruptive tactics they were barred from Quaker meetings. A Frenchman who was one of the singing Quakers told Bullivant that Quakers had fallen from the Light and they were to be reproved for their apostasy. The Quakers, on the other hand, admitted that the singing Quakers were of old standing among them but they had fallen into licentious practices. They may have been remnants of Nayler's followers or part of the 'Church of the Firstborn' once mentioned by Robert Rich. Quakers like George Keith generally responded by disavowing these people as Quakers at all but later, when Keith was disowned, he made an about face and used these instances against Quakers [Increase Mather, *An Essay for the Recording of Illustrious Providences* (Delmar, New York: Scholars Facsimiles and Reprints, 1977/1684), pp. 338-61; W. Andrews, "A Glance at New

52

meeting at Hooten's house in Skegby with the specific aim of setting the woman free:

> and there were many Friends almost overcome by her with the stink that came out of her; roaring and tumbling on the ground, and the same day she was worse than ever she was, and then another day we met about her: and about the first hour the life rose in Friends, and said it was done, and she rose up, and her countenance changed and became white and before it was wan and earthly and she sat down at my thigh as I was sitting and lift (sic) up her hands and said ten thousand praise the Lord and did not know where she was and so she was well.[14]

The casting out of demons was a sign of the open conflict between the Kingdom of God and the Kingdom of Satan. Jesus himself had seen the dawn of the Kingdom of God in the fact that he expelled demons. The Kingdom was an absolutely miraculous event. Fox taught that the New Testament parables of the mustard seed and the leaven carried this message

---

York in 1697: The Travel Diary of Dr. Benjamin Bullivant," *New York Historical Society Quarterly*, 40 (1956), pp. 55-73. George Keith, *The Presbyterian and Independent Visible Churches in New England* (Philadelphia, 1689), pp. 215-17 and *A Third Narrative of the Proceedings at Turner's Hall*, (London, 1698), p. 28]. *See also* K. Carroll, "Singing in the Spirit in Early Quakerism," *QH*, 13 (1984), pp. 11-12 and H. Cadbury, "Glimpses of Quakerism in America in 1697," *BFHA*, 53 (1964), p. 38, and *Narrative Papers*, p. 225.

[14]Nickalls, *Journal*, p. 43. *Short Journal*, p. 3. There is already here a blurring of the distinction between the source of the miraculous power and the worker of the miracle. The healed woman sat at Fox's thigh and sang praises to the Lord. Ellwood edited the miracle accounts in Fox's *Journal* so as to ascribe the power to God the Creator and not to Fox the creature. Edward Grubb also followed this line of reasoning in *Quaker History and Thought* (London, 1925), pp. 153-54, 159-61. Fox did not always attribute the power to God (that is, an external God) but often left the impression that the power was coming directly out of him. An excellent example of his attitude occurred in the *Spence MS*. In the fragment in question, written in 1676 and ignored by Ellwood, Fox made the sweeping statement that during the Commonwealth years he was called for to heal many sick people. Once he was called to Whitechapel at three o'clock in the morning to heal a woman and her child, both who were dying. He spoke to the woman and both were healed "to the astonishment of the people" (*Cambridge Journal*, 2, p. 342. This fragment is also contained in *Epistles*, 7, p. 14). The whole story was a recollection of biblical epiphany and left the onlooker and reader to make the essential connection between Christ and Fox. Other notable miracles are known for 1649 as well. Some were undoubtedly contained in the now lost opening pages of the *Spence MS*. Why were these pages (in addition to Fox's *Book of Miracles*) lost when so many other less notable items were so meticulously preserved? Thomas Ellwood had access to these pages (which must have been full of references to miraculous phenomena) since he did allow some of these miracles to remain in his 1694 edition of the *Journal* (*see* Ellwood, *Journal*, 1, pp. 95-98).

as did the parables of the wheat and the tares, the treasure hid in the field, the pearl of great price, the drag net, the wicked servant, the labourer in the vineyard, the marriage feast and the ten virgins. The order of God's Kingdom was incalculably and overwhelmingly present within the signs in which it lay enclosed, initially in the activity of the prophets and of Jesus and then in God's final revelation - George Fox. At Firbank Fell in 1652 Fox told the crowd of over a thousand people that had gathered to hear him that the Kingdom of God had come in the same spirit and power that it had in the time of Jesus and it was evidenced in the casting out of demons and a multitude of signs and wonders.

We have only to turn to the testimony of several magus Quakers to realize that early Quakerism was a fully Spirit-led, charismatic movement. Edward Burrough prefaced Fox's book *The Great Mystery of the Great Whore* (1659) with these words:

> And waiting upon the Lord in silence, as we often did for many hours together ... we received often the pouring down of the Spirit upon us ... as in the days of old, and our hearts were made glad, and our tongues loosed, and our mouths opened, and we spake with new tongues as the Lord gave utterance, and his spirit led us, which was poured down upon us, on Sons and Daughters ... and things unutterable was made known and manifest.[15]

This last days' outpouring of the Spirit included prophecy and even *xenoglossa* which was yet another miraculous sign of the presence of the Kingdom.[16] Richard Farnworth said in plain language that God, through the

---

[15]E. Burrough, *Epistle to the Reader* a preface to G. Fox, *The Great Mystery of the Great Whore Unfolded and Antichrist's Kingdom Revealed Unto Destruction* (London: Thomas Simmonds, 1659), pp. b1v-b2r.

[16]That early Quakers used *xenoglossa* is confirmed in a report from Charles Perrott in Paris. He says that two Quakers, followers of James Nayler, had gone to Paris as missionaries and while there utilized the gift of tongues presumably for the success of their ministry in a foreign land [N. Penney, ed., *Extracts From State Papers, 1654-1672* (London: Headley Brothers, 1913), p. 24]. Quakers, like modern day followers of Charles Parham (the founder of Pentecostalism) believed that through the miraculous speaking of a previously unknown foreign language they would evangelize the world. Certainly in known cases where this occurred among Quaker missionaries the phenomenon of *cryptonesia* cannot be ruled out (hearing foreign words and phrases which become locked in one's unconscious). Edward

power of the Holy Ghost, enabled any "to lay hands on the sick, and recover them, as the Apostles did, and as Christ said should be done."[17] Richard Hubberthorne wrote in even more convincing fashion:

> this power we have received from Christ ... this is the same power that ever was and the same Christ as ever was; and the same eternal words of God ... which word is Christ; and we do speak it forth in his own power, as we have received it; and this word of power we have, which makes the devils to tremble ... and by it marvellous works are wrought; for now do the blind see, and the deaf hear, and the lame walk; and they who many years have walked in darkness and trouble of mind, and terror of conscience, and under many infirmities, who have spent their time and money upon physicians and parish priests, and have not been healed or cured, are now restored and healed freely, without money and without price, and the lepers are cured, and the leprosy is taken away, and the poor receive the Gospel: and this we witness to be fulfilled in us, and in the world where this Gospel is, and where it hath been preached; and this is the everlasting Gospel which is now preached ... and this Gospel is not the letter ... but the spirit which gave it

---

Beckham implied that some Quakers, including Fox, thought they had the gift of tongues, not in the modern sense of *glossalalia*, but the ability to speak other languages at some supernatural prompting or to understand other languages (Beckham, *The Principles of the Quakers*, p. 42). Other sectarians used *glossalalia* as well. The Ranter John Robin used it and his follower, Joshua Garment tried to interpret it (Smith, *Perfection Proclaimed*, pp. 302-3). Geoffrey Nuttall dismisses the idea that Burrough could have been referring to *glossalalia* because, he said, there was no evidence for it in Quakerism. However, Nayler's followers and other early Quaker missionaries conclusively used *xenoglossa*, which is but a variant of *glossalalia*. Still, Nuttall's interpretation of Burrough is useful: that is, the idea that Burrough spoke of tongues loosed in Paul's sense (*parrhesia*) - "they found their tongues". The string of the tongue was loosed and they spoke in plain language ("Puritan and Quaker Mysticism," *Theology*, 78 (Oct., 1975), pp. 530-31). Early Quakers also practised a form of 'singing in the spirit'. This seems to have been part of a wide-spread non-conformist reaction to the unaccompanied singing of "metrical versions of the Psalms" decreed by Parliament and in force from 1644 to the Restoration. At times Quakers would simply sing the Psalms in their own inspired way but at other times their singing seemed to take the form of sweet harmonious melodies of praise which were quite audible but not understandable - it took the form of humming or toning in unison. Nayler and his followers entered Bristol singing in a loud humming noise. This form of what we might call today charismatic worship actually lasted in Quaker meetings until the beginning of the 18th century [See K. Carroll, "Singing in the Spirit in Early Quakerism," pp. 2, 5, 8, 11-13; Barclay, *Apology*, pp. 250-1, 297-8; "Thomas Holme to Margaret Fell," (1653), *Swarth. MSS.*, 1, No. 190; *Cambridge Journal*, 1, p. 246, 329-31; 2, p. 141].

[17]Richard Farnworth, *Antichrist's Man of War* (London, 1655), p. 62.

forth, and this spirit is within which is our rule ... and the same speaks now on sons and daughters as they are moved.[18]

William Caton and William Dewsbury were among other leading Quakers to affirm the role of miracles in Quaker ministry. Caton said that Quakers "have revelations by the same spirit which revealed the mysteries of God in former ages to the saints ... and by the mighty power of God miracles have been wrought among them."[19] Just before his death William Dewsbury had these reflections: "I can never forget the day of his great power and blessed appearance, when he first sent me to preach his everlasting gospel ... also he confirmed the same by signs and wonders."[20] Quakers anticipated signs and wonders as a confirmation of God's presence and power among them. Not only had Joel's prophecy been fulfilled in their own time but they believed they were living in the same spirit and power as Jesus and the apostles. They were a witness to the fact that Christ had come and was restoring His kingdom in both the inward and outward orders.[21] John Toldervy testified upon his conversion to Quakerism that, "it was the purpose of God, that I should be serviceable in the healing of the lame, the sick, the blind ... as Christ did heal the imperfect parts of the visible body; and that all the visible miracles wrought by him, did signify what was to be effected miraculously in the invisible parts of every man."[22] Signs and wonders were normative for

---

[18]Richard Hubberthorne, *A True Separation Between the Power of the Spirit, and the Imitation of Antichrist* (1654), p. 7.

[19]William Caton, *The Moderate Enquirer Resolved* (1671), p. 13. First published in 1658.

[20]He then recounted an occasion when he, George Fox and Richard Farnworth were instrumental in curing a lame woman: "as I cried mightily unto the Lord in secret that he would manifest himself among us at that time, and give witness of his power and presence ... R[ichard Farnworth] in the name of the Lord took her by the hand, and G[eorge] F[ox] after spoke to her in the power of God, and bid her stand up, and she did, and immediately walked straight, having no need of crutches any more." [William Dewsbury, *The Faithful Testimony of that Ancient Servant of the Lord ... William Dewsbury* (London, 1689), unnumbered page near the front]. Richard Farnworth also healed a woman in Derbyshire in mid-1652 ["Richard Farnworth to James Nayler" (July 6, 1652), *Swarth. MSS.*, 1, No. 372].

[21]*Gospel Truth Demonstrated*, 5, pp. 50, 56, 171-96; 6, p. 98.

[22]John Toldervy, *Foot Out of the Snare* (London, 1656), p. 31.

56

they testified to the great inner and outer transformation that had occurred and was occurring.

We cannot underestimate the profusion of miraculous phenomena that followed in the wake of George Fox's prophetic declaration that Christ had come again. Fox confirmed his teaching with a multitude of signs and wonders. He said it would be too tedious to mention all the miracles he performed so he recorded a representative sampling of over 150 miracles in his *Book of Miracles* in which he enumerated case after case of the blind made to see and the lame made to walk. A Baptist woman in Baldock was raised from a life threatening illness. Frequent sicknesses were Ague and fever combined, smallpox and distraction. Sometimes Fox was not actually present for a cure but like a true magus exercised his miraculous power from a distance. He did this through letters (as with Cromwell's daughter Lady Claypole) or through a messenger.[23] The patients were women more often than men and there were some children involved.

Nor was Fox the only Quaker to work miracles. John Taylor raised a dying woman to health on the Island of Nevis in 1662. When Samuel Hooten arrived in New England he says "the hand of the Lord was with me ... both in outward miracles and in the work of the Spirit." Richard Farnworth cured a woman from fever in 1652 and a little known Quaker from Gloucestershire, Mary Atkins, cured a Presbyterian woman who was so ill "she could stir neither hand nor foot."[24] There were even reports of painless child delivery - interpreted as a sign that God had removed the curse of Genesis 3:16 and was now present among his people with healing in his wings as prophesied in Malachi 4:2.[25] Stories of similar accounts would fill a large folio but the point was best made by two Quaker women who were probably part of a

---

[23]Cadbury, *George Fox's 'Book of Miracles'*, pp. 101, 111-12. Lady Claypole had shown sympathy for the Quakers.

[24]All these miracles are documented by Cadbury, *George Fox's 'Book of Miracles'*, pp. 9-10.

[25]Letter of Thomas Salthouse to Margaret Fell regarding Mary Clements ["Thomas Salthouse to Margaret Fell" (July 9, 1657), *Swarth. MSS.*, 3, No. 158]. There were also expectations of a miraculous birth of a child attributed to Margaret Fell and George Fox (Cadbury, *George Fox's 'Book of Miracles'*, p. 22).

Women's Meeting Fox founded in London to meet the needs of the sick and impoverished. Katherine Evans and Sarah Cheevers were prisoners of the Inquisition on the Island of Malta when they recounted this story (recalling Matthew 11:5) to their Roman Catholic captors: "We had thousands at our meetings, but none of us dare speak a word, but as they are eternally moved of the Lord; and we had miracles; the blind receive their sight, the deaf do hear, and the dumb do speak, the poor receive the gospel, the lame do walk, and the dead are raised."[26] In true Quaker style they were using biblical parallels to describe their own experience. There were even documented reports of women attempting to raise the dead.[27]

The aforementioned Women's Meeting was one of the great centres of spiritual power in early Quakerism.[28] Fox personally attested to this fact:

---

[26]*This is a Short Relation of Some of the Cruel Sufferings (for the Truth's Sake) of Katharine Evans and Sarah Cheevers* (London, 1662), p. 9. John of Salisbury used this same text from Matthew's Gospel when speaking of the multitude of miracles at Thomas Becket's tomb [Frank Barlow, *Thomas Becket* (Berkeley: University of California Press, 1986), p. 264].

[27]Cadbury, *George Fox's 'Book of Miracles'*, pp. 14-15.

[28]The origin of these Women's Meetings is uncertain. Two Quaker Women's Meetings (the Box Meeting and the Two Weeks Meeting) met alongside the Men's Meeting during the Restoration period. The Two Weeks Men's Meeting originated in London in 1656 and one of the Women's Meetings clearly originated in the pre-Restoration period. W. Crouch, *Posthuma Christiana* (1712, pp. 22-23) said "Now also some ancient Women-Friends did meet together ... to inspect the circumstances and conditions of such who were imprisoned upon Truth's account and ... the wants and necessities of the poor." Braithwaite says that "This passage is clearly placed in his narrative prior to the Restoration" (*Beginnings*, p. 340 n.4). This was probably the Box Meeting based on Fox's reminiscences: "[The next morning] there came in Sarah Blackberry to complain to me of the poor ... and the Lord showed me, what I should do ... So I spake to her, to bid about sixty women to meet me about the first hour in the afternoon. And ... I declared unto them, concerning their having a meeting once a week ... that they might see and inquire into the necessity of all poor Friends, who were sick and weak, and were in want, or widows and fatherless in the city and suburbs" [*A Collection of Many Select and Christian Epistles (1698)*, p. 6]. That this was the Box Meeting and not the Two Weeks Meeting may be deduced from a later report by a Friend named Mary Elson. She reported that there were offerings given at this meeting and according to Braithwaite the "Box Meeting gathered monies for poor relief in a box" (Braithwaite, *Second Period*, p. 272). In *A True Information of our Blessed Women's Meeting*, Elson referred to a women's meeting "gathered betwixt twenty three and twenty four years ago". Unfortunately this pamphlet contained no publishing date. Joseph Smith assigned a date of 1680 which was far too early (Joseph Smith, *Descriptive Catalogue of Friend' Books*, 1, p. 572). Cadbury more accurately assigned the publishing date to 1683, based on publishers dated imprints contained at the end of the pamphlet (*Book of Miracles*, p. 47 n.3). The Women's Meeting Katharine Evans and

"Great things have been done in their meetings by the Lord's power ... I believe that there are a thousand women [Friends] who have wrought miracles among them."[29] Even if Fox was referring to the meeting of peoples' spiritual and physical needs in general,[30] supernatural healings were involved. And Fox was not the only one to document this. Peter Briggins wrote that one member of the Women's Meeting, Mariabella Farnborough, was miraculously healed of lameness and was thus able to continue her work. He also identified another member of the Women's Meeting, Mary Elson, as one who "used to go and visit the sick" and she, too, experienced a miraculous healing.[31]

Knowledge of miracles in early Quakerism was not limited to the sect itself. However, in the wider community such reports were treated with skepticism and disdain. Fox's opponents used his claims to miracles as

---

Sarah Cheevers referred to, then, was the Box Meeting. Its origin may be dated as early as 1656 or as late as 1659. Whatever, one of the important mandates of this meeting was, said Fox, visiting the sick and, in the power God, healing (*Cambridge Journal*, 2, pp. 342-43, 484; Epistles, 7, pp. 14-15).

[29]Quoted in Monaghan, *"Dear George"*, pp. 258-59.

[30]Antonia Fraser pointed out that cure of the sick through the administration of herbal medicine, for example, was on a par with poor relief as one of the leading functions of women in seventeenth century English society [*The Weaker Vessel*, (New York: Alfred Knopf, 1984), pp. 49-50).

[31]Cadbury, *George Fox's 'Book of Miracles'*, pp. 16-17, 64a). Not all attempted cures were successful. In 1654 a disheartened Francis Howgill wrote to Fox for counsel after he and Edward Burrough failed to cure a lame boy ["Francis Howgill to George Fox" (1654), *A.R. Barclay MSS.*, No. 21]. The documents reveal that someone tried to erase this account from the record. The fact that Howgill looked to Fox for counsel is itself significant - Fox was looked upon as the authority in this realm. In another bizarre case, a Quaker named William Poole committed suicide (possibly expecting to be resurrected). A woman Friend, Susanna Pearson, promised to raise him from the dead, this being in February, 1657. She went to the gravesite with Poole's mother, dug up the corpse and proceeded to call it back to life, a scene that recalls Jesus and Lazarus. When Poole did not return to life they buried him again ["Thomas Willan to Margaret Fell" (Feb., 1657), *Swarth. MSS.*, 1, No. 217. Fox later remarked on the back of the letter "mad whimsey"]. In another case, unrelated to healing, a Quaker named John Toldervy laid down a bed of sticks and blew on it hoping to bring down the celestial flame, as in Moses' day. No such magical event occurred (Cadbury, *George Fox's 'Book of Miracles'*, p. 11). These were all replays of biblical epiphanies that belonged in the magical underworld of popular religion in seventeenth century England, a world that was entwined with early Quakerism.

fodder for denouncing him as an imposter.[32] Most notable among these was Francis Bugg, another erstwhile Quaker who became Fox's most virulent opponent. He compared Fox to Simon Magus, called him a "notorious liar" and said his miracles were a "legend of stories" and "counterfeit" since their description in his *Journal* lacked detail and witnesses, showed inconsistency and contradiction and were recalled only after great lapses of time. He also accused Fox and several other magus Quakers, including James Nayler and Richard Hubberthorne of laying claim to the same miracle-working power as Christ, a charge which was accurate and fully in keeping with statements made by Fox, Nayler and Hubberthorne.[33] Nor was Gerard Croese, who wrote the earliest extant history of Quakers, unaware of their claims to miracles. But he, too, took the approach of the skeptic and treated them as a farce.[34]

Fox's psychic experiences also added to his reputation as a magus. His altered psychic states began when he was a young man. In 1647, at the age of twenty-three, he had the first of several major trance-like experiences in which his body was altered in some way. A certain man, on his deathbed, had 'great prophecies and sights' and said that Fox would be an instrument of the Lord. Upon hearing of the man's death Fox went into a trance for two weeks "and was very much altered in countenance and person as if [his] body had been new-moulded or changed."[35] It was not uncommon for the words

---

[32]Francis Bugg, *New Rome Arraigned* (London, 1694), pp. 2ff.

[33]Francis Bugg, *A Finishing Stroke ... Whereby the Great Mystery of the Little Whore is Farther Unfolded* (London, 1712), pp. 192-97 wherein Bugg provides an exhaustive recounting of Fox's miracles. *See also A Modest Defence of My Book, Entitled 'Quakerism Exposed'* (London, 1700), pt. 3, pp. 8-9. He also compared Fox's miracles to those claimed for Ignatius Loyola [*The Quakers Set in Their True Light* (London, 1696), pp. 12-13, 16-18]. Edward Beckham also denounced the miracle accounts in Fox's *Journal* on the same premises - no one saw them, they were published well after the events and Fox was an imposter like Simon Magus [*The Principles of the Quakers Further Shown to be Blasphemous and Seditious* (London, 1700), p. 42]. Fox had his own view of Simon Magus. His magic, said Fox, was contrary to the religion of Christ and the Apostles [George Fox, *Old Simon the Sorcerer Who Hath Bewitched the Whole City of Christendom* (London, 1663)].

[34]Croese, *General History of the Quakers*, p. 28.

[35]Nickalls, *Journal*, p. 20.

of a dying person to have such an impact. Nigel Smith points out that "dying men's words were supposed to be prophetic, since they were coming close to the divine."[36] A similar experience occurred when Fox was forty-six years old and it lasted through the winter of 1670/71. This time he lost his hearing and sight and many thought he had died. When people came to visit him, though he could neither hear nor see them, he was able to discern their spirit.[37] According to Fox's followers these states were brought on by extreme sensitivity to the misery and sin around him which he took upon himself even as Christ bore the sins of the world. When Fox once fell into an illness during a trip to Barbados a Friend there wrote, "He bears the iniquity whenever he comes".[38] Like Christ, the weight of unrighteousness would at times press down that of God in him and he would enter a 'dark night of the soul'. At other times his illness was strangely linked to the fortunes of Friends. While in Reading in 1659, for example, he had another similar experience. The country was in a state of near anarchy and the Restoration seemed imminent. The Lamb's War was on the verge of collapse due to external political pressures brought to bear upon his movement. Fox only began to emerge from these illnesses when he sensed that the crisis or danger

---

[36]Smith, *Perfection Proclaimed*, p. 330.

[37]Nickalls, *Journal*, p. 570. This state may be interpreted with a psychological condition that is now known as catatonic. In C.L. Cherry's article "Enthusiasm and Madness: Anti-Quakerism in the Seventeenth Century," we find this insightful assessment from Anton Boisen: "the illness was a successful effort of psychological reorganization in which the entire personality, to its bottommost depths, is aroused and its forces marshalled to meet the danger of personal failure and isolation." Boisen characterized the upheaval experienced by Fox in his early twenties as "catatonic dementia praecox" and saw in this period characteristics exhibited throughout Fox's ministry: identification of himself as a "unique spokesman of the Lord", cosmic identification, receiver of direct revelations from God, obedience to "openings". Boisen was struck by the fact that, like other religious leaders, Fox overcame potentially disruptive disturbances and became not a madman, but a forceful, prophetic leader. William James was similarly struck by Fox's skirting a fine line between sanity and pathological behaviour. Had Fox not experienced an integration of personality through religion, James suggested, he would have suffered a breakdown (Cherry, "Enthusiasm and Madness," *QH*, 73 (1984), p. 6).

[38]Nickalls, *Journal*, p. 596. It was not uncommon, in the seventeenth century, for people to compare their sufferings to those of Jesus [*see*, for example, John Lilburne, *A Work of the Beast* (Amsterdam, 1638) and Charles I, *Eikon Basilike* (Royston, 1662)].

had abated. For example, he only emerged from his 1670/71 illness when the persecution of Quakers began to abate.[39]

Fox also had many prophetic insights. In fact, he had so many prophetic visions that the compiler of the *Annual Catalogue* considered making a separate collection of them. He foresaw the death of Cromwell.[40] He had visions of being taken prisoner, of escape from danger, of persecution, of the gathering of the elect in England, Scotland, Wales and Holland, and of impending divisions in his movement.[41] He applied a vision he had while in Lancaster Prison in 1665 to the Dutch War, the plague and the great fire of London.[42] Throughout his *Journal* he justified his every action with his prophetic prowess. On nearly every page we read "the Lord led me", "the Lord drew me", or "through the Lord's power I spoke". When healings failed (as with the death of Margaret Rous' daughter for whom Fox had prayed) or when untimely death occurred (as when a cook fell overboard and was lost on a ship on which Fox was a passenger) the spirits of the deceased would return to Fox shortly thereafter and he would be reassured that they were well.[43]

Prophetic insight also provided a divine stamp of approval on major decisions affecting his movement. He condemned James Nayler by saying "the Lord God moved me to slight him and to set the power of God over him."[44] When he organized his movement into Meetings for Discipline he was "moved of the Lord" to do so in order to control "unruly spirits" and those

---

[39]*Cambridge Journal*, 2, p. 169; Nickalls, *Journal*, pp. 570-73.

[40]Nickalls, *Journal*, p. 350.

[41]Cadbury, *Narrative Papers*, pp. 112, 233-37, 240-41; *Epistles*, 8, p. 245.

[42]*Gospel Truth Demonstrated*, 5, p. 7; *Cambridge Journal*, 1, p. 346; 2, pp. 89-90. The imagery of the glittering sword drawn against evil appeared frequently in Fox's writings. It was an important image for judgment. Quakers believed the plague and the great fire of London were God's judgment upon the sin of the nation [*See also* G.W. Edwards, "The Great Fire of London," *JFHS*, 51 (1966), pp. 66-67 and Humphrey Smith, *The Vision of Humphrey Smith, Which He Saw Concerning London* (London, 1660)].

[43]Cadbury, *Narrative Papers*, pp. 60, 144.

[44]Nickalls, *Journal*, p. 269.

62

who had "run out from the truth".[45] Practically, this was Fox's way of preserving the movement from anarchy. But he used direct inspiration to justify his actions and confirm his decisions. When Friends asked him about marriage he waited upon God and "saw" that Friends were to marry only after the matter was brought before an assembly of faithful Friends.[46] Fox also had visions about impending schisms and threats to his leadership in the movement. For example, he was so severely criticized for setting up separate Men's and Women's Meetings that he said a "dark power" was working against him. At this time (1666) he had a vision in which a fierce bull was chasing him and he was hard pressed to protect his children. Then, at one point when it seemed certain the bull would destroy him he "got a great hedge stake and chopped it down his throat to his heart and laid him still."[47] Fox was the great father protector of his movement. His visions confirmed his patriarchal status, his judgments and his victory over evil.

Visions and prophesies were normative in the early Quaker witness to the immanence of the Kingdom of God. They were a product of the last days' outpouring of the spirit prophesied in Joel 2:28. Fox said, "they that deny divine inspiration ... nowadays ... had better be still and wait upon the Lord for it, else they will be found of the number ... the Lord never sent."[48] Early Quakerism abounded with visionaries who were directly inspired by the word of the Lord in accordance with the prophetic declarations of Fox. Women, for example, who were otherwise denied a place in the ministry were given free reign when prophecy was involved. Of over 300 women visionaries who appeared in England during the Commonwealth, Phyllis Mack identified 220 as being Quakers, an astonishing total that confirms the receptivity of the sect to various charismatic phenomena including prophecy

[45]*Ibid.*, p. 404.

[46]*Epistles*, 8, p. 81; Cadbury, *Narrative Papers*, p. 238.

[47]Cadbury, *Narrative Papers*, pp. 238-39. The Shepherd of Hermas had a similar vision in which he escaped from a fearsome monster which he took as a symbol of persecution (Lane Fox, *Pagans and Christians*, p. 385).

[48]*Gospel Truth Demonstrated*, 5, p. 246.

through direct revelation.[49] One woman, Miriam Moss from Gloucestershire, even had a "prevision of the marriage of Margaret Fell with George Fox in the year before the death of Judge Fell," and "she felt free to speak of it before the marriage."[50]

This aspect of Quaker charismatic phenomena also came under Ellwood's editorial knife. For example, in 1671 when his movement was undergoing a massive transformation and his leadership was in jeopardy Fox had a remarkable vision concerning the rediscovery of the inward Christ.[51] It tends to suggest that Friends should stop tampering with his message of celestial inhabitation and this may have been the reason it was cut out of the Ellwood text of the *Journal* and therefore remained hidden from view until the *Spence Ms.* was published earlier this century. The hint of blasphemy at a time when Quakerism was in the process of distancing itself from its earlier excesses and 'enthusiastic' deportment was sufficiently scandalous for Ellwood to delete the whole prophecy. But once again, it was the essence of Fox's message about the inward Christ that was being tampered with.

Some of Fox's greatest visions were the 'openings' that confirmed his calling or, in Pauline fashion, revealed knowledge of the universe and the

---

[49]P. Mack, "Women as Prophets During the English Civil War," *Feminist Studies*, 8 (Spr., 1982), p. 24. Antonia Fraser said that apart from a few exceptions this brief outburst did not outlast the Commonwealth (*The Weaker Vessel*, p. 263).

[50]Cadbury, *Narrative Papers*, p. 77. Comments in "Miriam Moss and Her Vision of Matrimony," *JFHS*, 13 (1916), p. 143 and by Isabel Ross, *Margaret Fell: Mother of Quakerism* (London, Longmans, Green and Co., 1947), p. 143 say that this is either "strange" or "curious" but Cadbury accepts it "whatsoever our modern tastes" may be. This was Miriam Moss' vision: "In the year 1657 [it may have been 1658] I was coming to Swarthmore to visit M.F., I was moved of the Lord to go into her garden where I was sitting in the silence of my spirit. Then did the Lord let me see, that G.F. and M.F. were joined together in that eternal spirit, and that they should be joined together in that bond of love which could not be broken; which thing I resisted, but it sunk deep in me and I could not put it by, for in the light it rose often - then pondered I the thing in my heart, believing that the thing should be accomplished in its time." This vision applied to the marriage of Fox and Fell in 1669 and it was read at a meeting in connection with that marriage. ("Miriam Moss and Her Vision of Matrimony," p. 143). Some other Quakers who had visions were Humphrey Smith, John Rous, Thomas Holme, Margaret Fell, Ann Camm, John Camm, Mary Penington, Susanna Arnold, John Perrot and Prudence Wilson.

[51]*Cambridge Journal*, 2, p. 175. *See* chapter 7, p. 265 for a more detailed discussion of the vision.

unity of all things. Fox had one such vision at the age of twenty-four (1648) at which time he says he was transported to Paradise and perfected:

> Now was I come up in the spirit through the Flaming Sword, into the Paradise of God ... being renewed up into the image of God by Christ Jesus, so that I say I was come up to the state of Adam, which he was in before he fell. The creation was opened to me, and it was showed me how all things had their names given them according to their nature and virtue. And I was taken up in the spirit to see into another or more stedfast state than Adam's in innocency, even into a state in Christ Jesus that should never fall. And the Lord showed me that such as were faithful to him, in the power and light of Christ, should come up into that state in which Adam was in before he fell.[52]

Fox used the imagery of the flaming sword to symbolize God's wrath, the expulsion from Eden and ultimately the return to innocence, to Paradise.[53] He even inscribed "G.F. and the Flaming Sword" on his favourite seal. He was renewed into a pre-Fall state of perfection and more. He was renewed into a state from which he could never fall. This was not a state of future glory. It was a present reality. What Fox preached after this vision in 1648 was that the breach between heaven and earth had been repaired and man had regained the divine powers that he had lost at the time of the Fall and again at the time of the apostasy.[54]

The restoration of the divine in man involved an innate knowledge and power over the natural world as well. Fox calmed storms at sea and

---

[52]Nickalls, *Journal*, pp. 27-28. St. Paul, St. John, Mani and Jacob Boehme, to name only a few, all had similar life-changing mystical insights into the divine mysteries.

[53]See *Gospel Truth Demonstrated*, 4, p. 32. Fox once referred to this sword as that which cuts down earthly wisdom, and as that through which everyone must pass in order to return to Paradise (*Reynolds MSS.*, FRL, p. 95).

[54]Christian orthodoxy has always viewed Jesus as the last epiphany until the 'second coming' which is inevitably always put into the future. In the meantime Christ remains withdrawn from earth and there are no epiphanies. Fox, on the other hand, proclaimed that Christ had come and he was an epiphany of the divine, the one chosen to declare that fact after 1600 years of apostasy.

wrote of miraculous deliverances from pirates.[55] He used his unusual knowledge of the curative properties of herbs (which he received, he said, after the 1648 vision) to heal.[56] Astrologers were known to consult him and doctors from Germany, Poland and Holland requested to see him.[57] The well-known physician, Edward Bourne, recorded a conversation with Fox as the two were riding on horseback from Worcester to near Tewkesbury in 1655. Fox spoke of "the glory of the first body, and of the Egyptian Learning, and of the language of the birds."[58] From where did Fox receive these insights? One explanation is that all these esoteric interests were rooted in the great 1648 vision in which Fox was transported to Paradise. It was this idea of the 'hidden unity of the eternal being' that linked the aeons between Fox and the Egyptian Learning, which was probably the mystical philosophy of Hermes.[59]

---

[55]While there are no reports of miraculous deliverances from prison two Quakers who were in prison in Chester sang Psalms in the Spirit and reported that such a great light shone in the prison that a trembling jailor came and fell before them, both he and his household being converted that day - recalling the biblical epiphany of Paul and Silas singing hymns and being miraculously released following the conversion of the jailor and his household (Acts 16), [Jonathan Clapham, *A Full Discovery and Confutation of the Wicked and Damnable Doctrines of the Quakers* (London, 1656), p. 45; "Thomas Holme to Margaret Fell" (1653), *Swarth. MSS*. 1, No. 190 for a similar account].

[56]Cadbury, *Narrative Papers*, pp. 146, 204-5.

[57]Cadbury, *George Fox's 'Book of Miracles'*, pp. 54-55.

[58]H. Cadbury, "Early Quakerism and Uncanonical Lore," *Harvard Theological Review*, (1944), p. 191.

[59]Cadbury, *George Fox's 'Book of Miracles'*, pp. 192-93. One of the places Fox would have contacted Hermetic philosophy would have been at Lady Conway's home, Ragley Hall. There he would have met, on occasion, Francis Mercury Van Helmont when both were guests there. Van Helmont was an eager student of the mystics, neo-Platonists, occult, Paracelsans, Rosicrucians, Pythagoreans and the Hermetic writings (Nicolson, "George Keith and the Cambridge Platonists," pp. 49-50). Cadbury confirms that Fox was at least once in Van Helmont's company at Ragley - in 1678. They were together again in James Claypole's house - the same James Claypole whom Fox healed of a lame arm. Although Fox criticized Van Helmont's occult writings in the 1680's their relationship seems to have been one of "mutual satisfaction" [Cadbury, George Fox's *'Book of Miracles'*, p. 54 and Fox, Box A, Portfolio 10 (November 19, 1683) at FRL where Fox outlined rules by which Friends' books were to be printed and cautioned about the books of Van Helmont]. John Everard had also made

Miracles and visions were not the only witness to the presence of the Kingdom. The judgment and reproof aspects of the everlasting gospel, for example, were publically proclaimed through a host of metaphorical signs that were acknowledged and supported by Fox.[60] Of these signs going naked was the most prolific and the most controversial. Indeed, it was much more prevalent than Quaker historians, until recently, have preferred to admit. Janney minimized it to a "few instances of indecorum".[61] Jones said that it was the activity of a few "misguided people" who were "driven over the verge of sanity by the fury of persecution."[62] This can only be interpreted as being said in the interests of respectability. Going naked was not only a frequent event in early Quakerism but it was an accepted part of the Quaker repertoire of prophetic signs.[63] Fox, though never enacting such a sign

---

Hermes Trismegistus' *Divine Pymander* and *Asclepius* available in translation (London, 1649, 1657).

[60]These signs and their meaning and significance are dealt with at length by R. Bauman, *Let Your Words be Few*. Early Quakers also collected examples of judgements (disasters) that befell persecutors (see Cadbury, *Narrative Papers*, pp. 209-32). I have discovered, in unindexed volumes at FRL, that one such manuscript collection was in existence until the time the Gracechurch Street Meeting House and its considerable library were destroyed by fire in 1821. There are five unnumbered volumes which contain the indexed contents of the library. Listed therein is: "Exemplary Deaths of Persecutors." Might this be the missing "Examples Fallen Upon Persecutors" Cadbury was unable to trace, or even the *Book of Examples* mentioned by Fox? *Ibid.*, pp. 216-17).

[61]S. Janney, *History of the Religious Society of Friends* (Philadelphia: Zell, 1861-68), 1, p. 476.

[62]R. Jones, *The Quakers in the American Colonies* (London: Macmillan, 1919), pp. 108-9.

[63]There were two outbreaks of Quakers going naked as a sign. The first was between 1652 and 1655. The second occurred in the waning years of the Commonwealth when there was a heightened eschatological consciousness brought on by political turmoil. Sporadic cases continued into the mid-1670's. In addition to Fox, going naked received the approval of most other Quaker leaders, including Nayler, Howgill, Farnworth, Hubberthorne, George Whitehead and even Thomas Ellwood. In the *First Publishers of Truth* there are four specific accounts of going naked [N. Penney, ed., *First Publishers of Truth: Being Early Records (Now First Printed) of the Introduction of Quakerism into the Counties of England and Wales* (London: Headley Brothers, 1907), pp. 71, 213, 259, 308]. William Simpson, who had the longest career of going naked as a sign, wrote a short tract on the subject [William Simpson, *Going Naked, A Sign* being the last part of his pamphlet *A Discovery of the Priests and Professors* (London, 1660), pp. 7-8. Also appended to *A Short Relation of the Life and Death of ... William Simpson* (1671)]. He went naked and in sackcloth for three years with George

himself, approved its use among Friends.[64] The earliest recorded incidence of going naked comes from the pen of Fox himself in 1652, at which time he wrote that it was a sign of people's nakedness before God and a sign of

---

Fox's full support. He reminded his accusers that Isaiah, too, had walked naked and barefoot for three years as a sign of God's impending judgment against Egypt [William Simpson, *From One Who Was Moved of the Lord God to Go as a Sign* (London, 1660), p. 8. *See also* Soloman Eccles, *Signs are From the Lord ... to Forewarn Them of Some Imminent Judgement Near at Hand* (London, 1663)]. In 1654 fourteen year old Elizabeth Fletcher went topless in Oxford as a sign against false religion and was whipped for blasphemy at the behest of the vice-chancellor of Oxford (Fraser, *The Weaker Vessel*, p. 264). Another Quaker once paraded naked in a church attended by Oliver Cromwell [D. Neale, *History of the Puritans*, 4 (London: William Baynes, 1822/1732), p. 139]. Samuel Pepys sighted Soloman Eccles running naked through Westminster Hall and had this to say: "One thing extraordinary was, this day, a man, a Quaker, came naked through the Hall only very civilly tied about the loins to avoid scandal" [Samuel Pepys, *Diary and Correspondence of Sammuel Pepys*, 3 (New York: Bigelow, Brown and Co., 1848), p. 204]. The sign was rarely performed stark naked. Running about in undergarments was enough to draw charges of nakedness in seventeenth century England. When Thomas Holme went naked as a sign in Chester he was severely persecuted for it, prompting him to say that he had borne the iniquity of the city and now their blood was on his head (Penney, *First Publishers of Truth*, p. 368). When going naked is linked to suffering and bearing the iniquity of the people in this way it suggests that the sign, for some, went beyond mere illustration and became an actual epiphany. Most cases, however, were simple illustrations of impending divine judgment or signs against false religion [*see* James Nayler, *A Short Answer to a Book Called The Fanatick History* (London, 1660), p. 5]. In 1673 Daniel Smith disrupted a church service by taking off his clothes and standing on a seat and declaring that his naked body was a sign against false and hypocritical religion. As he was naked so too was the congregation before God (Carroll, "Early Quakers and Going Naked as a Sign," p. 71). *Nudas veritas* was a confronting of calumny and deceit. But, as Bauman points out, the situational context was often left ambiguous. Streaking in seventeenth century England so shocked onlookers that they were unable to go beyond the flagrant flouting of decorum to look for the metaphorical meaning (Bauman, *Let Your Words Be Few*, p. 72). In a society that paid an inordinate amount of attention to attire the practice was labelled as "immodest", "impudently bold", "obscene", "uncivilized", "heathenish", "brutish", "shameless", and "unseemly" (*Ibid.*, p. 92). Indeed, to go about naked (ie. partly dressed) was evidence of being "Bedlam mad" (Hume, *History of England*, 5, p. 523). Lunatics would rend their clothes and partially disrobe and the seventeenth century Englishman was not prepared to make a distinction between lunatics and Quakers. Both were accused of "repudiating their social pretentions". As MacDonald writes, "By reducing apparel to rags, the lunatic repudiated the hierarchical order of society and declared himself a mental vagrant, by casting away all artificial coverings, he shed all trace of human society. These gestures appeared to normal men and women to be acts of self-destructive violence, a kind of social suicide" (Macdonald, *Mystical Bedlam*, pp. 130-31). Quakers worked from the premise that "the Inward Light was the source of all spiritually informed communication" (Bauman, *Let Your Words Be Few*, p. 92). The Quaker who went naked was simply a communicative agent in the process.

[64]*See* especially *The Great Mystery of the Great Whore*, 3, pp. 137, 148, 353, 376, 495.

68

impending judgment.[65] In 1654 he wrote, "many hath the Lord moved to go stark naked amongst them ... [as] a figure to show them their nakedness." They were moved by "the Lord in his power", and "they were true prophets and prophetesses to the Nation."[66] He also gave a fairly extended treatment of William Simpson's practice of going naked.[67] Quakers used prophetic signs like this to demonstrate to political and religious leaders that the Kingdom of God had invaded the temporal realm and judgment of apostasy, oppression and injustice was imminent. Going naked was a sign first of impending judgment upon hypocrisy and second that Quakers were covered with the truth whereas their opponents were covered with falsehood and deceit.

Fox's prophetic proclamation of the everlasting gospel, then, was accompanied by a host of miracles, prophecies, visions and signs which were interpreted by Quakers as proof of the immediate presence of the Kingdom of God. On the other hand, this same outpouring of charismatic phenomena was interpreted by opponents of the sect as a flagrant flouting of decorum. Many approaches have been taken to explain the miraculous phenomena that accompanied the ministry of George Fox. The skeptic (like Bugg or Croese) took a satirical approach and lampooned the claim to miracles. Others, like Cotton Mather and more recently Ronald Knox, said that it was a product of excess enthusiasm. Seventeenth Century Anglican polemicists and contemporary scientists, like Rosen, interpreted it as a sign of insanity while still others (especially contemporaries of Fox) attributed it to witchcraft. Modern medicine (preceded in this case by Casaubon) has looked for the psychosomatic factor in illness and healing. A more sensitive and contemporary approach is that of Nigel Smith. Dreams, visions and prophecies expanded the use of figurative language, liberated it from conventional forms and gave freer reign to the work of the Spirit. The

---

[65]Fox, *The Rise of Friends and Truth*, in Cadbury, *Narrative Papers*, p. 27.

[66]Quoted in K.L. Carroll, "Quaker Attitudes Towards Signs and Wonders," p. 71.

[67]*A Short Relation Concerning the Life and Death of William Simpson* (1671) in Cadbury, *Narrative Papers*, p. 183.

expanded use of figurative imagery enabled the radicals to assume a new and peculiar deportment which implied, among other things, perfection.[68] Indeed, the best approach may be the all purposive one. Our interest here is to avoid the question of the truth of miracles in favour of an explanation, or, to avoid discussing the validity of miracles in favour of their impact, meaning and significance.

R.F. Holland, in his article "The Miraculous", defined miracles by using the 'contingency' and 'violation' concepts. According to the former a miracle may be the product of an unexpected conjunction of natural phenomena, without detracting from the sign significance. Some miracles have good historical explanations. Other miracles violate natural law. In Holland's terms an event may *occur* (that is empirically certain) that is *impossible* (that is conceptually impossible). David Hume argued that no such event could ever be proved, and thus could not be made a "just foundation" of any religious system. Miracles, he said, lacked any competent witnesses, enlarged on the truth, abounded among the ignorant and finally, miracles of rival religions cancelled each other out. All revealed religion resting on the miraculous was contrary to reason. This was the interpretation of the skeptic.[69]

Other interpreters, informed by a different set of presuppositions, would accept either of Holland's two categories. Miracles were 'signs' which, in a particular context, had meaning. If the contingency concept applied to a miracle, as for example when Fox 'miraculously' healed a man with a severely sprained neck by using a natural technique to realign his neck,[70] even though Fox was acting more as a 'manipulative surgeon' the miracle still did not lose its sign-like significance in its historical context.

Not all Fox's peers, however, were willing to assign value to his miracles and they assailed the doctrine of direct inspiration as the root of all

[68]Smith, *Perfection Proclaimed*, p. 308.

[69]*See* R.F. Holland, "The Miraculous", *American Philosophical Quarterly*, 2 (Jan., 1965), pp. 43-51.

[70]Nickalls, *Journal*, pp. 631-32.

religious enthusiasm. In seventeenth century England a new educated elite was heralding the virtues of scientific materialism, which was used as a tool to combat the claims of the religious enthusiasts. Direct inspiration was a sign of insanity or deep religious melancholy. No rational person spoke to God directly. Burton and Napier did entertain the possibility that the strange psychic states of Fox might just be "genius glimpses of the unseen world"[71] but it was the argument for the link between direct inspiration and madness that became prominent between 1650 and 1750:

> When the educated elite abandoned their beliefs in divine inspiration and demonology, they also elevated delusion to a prominent place among the signs of madness. These two changes were closely connected. For more than a century after the English Revolution, the governing classes assailed the religious enthusiasm of the sects. Anglican propagandists declared that the visons and inspirations of radical Dissenters were insane delusions based on false perceptions and diseased imaginings.[72]

These characterizations retained their potency because they contained a kernel of truth. When intellectuals of considerable social standing, like Cotton Mather, wrote of Quakers as "the sink of all heresies" they were repudiating the flouting of decorum, disruption of the social order, the

[71]MacDonald, *Mystical Bedlam*, p. 170.

[72]*Ibid.*, p. 170. The clash between the magic of exorcists and faith healers and rationalists continued well after Fox's own lifetime as illustrated by the well known dispute between the popular exorcist Gassner and the physician Mesmer in 1775 best described by Henri Ellenberger. Eyewitness accounts of Gassner's healings and exorcisms are almost identical to those associated with Valentine Greatrakes and George Fox. His personal influence over people was profound. However, like Fox, he lived in an era when Enlightenment forces were struggling to overthrow the magic in religion. Mesmer heralded the same healing powers as Gassner but he wrapped them in a non-religious, scientific cloak. By experimenting on his own patients he discovered that he could treat them by facilitating special powers in each person - powers which he called animal magnetism. With a touch, or even a gesture of his hand, Mesmer could influence people, even at a great geographic distance. He became known as a 'magnetizer' or 'hypnotizer' of people. He explained the healing process scientifically rather than mystically and he became known as one of the fathers of 'dynamic psychiatry'. Mesmer's abilities to heal at the touch or stroke of his hand, his hypnotic effect on people are all too reminiscent of Fox and later, the great nineteenth century seer Fredericke Hauffe [*see* Henri Ellenberger, *The Discovery of the Unconscious* (New York: Basic Books, 1970), pp. 53-102 and Robert Darnton, *Mesmerism and the End of the Enlightenment in France* (Cambridge: Harvard University Press, 1968)].

blasphemy, the miracles and the mad acts of running through the streets naked. There was a freedom and 'wildness' spawned by the idea of direct revelation that challenged 'orthodoxy' by going its own way and forming opinions that clearly flouted decorum and it is worthy of repetition that "religious excess" in seventeenth century England was "identified with social and political chaos". Religious enthusiasm was equated with "deviation from social norms" which led to the disruption of the social order.[73]

Other modern interpreters have provided physical or psychological explanations for Fox's healing powers. Jones said that miracles of healing could be attributed to a 'faith attitude' or an 'expectant state of mind'. Endocrine glands of the body could play an enormous role in the healing process. The glowing in Fox's eyes (which had such a hypnotic effect on people) may have been produced by a virile blood supply or active glandular secretions. Fox, continued Jones, may also have had a natural capacity for "awakening faith and of carrying suggestive attitudes irresistibly into action."[74] Cadbury suggested that many of Fox's cures could be treated as the product of a "strong personality", a "commanding presence", a "piercing eye" and a voice of "absolute assurance."[75] He was, said Steven Kent, able to

[73]Cherry, "Enthusiasm and Madness," p. 23. Still, belief in supernatural portents remained widespread among the lower orders where the signs and wonders of maguses like George Fox were accepted.

[74]R. Jones, Foreward to Cadbury, George Fox's 'Book of Miracles', p. xiii. Fox's eyes had a definite hypnotic quality. An angry deacon once said to Fox "Do not pierce me so with thy eyes; keep thy eyes off me" (Jones, George Fox: An Autobiography, 1, p. 187). He quieted a crowd in Lancaster by telling them to look at his eyes (Ibid., p. 344) and in Holland the well-known Mennonite and Collegiant, Galenus Abrams, bade Fox to keep his eyes off him, for they pierced him (Ibid., p. 556). Untreated thyroid irregularities can also have an enormous effect on the eyes.

[75]Cadbury, George Fox's 'Book of Miracles', p. 60. Cadbury did not discount the validity of miracles altogether. His New Testament writings suggest he believed they served a purpose for their time. They were signs, a dramatization of religious experience. He does not want Quakers to be embarrassed by the miraculous in their own history. In early Christian times they were proper New Testament idiom. He suspends judgement on their reliability and interprets them as idiomatic expressions of God's will. The light of conscience adopts the same idioms. Miracles dramatize God's work. From age to age the language and symbols may change but the work of God in the conscience is ongoing. Miracles, in any age, are idiomatic. They are a form of dramatic language for one who is trying to do God's will. Cadbury's reconstruction of Fox's Book of Miracles was done from the perspective that the

72

establish a special bond between himself and people and this seemed to be especially true of his dealings with distracted people.[76]

Brayshaw interpreted Fox's prolonged illnesses as "psychic states of misery"[77] brought on by external forces of injustice and sin around him. His trances were like deep depressions. His premonitions, however, are more difficult to explain - like his premonition of the hanging of Quakers on Boston Common long before the news of the event actually reached him.[78] We cannot scientifically test these things. We only have his *Journal* record and other fragmentary evidence to rely on. This has led some interpreters to take a linguistic approach to his language. Fox's language, said Knight, was a

---

miracles in early Quakerism were historically conditioned language. Anyone informed by the light acts in God's will and miracles can be idiomatic expressions of God's will.

[76]S.A. Kent, "Psychology and Quaker Mysticism: The Legacy of William James and Rufus Jones," *QH*, 76 (Spr., 1987), p. 16. Prayer and visions can have a certain therapeutic function, especially when a powerful personality is addressing itself to the mind in a high state of religious excitement. Once, when a 'distracted' man was intent on beating Fox, he spoke to the man and "chained him" (*Religion and the Decline of Magic*, p. 150; *Cambridge Journal*, 1, p. 72). Mesmer was able to establish a high degree of rapport with his subjects. He had a compelling mixture of charm and authority. He even claimed to magnetize the sun. Ellenberger said he "is closer to the ancient magician than to the twentieth century psychotherapist" but in him were "the seeds of several basic tenets of modern psychiatry - namely, healing can only be accomplished when a "rapport" is established with a patient." Healing occurs, in large part, due to the subjects' attitude toward the healer (think for example of those who were healed after touching the blood stained garments of the freshly slain Thomas Becket). The theory of magnetism outgrew Mesmer and was subjected to serious scientific scrutiny. What remains today, as the fundamental modern explanation for healing is the concept of "rapport" or "reciprocal influence between the patient and the magnetizer." Among twentieth century charismatic faith healers Oral Roberts, Kathryn Kuhlman and William Marrion Branham stand out. Branham's left hand would quiver in the presence of disease and he was known for his ability to discern people's hearts, not unlike the supernatural power attributed to the *starets* or Holy Man in the Russian Orthodox tradition. An angel was once said to have proclaimed Branham's special status as a prophet and some of his followers even believed he was the Messiah [C.D. Weaver, *The Healer-Prophet, William Marrion Branham: A Study of the Prophetic in American Pentecostalism* (Macon, Georgia: Mercer University Press, 1987); D. Harrell, *Oral Roberts: An American Life* (San Francisco: Harper and Row, 1987) and J. Brown (trans.), "Russia's Spiritual Traditions Live On," *Religion in Communist Lands*, 10 (1982), pp. 96-100].

[77]Brayshaw, *The Personality of George Fox*, p. 88.

[78]*Cambridge Journal*, 2, p. 5. Compare with Ellwood's extended account and additions to the *Spence MS*. (*Journal*, 1, p. 430).

"sign and symbol of his mental state."[79] He lived, moved and worked as if it were God himself working. Knight pointed out that Fox rarely differentiated his actions from God's actions. The two were inextricably interwoven. His person could quiet crowds, "chain" lunatics and even cause people to think they had seen an angel.[80] Washburn and Starbuck thought that these were all bodily reactions to Fox's mental life. He was "moved", "led", "constrained" and "drawn" by God to such a degree that some said the places where he prayed 'seemed to be shaken'.[81] Unlike us, Fox did not stop to analyze where this power came from. It had but one source - the Lord who speaks within. Fox energized in a level of consciousness that was above the ordinary, yet, the trend of his life, when taken as a whole, was not irrational. His organizational skills attest to his practical and efficient side - something which prompted Macauley to grudgingly admit that while Fox was "too much disordered for liberty" he was "not sufficiently disordered for Bedlam."[82]

Finally, the true *significance* (that is, sign meaning) of Fox's miracles in their mid-seventeenth century Quaker setting was informed by his Kingdom theology and his prophetic role in its proclamation. What is certain about the miracles he performed is that they were bound up with the literal presence of the glorified body of Christ in the believer. What Barth said about the ministry of Jesus may be equally applied to the ministry of Fox -

---

[79]R. Knight, *The Founder of Quakerism: A Psychological Study of the Mysticism of George Fox* (London: Swarthmore Press, 1950), p. 59.

[80]At Cambridge, where theological students were preparing to attack Fox they were, he records in his *Journal*, arrested by a glow - "O", they said, "he shines, he glistens" (*Cambridge Journal*, 1, p. 190). He once spoke to a congregation at Beverley after which a woman later reported "there was an angel or spirit came into the body of the church ... and spoke strange things, and the wonderful things of God ... and when he had done it he passed away" (Nickalls, *Journal*, p. 75).

[81]M.F. Washburn, *Movement and Mental Imagery* (New York: Arno Press, 1973); E.D. Starbuck, *Psychology of Religion: An Empirical Study of the Growth of Religious Consciousness* (London: Walter Scott, 1899).

[82]Macauley, *The History of England*, 7, p. 163. William James recognized Fox's religious genius as being the result of a pathological personality that gave him his "religious authority and influence", that is, the tendency to depressions, fixed ideas, trances, voices and visions [*The Varieties of Religious Experience* (London: Longmans, 1915), p. 7].

74

miracles were an epiphany of the Son of Man and were prophetic signs and anticipations of the restoration of the world.[83]   They linked the verbal message and the prophetic act and functioned as signs of the eschatological prophet, which both Jesus and Fox were.[84] The expelling of demons and the healing of the sick were never separate from the preaching of the Kingdom or, in Fox's case, the everlasting gospel.[85]

---

[83]C. Brown, *Miracles and the Critical Mind* (Grand Rapids: Eerdmans, 1984), p. 244.

[84]*Ibid.*, p. 263. Following Alan Richardson.

[85]Fox's life had all the ritualistic characteristics of the traditional magus, like Appollonius, Jesus, Mani, Montanus and even the not so well known Hanina ben Dosa, the first century Galilean charismatic who lived in total poverty, survived the bites of poisonous snakes, healed at a distance (like Fox), interceded for rain (like Fox), cast out evil spirits (like Fox) and in whom there was deep concern for moral reform (like Fox).

4

AVATAR

Signs and wonders alone were not conclusive evidence that Fox was an avatar. This brings us to the central part of the study - that Fox was more than a miracle-worker. By his own account he was the Son of God. No sectarian, to my knowledge, ever expounded a similar form of Christ inhabiting and thus divinizing the saint. Neither was it foreshadowed in exactly the same way in Continental concepts of celestial flesh. One even searches in vain for a hint of it in Thomas Edwards' comprehensive commentary on sectarian errors.[1]

---

[1]In Thomas Edwards' expanded edition of *Gangraena* he did mention the heresy "that God is in our flesh as much as in Christ's flesh" (*Gangraena*, revised edition, vol. 2, p. 10) but this was not exactly the same as the inhabitation of the celestial, glorified flesh of Christ in the believer. At the end of the seventeenth century the French Calvinist Pierre Jurieu, "le pape des réformés", reproached Catholicism for never having condemned the tendency of some in the tradition of mystical devotion to teach "l'idée d'une déification parfaite de l'homme". On this point Leszek Kolakowski said Jurieu was wrong since the possibility of deification, in at least one form, was condemned by Pope John XXII in his Bull *In Agro Domini* (1329) [Lescez Kolakowski, *Chrétiens sans Eglise* (Paris: Gallimard, 1969), pp. 551, 554, 566n.127. I am indebted to Stephen Davidson for bringing this item to my attention]. Fox's notion of celestial inhabitation was far more literal than similar concepts in the medieval mystics who were far more speculative. It was a case of differing 'forms' of deification. Fox, for example, spoke of deification in the novel form of Christ's glorified body literally inhabiting the saints. Fox pressed his idea well beyond the Augustinian tradition of "illuminationism", but so then did some mystics. Meister Eckhardt comes closest to Fox but even Eckhardt's two leading notions - the 'divine spark' and the 'birth of God in the soul' - were informed by a distinction between the creator and the created. There was an "existential detachment" (an emphasis on the nothingness of the creature and the passivity of the will) in Meister Eckhardt's theology that

76

The implications of Fox's claims to divinity were a challenge to orthodoxy that far outweighed, in importance, the social disruptions caused by anti-tithe agitation and disruption of church services. Yet even the most recent works on Fox, Nayler and early Quakerism have seriously failed to confront and interpret the issue of blasphemy.[2] This chapter will demonstrate that the suppressed declarations of Fox will make the Palm Sunday reenactment of Nayler look less extravagant and more representative of informed Quaker teaching of the time.

Fox openly proclaimed himself to be the Son of God and that bold and contentious proclamation was another bowdlerized feature of early Quakerism. Some Quaker authors have made passing reference to these exalted claims but they have reasoned that the claims were part of an inadequate view of Christ's work, the initial flush of a new experience or the immaturity of new beliefs.[3] Quaker interpreters from as early as the 1670's have chosen to explain Fox's exalted claims by excusing them. Even their opponents accused them of excusing Fox.

Why the attempt to excuse, misconstrue and even bowdlerize these features of Fox's theology? The charge of blasphemy against Fox (and numerous other Quakers) became such a sensitive issue, especially after the Nayler incident and in the 1670's, 1680's and 1690's when a new generation of leadership was attempting to relocate Quakerism within the pale of respectable English non-conformity, that it was judged appropriate and safer

wasn't there in Fox [On Eckhardt *see* Oliver Davies, *God Within: The Mystical Tradition of Northern Europe* (London: Darton, Longmans and Todd, 1988), p. 72].

[2]Gwyn, *Apocalypse of the Word* on Fox; W.G. Bittle, *James Nayler, 1618-1660: The Quaker Indicted by Parliament* (Richmond, Indiana: Friends United Press, 1986) and on early Quakerism, H. Barbour and J.W. Frost, *The Quakers* (New York: Greenwood Press, 1988).

[3]Braithwaite, *Beginnings*, p. 109; Barbour, *Quakers in Puritan England*, pp. 146-47 and Barbour and Frost, *The Quakers*, pp. 26 and 40; K. Carroll, "A Look at James Milner and his "False Prophecy"," *QH*, 74 (1985), p. 23. The idea expressed by "inadequate christology" is that George Fox and early Quakers were insufficiently confident of the historic sufficiency of Christ's work. So imagined, Christ's work had to be added to in order to be completed. Saying that early Quakers had a weak view of Christ's historic work is to excuse them and especially Fox for his excessive claims. The rewriting of early Quaker theology (to be discussed in chapter seven) was more than a matter of editing words. It was a widespread and lasting paradigm shift that realigned Quaker theology with more orthodox conceptions of the historic Christ and his work.

to delete all questionable references from the relevant literature. In Fox's *Journal* Thomas Ellwood, under the direction of the Second Day Morning Meeting, deleted all references where Fox called himself the Son of God, the entire text of the Lancaster blasphemy trial, references to the Nayler incident and the aforementioned vision seen by Fox in 1671. Early Quaker authors like John Whiting and George Whitehead did their best to reinterpret, in an orthodox way, the exalted claims of Fox and other early Quakers. They in turn accused anti-Quaker apologists of using the exalted language in devious ways to discredit the movement.

It is necessary, therefore, to grasp as clearly as we can the precise nature of Fox's christopresent theology before proceeding on with the discussion of the blasphemy trials. Fox's doctrine of celestial inhabitation was the hub of his entire world of thought. The radicalness and the novelty of his christopresentism is missed when it is given a spiritualistic or mystical reading.[4]

As we saw in chapter two, Fox's inner light was the inner Christ and the inner Christ meant, quite simply, the presence of Christ's heavenly flesh and bone in the believer. Fox spent a great deal of time elucidating this point:

> The scripture saith God will dwell in men, and walk in men ... Doth not the Apostle say, the saints were made partakers of the divine nature? and that God dwells in the saints, and Christ is in them, except they be reprobates? And do not the saints come to eat the flesh of Christ? And if they eat his flesh, is it not within them?[5]

One opponent, Christopher Wade, understood Fox to imply that Christ's person was in the believer, which "is a false thing". Fox scoffed at Wade's skepticism and replied: "which is as much to say, none are of his flesh, of his

---

[4]As we saw in chapter one, Creasey, Benson and Gwyn all brought material forward about Fox's christology but they failed to satisfactorily interpret his doctrine of celestial flesh inhabitation.

[5]*Great Mystery of the Great Whore*, 3, pp. 181-82. For other examples of "flesh and bone" statements *see Cambridge Journal*, 1, pp. 68-69 and *Great Mystery of the Great Whore*, 3, p. 505.

78

bone, nor eat it, nor had his substance".[6] This was an affirmation of the doctrine ridiculed by Wade. Christ's body was in the believer. Christ was not distinct from the believer, their body or their spirit. This is not to suggest that celestial flesh is of man. Of course it is "of God" in man.

Nor was a disembodied Christ within: "Doth not Christ dwell in his saints, as he is in the person of the Father, the substance? and are they not of his flesh and bone"?[7] Fox did not hold orthodox Trinitarian views which represented the three persons of the Trinity to be coeval. Fox made rich use of the word "spirit" in his writings in a wide sense of contexts, shades and ambiguities but central to this discussion was his lack of distinction between Father, Son, Spirit and believer:

> Christ saith he is in the Father, and the Father is in him, and he will send them the spirit of truth, the comforter, that proceeds from the Father and the son; and Christ saith, he was glorified with the Father before the world began; and yet ye say, the son is distinguished from the Father in eternity. And the son saith he is in the Father, and the Father is in him. And you say the spirit is distinguished from the Father and the son from eternity, and Christ saith it proceeds from him and the Father, and he is the God and father of the spirits of all flesh, and the substance of all things ... And are there not three that bear record in heaven, the Father, the word, and the spirit, and are they not all one? How then are they distinct? ... And Christ saith, 'I and my Father, are one' ... and he is in the saints and so not distinct.[8]

The operative theme in Fox's notion of celestial inhabitation was that there were no distinctions in the Godhead and this is important when we come to discuss the blasphemy trials, especially at Lancaster, for Judge Fell's defence of Fox was based on the idea that there was no distinction between Christ and saint and therefore the notion of equality could not be properly defined and applied. Furthermore, where Christ was present the fulness of the Godhead was always present, for there were no distinctions in the Godhead.

[6]*Great Mystery of the Great Whore*, 3, p. 399.

[7]*Ibid.*, 3, p. 397.

[8]*Ibid.*, 3, p. 180. *See also* pp. 206, 243-44, 291-92, 340, 397, 399, 402.

Christ within the believer meant that the fulness of the Godhead dwelt in the believer and they were not distinct. Christ did not have a separate bodily existence in a faraway heaven while his Spirit dwelt in the believer. Fox repeatedly spoke of the cohabitation of Christ and believer in familiar eucharistic terms only he interpreted it much more broadly. And the saints were not only inhabited by Christ's flesh and bone but they fed on his celestial flesh[9] and in so doing they became divine creatures. Christ may be said to have been transubstantiated in them, although there are dangers to this crude analogy. According to Fox the inner body seems in the saint to have been displaced and replaced by celestial flesh substantially. By substantially we mean something like "in the flesh and bone" or "in fact" rather than "in essence". A too strict analogy with transubstantiation (and the circumscription of Christ to the wafer) puts us in danger of losing Fox's far-reaching literalness. With Fox more than grace is infused into the believer. The inhabitation of the celestial Christ within effects a pervasive and permanent transformation wherein the saint is divinized. Perhaps the notion of the permanent transubstantiation of the believer into Christ – so the believer becomes the sacrament – is closer to the mark if we use the terms "transference" or "transposition." Whatever, Fox's inner Christ was a celestial (not a "spiritual") Christ with an immaterial "flesh and bone." He was not the corporal Christ (with the historic "body and blood") of late Medieval Catholic sacramental theology. A fundamental source of conflict between early Quakers and their learned opponents was over their different conceptions of Christ – who He was, how He was formed, where He resided.

For Fox, the presence of this celestial Christ was concrete, graphic and visceral.[10] It was not a figurative presence. Nor was it a disembodied Spirit presence. This is the crucial interpretive point. Leading early Quakers refused to separate Christ's body and Christ's spirit. This has nothing to do with an inadequate or immature theology. It was another view of Christ.

---

[9]*Ibid.*, 3, p. 183.

[10]Visceral: arising from within: pertaining to the interior or inner parts of the body.

Nayler repeatedly said, "Christ is not divided".[11] Howgill put it most clearly: "But maybe thou will say as thy generation does, that Christ is in the earth by his spirit, and in heaven by his body and person, distinct from his spirit. If so, then you divide Christ, and a person without a spirit, and not Christ."[12] The failure to understand that early Quakers did not disembody the spirit has been an obstacle to overcome when interpreting the christopresentism of Fox. Not only was the spirit of Christ not disembodied but the saints were inhabited by the heavenly body of Christ. They were equals in the Godhead. As Howgill wrote to an adversary,

> And the first thing that thy dark mind stumbles at is, that some have said, that they that have the spirit of God are equal with God. He that has the spirit of God, is in that which is equal, as God is equal, and his ways equal. And he that is joined to the Lord is one spirit, there is unity, and the unity stands in equality itself. He that is born from above is the Son of God, and he said, I and my Father are one. And when the Son is revealed, and speaks, the Father speaks in him, and dwells in him, and he in the Father. In that which is equal in equality itself; there is equality in nature, though not in stature. Go learn what these things mean, the understanding and learned will know what I say, and this is neither damnable nor blasphemous; but on the contrary, it is saving and precious to them that believe. And thou concludes, though they be glorified in heaven, yet are not equal with God. Here thou blasphemes. The Son of God is glorified with the Father in the same glory he had with him before the world began; the glory is in purity, equality, immortality, and eternity.[13]

In 1699, after the transformation of Fox's doctrine of the inner light, George Whitehead commented on this passage. He said that Howgill was only

---

[11]Fox and Nayler, *Saul's Errand to Damascus*, pp. 594, 610.

[12]Howgill, *Darkness and Ignorance Expelled*, p. 23.

[13]*Ibid.*, p. 21.

speaking of the unity between Father and Son.[14]   He was only partially correct. Howgill was trying to demonstrate that the saints participated in the same unity and equality that existed between the Father and the Son precisely because they had the Spirit of God in them - not the disembodied Spirit but the heavenly body of Christ. He that had the Spirit of God within was in that which was equal; equal in nature though not in stature, that is, each believer was not the sum total of what God was but each shared in the equality within the Godhead.

Even if we understand that the early Quakers did not disembody the Spirit it is difficult to grasp the idea of celestial flesh. It is difficult to imagine just how heady and exhilarating this celestial inhabitation must have been. Exactly how it was felt may escape us but some idea is conveyed through the interrogations and questionings of leading Quakers around Fox, for Fox's views informed his followers and some went to great lengths to define the unity of the celestial flesh of Christ and the saint. Howgill, Farnworth and Nayler believed it and expounded on it. So, too, did Josiah Coale who said that the glorified body of Christ was not separate from the saints who "were flesh of his flesh and bone of his bone ... members of his body, of his flesh."[15] Deification was a natural corollary to christopresentism. This general conjecture was shared by Henry More who was the most discerning critic of early Quakerism. More was able to exert some influence on George Keith, William Penn and Robert Barclay but none on Fox. He spoke kindly of the former but never of Fox with whom he associated primitive, early Quakerism which held "nebulous and confused" Familist ideas about the inner light - ideas which compelled "silly-minded" Quakers to think of themselves as gods.[16]   Throughout his writings, whenever he discussed Quakers, More

[14]George Whitehead, *Supplement* to Joseph Wyeth's *Anguis Flagellatus; or, A Switch for the Snake* (1699), p. 20.

[15]Josiah Coale, *A Vindication of the Light Within*, in *The Books and Diverse Epistles of ... Josiah Coale* (1671), p. 332.

[16]Henry More, *An Explanation of the Grand Mystery of Godliness* (London, 1660) Book 1, chapter 6, p. 14. Once, at the request of Lady Conway, More did meet with Fox and other leading Quakers, this being in late 1677. According to Powicke Fox apparently repelled More for after conversing with the Quaker leader he reportedly said "he felt himself as it were

82

implied that the *majority* of Quakers were hopelessly committed to Fox's primitive 'Familist' vision while the "well-meaning" Quakers like Penn and Barclay were part of a select few sensible ones who held out some hope that in time the rest would follow Barclay's example and return to a more balanced and orthodox position on the historic Christ.

The question of whether Fox thought of Christ's indwelling figuratively or literally is the most contentious point raised by this study. More, I think, had a correct sense of things. If we divide early Quakers along the lines of contiguous and metaphoric ways of thinking, far less interpreted the inner Christ metaphorically at least until the 1670's. Contiguous thinking may not be the preference of the educated elite but it is not faulty or inadequate. George Whitehead, Edward Burrough, Samuel Fisher, George Keith, William Penn and Robert Barclay thought metaphorically. Generally they were better educated than most Quakers and in some ways more orthodox. More recognized this. But contiguous thinking (literally touching the non-physical substance of the inner Christ) predominated in early Quakerism.

Critics of Quakerism often critiqued the literalist notion of celestial inhabitation, the notion of a spiritual and immortal body inhabiting the physical body of the believer. No contemporary grasped the nature of the problem as well as the Muggletonian prophet John Reeve. In a letter contained in a group of letters directed to or about Quakers he said that it was an error to deny that a spirit had to have a body.[17] He wanted to give God a body and would not separate body from substance. He derided the view that immaterial substances exist, that is, that something immaterial could have a substance without a body or, that a spiritual body could consist of a formless 'stuff'. To say that a spirit had neither shape nor substance

turned into brass (so much did the spirit, crookedness, or perverseness of that person move and offend his spirit)". The feeling may have been mutual with Fox being repelled by More's superior air [F.J. Powicke, *The Cambridge Platonists: A Study* (London: J.M. Dent, 1926), p. 167. For the quote *see* F.J. Powicke, "Henry More, Cambridge Platonist; And Lady Conway, of Ragley, Platonist and Quakeress," *Friends Quarterly Examiner*, 55 (1921), p. 213].

[17]John Reeve, *The Prophet Reeve's Epistle to his Friend, Discovering the Dark Light of the Quakers*, pp. 11-12. Nigel Smith accepts the content of this material as being directed toward the Quaker notion of immaterial bodies (*Perfection Proclaimed*, p. 240).

implied that it was no more than a shadow.[18] He was concerned to safeguard the notion that a mortal soul was embedded in a mortal body and both would see resurrection together.

Celestial flesh provided the early Quaker with an immortal soul and suggested they were deified and resurrected while still in their mortal bodies. Reeve had grasped the idea that early Quakers held a view about immaterial bodies that was unusual, unorthodox and worrying. The metaphysics bear on doctrines of the soul in animate creatures from Greek times on. The notion of whether a body could be material or immaterial had roots in the debate between Plato and Aristotle.[19] Fox was not involved at this level of argument but Reeve did charge that belief in spirit as an immaterial substance was to believe in a bodiless God and a bodiless soul and that, he said, was akin to the philosophical notions of the "Heathen Philosophers", who were known to his respondent.[20] In Reeve's orthodox view of things spirits had to have bodies to exist. Every spirit had to have "form, substance and shape" and God "is no other but the form of a man."[21] Christ had a glorified body with substance, form and shape. Reeve could, understandably, not conceive how such a body could inhabit the mortal body of the believer since nothing immaterial could have a substance. The only way an immortal soul could inhabit a mortal body was after the resurrection. Quakers, on the other hand, believed spirits were immaterial substances that could inhabit the mortal body. Specifically, Christ's body was an immaterial substance that

---

[18]Reeve, *The Prophet Reeve's Epistle*, 12.

[19]Plato said that real substance exists outside a body while we could understand Aristotle to say that there could be no substance without a body. Catholic sacramental theology was based on the first of Aristotle's categories. The substance of the body and blood of Christ was in the wine after consecration. This was transubstantiation. The corporeal body of Christ was imbibed. After the change the sacrament had a corporeal body; a physical, visible body.

[20]Reeve, *The Prophet Reeve's Epistle*, pp. 12, 13 and 15. Fox's spirit as "stuff" may not have been the same as Augustine's ontological sense of spirit as "substance" but the debate over the nature of the "unseen", the nature of "invisibility" has genealogy that goes back to the ancient authors.

[21]Reeve, *The Prophet Reeve's Epistle*, p. 11.

84

could inhabit, divinize and resurrect the believer even while the believer retained the mortal body.

We are here at the heart of Fox's theology of celestial inhabitation and the majority of early Quakers subscribed to it. If we understand early Quaker notions about immaterial bodies then we have gone a long way toward explaining heretofore unexplainable aspects of early Quakerism - especially the exalted language and the Nayler incident. It helps, too, to explain the general direction of the blasphemy trials and the critiques by Reeve and More as well as Bunyan, Baxter, Owen and innumerable other seventeenth century Puritan divines whose arguments were put forth and answered by Fox in his *Great Mystery of the Great Whore*. If it can be shown that some early Quakers interpreted Christ's indwelling metaphorically, it can equally be shown that many more interpreted it literally based on the understanding that Christ's glorified body was an immaterial substance. Fox's idea of the inner Christ must be radically reoriented away from the spiritualistic and highly esoteric interpretations that became a part of the later story, towards a qualitative, corporeal presence.

We have established, then, that Fox conceived of Christ's flesh as an immaterial substance that could inhabit every particle of the mortal body of the believer. It was but a short step to the exalted claim that Nayler was Jesus reincarnate. Fox, however, made a fundamental distinction between outer, human flesh and inner, heavenly flesh and it was the heavenly body of the pre-existent Christ within that concerned Fox. The mortal vessel that contained the heavenly body was of no consequence for it was not the vessel of human flesh that was sinful or glorified, it was the inner body. Every person (except Jesus and those who were born of believers who were thus glorified and had no body of sin left to pass on) had an inner, "carnal" body of sin that had to be shed if the glorified body of Christ was to dwell in and glorify the believer. When the saints fed on the heavenly flesh of the inner Christ they were resurrected.[22] These glorified, celestial bodies were

---

[22]On recreation *see* Fox, *Great Mystery of the Great Whore*, 3, pp. 269-70, 411-12, 466-67, 505 and *A Testimony of What We Believe in Christ* (1675) in *Gospel Truth Demonstrated*, 5, pp. 84-154 (*see also* p. 226, *Gospel Truth Demonstrated*, 6, p. 299 and Fox, Box A, Portfolio 10, No. 58 at FRL). George Bishop: "When the body of sin is shed and the exalted body put on

assumed while the saints remained in their human, earthly vessels. The Apostles of old, said Fox, were glorified yet they remained in their earthly vessels. Howgill further explained this concept by saying that when Christ changed the body he did not change its "form" but its "quality". When Adam degenerated from his glorified state the form of his body did not change but it changed nonetheless - substantively. Likewise, when the believer was restored to the glorified state he was resurrected not in form but in substance.[23] This was how Christ's heavenly body dwelt in and substantively transformed the saints.

The distinction between the inner body and the outer garment was a fundamental one and all early Quakers used it in one form or another. The standard early Quaker response to their interrogators was 'as the world knows me I am George Fox, James Nayler, Francis Howgill, Richard

---

this is the resurrection. In this life we pass from one side of corruption to another" [*A Treatise Concerning the Resurrection* (London, 1662), p. 11]. The anti-Quaker apologist Richard Sherlocke said that it was inconceivable that recreation could occur on such a complete and widespread scale in this life since the inner sanctuary and the light in it was profaned [*The Quakers Wild Questions* (London, 1654), p. 110]. Braithwaite tended to agree with Sherlocke's conclusions (both were working with an orthodox view of God and God's salvatory work in the creature) when he said that early Quakers had an "inadequate recognition of the earthly character of the vessel" and this led to excesses (*Beginnings*, p. 110). Fox knew only too well that an inner body of sin defiled the inner sanctuary but he said that it was possible and biblical to believe that the inner body of sin could be totally shed and the glorified body of Christ assumed in this life. On perfection *see* Fox, *Gospel Truth Demonstrated*, 4, pp. 45, 128, 159, 188, 283, 317; 5, pp. 44-5, 48, 94-5, 100-1, 109, 118, 175, 226, 267, 309, 379; 6, pp. 20, 22, 422, 429, 440, 443, 478; *Epistles*, 7, pp. 231-33, 251 and Nayler, *A Discovery of the Man of Sin* (London, 1654), p. 6. There was no redemption or perfection beyond the grave [Francis Howgill, *The Invisible Things of God Brought to Light* (London, 1659), p. 27]. An interesting consequence of the perfection of the saints and the assuming of a glorified body was that children of the saints were sanctified and perfected in the womb suggesting that in time a small army of saints could grow and one day cover the whole earth (*see* Fox, *Great Mystery of the Great Whore*, 3, pp. 421, 423, 449, 554). Nor was there any need for purgatory. The saints were only to pray for each other while they were alive. When they died or "fell asleep" they were no longer able to intercede. When the saints died they simply discarded their earthly tabernacle and returned to the God who made them (*Gospel Truth Demonstrated*, 5, p. 455 and 6, pp. 110-11, 362). There was some ambivalence among early Quakers about whether total perfection occurred at the instant of regeneration or not. Some, like William Dewsbury and Alexander Parker believed that it was slow process since different people had different measures of light and different measures of good and evil in them. This was a more realistic view (and eventually the predominant view) since so many Quakers had trouble with the carnal nature long after regeneration.

[23]Howgill, *Invisible Things of God Brought to Light*, p. 26.

Hubberthorne, etc., but to the saints we are known by a new name that the world knows not' [i.e. as sons and daughters of God].[24] The name George Fox was according to the flesh and it was not the human flesh that was glorified - not in the patriarchs, prophets, Jesus, the Apostles or Quakers. Human flesh was a neutral entity, neither good nor bad, sinful nor glorified. It was merely an earthly tabernacle and earthly names were attached to the earthly tabernacle. However, when the saints shed their inner, "carnal" body of sin and returned to the pre-Fall state of glory by assuming Christ's glorified flesh they also assumed new names.[25] As early as 1652 Fox was using language that implied he held the same notion of celestial inhabitation for the Apostles:

> Did not [Christ] say he would come again to [the Apostles]? did he not say he was in them, "I in you"? and did not the Apostle say Christ was in them, the hope of glory, except they were reprobates? was he not revealed in the Apostle, and so in him? and did not the Apostle preach Christ within? and you preach Christ without.[26]

and again, "doth not the Apostle say, they are of his flesh and bone, and sit with him in heavenly places ... And Christ saith, they must eat his flesh, and he is in them".[27] In his writings Fox equated the glorified Christ in the

---

[24]See, for example, the answers of William Dewsbury, John Whitehead and Francis Ellington in Dewsbury, *A True Testimony of ... the General Assizes ... at Northampton* (London, 1655). Fox cited the case of Cotton Crossland in his *Great Mystery of the Great Whore*. Crossland was another erstwhile Quaker who was present at some meetings Fox held in Gainsborough in 1652. At one such meeting Crossland declared that he believed Fox was saying that he was Christ. This provoked an unruly mob which turned on Fox. Fox called Crossland "Judas" (a metaphor of judgment in this case) and the unfortunate Crossland apparently did go and hang himself (p. 471, *Cambridge Journal*, 1, p. 34 and Gilpin, *The Quakers Shaken*, p. 21.). Fox eventually calmed the crowd by saying that he never said George Fox was Christ, nor was he referring to the creature when he said that the saints were equal with Christ.

[25]Consequently the saints were resurrected and perfected in this life. Death was only a passage through the resurrected life they already fully participated in.

[26]An answer to John Bunyan in *Great Mystery of the Great Whore*, 3, p. 344. *See also* p. 401.

[27]*Ibid.*, p. 345.

Apostles with the spirit and power of the Apostles which was, in turn, the same spirit and power and the same glorified Christ that was in Quakers:

for the Lord had said unto me: if I did but set up one in the same spirit that the prophets and Apostles was [sic] in that gave forth the Scriptures he or she should shake all the country in there [sic] profession ten miles about them. [And if they did own God and Christ and his prophets and Apostles: they must own him or her].[28]

To be in the spirit and power of the Apostles meant to have the same glorified Christ within that the Apostles had. In the *Great Mystery of the Great Whore* Fox cited the Apostle Paul who preached that Christ was in the saints and of His flesh and bone.[29] In his appendix to the *Great Mystery* he examined Scriptural phrases about the location of Christ and concluded in each case that the phrases about Christ in the Apostles had been corrupted in the text (the preposition "in" was replaced by "to") to detract attention away from any notion of blurring distinctions between Christ and the believer.[30] But as the Apostle John said, "The Word was made flesh and dwelt in us",[31] that is, according to Fox's understanding, the glorified body of Christ made its abode in the mortal bodies of the Apostles and the saints and this was precisely what it meant to be in the spirit and power of the Apostles. In *Saul's Errand to Damascus* Fox said that the Apostles taught clearly that God dwelt *in* the Apostles and saints (2 Cor. 6:1; Eph. 4:6; 2 Pet. 1:4).[32]

---

[28]*Cambridge Journal*, 1, p. 39.

[29]*Great Mystery of the Great Whore*, 3, pp. 344-45.

[30]Most, if not all translations of the Bible in Fox's day (and our own) translated Paul's frequently quoted phrase "Christ in me" as "to me". This was incorrect said Fox. It was a theological gloss to change the preposition and it demonstrated a theological prejudice of the translators. How could it be blasphemy to preach Christ in us, asked Fox, when Paul himself proclaimed this very doctrine? Fox has one ally in the modern biblical scholar Gustav Diessman who said "There cannot be any doubt that 'Christ in me' means the exalted Christ living in Paul" [Quoted in H.E. Dana and J.R. Mantey, *A Manual Grammar of the Greek New Testament* (Toronto: Macmillan, 1957), p. 106].

[31]*Great Mystery of the Great Whore*, 3, p. 582.

[32]*Ibid.*, p. 594.

Again in 1675 Fox wrote that the Apostles and saints possessed the glorified Christ. They "owned" Him and the Scripture as Fox said on other occasions. If the saints did not have the Son of God within "then they cannot succeed the Apostles".[33] To say the saints lived in the same spirit and power as the Apostles was to affirm the notion of celestial inhabitation for the patriarchs, prophets, Apostles and all saints. Consequently, Quakers became known as sons and daughters of God - something the "carnal" world was unable to see or comprehend.

Orthodoxy was not theologically equipped to comprehend any believer being occupied by the glorified body of a Christ who existed in a very distant and remote heaven. Specifically, in the context of seventeenth century English Protestant theology, Baxter, Bunyan and Owen preached very different theologies. The certainty of Quakers, based on their notion of celestial inhabitation, constrasted starkly with the necessity of doubt about salvation outlined in the theology of Ames and Gouge, as did the normal Reformed sacramental insistence that the body of Christ remained in heaven.[34] Fox became enraged at his accusers who persistently charged him with saying that he, George Fox, was Christ. They failed, he said, to comprehend him and apart from a few notable exceptions this was true. The world, said Fox, only saw the human creature and was unable to make any further distinctions. On the other hand, when the saints claimed to be equal with Christ they spoke "beyond all creatures and out of all creatures".[35] No outward garment could be equal with Christ. That was inconceivable since

---

[33]*Gospel Truth Demonstrated*, 5, p. 190.

[34]*See*, for example, the relevant discussions of orthodox doctrine in the Puritan England of the 1640's and 1650's in Perry Miller, *The New England Mind: The Seventeenth Century* (Cambridge: Harvard University Press, 1954); Edmund Morgan, *Visible Saints: The History of a Puritan Idea* (New York: New York University Press, 1963); Tai Liu, *Discord in Zion: The Puritan Divines and the Puritan Revolution, 1640-1660* (The Hague: Nijhoff, 1973); Nicholas Tyacke, *The Anti-Calvinists: The Rise of English Arrnenianism, 1590-1640* (Oxford: Oxford University Press, 1990) and Dewey Wallace, *Puritans and Predestination: Grace in English Protestant Theology, 1525-1695* (Chapel Hill: University of North Carolina Press, 1982). Richard Greaves "The Puritan-Nonconformist Tradition in England, 1560-1700: Historiographical Reflections," *Albion*, 17 (1986), pp. 449-86 is also helpful.

[35]Fox, *Great Mystery of the Great Whore*, 3, p. 221.

Christ had a heavenly, glorified body. What Quakers saw when they were in the presence of Fox (and each other) was the inner deified person.

Thus, when Fox spoke he spoke not as George Fox but as Christ. He spoke as one who had transcended the carnal state. He spoke as one who was literally inhabited by the glorified Christ. He spoke as the glorified Christ. No one put this concept forth as clearly as James Nayler. George Fox was dust, he said, "but the spirit that spoke in him is equal with God". This was not a disembodied spirit but the very heavenly Christ within who spoke through Fox. Said Nayler, the words of God simply pass through the outward garment named Fox as a channel of the divine.[36]

When Fox spoke of Christ's heavenly flesh, then, he was not referring to the outer flesh-of-Jesus flesh but to the heavenly body that had always been a part of the pre-existent Christ. At the moment of incarnation this heavenly flesh came down from heaven, not up from the ground, to inhabit the earthly vessel: "He was from heaven, His flesh came down from heaven, His flesh which was the meat, came down from heaven."[37] There was a strong distinction between Christ and the earthly garment he took. Fox never discussed the implications of Christ assuming the flesh of the Virgin Mary, as many Medieval and Reformation exegetes of the heavenly flesh doctrine did but it is clear that his heavenly flesh christology differed from earlier Anabaptist notions while still contending for a heavenly origin for the flesh of the pre-incarnate Christ. The earlier views were preoccupied with the nature of Christ's historical flesh, and specifically, with the heavenly or sinless origin of his historical flesh.[38] Fox, on the other hand, was exclusively

---

[36]Nayler, *A Discovery of the Man of Sin*, p. 13 and *An Answer to the Book Called "The Perfect Pharisee"* (1655), p. 4.

[37]Fox, *Great Mystery of the Great Whore*, 3, p. 505.

[38]Melvin Endy found heavenly flesh notions in Fox. However, he was concerned with heavenly flesh only as it bore on traditional theological concerns - as it bore on the nature of the historic Christ and the flesh he brought with him from heaven. He was not preoccupied with heavenly flesh as it literally inhabited the believer largely because he approached the matter through Penn's spiritualistic reading of things. Endy's is a sophisticated discussion of Penn's view of the nature of Christ and the relationship of the divinity and humanity of Christ, especially as it related to ancient Christian heresies. Endy does sense that Fox's views on the heavenly flesh of Christ went beyond metaphor but he did not extend the notion far enough to

preoccupied with the ever-present and palpable pre-incarnate celestial flesh of Christ in Jesus and all the saints. Fox never considered the flesh of Mary to detract from or add to Jesus' inner heavenly body or his work on earth. Thus the disputes over the two natures of Christ or the inbibing of Christ's flesh at the sacrament of the supper were of no consequence to him. It would misleading to link Fox's heavenly flesh views to Continental radical reformers like Melchior Hoffman, Caspar Schwenckfeld or Valentin Crautwald. Fox did not share their concern about preserving Christ's human body from corruption.[39]

One needs, with effort, to strip one's mind of modernism to come to grips with celestial inhabitation and what it meant to Fox and early Quakers. Celestial inhabitation is a difficult concept to understand, especially for the

---

work out all that celestial inhabitation implied for the early Quaker (*William Penn*, pp. 187-88, 277-79).

[39]Fox's doctrine may have been anticipated by but was not the same as medieval and Anabaptist views on the heavenly flesh of Christ. There is no evidence of direct connection or lineal descent of the idea to Fox although Endy suggests there *may* have been a link through "Giles Calvert's translation of Valentine Weigel's *Life of Christ*" which was published in 1648 (*William Penn*, p. 277). Two notions of the celestial flesh of Christ were prevalent in the Middle Ages and in Anabaptist thought. Both, as G.H. Williams has pointed out, represented "a revival of ancient Gnostic and Monophysite Christology" [*The Radical Reformation* (Philadelphia: Westminster, 1962), p. 326]. The first notion was that Christ's flesh as it became visible in Mary came from heaven and assumed nothing of Mary's substance. This view was adopted by the Anabaptist Melchior Hoffman (see my "The Melchiorites in the Netherlands: Origins and Developments to 1533", M. Phil. Thesis, University of Waterloo, 1985, pp. 140-45 and 170-74 for a fuller discussion of Hoffman's heavenly flesh notions and their origins). The second notion did not deny that Christ assumed his flesh from the substance of Mary but de-emphasized the creatureliness of Christ in favour of his divine and pre-existent sonship - a recovery of Docetism it would seem. This was the position of the great sixteenth century spiritualist Caspar Schwenckfeld [*See* Williams, *Radical Reformation*, pp. 332-35 and A. Sciegienny, *Homme charnel, homme spirituel: étude sur la christologie de Caspar Schwenckfeld, 1489-1561* (Wiesbaden: Steiner, 1975]. Schwenckfeld's christology owed much to Valentin Crautwald. Crautwald, who worked with a Neo-Platonic epistemology, believed that Christ's resurrected body assumed a spiritual and heavenly form which was imparted to the Church and the saints. The believer actually fed upon Christ's glorified body and was thereby renewed. Crautwald's christology was developed strictly within the formulation of eucharistic doctrine and his concept of the "new man". Even though the saints shared in the divine life they were in no way divinized or even perfected in this life. The most recent work on Crautwald's Christology by D. Shantz unfortunately leaves unanswered in specifics the tantalizing question of exactly how, in Crautwald's terms, Christ shared his body with believers and how the saints shared in the divine life ("Cognito et Communicato Christi Interna: The Contribution of Valentin Crautwald to Sixteenth Century Schwenckfeldian Spiritualism", Ph.D. thesis, University of Waterloo, 1986. *See* pp. 249, 287, 319, 337, 367).

majority of those within the Western Christian tradition who work with a disembodied Spirit theology. It is necessary, however, not to consider the doctrine of celestial inhabitation as the product of an inadequate christology. It was no more inadequate than Plato's view of reality, Eastern Christian views on deification or Catholic sacramental theology even though each may differ somewhat from Fox's notion of celestial inhabitation. We are dealing with a different view of God and God's work in creation which ultimately led to the creation of new forms of exalted language that eventually precipitated a necessary transformation of the movement.

One also needs to strip one's mind of orthodox conceptions of God and God's work in the person and in history. Modern secular thought is generally hostile to spiritual entities; and modern theological thought seems inclined, at least, to disembody spiritual entities. Paul Tillich's docetism or Karl Barth's inability to accept the resurrection of the body, in an ordinary sense, is an indicator of this. This is not to deny them their rightful place in the history of Christian thought. It is only to say that George Fox should not be interpreted through them, through modern secular thought or through modern mystical and evangelical thought. Celestial flesh appears to the modern mind as an impossible paradox: the inhabiting of the earthly flesh with a spiritual 'stuff' like the heavenly body of Christ. Anthropologists who talk of endogenetic[40] notions come close. Christ's celestial flesh was seen to work from within and the saints who fed on that flesh were recreated and regenerated by it. This feeding on the heavenly flesh of the pre-existent Christ, who inhabited Jesus and the believer similarly, reached quite literal heights in Fox since Christ inhabited the believer in a sensible (perceptible to the senses) manner. Christ and the saints were all one. One never was where the other was not. For Fox the inner Christ was much more than is intended by the idea of 'spirit' as insubstantial today: his celestial presence was much more graphic and visceral.

We are now ready to investigate some other early Quaker views on celestial inhabitation, especially those of Fox's leading followers. Following

---

[40]Endogenesis: originating or growing from within. In biological terms the formulation of new tissues by growth from within.

92

his apprehension at Orton, for blasphemy, Nayler was asked if Christ was in him as a man. He replied, "Christ is not divided, for if he be, he is no more Christ; but I witness that Christ is in me in measure, who is *God and man*" (italics mine). His questioner said Christ was in heaven with a carnal body. Nayler responded, "Christ fills heaven and earth and is not carnal, but spiritual: for if Christ be in heaven with a carnal body, and the saints with a spiritual body, that is not proportionable." In his defence at the Appleby Sessions Nayler argued that it was not "proportionable" for Christ to be in heaven with a carnal body (as his opponents thought) while the saints were on earth with glorified bodies.[41] We discover in Nayler a notion of Christ's glorified body as an immaterial substance that inhabited the believer in measure, that is, the sum total of what God was did not, of course, inhabit only James Nayler. Howgill, as we have seen, provided a similar argument in his pamphlet *Darkness and Ignorance Expelled*.[42] Both were apprehended at Orton for preaching that Christ was in them as God and man. They had no less graphic and substantial a notion of celestial flesh than George Fox.

The idea that Christ's heavenly body was not limited to heaven but inhabited every particle of the saint's body tends to support celestial inhabitation. By their very nature, then, the saints were divine and consequently they shared God's "purity, equality, immortality, and eternity", as Howgill said. Robert Rich made an equally clear statement on behalf of celestial inhabitation as late as 1679. The divine nature of which the saints are partakers, he said, "is one and the same thing with that person of Christ".[43] The fact that he called it a "spiritual indwelling" should not mislead us into thinking that early Quakers spiritualized the presence in the believer in such a way that it made Christ and saint separate and distinct. They did not spiritualize (in the sense of some modern usages of the term - turn into a mystical, insubstantial doctrine) celestial inhabitation and Robert

---

[41]For an account of these sessions *see* Besse, *Sufferings*, 2, opening pages and *Memoirs of the Life, Ministry, Trial and Sufferings of ... James Nailor (London, 1719)*, pp. 1-16.

[42]Howgill, *Darkness and Ignorance Expelled*, pp. 22-24.

[43]Robert Rich, *A Testimony to Truth, as it is in Jesus ... or, The Spiritual Appearance and In-Dwelling of Jesus Christ in Believers* (1679), pp. 8-9.

Rich was one of the last Quakers to confirm the notion that sanctifier and sanctified were one and the same substance - the very point that Fox made at his blasphemy trials.[44]

Opponents of Quakerism pressed home the view that Quakers somehow believed that the carnal body of Christ inhabited the believer. This was because Quakers and their opponents worked with different concepts of how Christ's risen body was formed and where it was located. If Christ was limited to a distant heaven with a risen but nonetheless material body that had form, substance and shape then it would be difficult indeed to conceive of such a body inhabiting the believer. If, however, Christ's glorified body was an immaterial heavenly body (but nonetheless a real entity) that was not limited to heaven but instead filled heaven and earth as Nayler said[45] then it is less difficult to conceive (at least for the primitive Quaker) that such a body could inhabit and deify the believer. Fox, Nayler, Howgill and Farnworth consistently answered the persistent questions about the location and nature of Christ's body by saying that it was the heavenly, celestial and spiritual body of Christ that was in them. Farnworth was pressed by Hugh Bealand to explain how it was that Quakers fed on Christ's body.[46] And Thomas Moore chastised Nayler for believing that it was the carnal Jesus of Nazareth that inhabited him.[47] Generally, these were misconceptions of Fox's notion of celestial inhabitation. Fox, Nayler, Farnworth and Isaac

---

[44]Fox and Nayler, for example, were far more than Geoffrey Nuttall's "spiritualists" [Nuttall, *Holy Spirit in Puritan Faith and Experience*, pp. 181-84 and *James Nayler: A Fresh Approach* (London: Friends' Historical Society, 1954), p. 16]. Nigel Smith continues to follow Nuttall's spiritualistic interpretation *(Perfection Proclaimed*, p. 144). Nayler, as they point out, moved in a Familist milieu that belonged within the framework of the great spiritualist movement of the sixteenth and seventeenth centuries. Nayler needs to be re-interpreted along the lines of Fox's own doctrine of celestial inhabitation which would be a continuation of our understanding of Nayler's thought and a radical extension of spiritualistic notions - more radical than any previous interpreters of early Quakerism have implied.

[45]Nayler at the Appleby Sessions, in Besse, *Sufferings*, 2, pp. 2-3.

[46]"Hugh Bealand to Richard Farnworth", *Samuel Watson MSS.*, p. 87.

[47]Thomas Moore, *A Defence Against the Poison of Satan's Design* (London, 1656), pp. 61-62 and *An Antidote Against the Spreading Infection of the Spirit of Antichrist, Abounding in These Last Days* (London, 1655), "Epistle to the Reader", p. 17.

Penington unanimously agreed that Jesus' glorified body was not human or carnal.[48] It was spiritual. But as a spiritual body it had a very tangible substance or quality to it. Nayler was most specific on this point. The glorified Christ, Jesus the Son of God who had become flesh, died, rose again and ascended to heaven was the same glorified Christ who returned to inhabit the Apostles and saints and that, said Fox and Nayler is "a *substance*" (italics mine).[49] Howgill said that the Scriptures did not use the words "human" or "mystical" to describe Christ's glorified body. It was a spiritual body (a real entity) that shared in God's glory before the world began. It was this immaterially fleshed spiritual body of Christ that literally inhabited the saints.[50] This idea of celestial inhabitation was far headier and more exhilarating to Quakers than if it had been the historic Jesus-of-Nazareth-body within, which some of Nayler's followers seemed to propose on his behalf.

Josiah Coale, remarking on the phrase "flesh of his flesh and bone of his bone" bluntly declared that the glorified body of Christ was not distinct from the saints and if it was the saints would no longer be perfect - as clear a statement affirming Quaker endogenetic beliefs as exists.[51] Farnworth's

---

[48]Although Penington's two leading works on christology (one earlier and one later in his career) implied that he believed Christ's heavenly flesh was distinct from the believer a careful reading of these works suggests that he was informed by the classic Quaker distinction between outward and inward. The believer had an outer tabernacle that housed the inner body which, at the time of the new birth, became flesh of Christ's flesh and bone of his bone. This, said Penington, was a mystery but the believer did assume Christ's nature, spirit, light and life [Isaac Penington, *Divine Essays* (London, 1654), pp. 16, 26, 66, 75, 78 and *The Flesh and Blood of Christ* (London, 1675), pp. 1-2, 7, 24-25]. A careful revision of his christology needs to be done, testing it for consistencies with Fox and other early Quakers who clearly understood the new birth as the formation of Christ in the believer in a very tangible way [*see*, for example, James Nayler, *An Answer to a Book Called the Quakers Catechism Put Out by Richard Baxter* (London, 1655), p. 49 and *Weakness Above Wickedness* (London, 1656), p. 14]. Endy's discussion of Penington's heavenly flesh christology is limited to the historic Christ and Schwenckfeldian influences (William Penn, p. 279).

[49]Fox, *Great Mystery of the Great Whore*, 3, p. 397 and James Nayler, *A Public Discovery* (London, 1656), pp. 16, 48. Presumably a spiritual, heavenly substance but still a substance, a spiritual 'stuff'.

[50]Howgill, *Darkness and Ignorance Expelled*, p. 23.

[51]Coale, *A Vindication of the Light Within*, p. 332.

response to Bealand was simply that the feeding was not on the outward body but on the inward "glorious" body and by so feeding on this body the saints assumed bodies of glory, which was also in harmony with Fox's own endogenetic views.[52] Nayler concurred fully with this line of thinking. "The flesh of Christ is the food of my inward man," he said.[53] The Christ in him was the spiritual (heavenly) Christ who inhabited him both as God and man and could not be seen with human eyes. It was not human flesh that saw the Christ within, it was the spirit.[54] What the believer saw within, however, was not the disembodied Spirit but Christ the very God-man in all his glorified and celestial splendor.[55]

The idea of Christ's glorified body being a spiritual body does not diminish the exalted claims of early Quakers. Leading Quakers confirmed and even expanded on Fox's idea of an almost corporeal presence. They agreed that Christ's glorified body could not be isolated in a faraway heaven. It could not be divided. His spirit could not be disembodied. Rather, the glorified Christ as the God-man inhabited every particle of the saints' body. As a result the saints could be glorified and perfected. They could be made sons and daughters of God. And they could be made fully equal with God in nature. This explains how Edward Burrough and Francis Howgill were able to unreservedly write to Fox: "Dearly beloved one, in whom the Father is well pleased, and in whom the godhead dwells".[56] Any idea that Christ was on

[52]"Richard Farnworth to Hugh Bealand", *Samuel Watson MSS.*, p. 88. *See also* p. 65 where Farnworth again comments on Christ's phrase "except ye eat my flesh".

[53]James Nayler, *Satan's Design Discovered* (London, 1655), p. 4.

[54]Nayler's defence at Appleby Sessions, Besse, *Sufferings*, 2, pp. 2-3.

[55]Nayler, *Satan's Design Discovered*, p. 18 and *A Second Answer to Thomas Moore* (London, 1655), p. 24.

[56]"Edward Burrough and Francis Howgill to George Fox" (January 21, 1656), *Barclay MSS.*, No. 34.

earth and in the believer by his spirit alone is quickly dispelled by the notion that the Godhead dwelt bodily in the saint.[57]

Leading Quakers around Fox affirmed the doctrine of celestial inhabitation and it bears repeating that instead of being characterized as an inadequate theology it was a new way of viewing God and God's work in creation. The use of the word 'spiritual' to describe Christ's glorified body was interchangeable with the notion that Christ's glorified body in the believer had substance - a type of spiritual 'stuff' that inhabited and deified the believer. It might best be described as a constant state of ecstasy, unlike the rare and momentary mystical experience of *raptus*. In Fox's case the saints permanently assumed the very substance of the glorified body of Christ.

Fox's interpretation of the biblical phrase "flesh of his flesh" was quite literal. Were it not for distortions of "possession" by the lurid tabloid press and popular horror films one might talk here of celestial *possession*.[58] Popular notions imagine that all possession is demonic, rare and sporadic. David Lamm's play, *Desire*, set in Zimbabwe and exploring beneficent possession is a partial modern exception. In Fox, the possession was divine, widespread and enduring. Quakers were literally transformed into heavenly beings, that is, although the forms of their bodies did not change their inner beings were qualitatively deified.

So conceived, the inner light was a challenge to orthodoxy at its very roots. Fox's opponents knew well enough that his doctrine of celestial inhabitation had revolutionary implications both theologically and socially and they tried to silence him on well-founded charges of blasphemy.

---

[57]Edward Cockson, *Quakerism Dissected and Laid Open* (London, 1708), p. 4. Cockson incorrectly reported that William Dewsbury, in his testimony to Burrough "before E.B.'s Works", said the Godhead dwelt bodily in Edward Burrough. Dewsbury does not have a testimony before Burrough's *Works* (unless it too was edited out). Francis Howgill, Josiah Coale and George Whitehead do. Cockson may have received his information through another source and incorrectly cited it. Nonetheless, the notion of the Godhead dwelling bodily in the believer is consistent with early Quaker views on celestial inhabitation.

[58]The idea of 'possession' was foreshadowed in Thomas Edwards' catalogue of heresies - the idea that "God is in our flesh as much as in Christ's flesh" although Fox's idea of celestial inhabitation took a very different form which was quite novel.

Invariably, they laid out the circumstantial evidence for blasphemy by trying to prove heresy on the location of Christ. Their arguments revealed their differing perceptions of Christ. The Puritan Christ was far removed from humankind, a just judge, harsh and merciful only to an elect few. Their Christ was kept distinct from the saints (if he was in a distant heaven how could he be on earth in the saints) and it was blasphemy to suggest otherwise. The Kingdom of God, which had not yet come, was shut up to humankind. No person could see the Father or Christ or the New Jerusalem until they had ascended up into a distant heaven. What orthodoxy was careful to do, throughout Christian history, was keep Christ separate from creation. Great efforts were made to keep the distinctions within the Godhead and the distinctions between the Godhead and creation intact. There was no possibility of Christ's glorified body inhabiting the believer in such a literal way since it was not only distant but it was a glorified (material) body with form, substance and shape.

Fox's Christ was near to and in the saints, egalitarian, merciful to all and pacifist. He repeatedly said that the saints saw the face of Christ within them, most notably at his blasphemy trial in Carlisle in 1653.[59] Men of the stature of John Owen, Richard Baxter, John Bunyan and Henry More all recognized that Fox's notions about celestial inhabitation had radical implications for the orthodoxy of the day.[60] Nor was it an altogether unfair inference on their part that if Christ was not above and distinct from creation but actually inhabited the saint (so that the distinction between God and saint was negated) then Fox or anyone else could imagine they were Christ and embodied the characteristics of Christ.

---

[59]Nickalls, *Journal*, p. 159.

[60]Opponents of Fox generally recognized that the logical *terminus* of the inner Christ doctrine was blasphemy - the deification of the saints. Richard Sherlocke wrote: "And for our new sect of Enthusiasts had they the Spirit of God as they pretend abiding in them and speaking in them personally and essentially, this blasphemy must necessarily follow, that they are equal with God" (*The Quakers Wild Questions*, pp. 66-67). Henry More concurred. The logical result of the Quaker claim that Father, Son and saint were equal was that they would be God and deserving of divine adoration (More, *Grand Mystery of Godliness*, Book 1, chapter 6, p. 14).

By orthodox views of the Trinity it was also possible to infer that the plaintiff (ie. George Fox) professed equality with God or even professed that he was Christ[61] and that was exactly how the blasphemy trials proceeded. It will become apparent in the following discussion of the blasphemy trials that Fox's opponents were prepared to go to any length to silence him. We cannot underestimate the uncontrolled rage he often evoked from them. Utilizing the full force of the *Blasphemy Act* which provided legal sanctions for imprisonment or banishment under a threat of death, Fox's opponents made the charge of blasphemy the best place to begin the indictment against him, especially since his own theology implied that he claimed equality with God.

English law allowed for the strict punishment of anyone convicted of blasphemy, first under the *Blasphemy Ordinance* of 1648 and then under the less severe *Blasphemy Act* of 1650. Under the latter, a first conviction brought with it a six month prison term and a second conviction meant banishment from the Commonwealth under threat of death.[62] Fox was charged three times under the first part of the 1650 *Act*[63] which specified that all who,

> presume avowedly in words to profess ... to be very God, or to be very infinite or almighty, or in honour, excellency, majesty and power to be equal, and the same with the true God, or that the true God, or the eternal majesty dwells in the creature and no where else ... All ... persons so avowedly professing ... the

---

[61]Fox, *Great Mystery of the Great Whore*, 3, p. 471; *Cambridge Journal*, 1, p. 34.

[62]C.H. Firth and R.S. Rait, eds., *Acts and Ordinances of the Interregnum, 1642-1660* (London: Wyman, 1911), 2, p. 411. By comparison, in France for example, the first four offences for blasphemy were punishable by imprisonment with bread and water. The fifth offence was a slit lip. The sixth was a cut lip so the teeth could be seen. The seventh offence was the boring of the tongue and the eighth was punishable by death.

[63]Nayler was charged and imprisoned twice, Francis Howgill and William Dewsbury were charged and imprisoned at least once (Howgill in Appleby in 1653 and Dewsbury in Northampton in 1654) and others were accused of blasphemy. These included James Parnell, Solomon Eccles, George Whitehead, Ann Audland and Richard Farnworth [George Whitehead, *The Divinity of Christ* (London, 1669), p. 25 and *Serious Search into Jeremiah Ives' Questions* (1674), pp. 58, 75; William Dewsbury, *The Discovery of the Great Enmity* (London, 1655), p.11; Nayler, *Satan's Design Discovered*, p. 51; Robert Rich, *The Saints Testimony*

aforesaid ... blasphemous ... opinions ... upon complaint and proof made of the same ... before one or more Justice or Justices of the Peace ... by the oath of two or more witnesses ... the party so convicted ... shall [be] ... committed to prison.[64]

The intention of the *Act* was to prevent the spread of heresy and blasphemy in the realm and protect true religion - in short, to ferret out Seekers, Ranters, Quakers and people like Fox, who seemed to claim authority through parity with God. The core of the charges against Fox, in each case, specifically involved Fox's claims to divinity and equality with God.[65]

The first charge of blasphemy occurred in October 1650 in Derby. He was taken to appear before two magistrates (Gervase Bennet and Colonel Nathaniel Barton) for things he had said at a local meeting of army officers, priests and preachers.[66] According to Fox's account he was examined for eight hours during which time,

> The power of God was thundered among them, and they flew like chaff, and they put me in and out from the first hour to the nineth hour at night in examinations, having me backward and forward: and said that I was taken up in raptures, as they called it, and so at last they asked me whether I was sanctified? And I said, Sanctified? Yes, for I was in the presence of God. And they said, Had I no sin? Sin? said I. He hath taken away my sin (ie. Christ my Saviour), and in Him there is no sin.[67]

Since no-one but Christ had ever lived a sinless life the magistrates asked Fox and the two others with him (we do not know who they were) whether any of them were Christ. Fox replied "Nay, we are nothing, Christ is all". What Fox was implying was that as a creature he was not Christ (he was

---

(London, 1655), pp. 3, 39; Norman Penney, *First Publishers of Truth*, p. 248]. On Dewsbury *see* his January 7, 1655 letter in *Caton MSS.*, 2, p. 8 (formerly *Boswell Middleton MSS*).

[64]Firth and Rait, *Acts and Ordinances*, 2, p. 411.

[65]These items correspond with Francis Higginson's list of Quaker errors: a)Christ is come in their flesh, b) the soul is part of the divine essence, c) we can attain perfection in this life [*A Brief Relation of the Irreligion of the Northern Quakers* (London, 1653), pp. 4-10].

[66]Our only source for these proceedings comes from Fox's *Journal*. *See also* Braithwaite, *Beginnings*, pp. 54-55. According to Cadbury an independent account of this examination may once have existed, but it is no longer extant (*Ann. Cat.*, 1:27A, p. 32).

[67]*Cambridge Journal*, 1, p. 2.

100

George Fox) but Christ was in him and spoke through him. This, coupled with the claim to perfection[68] convinced the magistrates to convict Fox and one of his companions of blasphemy. In the Mittimus[69] they were committed to prison for six months for "uttering ... diverse blasphemous opinions contrary to the late Act of Parliament, which, upon their examination before us, they have confessed".[70] This sentence was eventually extended to a full year since Fox refused to allow his relatives to become surety for his good behaviour.[71] So novel was it that a man should appear claiming to be as perfect as Christ, that Fox reported that after he was in prison "many people came from far and near to see a man that had no sin", a phrase left out of the text by Ellwood.[72] Fox was leaving certain impressions with people, especially the impression that he was a sinless man and perhaps even Christ. Following his release in early October, 1651 Fox resumed his itinerant ministry and it was at one of his house meetings near Wakefield that he first met James Nayler fresh from his army tenure. This was in December, 1651 and within a year Nayler himself was before the Appleby Quarter Sessions for blasphemy as well.

Between Derby and Appleby lay another important blasphemy trial for Fox. It occurred in Lancaster in October 1652, only six months after Fox had been "moved to sound the day of the Lord" from atop Pendle Hill and five months after he first appeared at Swarthmoor Hall in Ulverston. Fox had stirred up the people in Ulverston and had more than once been mobbed or attacked for his exalted claims. A warrant was prepared for his arrest only this time Judge Fell of Swarthmoor came to his aid. Fell was a judge on the King's Bench, highly educated, landed, an Independent in religion, deeply

[68]Perfection was another heresy prefigured in Thomas Edwards' catalogue of sectarian heresies (*Gangraena*, first edition), p. 27.

[69]Mittimus: The commitment paper explaining to the gaoler the reasons for incarceration.

[70]Nickalls, *Journal*, p. 52; Ellwood, *Journal*, 1, p. 100.

[71]Braithwaite, *Beginnings*, p. 54.

[72]*Cambridge Journal*, 1, p. 2 and compare with Ellwood, *Journal*, 1, p. 100.

committed to liberty of conscience (for which he eventually sacrificed his career) and was well placed to intimidate others on the Sessions bench.[73]

The background to the Lancaster Quarter Sessions, which were a turning point in Fox's career and in the early history of Quakerism, were focused on events in Ulverston and Judge Fell's timely intervention. Fox had been severely beaten by his enemies and he had been taken to Swarthmoor Hall to recover. During that time Justices Sawrey and Thompson prepared a warrant for his arrest. However, before it was issued Judge Fell returned home from his circuit duties and it was withheld.[74] Fell was sufficiently enraged by the abuses of liberty of conscience in his territory that he issued warrants for all the "riotous persons" who had persecuted Fox and his appearance at the Sessions was clearly intended to strike a blow at what he perceived was unlawful and contemptuous conduct on the part of Fox's accusers who displayed a flagrant disregard for the laws of the land.

Since the warrant was not served Fox was not legally bound to appear at the Sessions.[75] His appearance was voluntary for a hearing or

---

[73]Judge Fell was a "member of the Long Parliament, Judge of Assize of Chester and North Wales Circuit, Vice-Chancellor of the Dutchy and Attorney for the County Palatine of Lancaster", in short, a very formidable ally. Braithwaite goes on to describe him as a "pillar of the State" (*Beginnings*, p. 99). It would have been unusual for a man of his stature to attend the Quarter Sessions at Lancaster.

[74]"The warrant was based on signed allegations dated Lancaster, 5th October, 1652" (Braithwaite, *Beginnings*, p. 556; *see also Ann. Cat.* 6, 167A, p. 39). Fell's homecoming, said Russell Mortimer, "prevented the serving of the warrant". Mortimer has provided a copy of the text of the warrant (in fact two warrants were prepared against Fox). It was made out by William Marshall, Thomas Whitehead, William Moore, James Schoolcrofte and John Jaques following written complaints of Fox's activity in Lancaster. Contained in the warrant were charges that Fox "did affirm that he had the divinity essentially in him"; "that he was equal with God"; "that he was the judge of the world" and "that he was as upright as Christ" - all being the same charges read against him at Derby. Three witnesses swore to the charges - Michael Altham, William Smythe and Nathaniel Atkinson. The warrant was then issued by George Toulnson and John Sawrey [R. Mortimer, "Allegations Against George Fox by Ministers in North Lancashire," *JFHS*, 39 (1947), p. 15.

[75]Quarter Sessions were not Assizes. The former were a continuous series of sittings or meetings run by Justices of the Peace. They were mainly used to initiate preliminary interrogations. If warranted the more serious crimes were referred to the Assizes which were presided over by the Circuit Judges (like Judge Fell) who had authority to assess, decide and judge. For the charges and Fox's answers *see Cambridge Journal*, 1, pp. 63ff.; *Swarth. MSS.*, 7, No. 55 and *Saul's Errand to Damascus*.

"examination" that could have theoretically led to a committal but was, in actual fact, an impossibility given Judge Fell's presence. As a senior circuit Judge he had the authority to rule on any decision. It was also an opportunity for Judge Fell to quash opposition to liberty of conscience in his county and humiliate those on the Sessions Bench by proving the warrant's illegality. Thus, on October 18, 1652 Judge Fell and George Fox rode together from Swarthmoor Hall to the Sessions held in Lancaster Castle. They discussed the matter together *en route* and upon arrival met Colonel West who was another Justice sitting on the Sessions Bench, and forty "priests" who had assembled to bring their case against Fox.

This was the best documented of all the blasphemy trials and again, it was deleted from the *Journal* in its entirety by Ellwood.[76] The local vicar, or by this time should we say minister of Lancaster, Charles Marshall, was chosen to speak on behalf of the forty clergy and it is clear that their intent was to silence Fox under the *Blasphemy Act*. Fox was brought before an examining committee consisting of Judge Fell, Colonel West and Justice Sawrey.

Three witnesses were called to testify against Fox and eight particulars were charged against him. Fox denied ever saying that he was equal with God. He did say that according to Scripture the saints were of Christ's flesh and bone, the Sons of God, and the Father and Son were one.[77] The

---

[76]The sources for the trial are: *Cambridge Journal*, 1, pp. 61-72; Thomas Aldham, et. al., *A Brief Discovery of the Threefold Estate of Antichrist ... Whereunto is Added the Trial of George Fox, in Lancashire, With His Answers to Eight Articles Exhibited Against Him* (London, 1653) also containing *A Copy of a Letter to Some Friends Concerning George Fox's Trial* by James Nayler, pp. 11-13 and *George Fox's Trial and His Answers*, pp. 14-15; Fox and Nayler, *Saul's Errand to Damascus*; Nayler, *A Discovery of the Man of Sin*; Nayler, *An Answer to the Book Called "The Perfect Pharisee"* and Higginson, *A Brief Relation*. Fox's record of the examination which he inserted in his *Journal* "was taken out of an old torn book" which is still extant. Fox did not write this document but it came into his possession possibly through Thomas Lower, his son-in-law, and the author of a revised version of the trial. There is another fragment containing scribes notes on the trial but is is largely illegible. What is notable about the latter fragment is that it contained the questions of three of the priests who helped prepare the warrant against Fox - William Marshall, James Schoolecrofte and John Jaques (*see Cambridge Journal*, 1, pp. 63 and 67). Fox's version of the trial is corroborated by other extant accounts from Nayler and the anti-Quaker apologist Francis Higginson.

[77]*Cambridge Journal*, 1, p. 65.

operative aspects of his thought as he was presenting them to his accusers, were the lack of distinction between Christ and believer which ultimately implied unity, if not equality. At this point Judge Fell began to press home his case that unity was not equality; and it was equality, not unity that was condemned by the statute. "Equality shows two distinct",[78] he said, to which Marshall replied that if they were one they were equal. Judge Fell then pointed out that the idea that Father and Son were equal did not implicate Fox, who never exactly said that he was equal with God.[79] Throughout the entire hearing Fox never once said the exact words although his doctrine of the unity of Father, Son and saint implied as much. Marshall then recalled Fox's words that the sanctifier and sanctified were one and equal. There is a further sheet to the fragment Fox was using and it was written by Fox. In this fragment he said that he never said he was equal with God but "he that sanctifieth and the [sic] that are sanctified are all of one in the father and the son and that you are the sons of God and the father and the son is one (and we) of his flesh and of his bones..."[80] George Fox was not one with God but his re-created, resurrected, and transformed inner body was none other than the exact celestial flesh of Christ and that body was one with God.

Marshall then reiterated his statement that if sanctified and sanctifier were one then they were equal. Fell replied that this was a strange idea since the "the same thing cannot be equal" to which Marshall said "many may be one". Judge Fell responded again by saying "but they are not equal, oneness argues unity, there's a unity with God, and where there is unity there may be equality."[81] If the equality occurred within the framework of unity then it was a permissible equality. Judge Fell was being very finely discriminating here. To be equal to something, as he must have thought the statute required, implied discreteness - separate, distinct entities: "Equality shows

[78]*Ibid.*, 1, p. 65. The ensuing dialogue is drawn from the text in the *Cambridge Journal*, 1, pp. 63-67.

[79]*Ibid.*, 1, p. 65.

[80]*Ibid.*, 1, p. 69. *See also* Nayler, *A Copy of a Letter*, p. 11.

[81]*Cambridge Journal*, 1, p. 65.

two distinct". One can equal one but the ones, the units of one, must be separate entities. If the entities, or some important aspects of those entities were fully merged or involved in a unity of being then they were not sufficiently distinct to be compared. There was unity in the identity of saint with Son and the dominant operating quality here was unity.

The question about unity and equality continued with the charge that Fox said he was as upright as Christ. Fox replied "as he is so are we in this present world ... the saints are made the righteousness of God". Judge Fell spoke again to clarify and confirm Fox's original position: "He that sanctifieth and they that are sanctified are one, they are united"[82] to which Colonel West added "this is not to say that he is equal with God". They were finding a shared essence which, it seemed, a strict interpretation of the statute did not cover.

Marshall then asked Fox outright "Art thou equal with God"? Fox answered "My Father and I are one". Unity implied identity. But could the claim of identity evade that of equality? Fox's answer threatened to jeopardize his case since the assumption could clearly be made that he, George Fox, was identifying himself with Christ. At this point Nayler interjected on Fox's behalf to ask Marshall "Dost thou ask him as a creature or as Christ dwelling in him"? Nayler's remark, which embodied the classic early Quaker distinction between the earthly tabernacle and the inner glorified body, was a further point of clarification and another subtle way of evading the blasphemy charge. Nayler was being very astute here for Marshall had reopened the questioning about equality with a fresh approach, possibly even to trick Fox into admitting Trinitarian heresy. Trinitarianism (the notion that all three persons of the Godhead are coeval) was a leading characteristic of orthodoxy and Parliament had censored various people, like John Biddle, for holding to a subordinationist heresy. Nayler picked up the drift of Marshall's goading and replied with a question that restated Quaker belief in the full unity of Father, Son and glorified saint (as distinct from the

---

[82]*Ibid.*, 1, p. 65.

human tabernacle).[83]   As Fox often said, as the world knew him he was George Fox the earthly man but in the Kingdom of God he was a heavenly man and was known by another incorruptible and glorified name[84] - ie. the Son of God. This fine distinction was not covered by the *Blasphemy Act*, something Fox (and even Nayler who was at Swarthmoor as well) must have discussed with Judge Fell before the hearing began.

Considering these facts, and given Marshall's concerns, it appeared that the *Act* had been poorly drafted. Fox as a creature was not equal with God but the Christ in him was. At the same time the unity between God and saint did not necessarily imply equality. These were subtle distinctions with blasphemous implications (according to orthodoxy) but they were worded in such a way that no blasphemy charge, strictly speaking, could be made to stick. Marshall said that he was sorry that such distinctions were not included in the *Act* for it was certainly blasphemy to assert such things and they should be added to the *Act*. Colonel West chastised Marshall, saying that the issue was being judged by the law as it had been written. Undaunted, Marshall

---

[83]On Biddle *see* R. Greaves and R. Zaller, *A Biographical Dictionary of British Radicals in the Seventeenth Century* (Brighton, Sussex: Harvester Press, 1982-84), vol. 1, pp. 62-63. Fox's opponents were intent on proving that his view of celestial inhabitation was blasphemous because unity implied equality and equality was condemned by the statute. They did not make the fine distinctions made by Judge Fell or other Quakers. To say that the inner body was Christ was to say that George Fox was Christ. Richard Sherlocke said that they failed to distinguish between personal essence and the Spirit's "qualifications" - that is, God spoke within through the Spirit but the saint never assumed anything of the Spirit's divine essence (*The Quakers' Wild Questions*, p. 67). On the other hand Quakers explained Fox's exalted claims by making the distinction between outer and inner. Fox was dust and could not have been equal with God. The Christ in him was equal with God and Fox's inner body had assumed the divine nature of the glorified Christ. There was no metaphorical understanding involved in this unity. It was a literal transformation to the extent that no distinction between the inner body and God existed. Fell's distinction between equality and unity, when coupled with Nayler's distinction between outward creature and inward Christ, was important when it came to applying the strict letter of the law. Some opponents of Quakerism were astute enough to see Nayler's distinction and its blasphemous implications [Thomas Welde, *A Further Discovery of ... Quakers: By Way of Reply to an Answer of James Nayler to the Perfect Pharisee* (Gateside, 1654), pp. 7, 28ff]. Fox's theology of celestial inhabitation always implied that he was a fully divinized creature. Many actually bowed, kneeled and fell prostrate before him in the belief that he was the Son of God and it was this very behaviour that opponents said was prompted by the blasphemous claims to equality with God.

[84]*Cambridge Journal*, 1, pp. 161-62.   Others used this testimony for Fox as well [Ellwood, *Journal*, 1, p. 186; Solomon Eccles, *The Quakers Challenge* (1668), p. 6].

replied that it was a pity that such ideas were not included in the *Act* since they were "diametrically against that which is God's glory", and the *Act* had been drafted "that God may be truly glorified".

Marshall then returned to the topic of unity and equality. This time, in what seemed an odd reversal, he argued that to be one and equal was not necessarily the same thing while Nayler argued *for* equality. Marshall's remark was a logical possibility, but given the animosity of the debate it seems likely that he was trying to lead Fox or Nayler into an admission of error about the Trinity, namely, to own up to being subordinationists (or worse!).[85] Nayler's argument for equality, however, was really a re-emphasis on unity and the oneness of the Father and Son and the Son and saint. Nayler's defence was that nothing was "sanctified but the Son, and if nothing be sanctified but the Son and the Son being one in all, then the thing sanctified is equal in all; and it is not of the seeds, but one". The Son was Christ the seed (singular, one) who dwelt in all the saints and all the saints were at once sanctified by the presence of Christ in them and united with the Father by virtue of the fact that there was full unity in the Godhead. Justice Sawrey declared that this statement proved blasphemy. If Christ was within and not above this inferred deity and could even infer that the plaintiff imagined that he was Christ. The *Act*, after all, did stipulate that it was blasphemy to say that the eternal majesty dwelt in the creature. Judge Fell quickly responded that the issue at hand was to determine whether the exact words (i.e. that sanctified and sanctifier were one) were, strictly speaking, covered by the *Act* and he concluded they were not. He warned Justice Sawrey not to persist on the point of blasphemy for his interpretation of matters was, quite bluntly, erroneous.[86]

As it was the *Act* had been poorly drafted and Fell was able to get Fox off the hook. And if Fell concluded that the words were not included in the *Act* then the matter could have been safely laid to rest at that point. But

---

[85]Origen was an early Christian exponent of this "heresy" in which the Son was deemed subordinate to, rather than coeval with the Father. Milton held this view very clearly in his posthumous *De Doctrina Christiana* and rather more mutely in *Paradise Lost*.

[86]*Cambridge Journal*, 1, p. 67.

Judge Fell did not let matters rest on that point of interpretive judgment. He next proceeded to destroy the whole case against Fox on matters of procedure. Throughout the hearing he had succeeded in discrediting the testimony of all but one witness called against Fox. He pointed out that since they were only able to produce one credible witness (and not the two required by the *Act*) to confirm that Fox actually said he was equal with God, Fox's accusers were acting illegally and contrary to the *Act* itself:

> I ask this question, when you see you should have two witnesses, and you see there is but a single witness ... I think your proceedings have been very illegal and unjust; and contrary to the law of the Romans and the Act is by two or more witnesses: I conceive you may consider whether you have dealt according to justice in this or no: you see here should be two witnesses, and ye have but one, and yet will persist in it ... and so it is clear that the warrant which is out is very illegal.[87]

Judge Fell was at pains to uncover the malice of the witnesses and show that by a strict interpretation of the law Fox was not guilty. His recourse to Roman Law (the necessity of two witnesses in Roman Law harked back to St. Paul) clinched his case.[88]

One might say that a truly just judge would have discovered the malice of the witnesses and would have noticed that there was but one witness when the *Act* required two and left the matter at that. There was no need, legally, to proceed any further. But by taking such a narrow view of the statute and exonerating Fox on the logical/philosophical grounds that equality implied discreteness rather than unity Fell seemed to be going beyond impartiality to pure partisanship to quash his lesser adversaries. This is not to mention the

---

[87]*Ibid.*, 1, p. 67.

[88]Common law was really only as far as Judge Fell needed to go. As the law of the land it was based on custom and precedent, in which the decision of a higher court was binding on a lower court which faced a case with similar facts. Roman Law, on the other hand, required the simple (some thought slavish) application of a legal code. Roman Law was enjoying a vogue in Renaissance Europe and Fell's use of it may have been 'in the mode'. Reference to Roman Law was common in mid-seventeenth century England and most people knew of it from St. Paul. The not so learned young John Lilburne made this point in his account of his trial before the Star Chamber in 1638. Roman Law was taken by some as a guide to the law of nature or nations, the *lex gentiles*.

conversations Judge Fell held with Fox prior to the Sessions. It would appear that Judge Fell had already decided on the case before he sat on the Bench (an act which surely required impartiality from a Judge of Fell's stature) to hear the witnesses against Fox. Fox was fortunate to have had such a powerful ally. The warrant was rescinded and Quakerism was saved if only because its charismatic leader was saved from almost certain banishment under threat of death.

Fell's argument that equality implied discreteness while identity implied unity was clever legerdemain. By a broad view of the *Act*, which Fox's opponents took, Fox was probably guilty, and in different circumstances Justice Sawrey's and the clergyman Marshall's views could have carried the day. Certainly many observers would think and did think Fox guilty by any broad reading of the *Act*. Putting the law aside, what he argued for himself and the saints was, strictly speaking and according to orthodoxy, blasphemous. By assuming the heavenly body of Christ Quakers did become divine and equal with God. Furthermore the majesty of God was resident within them, and this was blasphemy according to the *Act*.

The fact that Fox and Fell rode together to Lancaster is significant. Fell was able to formulate his arguments in advance and deal a blow to the contemporary forces working against liberty of conscience. Fox, for his part, received permission to do what he wanted - speak before the assembly as Paul had before Agrippa.[89] Thus, at the end of the hearing Fell allowed Fox to stand up (Fox said he "was moved of the Lord to speak") and expound the Scriptures to the assembly. This provoked the clergy into a predictable rage at which time they were soundly reproved by Judge Fell. Allowing Fox to preach at the end of the hearing can only have been a final affront and a final upstaging of Fox's accusers. In the ensuing years (and to the present) Quaker apologists said that because Fox had been cleared of all charges at Lancaster the issue of blasphemy was a closed matter. But the case was not definitively settled and had Judge Fell not been present the history of Quakerism may have been vastly different.

---

[89]*Cambridge Journal*, 1, p. 62.

There are those who continue to range on the side of respectability today. In effect they accept the grounds for the notion of blasphemy, as defined by Fox's enemies. That is, they accept orthodox definitions of God. In the not so distant past they even accepted the notion that one could and should level wounding charges against those who contravened those accepted definitions. Doing this they deny that Fox contravened. They deny that Fox emitted even a whiff of blasphemy. Different assumptions are clashing here. One point of view has been to argue that Fox's view was, at bottom, a reasonable and orthodox one and the epithet of "blasphemy" was just vicious pejorative slang on the part of his enemies. Blasphemy was (and is) a misuse of power no matter who was wielding it - Catholic, Protestant, Quaker or Muslim. In our view there is more to it than malice and it would be wiser not to accept the definitions of God sustained by the dominant parties and let Fox present his own vision of a different kind of God who worked salvation in a different kind of way. By celestial inhabitation Fox meant no disrespect for God and he did not mean to impugn God's glory. From his perspective celestial inhabitation elevated God's glory because He was so gracious as to deal with the saints so generously and intimately. "Christ is exalted by his saints and members here", said Fox.[90] Those who blandly deny that Fox contravened accepted definitions of God and His work deny the depth of his challenge to orthodoxy, to "steeple-house" Christianity and to the very fabric of seventeenth century English society. They make Fox into a shallow reformer.

Fox's enemies did not rest content with the decision at Lancaster. They continued to pursue the case through other legal channels. At the ensuing Assizes the opposing Justices led a case against Fox in spite of the findings at Lancaster. But Colonel West, the clerk of the Assize and one of the Justices who ruled in favour of Fox at Lancaster, refused to make out a warrant.[91] Following the Assize a group of Lancashire Justices and ministers drew up a petition against Fox and Nayler which was to be sent to the

---

[90]*Gospel Truth Demonstrated*, 5, p. 298.

[91]Braithwaite, *Beginnings*, p. 108.

Council of State. In the petition, which was never sent, Fox and other Quakers were again charged with professing equality with God and claiming to be Christ "contrary to the late Act".[92] Fox and Nayler answered these charges in *Saul's Errand to Damascus* (1653). Christ dwelt in the saints and where Christ dwelt divinity was resident. "He that hath the same spirit that raised up Jesus Christ", said Fox, "is equal with God".[93] So now, in 1653, Fox openly used the phrase "equal with God". To have the Spirit of God was to have the fulness of the Godhead within. This was an identification of *unity* with the divine and where there was unity there was equality. The believer participated in the equality that existed in the Godhead. We may now conclude that Fox's own words were in clear contravention of the Blasphemy Act and it becomes increasingly evident that it was Judge Fell's clever legerdemain that got Fox off the hook.

Following the Lancaster Sessions Nayler went on to Westmorland where he and Howgill met hostile people in Orton in November, 1652. Both he and Howgill were charged with blasphemy and committed to Appleby prison to await the January Sessions.[94] The clergy in the area, still stinging from their defeat at Lancaster and convinced "that Parliament had opened the gap for blasphemy"[95] with the *Instrument of Government*, prepared as damning a case as possible. In spite of the precedent set at Lancaster the majority of justices at the Sessions reached a decision to keep Nayler and Howgill in prison until Easter, 1653.[96]

---

[92] *Ibid.*, p. 108.

[93] Fox and Nayler, *Saul's Errand to Damascus*, p. 592.

[94] The sources for the trial are: "James Nayler to Margaret Fell" (November, 1652), *Swarth. MSS.*, 1, No. 85; 3, No. 66; "James Nayler to George Fox" (February, 1653), *A.R. Barclay MSS.*, Nos. 18, 19, 74; George Fox and James Nayler, *Several Petitions Answered that were put up by the Priests of Westmoreland Against J. Nayler* (London, 1653); James Nayler, *A Collection of Sundry Books, Epistles and Papers Written by James Nayler*, edited by George Whitehead (London, 1617), pp. 1-16; Penney, *First Publishers of Truth*, pp. 248-49; Besse, *Sufferings*, 2, pp. 3-6.

[95] Fox and Nayler, *Saul's Errand to Damascus*, p. 604.

[96] Braithwaite, *Beginnings*, pp. 111-12. During the Sessions Nayler's defence was so compelling that one Justice, Anthony Pearson, became a Quaker while he sat on the Bench.

In mid-1653 Fox left his comfortable confines at Swarthmoor Hall for a missionary journey into Cumberland. For a third time, this time in Carlisle, a warrant was issued for his arrest on charges of blasphemy. He was called to appear before the Bench to defend himself and as at Lancaster the charges were serious since he could have been convicted as a second offender under the *Blasphemy Act*. If he refused banishment he would have been hung as a felon as the *Act* specified, and this was the rumor that was reportedly about at all the Assizes.[97]

Fox was subjected to another lengthy examination before the magistrates during which time he answered questions from Independents and Presbyterians.[98] Our only source for this examination is in Fox's *Journals* and it is very brief. But it provides a sense for how the questioning proceeded. Fox was asked if he was the Son of God. He said "yes". Had he seen God's face? "Yes". These were leading questions, designed to entrap Fox. From the orthodox point of view only Jesus (who was bodily removed from earth and in a distant heaven) could be called the Son of God and only the glorified Christ could see the face of God since he was present with the Father. According to Fox's radically different view of God the glorified Christ inhabited him and because he had assumed the very nature of Christ he was justified in calling himself the Son of God. If Christ was within then God's face could be seen within. Fox was making his distinction between creature and inner Christ and whenever he answered questions like this he answered as the Christ who inhabited him and spoke through him.

Another, Gervase Benson, who was already a Quaker, concluded that the words spoken by Nayler "were not within the Act against blasphemy nor against any law" (Fox and Nayler, *Several Petitions Answered*, p. 52). The precedent set by Judge Fell at Lancaster had an effect on future decisions.

[97] Fox, *Short Journal*, p. 33; *Cambridge Journal*, 1, pp. 119-25.

[98] The sources for the trial are: *Cambridge Journal*, 1, pp. 116-25 and the *Short Journal*, pp. 32-33. Ellwood added several letters from the time which were not contained in the *Spence MS*. and which exonerated Fox of any wrongdoing. The Baptists were not among the crowd that sought to have Fox imprisoned, tried and even executed. The reason for this may have been that the Baptist congregation in Carlisle "went over en bloc to the Friends, including the 'Pasteure'" following Fox's preaching at that time (from a source reported by the *Baptist Historical Society* in 1923. See *Short Journal*, p. 285).

Although the legal precedent set at Lancaster was in his favour Fox was sent to prison and put in a dungeon with felons and moss-troopers[99] to await trial at the next Assizes. While Fox was in prison many, especially curious noblewomen, came to visit him - a perfect and sinless man who was about to die. This, it will be remembered, occurred at Derby as well. Fox was leaving impressions with people about his divine status.[100] The clergy, said Fox, would then mock him and ask him if he was going to die for the sins of these visitors. Fox then compared these scoffers to those who crucified Christ. As with the Derby statement, Ellwood left this revealing comparison out of the text, leaving in only the material that exonerated Fox of blasphemy, lies and slander.[101]

When the Assize arrived the presiding Judges refused to hear the case, leaving Fox's fate in the hands of the local magistrates. This was probably because the Assize Judges knew, from the binding precedent set at Lancaster, that strictly speaking Fox's doctrine of celestial inhabitation could not be condemned under the existing *Blasphemy Act*.[102] Fox was held for another seven weeks without warrant and for no good reason. Two Justices who were favourable to Quakers, Gervase Benson and Anthony Pearson, wrote to Parliament saying that Fox was about to die for religion.[103] Margaret Fell wrote to Colonel West and charged Fox's enemies with

---

[99]Moss-troopers lived on the 'mosses' or borderlands between England and Scotland. Friends were noted for their success among these marauding outcasts of society. The Earl of Carlisle told King Charles II that "Quakers had done more to suppress them than all his Troups could do" (*see Short Journal*, p. 285).

[100]By analogy, Fox was not unlike the itinerant Christian wonder-workers or roving Apostles who proliferated throughout the Roman world in the second and third centuries and who were often the focus of female religious communities known for their sexual continence, independence and reactionary attitude toward patriarchalizing trends in the early church [S. Davies, *The Revolt of the Widows: The Social World of the Apocryphal Acts* (Carbondale: Southern Illinois University Press, 1980)].

[101]*Cambridge Journal*, 1, p. 125. Compare with Ellwood, *Journal*, 1, pp. 179-88.

[102]Justice Anthony Pearson, by this time a Quaker, had also written to the Judges of the Assize and specifically pointed out that the charges were not covered under the *Blasphemy Act* (Ellwood, *Journal*, 1, p. 181).

[103]*Ibid.*, 1, pp. 186-87.

blasphemy for professing "a god in words" but denying it in actions.[104] In time a letter came down from Westminster to the Sheriff and magistrates in Carlisle ordering Fox to be released. This was Fox's last imprisonment for blasphemy and only one other such trial lay ahead, the most famous one of all - Nayler's blasphemy trial before Parliament in 1656.

The blasphemy trials really settled nothing (although they were evidence enough of Fox's exalted claims) apart from proving the inadequacy of the *Blasphemy Act* and especially its failure to address the idea of celestial inhabitation. Fox's christology clearly implied blasphemy when measured against seventeenth century orthodox Puritan theology although it was established (thanks to Judge Fell) that Fox could not be charged under the strict letter of the law. But the issue, though settled legally for the moment, continued to have corrosive implications within Quakerism and within the socio-religious milieu in which they moved. The purpose of the following part of this discussion is to search out the sources to determine what Fox said about himself and what others inside and outside his movement said about him. The best place to begin is with Fox's own claims to divine sonship.

Traditionally, church theologians (including the seventeenth century Puritan divines) have kept the sonship attributed to Jesus and the sonship attributed to the saints separate. Jesus' sonship was not democratized and its uniqueness was preserved in three basic doctrines - his pre-existence, the expiatory character of his death and his resurrection. These basic doctrines were initially a post-Jesus outgrowth of early Christian apologists who were concerned to convey the idea that as the Son of God Jesus was unique and divine. These doctrines were affirmed at Nicea and Chalcedon.

Established Jewish usage of the time did not convey personal deity but simply rendered 'Son of God' in a nativistic sense - one who was God's representative on earth, a righteous servant with special authority and one who stood in a filial relationship with God. When Christian apologists filled the term with new meaning and identified Jesus with the pre-existent Christ, Jesus became more than just a prophet, magus or teacher of divine wisdom. He became a revelation of divine nature. He was both Christ and Son of

---

[104]*Cambridge Journal*, 1, p. 117.

God, the *logos* and the pre-existent creator who became incarnate and revealed himself to humanity. He did not become the Son because he always was the Son who had always lived in a pre-existent filial relationship with the Father. He was a unique event in history. The Church then established strict limits against democratizing Jesus' sonship. The saints were not sons of God in the same sense that Jesus was.[105] Any sonship that was attributed to the saints could only be actualized eschatologically. Their sonship was to be awaited as part of the future *eschaton*.

Fox challenged this traditional view with his doctrine of celestial inhabitation. The sonship of the saints was realized in the present.[106] There was no future *eschaton*. The saints, like Jesus, became sons of God by adoption after the inner body of sin was shed. Those born of the saints, like Jesus, were already born with a glorified body. Thus Fox could say "according to the spirit I am the Son of God, according to the seed I am the seed of Abraham and David, which seed is Christ, which seed is but one in all his saints".[107] When the saints became sons of God through the indwelling Christ they became indivisibly united with the divine nature. This was what celestial inhabitation meant to the early Quaker - the pre-existent Christ inhabited the believer, as he had inhabited Jesus, in such a sensible manner that the believer actually thought he was a Son of God. In this sense the Jesus of history was not the unique and final revelation in history for the pre-existent Christ was revealed in and through the saints in new modes of revelation.

What claims did Fox make for himself as the Son of God? In nature, no more than other saints. In stature he adopted manners, customs, phrases, images and actions that constantly called people to reflect not only on the similarities between Christ and himself but on his special divine authority as the first among equals. His claims to sonship never wavered. They were

---

[105]This was Jeremiah Ives' point against the Quakers [*The Quakers Quaking* (London, 1656), p. 6].

[106]*Gospel Truth Demonstrated*, 5, p. 226.

[107]*Caton MSS.*, 2, p. 48. Formerly *Boswell Middleton MSS.*

always absolute and authoritative. They carried an aura of a great, charismatic power, power that far surpassed that claimed by any other Quaker except, briefly, for James Nayler. Wherever he went he was thought to suffer on behalf of the sins of the world. If Fox democratized the potential for divine sonship he reserved for himself the pre-eminent status of avatar - a special manifestation of the divine in the last days. His psychic states, sufferings, miracles, youthful wanderings, fastings and ascetic holiness were all intended to mean something. They were the signs of one who had come with great authority and deserved pre-eminent status. He was the first proclaimer of the everlasting gospel since the days of Jesus. He was the first one to proclaim the Day of the Lord and lead the saints in hewing down Babylon's priests and temples. He was the teacher of righteousness so many Collegiants and Seekers had waited for for so long. All this meant something to Fox and he intended it to mean something to his followers. It meant that Fox was a new and final revelation of the divine. He had a special place in the divine order of things. And this special place brought with it a regal attitude (imparted to others around him) and the impression that he had more of the divine in him than others. He, it was implied, had fully returned to the pre-Fall state of innocence and perfection. His return to Paradise was complete. He was fully divinized. No other Quaker dared to make such claims with the certainty of Fox. Other Quakers used exalted language among themselves and some, like Nayler and Milner, even briefly claimed messianic status. But it was Fox who was the recipient of the most widespread worship, adoration and pseudo-messianic language.

When Fox used the term 'Son of God', as he applied it to himself, it gave added authority to his person and message. In 1652, at Pendle Hill in Westmorland/Yorkshire, Fox sounded the Day of the Lord after having a momentous vision (the view from atop Pendle Hill is the stuff visions are made from) of a great people in shining white raiment coming forth from the North. Soon after this vision he passed through Hawes (a nearby town) and entered an alehouse where he began to preach the Day of the Lord. For this he was viciously attacked. However, he remained at the Inn and the following morning he went to the man of the house and told him "that I was the Son of God and was come to declare the everlasting truth of God".[108] In light of the previous discussion, what Fox meant was that his inner body had been transformed into the glorified body of Christ with whom he was now unified and equal. But in this context it was also intended to imply that Fox carried with him a special divine authority. The reference to divine sonship, so specific in its implication, was omitted from the Ellwood, Cambridge and Nickall's editions of the *Journal* (all which dipped freely into the *Short Journal* where the incident is recorded).[109] The actual *MS.* of the *Short Journal* where these words appeared was not in the handwriting of George Fox but it was endorsed by his own hand at the end. There is another very old *MS.* of seventeenth century vintage which closely parallels the narrative in the *Short Journal*. In this *MS.*, entitled *This is a Book of the Travels and Passages of George Fox*, the original words "ye Son of God" were tampered with. The "ye" was obscured and a small "a" appeared above the "ye" - an attempt on the part of an early Quaker scribe to minimize Fox's exalted claims.[110] But even the scribe or scribes were uncertain whether he was "A Son of God" still suggesting pre-eminence or "a Son of God" following the more democratic and egalitarian Pauline concept found in Romans 8.[111]

In 1653, at his trial for blasphemy in Carlisle, Fox again unhesitatingly and definitively replied that he was the Son of God. Ellwood deleted this dialogue from the text altogether. Fox was sent to prison "as a blasphemer, a heretic, and a seducer", words which Ellwood did allow to remain in the text.[112] Theologically Fox did not make a distinction between his sonship and the sonship of the other saints. To do so would have undermined the

---

[108]*Short Journal*, p. 17.

[109]Ellwood, *Journal*, 1, p. 41; Nickall's, *Journal*, p. 106.

[110]*This is a Book of the Travels and Passages of George Fox* (date unknown), p. 21.

[111]There were times when Fox used the Pauline concept as it applied divinity to all the saints (*Gospel Truth Demonstrated*, 5, p. 90; *Epistles*, 7, pp. 57, 85, 206, 217, 290, 321-22; 8, pp. 28, 33, 159; Cadbury, *Narrative Papers*, p. 169). Most Quakers applied the Pauline concept to themselves as well: "to them he gives the power to become sons of God" [*see*, for example, James Parnell, *A Shield of Truth* (London, 1655), p. 10].

[112]Ellwood, *Journal*, 1, p. 180.

egalitarian edifice upon which his doctrine of the inner Christ in everyone was based. But he did make a functional distinction. He was the first among equals and he expected, even demanded, the respect (even adoration) that came with that position. This will become increasingly evident when we discuss the Nayler incident. Sonship could be democratized, as Fox explained to his interrogators at Carlisle, while his avatarial status as a unique revelation of the divine was preserved. The thaumaturgic aspects of his own life were a sign and confirmation to others that he had a special divine anointing, beyond the normal given to all the saints, and that provided grounds for his personal exalted claims and the adoration of others towards him.

Fox continued to apply the term 'Son of God' to himself after the 1653 trial at Carlisle. He used the term explicitly in a 1653 epistle to Margaret Fell and other Friends.[113] In January, 1654 he boldly used the term in a letter to Cromwell. Again this material was deleted from Ellwood's edition of the *Journal*. The background to this incident lay in a confrontation between Fox and the authorities at Whetson. Rumors of a plot against Cromwell were abounding and Friends were suspected of collaborating. As a result Fox was asked to desist from all public activity in order to minimize the threat of violence. Since he refused to comply he was sent directly to Cromwell. Before meeting with the Protector he was required, at the express wish of Cromwell, to write a letter promising "that he would not take up the sword against the Lord Protector or the Government".[114] Fox complied, but not to be overshadowed by Cromwell's worldly stature he established in the letter that he was not writing in obeisance to Cromwell but as a sign of the heavenly kingdom. He was meeting the Protector on his terms - as the Son of God:

> I (who am of the world called George Fox) do deny the carrying or drawing of any carnal sword against any, or against thee Oliver Cromwell or any man in the presence of the Lord God. I declare it (God is my witness, by whom I am moved to

[113]Larry Ingle has recently pointed this out in "George Fox as Enthusiast: An Unpublished Epistle", *JFHS*, 55 (1989), pp. 265-70.

118

give this forth for truth's sake, from him whom the world called
George Fox who is the son of God), and who is sent to stand a
witness against all violence ... my kingdom is not of this world,
therefore with carnal weapons I do not fight. ff.G. [Who is of
the world called George Fox and a new name hath which the
world knows not. We are witnesses of this testimony whose
names in the flesh is (sic) Thomas Aldham Robert Craven].[115]

The original copy of this letter was endorsed by Fox. Another copy, in the
handwriting of Thomas Aldham, also contains the phrase "who is the Son of
God".[116] Ellwood had the original copy but edited out the blasphemous
phrases or rephrased things in a more innocuous way. Charles Leslie also
had a copy of the original letter and he accused Friends of altering Fox's
work to "obviate the objections against their horrid blasphemies".[117] Friends
were, as an anonymous writer wrote a century later, "ashamed ... of the
blasphemy imputed to them".[118] Friends' response, in 1796, was to vindicate
the character of George Fox by standing by the trustworthiness of the
Ellwood version and judging Leslie's version to be spurious. If it was not,
they concluded, then there were grounds "for calling Fox a senseless
enthusiast".[119] As it turned out a Friend, Elisha Bates, was allowed access to
the original *Journal MSS.* and he discovered the original letter and used it as

[114]*Cambridge Journal*, 1, p. 161.

[115]*Ibid.*, 1, pp. 161-62.

[116]This document was also referred to by the anti-Quaker pamphleteer Charles
Leslie in *The Snake in the Grass* (London, 1697), p. 113 and *A Defence of ... the Snake in the
Grass* (London, 1700), last part, pp. 39-41. It is also referred to in Joseph Wyeth's answer to
The Snake in the Grass, being *Anguis Flagellatus*, p. 175. Leslie drew much of his knowledge of
Quakerism from Francis Bugg, Thomas Crisp, George Keith and other opponents of
Quakerism. For a critical discussion of how Ellwood's editing of the letter influenced the
views of subsequent generations of Friends *see* Cadbury, "The Editio Princeps of Fox's
Journal", *JFHS*, 53 (1974), pp. 216-18.

[117]Leslie, *Snake in the Grass* (1698 edition), p. 113. Leslie also accused Fox of
applying the phrase "my kingdom is not of this world" to himself, with christological
implications [*Ibid.*, pp. 109-10 (1697 edition)].

[118]Quoted in Cadbury, "The Editio Princeps of Fox's Journal", p. 217.

[119]*Ibid.*, p. 218.

part of his attack on what he perceived were the results of excessive spiritualism among Friends.[120]

The use of the term 'Son of God' in the letter to Cromwell was significant because it implied, before Cromwell, that Fox was claiming authority through equality with God. He, too, was a King in his kingdom and he went to Cromwell not as an inferior but as an equal and even greater than an equal, for he was the very Son of God. Fox's claim to divine sonship gave him added stature and authority when addressing his adversaries and those who were in worldly authority over him. It enabled him (and other Quakers) to carry himself with divine and regal stature before the Kings and nobles of the realm.

The last time we know Fox applied the term to himself in public was in 1660. In May of that year, at a time when the nation was rife with plots against the returned King, George Fox and Margaret Fell were committed to Lancaster Prison. In the Mittimus Fox was accused of being an enemy of the King and endeavouring to raise local insurrections throughout the country. Fox answered these charges much as he had answered similar charges before Cromwell. In a letter to the King he said:

> I am as innocent as a child of all these things, who witnessed the power of God, and am in that which was before wars was [sic], or carnal weapons either ... and my kingdom is not of this world ... my weapons are not carnal but spiritual, who am led by the Spirit of God, so the Son of God, who am not under the law nor its weapons, but am come to the love which fulfills the law.[121]

In the *Spence MS.* this was the middle portion of a longer letter which was separated from the main body of the letter by several pages. Ellwood chose to keep the main body of the letter (which had no incriminating material) but neither he, nor Nickall's, retained the fragment quoted above.[122] The

[120]See note 149.

[121]*Cambridge Journal*, 1, p. 381. *See also The Sum of Such Particulars as are Charged Against George Fox in the Mittimus by Which He Stands Committed* (London, 1650).

[122]Ellwood, *Journal*, 1, pp. 406-9 and Nickall's, *Journal*, pp. 370-82. Compare with *Cambridge Journal*, 1, pp. 375-78, 381.

deleted portion was accepted as authentic by Norman Penney who identified it as belonging to the longer letter.[123] The deletion was part of Ellwood's agenda to bowdlerize exalted language and contentious phrases contained in the *Journal*.

And yet it was the essence of Fox's message that was being tampered with. When Fox used the term 'Son of God' he was conveying a sense of divine authority and kingship to Charles. The notion of sonship, so bold in its pretentions, had serious implications not only for religious orthodoxy but for the stability of the social and political orders. As a Son of God (and for all Quakers as sons and daughters of God) the claim was made that Fox was a King in a higher kingdom. In his divinized form he was not even "under the law". Even though Fox demanded immaculate behaviour from his followers, theoretically he and they were above the law and their feared social and political radicalism springs from this source. Fox's antinomian statement was rooted firmly in the doctrine of celestial inhabitation. This was a bold statement to make at such a sensitive moment in Quaker history, even if the implications were somewhat muted by the implied reference to Romans 8.

Fox's claims to divine sonship are not the only clues to inform us about what he thought of himself. All Quakers may have been sons and daughters of God in accordance with Pauline teaching but Fox made larger claims for himself that suggest his claim to divine sonship superseded all others, at least in stature. This demeanour was revealed in small ways and finally became the bone of contention in the Nayler affair.

For example, because Fox was living in the pre-Fall, paradisiacal and glorified state he considered certain things to be "below" him. He set a higher ascetic standard for himself than he did for his followers. One such thing was total abstention from sexual conduct. In 1669 when he was married to the widowed Margaret Fell (a marriage designed to quell scandalous rumors about their relationship which threatened the purity of the movement) an old Puritan asked Fox why he had married. Fox replied that it was a sign to the world that "all might come up out of the wilderness to the marriage of the Lamb" - a revealing statement given Margaret Fell's views

---

[123]*Cambridge Journal*, 1, p. 467.

that Fox was the Lamb of God. The Puritan replied that he thought marriage was only for procreation to which Fox said that he judged such things below him.[124] Sexual activity even within marriage was obviously not acceptable for one who was living in a fully glorified state. Since most other Quakers married and had children (unlike the later sect known as Shakers) either Fox did not require the same celibate conduct from his followers or by implication they had not yet attained as high a glorified state as he had, not unlike the relationship between Cathar *perfecti* and Cathar believers.

In another instance the sources provide us with a glimpse into the kind of divine authority and stature Fox reserved for himself. There is no indication that Fox ever personally forgave James Nayler for trying to steal away the leadership of the movement and in the process discrediting Quakerism in the eyes of the world, but he begrudgingly allowed the breach between them to be publicly healed through the mediation of William Dewsbury.[125] The 1660 event was staged strictly on Fox's terms and in a manner that confirmed his exalted status in the movement. Nayler was made to bow before Fox and kiss his hand and afterward his foot, something Nayler had refused to do in 1656 when Fox demanded the rebellious Nayler's subjection. Robert Rich, a London clothier, follower of Nayler and no friend of Fox criticized Fox for asking for himself what honour belonged to God alone.[126] Every Quaker was a son and daughter of God according to Fox's doctrine of the inner Christ but the stature of Fox's sonship required an obeisance no other Quaker (apart briefly from Nayler) could demand. The Nayler incident clearly demonstrated that one challenged Fox's authority only at great risk. To borrow Howgill's phrase and apply it to Fox - there was equality in nature though not in stature. Fox's special claim to divine sonship put him 'above the crowd' and made him a first among equals. He was a

---

[124]Nickalls, *Journal*, p. 567. Cadbury, *Narrative Papers*, pp. 78-79 for the full text of his letter to Friends on the matter of his marriage.

[125]Braithwaite, *Beginnings*, p. 274. The incident is not mentioned anywhere by Fox.

[126]Robert Rich, *Hidden Things Brought to Light or the Discord of the Grand Quakers Among Themselves, Discovered in Some Letters, Papers, and Passages Written to and from George Fox, James Nayler and John Perrot* (London, 1676), p. 40.

Quaker but more than a Quaker as evidenced by his refusal to ever belong to a Yearly Meeting. He was an avatar, a special revelation of the divine in the last days.

Another curious instance of Fox's use of divine language leaving questionable impressions occurred in 1673. While in America he wrote a small book entitled *The Types, Figures and Shadows in the Old Testament Fulfilled by Christ in the New: and Many More Precious Things Very Serviceable to be Printed Which Many are Ignorant Of.* This little book was never printed and was subsequently lost. The title page is preserved and it contained an interesting monogram in Hebrew. The upper line consisted of Fox's initials repeated. The lower line was the Hebrew term for God. I do not claim to understand what Fox's intentions were here but once again we are left with impressions, which, when viewed in the whole context of his theology of celestial inhabitation and his exalted conduct among his followers and before Kings, suggest that he was claiming deity. One wonders why a manuscript with such an important content was lost.[127]

Exalted language as it was used by Fox often left some doubt in the mind about whether he was referring to himself or Christ. Two such examples were repeatedly cited by his opponents as evidence of his blasphemous claims. The first quote was from his pamphlet *The Pearl Found in England*; the second from *The Teachers of the World Unveiled*:

> I'll make nations like dirt: I'll tread them into mire; I'll make religions, professions and teachings ... gatherings on heaps: gatherings of multitudes; gatherings which they call churches ... I'll make mire of them: I'll make mortar; I'll make dirt of them. The wrath of the Lamb is risen upon all apostates.

And,

> I am the light of the world, him by whom the world was made ... if you love the light ... you love Christ ... if you hate that light, there is your condemnation: From him who is one with

---

[127]Reference to the book appears in the *Ann. Cat.*, No. 12, 68F on p. 122. On Fox's elementary knowledge of Hebrew *see* Cadbury, "Hebraica and the Jews in Early Quaker Interest", pp. 145-48.

> the truth in every man; who of the Lord was moved this to
> write, whose name of the world is called G.F.[128]

Fox's opponents saw in this a blurring of the distinction between creature and creator and they charged blasphemy. Not all were being purely vindictive on this point. Henry More, for example, was not necessarily being malicious when he said that the primitive Quaker notion of celestial inhabitation logically resulted in the use of this kind of language. Those who came to Fox's defence repeatedly said that he was not applying christological titles to himself but to the Christ in him, which, when understood in the context of celestial inhabitation really implied deification at least until the time of the transformation of the doctrine of the inner light.[129]

After considering the evidence so far it is apparent that Fox believed he was the Son of God (a divine creature of great authority and stature) and he was able to base this claim on his doctrine of celestial inhabitation. When pressed by opponents he was able to make his claims appear orthodox enough to escape the charge of blasphemy (barely) without betraying his own radical theology. But the larger question now is not what Fox meant (for that question can all too often devolve into finely tuned definitional arguments as it did at the Lancaster Sessions) but how others inside and outside his movement interpreted his exalted claims. How did Quakers think of

---

[128]George Fox, *The Pearl Found in England* (London, 1658), pp. 15-16 and *The Teachers of the World Unveiled* (London, 1655), p. 27. The contentious statement made by Fox in the latter pamphlet was inserted into the text in italics at the point where he is railing against teachers. The effect is that it is Christ himself who is speaking the warning. It captures the reader's attention concerning the seriousness of what is being said.

[129]Edward Beckham, *A Brief Discovery*, pp. 3-4. George Whitehead's partisan view may be found in his *Supplement* to Wyeth's *Anguis Flagellatus*, p. 20. Later Quaker authors did their best to minimize these exalted claims. George Whitehead did not deny the fundamental principle that there was something of God in every person but he did deny that Quakers meant what their opponents said they meant. He tried to clarify Howgill's statement that there was "equality in nature though not in stature" by saying that Howgill was referring to the equality in the divine nature between the Father and the Son only, of which nature the believer partook in measure (*Supplement*, p. 20). Our previous discussion of this passage suggested that Howgill implicated the saint in the full nature of the Godhead. There was no distinction and it was not in measure only. The fullness of the Godhead dwelt bodily in the believer and every part of their being was inhabited by the celestial flesh of Christ. Could early Quakers have been any clearer on the subject of deification than that?

themselves?   What did they think of Fox? He was leaving enough impressions with people that many actually believed he was claiming to be a 'god'. Nathaniel Stevens, a minister in Fox's home town of Fenny Drayton, thought that Fox was saying he had gone to heaven and returned exalted.[130] He was arrested in Derby and Carlisle, called to account in Lancaster, and caused riots in many other places because he said was perfect, sinless and equal with God. Some even thought he was an angel who could appear and disappear at will.[131] Because Fox left the impression with people that he was a theophany (and that was an impression he meant to leave) he evoked a wide range of responses from people. Some rebuked him and shouted blasphemy. Some of his followers exalted him. And in one case a Ranter named Thomas Bushell mocked him by bowing to the ground before him provoking Fox to say "Repent thou (swine and) beast".[132]

Fox was not the only Quaker to leave impressions with people that he was divinized, although he was the recipient of the most widespread worship. The charge was made by Richard Sherlocke, Ralph Farmer, John Gilpin, Francis Higginson, Henry More and Charles Leslie that the very notion of the saints being one and equal with God not only led to the use of rapturous language but the notion that they were deserving of divine adoration.[133] Enough examples remain in the sources to confirm this point of view. Richard Farnworth, William Dewsbury, Leonard Fell and Thomas Holme all used exalted language towards Margaret Fell.[134]   Extravagant pseudo-

---

[130]*Short Journal*, p. 4.

[131]*Ibid.*, p. 6.

[132]*Ibid.*, p. 8. The act of bowing to the ground in mockery was common among Ranters.

[133]Sherlocke, *The Quakers Wild Questions*, pp. 66-67; Ralph Farmer, *The Great Mysteries of Godliness* (London, 1655), p. 84; Gilpin, *The Quakers Shaken*, pp. 6-8; Higginson, *A Brief Relation*, p. 3; More, *Grand Mystery of Godliness*, Book 1, chapter 6, p. 14; Charles Leslie, *Primitive Heresy Revived* (London, 1698), p. 74.

[134]"Richard Farnworth to George Fox and Margaret Fell" (April, 1653), *Samuel Watson MSS.*, p. 26; "William Dewsbury to Margaret Fell" (March, 1660), *Swarth. MSS.*, 4, No. 134; "Leonard Fell to Margaret Fell" (1658), *Swarth. MSS.*, 2, No. 129; Thomas Holme

Messianic language was directed towards James Milner and James Nayler. Quakers like Gilpin, Toldervy, Milner, Nayler and the wife of one Mr. Williamson, a Quaker, also came to believe that they were Christ and many opponents of Quakerism viewed this as the logical *terminus* of their notion of celestial inhabitation.

The erstwhile Quaker John Gilpin heard a voice that said "Christ in God, God in Christ and Christ in thee" at which time he went out into the streets with a cross around his neck.[135] His identification with the glorifed Christ within was fully consistent with the teaching of Fox. His subsequent sign action was not an anomaly within the context of early Quakerism. And in a little known early Quaker incident the wife of one of James Milner's followers (Mr. Williamson) made the claim that she was the "eternal Son of God". One man who heard her replied that she could not be because she was a woman. Her response was "No, you are women, but I am a man".[136] This is not a statement to be quickly dismissed as silly or far-fetched. It was fully consistent with early Quaker beliefs and within the context of Fox's teaching about celestial inhabitation it was reasonable. It also had broad implications for seventeenth century women's rights, the question of who Christ represented generically,[137] as well as for the great liberating potential of celestial inhabitation not only for men but for women as well.

The doctrine of celestial inhabitation had the potential to liberate women from millenia of oppression and injustice. Women, like men, were divinized, freed from patriarchy and lived in the pre-Fall, glorified state. To

---

to Margaret Fell" (September 9, 1654), *Swarth. MSS.*, 1, No. 192 and "Thomas Holme to Margaret Fell" (April 16, 1657), *Swarth. MSS.*, 1, No. 196.

[135]Gilpin, *The Quakers Shaken*, pp. 6-8.

[136]Reported by Francis Higginson in *A Brief Relation*, pp. 3-4.

[137]For the contemporary debate on this issue *see*: Sacred Congregation for the Declaration of the Faith, "Declaration on the Question of the Admission of Women to the Ministerial Priesthood", reprinted in *Women Priests: A Catholic Commentary on the Vatican Declaration*, ed. by Leonard Swidler and Arlene Swidler (New York: Paulist, 1977), pp. 37-49. For the response *see* A. Farley, "Discrimination or Equality? The Old Order or the New"? in *Women Priests*, pp. 310-15. *See also* Rosemary Reuther, "Christology and Feminism: Can a Male Saviour Save the World", in R.R. Reuther, *To Change the World* (London, SCM, 1981), pp. 45-56.

believe that the flesh and bone of the heavenly man literally inhabited the person and transformed the inward body to the extent that the believer was transformed into the very flesh and bone of the glorified Christ meant exactly what Williamson's wife said - she became a man - a divinized man equal and identical with Christ himself. The statement recalls similar statements made in the Gospel of Thomas where Jesus said "Lo, I shall lead her, and make her male, so that she too may become a living spirit resembling you males. For every woman who makes herself male will enter the Kingdom of Heaven".[138] Williamson's wife surpassed ancient Gnostic androgeny by making men into women and thus excluding them from the redemptive process. As unbelievers they were women!

Although exalted language was used by Quakers among themselves the evidence demonstrates that Quakers used exalted language towards Fox both to a greater degree and in a qualitatively different sense. Fox was, after all, the father of the faith and the first and final public appearance of the pre-existent Christ since the days of Jesus and the Apostles. Fox was treated differently and he was exalted in a way reserved for no other Quaker. When Nayler was thought to usurp that special position he was shunned by Quakers for doing so.

Exalted language towards Fox was very widespread. It was used by Mary Howgill, Thomas Curtis, Ann Curtis, Richard Sale, Thomas Holme, Mary Prince, Ann Burden, Margaret Fell, Francis Howgill, Richard Hubberthorne, Edward Burrough, Solomon Eccles, Thomas Lower, Josiah Coale, John Audland and John Whitehead. These are only the ones recorded and extant, to my knowledge. In addition people were seen to bow and even fall down before Fox on at least two separate occasions.

How exalted could the language towards Fox become? Probably the best known occasion for the use of such language is Margaret Fell's letters to the young Fox, written shortly after she had first met him at Swarthmoor Hall. Note how the distinction between creature and Christ is very confused as she is obviously impressed by his doctrine of celestial inhabitation to the

---

[138]Quoted in Reuther, *To Change the World*, p. 50.

extent that she identifies Fox, or his inner glorified being with the glorified Christ himself:

> Our dear father in the Lord, for though we have ten thousand instructors in Christ, yet we have not many fathers, for in Christ Jesus thou hast begotten us through the gospel, eternal praise be to our Father. We, thy babes, with one consent being gathered together in the power of the Spirit, thou being present with us, our souls doth think and languish after thee ... O thou bread of life, without which our souls will starve. O forever more give us this bread, and take pity on us, whom thou hast nursed up with the breast of consolation. O our life, our desire is to see you again that we may be refreshed and established, and so have life more abundantly, and let not that beastly power which keeps us in bondage separate thy bodily presence from us, who reigned as King above it, and would rejoice to see thy kingly power here triumph over it. O our dear nursing father, we hope thou wilt not leave us comfortless but will come again; though that our sorrow be for a time, yet joy comes in the morning; O our life, we hope to see thee again that our joy may be full; for in thy presence is fullness of joy and where thou dwellest is pleasure forever more ... O thou fountain of eternal life, our souls thirst after thee, for in thee alone is our life and peace; for our souls is [sic] much refreshed by seeing thee, and our lives is preserved by thee, O thou father of eternal felicity.

In a postscript to the letter she added:

> My own dear heart ... my soul thirst to have thee come over, if it be but for two or three days ... I know it is a burden and suffering to thee, but thou hast borne our burdens and suffered for us, and with us, and now dear heart, do not leave us, nor forsake us for our life and peace is in thee.[139]

---

[139]"Margaret Fell to George Fox" (1652), *Spence MSS.*, 3, No. 24. "Dear Heart" was a commonly used greeting in seventeenth century England. Isabel Ross said that these words illustrated the "emotionalism" of the earlier years which soon "deepened and passed away" (*Margaret Fell*, p. 36). Braithwaite also explained this exalted language as an outgrowth of her new spiritual experience which "exalted her life, and caused her to rest herself in the young prophet's larger personality, which she felt was possessed by the living spirit of Christ. In giving expression to this feeling in an intimate letter, she inevitably made use of Biblical phraseology long familiar to her, and in her gush of feeling and poverty of vocabulary seems to have lost a due sense of the value of the words used" (*Beginnings*, p. 104). Both authors excused these exalted words as the excess emotionalism of a young convert. While sensible at one level this is a misunderstanding. Fox's own exalted claims prompted this response not only from Margaret Fell but from many others, and not only in the early years but as late as

128

The superlatives used of Fox in this letter were usually reserved for Christ and yet Fox did nothing to stop Margaret Fell from using this language. And why should have he? He understood her to be addressing the celestial flesh within. If there remained any doubt at all about her vision of Fox as a theophany and even the second appearance of Christ, such doubts are put to rest by her later comments about Fox during the Nayler incident. In one of the many letters written and passed between Friends at that time she referred to Fox as "him to whom all nations shall bow" and the one to whom God "hath given ... a name better than every name, to which every knee shall bow", language ascribed to Christ in the New Testament.[140] In the context of Nayler's challenge to the leadership of the movement the language was so shocking that George Bishop, who was delivering the letter to Fox, read it and withheld it lest it fall into the hands of the authorities and threaten Fox's reputation and safety. Early Quakers were acutely aware of the dangerous implications of such language and they hid it, as early as the mid-1650's.

Margaret Fell's exalted language was not an anomaly in early Quakerism and some were even more explicit in their exaltation of Fox. The following quotes illustrate how widespread the notion of celestial flesh was in early Quakerism. Howgill and Burrough addressed Fox as the one "who art one with the Father". Thomas Curtis called Fox the one "who was dead and is alive, and forever lives", while Ann Curtis wrote: "in thee is the everlasting being, the fulness of the fountain of eternity, in thy presence is life. O my dear father, bless me with thy presence and grant that I may live with thee forever." Mary Howgill wrote to Fox and used the word "life" interchangeably with his own name and person. Ann Burden called him "thou Son of God which the world knoweth not". Richard Sale wrote to Fox and called him "thou god of life and power ... glory, glory to thy name for evermore ... Praise, praises to thee for evermore, who was and is to come,

1674. Fox's theology of celestial inhabitation was not a superficial theology or an immature christology. Margaret Fell was writing to Fox in a gush of feeling but that gush of feeling was firmly rooted in an unwavering conviction that Fox's teaching on the inner Christ was the truth. And Fox was the teacher of righteousness that she had foreseen in an earlier vision. Fell persevered to the end of her days in her conviction that Fox was a new revelation of the pre-existent Christ.

[140]"Margaret Fell to James Nayler" (October, 1656), *Spence MSS.*, 3, No. 38.

who is god over all, blessed forever, amen". And Thomas Holme wrote to Fox as the one who "owns the world"; "to thee shall all nations bend"; "all things stand by thee" and "thou art the same that ever was ... among us ... the first and the last".[141] Unfortunately much of Holme's exalted language has been so severely edited (and literally ripped from the record) that it cannot be recovered. But enough remains in the sources to demonstrate that Holme's widespread use of exalted language towards Fox was more than salutary. Geoffrey Nuttall explained Holme's language as "rhapsodies" which were the result of extreme emotional enthusiasm. Even Holme's handwriting, said Nuttall, revealed an artistic temperament, one "liable, if the controls were loosened, to violent emotional outbursts".[142] To attribute such hysteria to Fox's followers fails to recognize that there were very real ideological reasons that prompted their behaviour. If one accepts the implications of celestial inhabitation these "rhapsodies" are less excessive than deservedly well-merited, for the body of the glorified Christ was within.

Quakers attributed titles to Fox that were, by orthodox standards, reserved for Christ alone ("Son of God", "god of life and power"; "the first and the last") and that is our best indicator that early Quakers subscribed to his doctrine of celestial inhabitation and in turn attributed a special status to Fox's divine sonship. The use of such exalted and messianic language towards Fox left the impression, both with Quakers and their opponents, that Fox was a new revelation of the divine in the last days. The best example of pseudo-messianic language applied to Fox appeared in a 1675 letter to Fox from Thomas Lower. The late date suggests that even after the first flush of

---

[141]"Edward Burrough and Francis Howgill to George Fox", *Barclay MSS.*, No. 154; "Edward Burrough and Francis Howgill to George Fox" (January 21, 1656), *Barclay MSS.*, No. 34; "Thomas Curtis to George Fox" (1658), *Swarth. MSS.*, 3, No. 87; "Ann Curtis to George Fox" (May 23, 1660), in Elisha Bates, *An Appeal to the Society of Friends* (London, 1836), p. 21; "Anna Burden to George Fox" (1663), *Swarth. MSS.*, 3, No. 102; "Richard Sale to George Fox" (October 25, 1655), *Swarth. MSS.*, 4, No. 211; "Mary Howgill to George Fox", (1656), *Barclay MSS.*, No. 41; "Thomas Holme to George Fox" (June 6, 1654), *Swarth. MSS.*, 4, No. 244; "Thomas Holme to George Fox" (September, 1654), *Swarth. MSS.*, 4, No. 249; "Thomas Holme to George Fox" (Winter, 1654), *Swarth. MSS.*, 4, No. 250.

[142]G. Nuttall, *Christian Enthusiasm: Illustrated From Early Quakerism* (Pendle Hill, 1948), p. 55.

emotionalism had disappeared Fox's doctrine of celestial inhabitation still continued to inform the beliefs of his followers. Lower's statement is surely one of the most shocking and unguarded statements by an early Quaker - a statement that indisputably confirmed the belief that Fox was identified with the appearance of the glorified Christ in the last days. In 1675 (supposedly well after the first gush of emotionalism should have worn off) Thomas Lower, a medical doctor and stepson-in-law of Fox, wrote a letter to his parents-in-law George Fox and Margaret Fell. Fox had always shown great interest in the Fell family and on many occasions he had been called upon to heal the Fell children and grandchildren.[143] In this case Lower was writing to Fox and Fell about the birth of a grandchild:

> We greatly rejoice to hear of our sister Rous's happy deliverance, and good hour wherein my father [George Fox] visited her, whose company is a blessing to all that see, know and receive him, as he is a blessing to the nations and the joy of his people, *the second appearance of him who is blessed for ever.* (italics mine)[144]

The specific identification of Fox with the second appearance of Christ, so forthright and bold in its unguarded openness makes the Nayler incident look less excessive and more congruous with the type of adoration that was given to Fox. Cadbury excused the statement as a simple example of "Fox's salutary influence on people".[145] Nuttall, while conceding a blasphemous tone to such language, described it as "hyperbolic language used by those whose minds were filled with biblical imagery".[146] To say that such language is merely salutary or hyperbolic is to miss the galvanizing truth of Fox's doctrine of celestial inhabitation, its electrifying impact on early Quakers and the large claims that Fox made for himself - claims subscribed to by many other leading Quakers. The mere fact that even at this late date there were

---

[143]Cadbury, *George Fox's 'Book of Miracles'*, 57C, 57D, 61-62, 63A, 66B, 66C, 67A.

[144]"Thomas Lower to George Fox and Margaret Fell" (January 4, 1675), *Spence MSS.*, 3, p. 174.

[145]Cadbury, *George Fox's 'Book of Miracles'*, p. 58.

[146]Nuttall, *Studies in Christian Enthusiasm*, p. 50.

still Quakers who privately believed that Fox was an avatar of the divine, is a matter of prime interpretive significance, not to be treated glibly or shrugged off as simple deferential respect towards Fox. It was more than that, much more than that, that Sale, Holme or Lower intended. And Fox accepted it. They were never disowned for their use of such excessive language.

Opponents of Quakerism like Jeremiah Ives, Edward Beckham, Francis Bugg, John Faldo and Edward Cockson always had a common stock of charges ready to be drawn up at any moment.[147] Wherever Fox went there was smoke and even smoldering embers ready to be fanned into flame. However the common stock of charges used on such occasions cannot simply be dismissed as groundless accusation on the part of vindictive opponents. Fox and his own followers repeatedly used the exalted language of celestial inhabitation and Fox was repeatedly the recipient of the kind of adoration that came with his own large claims for himself. Holme, for example, was paying homage to Fox as the highest revelation of Christ on earth. Only James Nayler was the recipient of similar worship and adoration. It is one thing to use language that displays the deepest respect for a person. It is quite another thing to say that a person in his glorified state will "rule the nations and establish his kingdom in peace" or to say that the glorified person is the second appearance of Christ!

Quakers were not being merely salutary when they used exalted language towards Fox. His doctrine of celestial inhabitation informed their thinking. Celestial inhabitation divinized the inner body and raised Fox and his fellow Quakers to a glorified status that prompted them to speak to each other as 'gods' and treat Fox as the greatest revelation of the divine among them. The exalted language of celestial inhabitation was not excessive emotionalism or immaturity and it was more than salutary language. It was the natural, indeed the only, reasonable language of divinized creatures. It

---

[147]The same list of charges and the same letters kept re-appearing over and over again - that Fox said he was equal with God, that he was Christ, that he was the light of the world, that he was the Son of God, that he was pre-existent and that he was in the state of Adam before before the Fall [see, for example, Cockson, *Quakerism Dissected*; Bugg, *Battering Rams Against New Rome* (London, 1690), pp. 28-29 and *New Rome Arraigned* (London, 1693), pp. 5-6].

was the language of a new view of God and God's work in history. By seventeenth century orthodox standards it was blasphemous language. Opponents of early Quakerism sincerely believed that Fox's notion of celestial inhabitation demonstrated deep disrespect for God. To believe that Christ sensibly dwelt in the creature was simply blasphemous. Quakers, on the other hand, thought it equally blasphemous to disembody the Spirit and imprison Christ in a distant heaven. Two different views of God were clashing. In fact, neither intended disrespect toward God and yet each, in the controversialist context of the age, used the cudgel of blasphemy to berate and demean the other.

What must it feel like to have the glorified body of Christ inside you? The idea, if it can be grasped, helps to explain the large claims of Fox and the exalted language of his followers. The mere fact that as Kings and Queens in a higher kingdom (realized on earth in their own day) Quakers saw themselves as above the law and greater than any earthly authority helps to explain why the authorities saw them as such a threat to the established order. Celestial inhabitation also helps to explain the Nayler incident and the subsequent necessary de-divinization of the inner light and the disembodying of the Spirit in the 1670's, to be discussed in a later chapter.

The fact that Fox did not deter the worshipful attitude towards him further confirms the case for his avatarial role and status in the movement. The Quaker Robert Rich testified that this was exactly how Fox was treated by his followers:

> when James Nayler and several others went down upon their knees before G.F. to confess, etc., etc. (and diverse have reported that were eyewitnesses) and what myself have seen at John Kilkams at Balby, a woman fall down before G.F. near an hour's time (he never so much as reproving her;) and is not this to worship men, which is idolatry: and when Solomon Eccles cryed up G.F. to be god, and not a man, whether this were not blasphemy against God, and to worship the creature more than the Creator, blessed for ever, Amen. And how can you believe

aright that thus seek and receive honour of one another and not the honor which comes from God alone.[148]

The doctrine of celestial inhabitation confused a good many people who did not comprehend the early Quaker teaching that distinguished between the earthly creature and the glorified inner being that had literally become the very Christ. This was understandable. Rich, however, was not being consistent in his accusations for he worshipped the Christ in Nayler in exactly the same way. Nonetheless his stinging indictment of Fox betrayed the glaring weakness in Fox's doctrine of celestial inhabitation - it lead to an all too prevalent tendency to confuse the creature and the glorified inner being of the believer. Fox and most early Quakers did not formulate a view of God that was based on the symbols and metaphors of their more educated opponents. The doctrine of celestial inhabitation, if correctly understood, was an alternative view of God, in a sense a more reasonable view of God, because it strove to close the yawning chasm between God and creation by divinizing the saints.

If Quakers had not stood so close to 'modernity' the notion of celestial inhabitation may have withstood the test of time and heavy persecution. As it was the very notion that Fox was a 'god' and was worshipped as such was rooted in a doctrine that Quakers were forced to rigorously extirpate from the sources. And with good reason. It has always been a potentially embarrassing topic for Quakers since their slow re-entry into the pale of respectable English non-conformity. The best example of this persistent thorn-in-the-side was the Beaconite Controversy in the 1830's when Fox's old claim to divine sonship was dredged up and used by Quakers against Quakers.[149]

---

[148]"A Letter From Robert Rich to George Fox", in Rich, *Hidden Things Brought to Light*, p. 40. This is the John Killam referred to by Fox in his *Journal* (*Cambridge Journal*), 1, p. 353.

[149]The heart of the controversy lay in a clash of views over ways of interpreting Scripture and the location of final authority. Those who followed the traditional Quaker understanding of that time tended to put more emphasis on the immediacy of the Spirit (the disembodied Spirit, not the inner Christ). The more extreme Evangelical Quakers, fresh from battles with American Hicksite Quietists, vigorously opposed the final authority of the inner light and upheld the literal authority of Scripture [for a discussion of the background of the

There are interpreters of Fox's thought who tend to argue that such approaches to Fox's christology are overdrawn. They simply accept, uncritically, the results of the Lancaster Sessions. Norman Penney, commenting on Fox's use of the term 'the Son of God' wrote, "probably more has been read into these words than they were ever intended to convey. It must be remembered that Fox's mind was not trained in accurate theological expression".[150] How could Fox have lacked theological accuracy after a decade of intense theological disputation with the leading Puritans of his day, including Baxter, Bunyan and Owen? A close reading of his answers to his opponents in the *Great Mystery of the Great Whore* quickly dispels the myth. It does not necessarily follow that if one is trained in sophisticated theological expression one would not hold to such a belief as celestial inhabitation although it would be more difficult, as Penn and Barclay discovered. But Fox knew exactly what he believed and he made no

---

controversy and the controversy itself *see* Elbert Russell, *The History of Quakerism* (Richmond, Indiana: Friends United Press, 1979), pp. 280-98 and 343-56. First published in 1942]. It was this latter group, and particularly Elisha Bates, who discovered Fox's letter to Cromwell and various examples of exalted language used towards Fox by early Quakers. He paraded this material publicly as an example of the danger of the doctrine of the primacy of the inner light. Here was George Fox, the very founder of Quakerism, proclaiming himself to be the Son of God. Fox's letter to Cromwell even found its way into the Preface of Bates' *Appeal to the Society of Friends* with the wry comment that "this piece, altogether, shows a disordered imagination, which I conceive is the only apology I can make for it" (Elisha Bates, *An Appeal to the Society of Friends*, p. 14. *See also* pp. 13, 19-22). Bates deserves the credit for being the first Quaker to attempt a return to the original manuscripts that were at Devonshire House. He uncovered, and made accessible to Friends, material on miracles and exalted language that had remained hidden from view for a century and a half [In relation to the Beaconite Controversy and further Quaker questioning of the use of exalted language towards Fox *see* J. Wilkinson, *Quakerism Examined: In a Reply to a Letter of Samuel Tuke* (London, 1836)]. Bates and other like-minded Friends in the 1830's understood the implications of Fox's exalted claims (even if they didn't fully understand his doctrine of celestial inhabitation) and they used it as an example of the excesses of the doctrine of the primacy of the inner light and immediate revelation. Bates' opponents were thoroughly dismayed by his public flaunting of these controversial and embarrassing aspects of Fox's message. He was soon excommunicated from the Society both for his divisive spirit and for receiving water baptism [*see* D.G. Good, "Elisha Bates and the Beaconite Controversy", *QH*, 73 (1984), pp. 38-39, 44]. Celestial inhabitation is a thorny issue. If it was a central doctrinal belief of early Quakers then it denies Quakers, above all else, a place within the pale of orthodoxy. Fox never sought that goal. Penn and Barclay did. Bates was excommunicated.

[150]*Cambridge Journal*, 1, p. 425.

apologies for it. The difficulties occur when celestial inhabitation is fitted into an orthodox christology, something Fox never intended.

Penney added, commenting on Fox's use of the phrase 'Son of God' that Fox may have had in mind Romans 8:14 - "As many as are led by the Spirit of God, they are the sons of God". He was partially correct but that approach simply glosses over the implications of Fox's doctrine of celestial inhabitation. One instance where the allusion to the Romans passage clearly lay behind Fox's description of himself as the Son of God, occurred in the 1660 letter to Charles II where Fox had already begun a subtle withdrawal from his earlier exalted claims, a direct result of the Nayler incident. The Romans text was used so self-consciously there that one cannot presume, as Penney did, that it implied the import of the other bolder usages. Geoffrey Nuttall also interpreted the exalted claims as the result of a "faulty psychology" that led to extravagance.[151] It was an exaggeration of the central Quaker belief that the Holy Spirit was in every person. Pneumatic theology informed Nuttall's entire interpretation of early Quakerism: however, it was not the disembodied third person of the Trinity but the exalted Christ that dwelt in the believer and that fact alone changes the entire complexion of early Quakerism and our understanding of it.[152] Even Braithwaite's allowing that Fox's doctrine of the inner Christ is "open to misconstruction" given the "first exhilaration of the experience of the indwelling Christ"[153] is inadequate given the evidence that has been presented here. The adoration of Fox did not disappear with the first flush of emotionalism. Even after Penn and Barclay disembodied the Spirit and thus de-divinized the inner light Fox never personally altered his theology. After the Nayler incident he struggled for years to arrive at a new and more acceptable 'formula' that would preserve his status and pre-eminence in the movement, but his authority and leadership were always based on the claim to be a living theophany. It had to

---

[151]Nuttall, *Studies in Christian Enthusiasm*, p. 88.

[152]Nuttall, *Holy Spirit in Puritan Faith and Experience*, pp. 181-84.

[153]Braithwaite, *Beginnings*, p. 109.

be and this becomes increasingly clear in the following discussion of his leadership conflict with James Nayler.

PART 2

THE UNMAKING OF A GOD

5

EMBARRASSMENT

Nayler's bid for the leadership of Quakerism by using bold messianic claims hurt Fox very badly.[1] The fallout cast an ominous shadow over Quakerism and cost Fox momentum, power, prestige and possibly even his divinity. The incident itself has been subject to certain patent anachronisms in the historical literature - Nayler was "deluded" and his mind "distorted"; his spiritual enthusiasm tended towards ranterism; his followers were disparaged as simple or credulous; Parliament was bigoted, or the whole event was a fanatic jester's caper that belonged on the fringes of early Quakerism.[2]

On one level Fox's claims for himself dictated the choreography of the debate over leadership. Nayler had to claim literal identity with Jesus in order to advance on Fox's own exalted claims. More broadly, and beneath

---

[1]Christopher Hill has stressed the rivalry between Fox and Nayler (*World Turned Upside Down*, pp. 231-32, 248-58).

[2]That Nayler was a deluded man was a common theme in the contemporary historical literature. Hume thought that Nayler's attempt to groom himself so that he would resemble common pictures of Jesus was a certain sign of his madness and delusion (Hume, *The History of England*, 5, p.523). *See also* W.C. Abbott, *The Protectorate, 1655-58*, vol. 4 of *The Writings and Speeches of Oliver Cromwell* (New York: Russell and Russell, 1947), p. 351; E. Brockbank, "Letter from Richard Hubberthorne Concerning George Fox and James Nayler," *JFHS*, 26 (1929), p. 12 and Geoffrey Nuttall, *Studies in Christian Enthusiasm*, p. 69ff. Kenneth Carroll pushes the event to the radical fringes of Quakerism ("Martha Simmonds, A Quaker Enigma," *JFHS*, 53 (1972), pp. 31-52). The most recent treatment of Nayler is Bittle, *James Nayler, see* p. 95.

138

this first level, lay the provocative doctrine of the celestial flesh inhabiting the believer, for potentially the inner Christ could be protean, that is, it could take any shape. The potentially protean quality of the doctrine of celestial inhabitation was as dangerous as Fox's own exalted claims.

Critics outside the movement were aware of the growing contention between Nayler and Fox throughout 1656 although they were not always explicit about its nature.[3] Nor were the rumblings peculiar to Nayler. Not every Quaker accepted Fox's exalted claims and autocratic control over the movement. And opponents of Quakerism likened Fox to a pope[4] and his preachers to bishops. Margaret Fell was said to consider him as infallible.[5] And Robert Rich accused Fox of contradicting his own principles with his practice of seeking dominion over others, and specifically James Nayler.[6] One incident in particular illustrated this point and additionally showed that the Nayler claim was not unique and *sui generis* but *sprang from a context* - the context of Fox's claims and the necessity of combating these claims with even larger claims if one was to challenge him for leadership.

In mid-1652 James Milner and his wife became convinced Quakers. In November of that year they reportedly "ran-out" from the Truth. Since we know so little of Milner from Quaker writers it is difficult to determine what his crime was but an anti-Quaker document by John Gilpin provides a curious list of twelve prophecies given by Milner between Nov. 14-16, 1652. Most notable among these prophecies was that he must suffer as Christ did; that Nov. 15 would be the Day of Judgment, the last day of the Old Creation and Nov. 16 would be the first day of the new Creation; that he was Adam and his wife was Eve and that George Fox was John the Baptist and he (James Milner) was the one to come after, whose shoe latchet Fox was not

---

[3]Edward Burrough in *Many Strong Reasons Confounded* (London, 1657), p. 15 replied to Richard Baxter's charge that "They are already in divisions among themselves, as the contention between Nayler and Fox, and their followers doth show."

[4]Mad-Tom, *Twenty Quaking Queries* (London, 1659).

[5]E. Fogelklou, *James Nayler: The Rebel Saint, 1618-1660* (London: Ernst Benn, 1933), p. 148.

[6]Rich, *Hidden Things Brought to Light*, p. 40.

worthy to unloose.[7] Milner's claim to usurp Fox may have been his ultimate crime, even though he had no great following, like Nayler, made no great stir and presented no real threat to Fox. Milner and his wife later repented of their crime[8] but the incident itself is a key to understanding the dynamic in early Quakerism - the tension between immanent and imminent, external eschatology so apparent in Fox's thought and the ferment caused by Fox's exalted claims for himself. The incident is important because it illustrates that Nayler was not an anomaly in early Quakerism and he emerged out of a double-layered context: that of Fox's own extravagant language, and the broader context of an evocative heavenly flesh theology.[9]

There is more, then, to the contention between Fox and Nayler than has been provided in the interpretive literature. Their dispute was waged through the language and symbolism of messiahship, which, it is suggested, was the necessary discourse for power in early Quakerism. Messiahship was the charismatic and epistemological symbolism used to maintain, or, in Nayler's case, usurp leadership in order to become the ideological head of the saints of the new age.

---

[7]John Gilpin, *The Prophecies and Other Passages of James Milner, a Tailor* in *The Quakers Shaken* (London, 1653), pp. 18-19. FRL-tract volume No. 533.

[8]Margaret Fell, *False Prophets, Antichrists, Deceivers, Which are in the World* (London, 1655), pp. 12-14.

[9]Carroll suggested that the Milner's behaviour was due to the fact that they were "young in the Truth" ["A Look at James Milner and his "False Prophecy"," *QH*, 74 (1985), p. 23]. This was true at one level but not when Milner's actions are interpreted in the larger context of Fox's exalted claims. We have already seen that Quaker exegetes explained these incidents as immaturity in the faith, "prophetic blunder" (*Ibid.*, p. 25), an incomplete view of Christ that led to excesses which in turn provoked charges of blasphemy or "delusion" (Barbour, "Quaker Prophetesses," p. 47). According to Carroll although Milner "probably never actually claimed to be the Christ, he undoubtedly spoke words which led others to believe that he was making such a claim" (*Ibid.*, p. 25). Why, given the climate of early Quakerism, could Milner not have made such an exalted claim? Given Fox's own claims, for example, and later those of Nayler, Gilpin was not exaggerating. The signs, symbols and metaphors which early Quakers literally appropriated from Fox and applied to their own religious experience help to explain, rather than excuse Milner's actions. The error may have been less the exalted claims and more the attempt to usurp Fox's role of pre-eminence in the movement. For Fox's view *see* Cambridge Journal, 1, p. 107.

James Nayler, who was six years Fox's senior, was the most prominent Quaker leader in London in the mid-1650's.[10] An ex-soldier who had supported the cause of Parliament[11] he left the army after a sickness and becoming somewhat disillusioned with Cromwell's betrayal of the 'Good Old Cause'. His dramatic call from behind the plough reminds one of Elisha or Amos. He never credited Fox with his conversion but claimed, instead, to be one of the many seeking spirits who arrived at his views independently. He was, however, one of the many seeking spirits whom Fox succeeded in gathering to his cause in the early 1650's. He was present with Fox and the Fells at Swarthmoor from the beginning.

There were indications that Fox became uncomfortable with Nayler's high place of authority among Quakers in London, where he had worked alongside Francis Howgill and Edward Burrough since June, 1655. In July, 1655 the two left London temporarily and Nayler became the chief spokesman for the movement there. In May, 1656 an uneasy Fox asked Nayler to leave London and return to Yorkshire to attend to some pressing

---

[10]Richard Baxter called Nayler the "chief leader" of the Quakers before Penn [*Reliquiae Baxterianae* (London: T. Parkhurst, 1696), Part 1, p. 77]. This may have been an attempt to discredit the movement. Baxter doesn't mention Fox at all. Fox was seldom in London during the 1650's and 1660's and therefore he did not command the high profile that Nayler did. The 'outside' perception of who the leader of Quakerism was may not have been self-evident, but it is still surprising Baxter never once mentioned Fox. Nayler's popularity and reputation, especially after his celebrated blasphemy trial, is beyond dispute. Within a year of his messianic ride into Bristol all Europe knew of Nayler and virtually nothing of Fox. In the German work *Quaker Greuel* Nayler is called the King of the Quakers [*Quaker Greuel* (Hamburg, 1702)].

[11]Nayler joined the Parliamentary Army in 1652. While in the Army he became an Independent and a preacher. One officer said "I was struck with more terror by the preaching of James Nayler than I was at the battle of Dunbar", a testament to Nayler's charismatic preaching abilities. He returned home to Yorkshire on sick leave in 1650 and there joined the local Congregationalist church. He became a Quaker during a visit Fox made to the Wakefield area in 1651. His Congregationalist church then expelled him on gossipy charges of adultery with a Mrs. Roper. This gossip eventually turned up in the report to Parliament during the blasphemy trial. *See* John Deacon, *The Grand Imposter Examined, or, the Life, Trial, and Examination of James Nayler* in *The Harleian Miscellany: A Collection of Scarce, Curious, and Entertaining Pamphlets and Tracts ... Selected From the Library of Edward Harley, Second Earl of Oxford*, 10 vols. (London, 1810), VI, pp. 429-30 and L. Stephen and S. Lee (eds.), *The Dictionary of National Biography*, 14 (London: Humphrey Milford, From 1917), pp. 130-33.

matters. Nayler was convinced that his place was in London but he reluctantly obeyed Fox, only to return to London as quickly as he could "still having", said Braithwaite, "the full confidence of his friends."[12] Upon his return he came under the influence of (or was reunited with) a small group of Quaker zealots led by Martha Simmonds,[13] a Quaker minister in London who was openly seeking to discredit Fox as leader of the movement, preferring instead to magnify Nayler whom she and her followers believed would soon be revealed as Jesus the Messiah.[14] Fox later called them "Ranters" and "loose persons" who came after Nayler.[15]

Martha Simmonds emerged as the real 'power-broker' in this struggle. Even though early Quakerism made radical claims for the equality of women in the Church, women were still only allowed to speak under direct impulse

---

[12]Braithwaite, *Beginnings*, p. 244. Also described in Bittle, *James Nayler*, pp. 83-84.

[13]She belonged to a prominent Quaker family in London and was a nurse to Cromwell's sister (Mack, "Women as Prophets During the English Civil War," p. 30). Her brother, Giles Calvert, was the leading printer of early Quaker pamphlets, including two of Martha's (Carroll, "Martha Simmonds, a Quaker Enigma," p. 31). She had, by her own account, spent many years searching for an "honest minister" and once groaned in great turmoil "When shall I see the day of thy appearance?" To this question, she said, it was slowly revealed to her that there was a measure of God in her and that by attending to that measure it would increase over time [Martha Simmonds, *A Lamentation For the Lost Sheep of the House of Israel* (London, 1656), pp. 4-5]. From the beginning her career as a Quaker had been characterized by the ecstatic. In 1655 she walked through London in sackcloth and ashes. She had an extensive itinerant ministry throughout the cities of England, during which time she prophesied of impending judgement, great tribulation and of the urgency of repentance for the Kingdom of God was at hand (*Ibid.*, pp. 2-3 and *When the Lord Jesus Came to Jerusalem*, pp. 5-6, appended as a separate tract at the end of *A Lamentation*). She did adopt Fox's doctrine that Christ had come to reign in his saints but her emphasis on imminent eschatology, a physical as well as a spiritual return of the Messiah, her charismatic excesses and her public disputation with leading male elders all brought her into disrepute among London Quakers [Martha Simmonds, *O England, Thy Time is Come* (London, 1656), pp. 1-5, to which is appended some postcripts of a prophetic nature by individuals who may have been part of a small conventicle of Quaker prophets and prophetesses].

[14]Deacon, *The Grand Imposter*, pp. 431-33.

[15]*Cambridge Journal*, 2, p. 314. Braithwaite and Carroll perpetuated the view that Nayler, overworked and "ensnared by trifles, vanities, and persons," was "drawn away from the Light and into darkness" (Braithwaite, *Beginnings*, pp. 243-44 and Carroll, "Martha Simmonds, a Quaker Enigma," p. 38).

of the spirit (ie. as prophetesses).[16] They were not allowed to engage men in reasoning or disputation. Martha Simmonds, however, did choose to engage both Howgill and Burrough in public dispute, probably on the topic of her favourite subject - eschatology. Her teaching called for an actual physical return of Jesus as Messiah to inaugurate the new age.[17] There was a drift here towards an external eschatology that must have worried Fox. She had already prospered to the point that she had gained a small following. But when she attempted to dispute with Howgill and Burrough, and even disrupt their meetings, she was severely reprimanded. She then turned to Nayler for a just and equitable hearing but Nayler "judged her, and told her that she sought to have the dominion and told her to go home and follow her calling."[18]

Unable to receive a hearing through rational argument she confronted Nayler with moaning and weeping and in a shrill and passionate voice cried out "How are the mighty men fallen, I came to Jerusalem and behold a cry and behold an oppression."[19] At this point, she said, her words, "pierced and struck [Nayler] down ... and he lay from that day in exceeding sorrow for about three days, and all the while the power arose in me, which I did not expect ... But after three days he came to me and confessed I had been clear in service to the Lord, and that he had wronged me."[20] Nayler lay trancelike

---

[16]Traditionally, in both Catholic and Protestant traditions, exegetes interpreted Paul's statement forbidding women to speak as a prohibition against teaching, especially in the ministerial role. Women were allowed to prophesy in the assembly.

[17]Deacon, *The Grand Imposter*, p. 431. Simmonds refocused Quaker eschatology away from its immanent nature towards an externalized, imminent appearance of the Messiah. She was in fact closer to the Fifth Monarchists and she tried to persuade Nayler to adopt this eschatology. She tainted Fox's eschatology by making it appear more 'orthodox' and this enabled her to work out her struggle for leadership in the movement in terms of messiahship. As a women she was unable to lead the movement but she was still able to pursue her goals through Nayler.

[18]"Richard Hubberthorne to Margaret Fell" (July 26, 1656), *Caton MSS.*, 3, pp. 364-65.

[19]R. Farmer, *Satan Enthroned in his Chair of Pestilence* (London, 1657), pp. 10-11.

[20]*Ibid.*, pp. 10-11.

upon a table in Simmond's home for that three days, trembling night and day.[21] Through her ecstatic behaviour Simmonds succeeded in gaining a hearing from the Quaker leader that she would otherwise have been denied. Hubberthorne concluded that "an exceedingly filthy spirit is got up in her, more filthy than any that yet departed out of the truth, and with it labours to break and destroy the meetings."[22] This "spirit" to which Hubberthorne referred was a divisive spirit that sought glory and dominion in the movement.

The episode, and what followed, has generally been treated as a sign of weakness on Nayler's part. His trancelike behaviour, it is said, exemplified a flaw in his character.[23] This shallow, late Victorian judgment fails to understand the mood of the seventeenth century. Moments of indecision were not necessarily moments of weakness. Neither Cromwell nor Fox were weak yet both were deliberately hesitant when great decisions had to be made. Cromwell often hesitated to wait upon Providence and Fox would enter deep trancelike states while seeking the leading of God. In his trance Nayler may be interpreted not as weak but as transparently receptive to the divine impulse. He was in a stage of preparedness, gathering strength for what he defined as the "suffering" that lay ahead.[24] It may also have been a way to find rest after prodigious troubles, labours and stress, and rest to summon the emotional energy and courage - sheer courage - for the next step. A trance, then, can be a way of focusing oneself intensely, like an

[21]"Hubberthorne to Fell", *Caton MSS.*, 3, p. 365.

[22]*Ibid.*, 3, p. 365.

[23]Fogelklou, *James Nayler*, p. 149. This interpretation that fear and doubt clouded his understanding and resulted in a loss of judgement first appeared among his contemporaries, like Hubberthorne. It was an obvious attempt to excuse his actions. Subsequent interpreters, beside Fogelklou, have uncritically accepted this view [M.R. Brailsford, *A Quaker From Cromwell's Army: James Nayler* (New York: Macmillan, 1927), p. 98 and Carroll, "Martha Simmonds, a Quaker Enigma," p. 41]. In later years, in hindsight, a regretful Nayler accepted this view. He said that during this time he lost his Guide and entered into a "Darkness". He let go of his guiding inner light and allowed himself to be "wholly ... led by others, whose work was then wholly to divide me from the Children of Light" (Nayler, *Works*, p. xlii). This was a statement from hindsight and did not annul his earlier endorsement of Simmonds.

[24]"Thomas Rawlinson to Margaret Fell" (June 23, 1656), *Swarth. MSS.*, 3, p. 12.

athlete before competition. In this sense it enabled Nayler to prepare, to cope and to replenish his spirit for the task of 'freeing' the world and leading it into a new age of peace, justice and equality.

Nayler's response to Simmond's ecstatic behaviour and his own trance did not occur in a vacuum. Many things had been weighing heavily upon his mind throughout 1656 and he was clearly in a state of spiritual crisis that was foreshadowed in several of his writings. He was severely tested by Jeremiah Ives, a Baptist minister of considerable controversial skills. In three public debates held at the Bull and Mouth, an inn turned Quaker meeting place in London, Ives assailed the credibility of Nayler's call to the ministry and he asked for a sign to prove that calling. He accepted none of Nayler's "proofs" (that he had been called from behind the plough like a prophet of old; that he had left family and home for the Lord) and his persistent refusal to listen to Nayler until he could prove his calling by working miracles was a source of great anxiety for Nayler. They finally exchanged pamphlets, each giving their own account of the disputations. In his pamphlet, *Weakness Above Wickedness*, Nayler accused Ives of being "worse than any that ever disputed with the Apostles". Why would Ives not put his faith on trial by Scripture rather than call for a miracle?[25] Nayler, who had performed no miracle to this point, was left groping for proof of his calling and his subsequent raising of a Quaker from the dead may be interpreted as a partial attempt to establish proof of his calling and confirm his status as a magus alongside Fox.

Nayler was not only groping for proof of his miraculous calling at this time. He also believed that he was being called to perform some kind of sign enactment that would rivet a stubborn and unbelieving world's attention on the fact that Christ had come and was in the process of judging the world.

---

[25]Jeremiah Ives, *The Quakers Quaking* (London, 1656), pp. 9-10 and *Innocency Above Impudency* (London, 1656), pp. 8-9. Nayler, *Weakness Above Wickedness ... an Answer to a Book Called "Quakers Quaking" ... by Jeremiah Ives* (London, 1656), pp. 17-18. Ives also challenged Nayler to confirm his calling by speaking with tongues like the Apostles and to perform a specific sign to prove that he was the messiah (Ives, *Quakers Quaking*, p. 10). These were revealing charges that suggest that Nayler was at least implying he had the same spirit and power as the Apostles. Later some of his followers would even claim to be above the Apostles. Certainly Nayler's inability to prove his calling was a matter that weighed heavily on his mind at the time he succumbed to Martha Simmonds.

This was a foreshadowing of his messianic ride into Bristol. In a prophetic postscript to one of Martha Simmonds apocalyptic tracts Nayler wrote: "In the days of my affliction, how have I roared from morning till night! Then did I seek death, but could not find it ... A sign and wonder thou hast made me ... Thou hast lifted me up, and I have been exalted; thou hast cast me down, and I have been despised."[26] This was like a premonition of what was to occur later in 1656 when Nayler made his exalted messianic ride into Bristol and then suffered his humiliating trial, punishment and imprisonment. In 1660 Nayler said that he had been made a sign to an evil generation that refused to see that Christ had come. The fact that the world was not hearing what Quakers were saying about Christ's return sorely distressed Nayler and seemed to throw him into times of deep despair and affliction which, he said in retrospect, made him vulnerable to abuse and manipulation by those around him.[27]

Nayler was also living in a state of heightened eschatological consciousness, primed by Martha Simmonds. Simmonds had been busy stoking the fires of eschatological excitement among Quakers in London at least since 1655, when she published a tract entitled *When the Lord Jesus Came*. This was followed by two more eschatologically oriented tracts in 1656, the year that Christ's coming was widely believed to occur.[28] Fox

[26]Simmonds, *O England*, p. 12.

[27]James Nayler and Richard Hubberthorne, *A Short Answer to a Book Called the Fanatick History* (London, 1660), p. 3.

[28]For those who were interested in numeric calculations, like Peter Sterry, the 1656 years between the birth of Jesus and the events of mid-17th century England corresponded to the 1656 years between creation and the Noachite Flood. One Quaker, Francis Ellington, did attach apocalyptic significance to the year 1666 - the number of the beast plus one thousand and the sum of the Roman numerals MDCLXVI (found on the title page of *A Christian Information Concerning These Last Times*). The Fifth Monarchy Men also looked for Christ's coming in 1666 (Ellwood, *Journal*, 1, p. 436). Most Quakers, however, were not given to this kind of prophetic calculation. But they would still have been influenced by the millenarian excitement of the time [*see* C. Hill, *Antichrist in Seventeenth Century England* (London: Oxford University Press, 1971), pp. 114-15]. There is some evidence that Quakers at that time gave some apocalyptic significance to the conversion of the Jews, for which reason a concerted effort was made to convert the Dutch Jews who were expected to be readmitted into England at any time [*See* R.H. Popkin, "Spinoza's Relations With the Quakers in Amsterdam," *QH*, 73 (1984), pp. 14-28]. Numerous pamphlets were written to the Jews in order to help facilitate

himself wrote, "The Baptists and Fifth-Monarchy Men prophesied that this year Christ should come and reign upon the earth a thousand years."[29] While Fox and most Quakers refrained from such speculation (their doctrine of immanence and their proclamation that Christ had already come rendered such speculation unnecessary) the idea of a physical coming was a particularly active force in Simmonds' small group which, as 1656 proceeded, came to believe that Nayler was the incarnation of Jesus. At the time of his trance this idea was not yet fully formed but he was increasingly receptive to the idea that he, and not Fox, had pre-eminence in the movement and this fact can only have added to the inner turmoil and stress that he was already experiencing.

Friends soon became concerned by what they perceived was Martha Simmonds' control over Nayler. Hubberthorne said that she had been filled by a "filthy spirit". William Dewsbury accused her of "sorcery" and others said that she had "bewitched" Nayler.[30] Phyllis Mack suggested that these leading Quakers entertained the possibility that the charismatic preaching of a woman, which always exposed the woman to the "danger of being taken as a witch", "had opened him to the sin of pride, which in turn made him vulnerable to invasion by evil spirits and finally caused him to commit a heretical act."[31] These accusations did nothing to deter Simmonds. She continued to disrupt meetings and engage in public debates with other Quaker leaders like Richard Hubberthorne. At one particular meeting Hubberthorne recorded that while Friends remained in silence she "fell on singing, with an unclean spirit. And the substance of that which she said in

their conversion. Quakers used Hebrew throughout their writings, Fox included. Some Quaker pamphlets were even translated into Hebrew. Cadbury said that the Quaker interest in the Jews coincided with a 1655 visit to England of the very learned Rabbi of Amsterdam, Mannaseh ben Israel, to whom Margaret Fell later addressed correspondence. He was especially noted for his interest in messianic prophecy and his belief in the imminence of the coming of the messiah occasioned a spate of Quaker tracts designed to prove to the Jews that the messiah had already come (*See* Cadbury, "Hebraica and the Jews in Early Quaker Interest," pp. 156-8).

[29]Nickalls, *Journal*, p. 261. Compare with Ellwood, *Journal*, 1, p. 287.

[30]Letter by William Dewsbury, *Markey MSS.*, p. 123.

[31]Mack, "Women as Prophets," p. 31.

her singing was, Innocency, innocency, many times over, for the space of one hour or more." Hubberthorne confronted her but this only made her more ecstatic and she took up singing again, saying "that we were all the beast, and [Hubberthorne] was the head of the beast."[32] Quaker leaders from all quarters began to condemn her. Burrough wrote to her that she was "out of the way, out of the power, out of the wisdom, and out of the life of God ... though some of you have prophesied in the name of Christ yet now are you workers of iniquity."[33] Dewsbury accused her of departing from the counsel of the Lord and using sorcery to abuse Quakerism.[34]

Nayler remained in his trance and spoke to no one. Friends finally kidnapped him from Simmonds' house and took him to Bristol.[35] All the while Nayler remained silent, even in the Bristol Meetings. Simmonds and her friends followed Nayler to Bristol and continued to disrupt meetings there. At one point she found Nayler and knelt at his feet, during which time he remained "silent and apathetic, but the sweat began to trickle down his forehead."[36] Quakers then tried to prevent her from seeing Nayler by hiding him in a Friend's house. When she discovered the house and tried to enter she claimed they treated her abusively and threw her down a flight of stairs, something George Bishop denied since, he said, there were no stairs at that particular house.[37]

News of the incident soon reached Fox who was, at that time, imprisoned at Launceston. He requested an immediate conference with Nayler, the consensus being that only Fox could remedy the situation and restore the wayward Nayler who was now threatening the unity of the

[32]"Hubberthorne to Fell", *Caton MSS.*, 3, pp. 366-67.

[33]Letter by Edward Burrough, *Markey MSS.*, pp. 120-22.

[34]Letter by William Dewsbury, *Markey MSS.*, p. 123.

[35]Farmer, *Satan Enthroned*, p. 11.

[36]Described by Fogelklou, *James Nayler*, p. 155.

[37]Farmer, *Satan Enthroned*, p. 11; George Bishop, *The Throne of Truth Exalted Over the Power of Darkness* (London, 1657), pp. 29-30.

movement. Fox told Friends to "be quiet" about the dissension in their ranks and work to get "dominion over it".[38] Nayler was to be taken to Fox as quickly as possible. On August 1, 1656, a small party of Friends set out for the journey from Bristol to Launceston. Nayler remained silent throughout the journey and at one point wept exceedingly. But the small party never reached Fox. Authorities had ordered the arrest of all Quakers travelling the Devonshire roads and a mere three miles from their destination Nayler and his party were arrested and imprisoned at Exeter. Here the silent Nayler, under great mental stress, began an immediate fast.

While he was imprisoned at Exeter Nayler seems to have reached the conclusion, under great duress, that God had manifested himself in a special way in the flesh of James Nayler.[39] The claim was not any more dramatic than Fox's own exalted claims but Nayler's careless resolve to openly challenge Fox by using messianic images not only created a serious leadership crisis but it scandalized Friends and led Quakerism into a credibility crisis from which it never fully recovered, short of retreat and major theological transformation.

Nayler's so-called "fall" or "spiritual collapse"[40] created a tumult in Quaker ranks, illustrated by the large amount of correspondence passed between Friends closest to the situation during this time.[41] Margaret Fell wrote to Thomas Rawlinson, "I have heard something which hath made my

[38]*Ibid.*, p. 114.

[39]The parliamentarian, Mr. Downing, made the statement at Nayler's trial that it was blasphemy to believe that "God came down in the flesh, at Exeter, in James Nayler" (Burton, *Diary*, 1, p. 60).

[40]Luella Wright interpreted Nayler's actions during this time as a "fall" and this was certainly how his peers interpreted it as well [L. Wright, *The Literary Life of the Early Friends, 1650-1725* (New York: Columbia University press, 1932), p. 48]. *See also* Nuttall, *Studies in Christian Enthusiasm*, p. 77 and Carroll, "Martha Simmonds, a Quaker Enigma," p. 45.

[41]Fox wrote a pastoral letter to Friends encouraging them to keep the incident to themselves and not make much of it. He bluntly told Nayler that he had betrayed the "Son of God" to the powers of darkness. And not only had he separated himself from Friends but he drew others after him. Some Quakers were led into doubt and despair. Thomas Salthouse confessed that "This business about J.N. hath made a great tumult in the minds of many weak Friends" ["Thomas Salthouse to Margaret Fell" (January 30, 1657) in Barclay, *Letters*, p. 228].

heart to ache."[42] Rawlinson magnanimously replied, "Believe not every spirit
... and believe not every report ... James saw this thing long before it came
and thou knowest he wrote to thee of it that there must be a suffering."[43] It
is not clear what this suffering was. Some Quakers interpreted God's
command to them to act as a sign to the world as a great suffering. That, for
example, was how William Simpson wrote of his call to go naked.[44] In some
cases such suffering even took on the dimensions of being an epiphany.
When Thomas Holme was beaten for going naked through Chester he
interpreted his sufferings as bearing the iniquity of the city. Fox, too, gave
the impression of bearing the sins of the world in his own suffering. Nayler
was going through a similar experience. He believed that God was calling
him to be a sign to an unbelieving world that Christ had come. And this sign,
according to his followers, was an actual epiphany whereby Nayler, by
following the path of the sufferings of Jesus, would be revealed as Jesus
himself.[45] Part of Nayler's sign enactment included allowing himself to be
exalted as Jesus.[46] According to Rawlinson's letter to Margaret Fell Nayler
had not kept his struggle over his special calling to act out this sign as a
suffering Lamb secretive.   Whether Margaret Fell, or any Quaker,
understood the full implications of Nayler's crisis at the time is not clear.
What is clear is that as time went on Nayler's sign became an actual claim to
'messiahship'.

Even Fox was not convinced that what Nayler was advocating was
theologically wrong. Rawlinson said to Margaret Fell, "George ... makes not
much of it and he bade that no Friends should be discouraged; he said the

[42]In Bishop, *The Throne of Truth Exalted*, p. 26.

[43]"Rawlinson to Fell," *Swarth. MSS.*, 3, p. 12.

[44]Simpson, *Going Naked, a Sign*, pp. 7-8.

[45]Deacon, *The Grand Imposter*, pp. 428-31.

[46]Later, during his celebrated blasphemy trial Nayler said he allowed his followers to
exalt him in such a manner because "I was commanded by the power of the Lord to suffer such
things to be done to me ... as a sign" [Thomas Burton, *The Diary of Thomas Burton*, edited by
John T. Rutt (London, 1828), p. 11. On the authorship of this *Diary see* S.C. Lomas, "The
Authorship of Burton's Diary," *Atheneum*, No. 3808 (Oct. 20, 1900), pp. 513-14].

wrong in them [Nayler and his followers] was got above and James Nayler had lost his dominion, but there was something in it."[47] Had Nayler lost his dominion because he committed the sin of coveting power and dominion, of coveting Fox's position as Milner had before him? If so there was still something to be redeemed in Nayler's actions - namely the idea of the divine in man. Fox never fought with Nayler over that issue. He only confronted Nayler on the issue of Nayler's stubborn refusal to submit to the authority of Fox and other Friends.[48] Theologically Nayler's claims to divinity were not challenged. Instead he was chastised for not acting in accordance with certain undefined rules of protocol that exalted Fox as 'first among equals'. No movement can be led by two avatars who claim prophetic pre-eminence.

While Nayler was in prison Martha Simmonds and her group wrote letters to him encouraging him to assume the mantle of leadership since he was "the most perfect in the movement".[49] God may have been present in everyone but "a double portion of that Spirit" was in Nayler. Martha Simmonds said: "There is a seed born in him which I shall honour above all men."[50] He was also encouraged in this way by three fellow prisoners who belonged to this group and were among those arrested as Nayler's travelling companions en route to Launceston. One was Dorcas Erbury, daughter of the famous Seeker, William Erbury. She apparently fell into a deep trance and her fellow prisoners believed she had died. Nayler came and touched her and in a replay of St. Peter's own great miracle said "Dorcas arise" at

---

[47]"Howgill and Audland to Burrough", *Barclay MSS.*, No. 114.

[48]It might be said that it was not a struggle for leadership since Nayler, while under the influence of Martha Simmonds, was not accepted by any major Quaker group as a "leader". Most of the Friends with whom he came into contact, tried to rescue him from the "evil spirits" (Simmonds and her supporters) who had "run out from the Truth". In answer, the discernment of "good spirits" from "evil spirits" was a rhetorical devise Fox and leading Quakers used to denounce all challenges to their movement from without or within. But Nayler was a major Quaker leader and Simmonds controlled a prophetic Quaker group in London. Nayler's challenge was doomed to fail given the fact he had no numerical support. Nonetheless his attempt to lead the saints of the new age was considered possible through divine intervention.

[49]Bittle, *James Nayler*, p. 95.

[50]Carroll, "Martha Simmonds, a Quaker Enigma," pp. 45-46.

which point she arose.[51] It was subsequently widely believed that Nayler had raised Dorcas Erbury from the dead. Nayler later denied performing the miracle[52] but at the same time it served a useful purpose (and perhaps at the time he really did believe he had performed it) - it confirmed his miraculous 'calling'. The issue here was not the truth of the miracle but its effects. It became a powerful sign that confirmed Nayler's status as the Son of God. Fox never performed such a miracle and Nayler clearly outstripped him as a magus in this respect. In addition it was the sign that his small band of followers had been waiting for. Hannah Stranger later said that the miracle proved to her that Nayler really was the Son of God.[53]

Meanwhile Martha Simmonds and her followers kept up their agitation. They travelled to Launceston where a very revealing confrontation occurred between them and Fox.[54] Fox recorded the incident:

> [she] bid me bow down and said I was Lord, and King, and that my heart was rotten, and she said, she denied that which was the head in me, and one of them said, she had stopped Francis Howgill's mouth and silenced him, and turned my word into a lie, and into a temptation, and she came singing in my face, inventing words, and Hannah [Stranger] boasted, and said, if they was [sic] devils make them to tremble, and she boasted what she would do, and cry against.[55]

---

[51]Deacon, *The Grand Imposter*, pp. 430, 433.

[52]James Nayler, *Glory to God Almighty Who Ruleth in the Heavens* (London, No Date), p. 3.

[53]Deacon, *The Grand Imposter Examined*, p. 427.

[54]Martha Simmonds had been nursing Major General Desborough's wife (Cromwell's daughter) during this time and through Desborough she received an order granting Nayler's release. It was *en route* to Nayler that she visited Fox in Launceston, a clear attempt to seize the moment by discrediting Fox's leadership while exalting her man.

[55]"George Fox to James Nayler" (1656), *Swarth. MSS.*, 3, No. 193. *See also* Bishop, *Throne of Truth Exalted*, p. 6.

Simmonds also believed and wrote that Fox "must come down out of his wisdom and subtlety".[56] For this Fox judged Simmonds to have an unclean spirit, an assessment he based on the way she exalted herself over him.[57]

This incident deeply wounded Fox and he harboured it as a bitter memory until his dying day. He also incorrectly believed that Nayler had put Simmonds up to it. Simmonds, in fact, had acted on her own in her attempt to dethrone Fox and exalt Nayler. The language used in this confrontation was focused on the issue of authority and leadership. Fox had accused Nayler of treachery for seeking the leadership of the movement. Now Simmonds was accusing Fox of exalting himself as the leader of the movement.

Simmonds then went on to Exeter where Richard Hubberthorne had been softening Nayler and slowly encouraging him to return to and make amends with Friends. But when Simmonds arrived, wrote Hubberthorne, she "called [Nayler] away and he was [made] subject to her." It would seem she needed Nayler to further her own apocalyptic crusade.[58]

Fox was released from Launceston on Sept. 9, 1656. On Sept. 20 he travelled to Exeter to see Nayler. It was at this time that a permanent falling out occurred between the two. That evening Fox and Hubberthorne met with Nayler whom Fox had already determined "was out and wrong and so was his company".[59] Fox and his companion, Hubberthorne, had but one mission - to secure Nayler's submission. Two things weighed heavily upon Fox during this time - Nayler and his cohorts were making a bad example of Friends[60] and Fox, who had been warring with the world for so long, was now

---

[56]"Richard Hubberthorne to Margaret Fell" (July 16, 1656), *Swarth. MSS.*, 3, No. 153.

[57]*Ibid.*, 3, No. 153.

[58]*See* Carroll, "Martha Simmonds, a Quaker Enigma," pp. 43ff.

[59]Nickalls, *Journal*, p. 268.

[60]Fox had written to Nayler at Exeter, "Thou hast satisfied the world, yea their desires which they looked for" (Bishop, *Throne of Truth Exalted*, p. 6). Fox wanted to keep Friends above all reproach in the eyes of the world - their unity and purity was always paramount in his mind. Nayler cast a shadow of suspicion over the movement at a time when it could least

warring with a divisive spirit among Friends. Fox always discussed challenges to his authority in the language of spiritual warfare. It enhanced his own leadership claims. The whole dialogue with Nayler was largely, but not exclusively (there was an important disagreement over eschatology and the meaning of the arrival of the Kingdom of God), over the practical matter of leadership and maintaining a public image of unity and integrity.

On Sept. 21, following a visit with Fox outside the prison, Richard Hubberthorne returned to the prison with Nayler and tried to convince him to disown the "filthy spirits" around him.[61] After a vicious exchange between Hubberthorne and these "filthy spirits" Fox arrived and called out to Nayler several times. Nayler refused to reply at which point Fox left the prison while Hubberthorne remained behind to continue the dialogue. At this time he encouraged Nayler to "see whom he was subject to and whom he rejected" and more significantly, "whom he should be subject to."[62] Hubberthorne had accompanied Nayler back to the prison to determine exactly where Nayler's loyalties lay - with Fox or the 'filthy spirits'. Both Fox and Hubberthorne were seeking Nayler's subjection not only in the best interests of the movement but because Fox, the self-proclaimed Son of God, was the single source of undisputed authority in the movement.

The next day Fox and Nayler met again outside the prison. At this time the first public breach occurred between the two. Some of Fox's remarks suggested that he believed certain unfavourable reports about Nayler. This prompted Nayler to hurl insults at Fox in public[63] which

---

afford any further ridicule and persecution. That was literally an unforgivable "sin" according to Fox and he never did privately forgive Nayler for it. Fox expected Quakers to adhere to his own strict sense of decorum, especially as it impinged on the unity of the movement.

[61]"Richard Hubberthorne to Margaret Fell" (October, 1656), *Gibson MSS.*, 5, p. 93. This important letter was a full report on events. It was reprinted by E. Brockbank, "Letter From Richard Hubberthorne Concerning George Fox and James Nayler," *JFHS*, 26 (1929), pp. 13-15.

[62]*Gibson MSS.*, 5, p. 93.

[63]This was not the only time Nayler was prompted to react angrily to Fox's unfounded charges. During his examination on charges of blasphemy before the Bristol magistracy he was asked why he called Martha Simmonds his mother "as George Fox affirms".

distressed Fox even more for now his authority was publicly challenged and the movement was seen to be in a state of division. For years Fox had preached unity as a major characteristic of the true people of God while schism and division was characteristic of the apostate church. Now that division had occurred in his own movement Fox had no other recourse than to portray Nayler as an evil spirit sent to disrupt the work of God and the growth of His Kingdom, while maintaining his own dominion by challenging Nayler through the discourse of messianic language. This would become clear in the final confrontation between the two.

Fox's last visit to Nayler was one of the most dramatic scenes in Quaker history. Fox approached the prison chamber Nayler and his companions occupied. They were, at that time, in a lower and much darker part of the chamber and Fox stood above them. He berated Nayler for his conduct in the street the previous day. Nayler wept and professed great love for Fox. Then,

> [he] offered Geo. an apple and said if I have favour in thy sight receive it: but he denied it and said if thou art moved of the Lord to give me it: James said would thou have me to lie. Then James having Geo. by the hand he offered him if he might kiss him, Geo. standing above the low place would have drawn Jas. out to him but he would not come out: but Geo. standing still would not bow down to him at his asking of him in this thing which if he had come out he would have suffered him to have done it. Then Geo. gave him his hand to kiss but he would not and then Geo. said unto him it is my foot.[64]

This discourse is full of hidden symbolism which suggests that the two men were posturing to solicit the submission of the one to the other. Many attempts have been made to interpret the 'hidden meaning' here, from contemporaries of Fox and Nayler to the present. What was undeniably at issue was Fox's unquestioned authority.[65] Fox's affront is not to be dismissed

---

Nayler replied "George Fox is a liar and a firebrand of hell; for neither I, nor any with me, called her so" (Deacon, *The Grand Imposter*, p. 430).

[64]"Hubberthorne to Fell", *Gibson MSS.*, 5, p. 93.

[65]Bittle made this point and said: "In a movement that placed so much stress on the basic equality of the individual ... it is difficult to imagine any action on Fox's part which would have wounded Nayler as deeply" (*James Nayler*, p. 99).

as a "half-humorous gesture", as Brockbank said,[66] nor is Fox to be exonerated because it was out of character for him to be party to personal homage, as Monaghan has said.[67] These interpretations excused Fox while turning a blind eye to the real context of the bitter struggle for leadership.

The very language of the dispute sets the context. Nayler's version, through Robert Rich (a London clothier and follower of Nayler) was that Fox came to Nayler that day to accuse and condemn. He also tempted Nayler with fair speeches and promises if he would bow down to him. Nayler remained silent and when Fox, thinking Nayler was ready to submit, gave him his hand to kiss Nayler refused. A hurt Fox then retorted that he should have given Nayler his foot to kiss instead.[68] Fox himself wrote, twenty years later, that Nayler was "dark and much out", "resisting the power of God in me" and thus "the Lord God moved me to slight him and to set the power of God over him."[69] Fox, rather than bowing down to Nayler to receive the apple or the kiss, stood in authority over him by setting the power of God over him. The final act of giving Nayler his foot to kiss was his final affront of Nayler and everything he stood for. Both men were locked in a struggle for leadership and both were soliciting homage one from the other. Nayler was trying to get Fox to bow before him by offering him the apple or by asking him to bend to kiss him.[70] When Fox refused Nayler broke down in weeping and Fox,

---

[66]Brockbank, "Letter from Richard Hubberthorne Concerning George Fox and James Nayler," p. 11.

[67]Instead Monaghan said that Fox spoke in symbols to Nayler. "Symbolically a foot is the power of grasping of understanding God's ideas." Nayler lacked understanding and this is what Fox meant - "Kiss me not, but the foot of understanding" (*"Dear George"*, p. 129). Another writer even suggested that this was all due to a bad temper on the part of Fox, or a genuine personality clash. All that was accomplished was that Nayler was turned "again towards his extravagant practices" (A. Blunden, "James Nayler," *Quaker Monthly*, 64 (1985), p. 224.

[68]Rich, *Hidden Things Brought to Light*, p. 37.

[69]Nickalls, *Journal*, p. 269.

[70]Fogelklou said that the kiss simply came at the wrong time for Fox. He believed that Nayler was wrong and a kiss at this time would have been a "Judas kiss". The two were "out of step" (*James Nayler*, p. 170).

sensing a moment of weakness, tried to draw Nayler up at which point Nayler could have kissed him. Nayler, keenly aware of what was at stake, refused. Fox then scorned Nayler by giving him his foot to kiss. He then hardened his heart and left the prison. He later justified his action by saying he did it at the "Lord's command".

What remains to be emphasized is the specific 'messianic' discourse of the incident. Hubberthorne encouraged Nayler to see "whom he should be subject to". Fox said that Nayler was "resisting the power of God in me". In two letters written by Fox after he left Exeter he accused Nayler of already having deceit in his heart when he would have kissed Fox "the innocent". In one of those letters, which reached Margaret Fell, through Hubberthorne, Fox said that Nayler had "caused the truth, the right way, to be evil spoken of."[71] Bittle said "the identification of George Fox with 'truth' in the letter is unmistakable."[72] On the other hand Fox called Nayler a "false Christ" and added, "James, thou separates thyself from Friends and draws a company after thee, and separated from the power of the Lord God, yet truth followed thee and bowed down under thee to recover thee. And you strike against it."[73] Fox, the truth, was not admitting that he bowed down to Nayler, only that he tried to overcome the evil in Nayler and redeem Nayler and his followers from the "cloud of darkness" that had risen up and betrayed him, the lamb.[74]

Margaret Fell's response to the matter, contained in a private letter to Nayler, confirmed the messianic nature of the discourse as a means through which authority and leadership was obtained and maintained in early Quakerism. Nayler had already written to her saying that Fox was trying to

---

[71]"George Fox to James Nayler" (September, 1656), *Fox Portfolio 24*, No. 36 at FRL.

[72]Bittle, *James Nayler*, p. 100.

[73]"Fox to Nayler", *Fox Portfolio 24*, No. 36.

[74]'Lamb' was a term Margaret Fell used to describe George Fox ("Margaret Fell to George Fox", *Spence MSS.*, 3, No. 24). Nor was it uncommon for Fox to attach such terms of divinity to himself. Robert Rich was still calling Nayler "the Lamb" in 1658 (*Hidden Things Brought to Light*, pp. 43-44).

bury him in order to raise his own name.[75] Fell then responded that it was Fox who should be exalted and Nayler who should unequivocally submit to Fox's will: "Since I have heard that thou would not be subject to him to whom all nations shall bow, it hath grieved my spirit."[76] Nayler was to cease his rebellion and subject himself to "Him who hath given him [Fox] a name better than every name, to which every knee must bow."[77] This piece of evidence which attributed messianic characteristics to Fox used language that was as dangerous as any used by Nayler's followers of him. All Quakers, indeed all nations and peoples, were to be subject to Fox who had been exalted by God and chosen by God to reveal the coming of the Kingdom and who had a greater measure of Christ to be subject to than any other creature. According to Margaret Fell George Fox's stature as the Son of God was greater than that of any other creature.

Nayler's followers, on the other hand, continued to exalt him as Margaret Fell exalted Fox. Both men had powerful women backers. Hannah Stranger called Nayler the "fairest of ten thousand" and the "only begotten Son of God". In language reminiscent of Fell's language towards Fox she wrote: "Oh, thou fairest of ten thousand, thou only begotten Son of God, how my heart panteth after thee. O stay me with flaggons [vessels used to hold wine], and comfort me with wine. My beloved, thou art like a roe, or young hart, upon the mountains of spices, where thy beloved spouse hath long been calling thee to come away."[78] In another letter she said: "All the wise men shall seek for him, and when they have found him, they shall open their ears, and shall give unto him of their gold, frankincense, and myrrh." Another member of this group, Richard Fairman, wrote to Nayler from Dorchester Prison: "I am filled with joy and rejoicing when I behold thee in the eternal unity. O my soul is melting within me, when I behold thy beauty and innocency, dear and precious son of Zion, whose mother is a virgin, and

[75]"Margaret Fell to James Nayler", *Spence MSS.*, 3, No. 38.

[76]*Ibid.*, 3, No. 38.

[77]*Ibid.*, 3, No. 38.

[78]Deacon, *The Grand Imposter*, p. 427.

158

whose birth is immortal."[79] These statements recall similar exalted language used towards George Fox. John Stranger, Hannah Stranger's husband, simply confirmed the others' certain belief that Nayler was Jesus reincarnate by writing to Nayler, "Thy name is no longer to be called James but Jesus."[80] In the minds of his followers Nayler had been transformed into Jesus. Nayler's followers even carried a copy of an apocryphal letter sent to the Roman Senate by Publius Lentulus, president of Judea under Tiberius Caesar.[81] The letter contained a description of Jesus' physical appearance which was transposed onto Nayler. His followers claimed he looked identical to Jesus. Others drew an analogy between Nayler's initials, J.N., and those of Jesus of Nazareth, also J.N.[82] Historians dismiss that information as silly, absurd or fatuous behaviour but it was a key ingredient in the struggle with Fox on the symbolic level. If it could be proved in this way that Nayler was Christ, then Fox could be deposed. At best Fox would have been rendered to subordinate status and this most likely would have split the movement.

The claim that Nayler looked identical to Jesus was a critical assertion in the dispute. It is a measure of their misunderstanding that some historians have seen this as lugubrious. Given Fox's own christological language and the exalted language of Margaret Fell this was the necessary language of the dispute. If Nayler and Martha Simmonds were to effectively challenge Fox's dominion then Nayler himself had to be exalted in even more specific and lofty terms - Nayler's very flesh and blood was transformed into that of the

---

[79]These last two quotes are from a Broadside published by the authority of Parliament and entitled *A Brief Account of James Nayler, the Quaker* and located in William Cobbett, *Cobbett's Parliamentary History of England*, 3 (London: R. Bagshaw), p. 1490.

[80]Deacon, *The Grand Imposter*, pp. 427-28. Nayler said of this latter statement: "that letter sent to me at Exeter by John Stranger ... this I judge to be written from the imaginations, and a fear struck me when I first saw it, so I put it in my pocket (close) not intending any should see it, which they finding on me spread it abroad, which the simplicity of my heart never owned." He acknowledged the titles Son of God and even Christ as they were applied to the Christ in him, not to James Nayler after the flesh (Nayler, *Glory to God Almighty Who Ruleth in the Heavens*, p. 1).

[81]Cobbett, *State Trials*, 5, p. 806.

[82]*See* Thomas Moore, *An Antidote Against the Spreading Infections of the Spirit of Antichrist* (London, 1655), p. 36.

historical Jesus himself,[83] an illustration of the protean quality of Fox's own doctrine of celestial inhabitation.

Fearing that Nayler would try to enhance and strengthen his position Fox immediately began to consolidate his support. Upon leaving Exeter Fox held a series of meetings throughout Somersetshire, Wiltshire and in Bristol. Daily meetings were held in London. A general meeting of leaders was convened in Cornwall in the Fall of 1656 after which Francis Howgill declared that everything was in order and Nayler and his group would miss their expectations.[84] Fox had emerged as the undisputed leader of Quakerism, at least for the time being. Nayler was accused of setting up the whole incident in his own interests, out of "prejudice and jealousy" and he was described as a "rebellious spirit whose bid for the leadership had finally been suppressed."[85]

Nayler, now the 'outcast' to all but a few loyal followers, had not completed his sign enactment and bid for the leadership of the movement when Fox left Exeter. Upon his release from prison he staged one more dramatic act which recalled the New Testament epiphany of Jesus' entry into Jerusalem. To his followers this was to be a final sign and proof not only of Nayler's messianic stature but of the fact that the Messiah had finally returned. Nayler and about six of his followers set out and moved from town to town seeking disciples to participate with them in the sign enactment.[86] It seemed the group was attempting to gather as large a following of saints as

---

[83]The fact that the language for this discourse was drawn directly from Fox has been briefly mentioned in the historical literature from time to time. In the *Dictionary of National Biography* we find these words: "To Fox, in his early career, was addressed language as exalted as any that was offered to Nayler. With very little encouragement Margaret Fell would have gone as far as Hannah Stranger. But Fox brought this tendency under control and subdued it, while Nayler was its dupe" (*DNB*, p. 133). And Omerod Greenwood wrote: "What made George hard was seeing in James a distorted reflection of himself; for if James had a woman follower who wrote to him 'thy name shall be no more James Nayler but Jesus', George had a woman follower ... who ... had written ... "O thou fountain of eternal life ... in thee alone is life and peace"" ["Letter from a Friend," *Quaker Monthly*, 51 (1972), pp. 79-80].

[84]"Francis Howgill to Margaret Fell" (August 21, 1656), *Etting MSS.*, p. 33.

[85]"Hubberthorne to Fell", *Gibson MSS.*, 5, p. 93.

[86]"Howgill to Fell," *Etting MSS.*, p. 33.

160

possible in preparation for the imminent eschatological transformation that was about to take place. Nayler's own transformation into Jesus, his followers believed, was the sign confirming this universal transformation.

The party set off in the general direction of London, which was believed to be the site of the revelation of the New Jerusalem. But then a disagreement occurred between Martha Simmonds and her husband as to the exact place of the New Jerusalem. Thomas Simmonds believed it was London and Nayler (whose name was now 'Jesus') was targeted as the sign of this dramatic eschatological occurrence. London would also have been the logical place to establish Nayler's leadership of the movement. However, Martha Simmonds, for reasons of her own, overruled her husband and directed the group towards Bristol. Thomas Simmonds then left the group and later testified that his wife was wrongly inspired. She directed the group herself, he suggested, when one would have thought that in the presence of glory (ie. of Nayler who was by now the Messiah) she would have remained silent and worshipful before him and let him lead the way.[87]

---

[87]In *Satan Enthroned* Ralph Farmer included the text of an actual letter sent from Thomas Simmonds to his wife after the split: "Had you stood in the wisdom and counsel of the Lord ... then the Lord would have brought you safe to this city [London], where he would have manifested his mighty power among us. Now thus it was, and I know it is so with you, you being all joined in love, when you wait on the Lord, there is a great power among you, and then when any thing arises in any particular as to speak or act which many times arises from the earthly dark principle, to this you all join although you see it not ... And hence comes all your cumber and trumpery without; which my soul was grieved to see it ... which the Lord delivered me from ... and he was with me in my journey and brought me in peace to this place, and warned me in the night at Exeter, not to return by Bristol, but to go the straight way to London ... and my love was to thee, none else did I see, which made me think thou was coming along towards London, surely thou wast the chief leader in that action. If there was such a glory amongst you, why were you not silent, and have let the people cry Hosanna. Oh how is dark night come upon the Prophets and those who once were honourable and glorious, are now fallen ... because they were in prosperity and the Lord honoured them, they forgot the Lord; therefore hath he darkened their understanding ..." (Farmer, *Satan Enthroned*, pp. 20-21). Thomas Simmonds attributed the ultimate failure of their sign enactment to their wayward desires and failure to listen to and be led by the glory in their midst - ie. Nayler the Messiah. The 'Prophets' whom he referred to is a curious term for which we have no further knowledge. Carroll speculated that Martha Simmonds belonged to a "band" of prophets ("Martha Simmonds, a Quaker Enigma," p. 46 n.2). More precisely, she and her followers were probably part of a highly charismatic group within early Quakerism that used prophecy as a guide and a confirmation in all matters of life and faith. Nayler's followers were also known to speak in other tongues.

As the small group moved from town to town other Quakers monitored their activities. Howgill reported to Margaret Fell that they were not getting disciples or adding to their small number. At one point they even met Fox and "judged him .. and boasted what J.N. would do." Howgill added,

> Truly my dear J.N. is bad, ... and there is such filthy things acted there in such havoc and spoil and such madness among them as I cannot write, but there is about 10 of them in all with him, and they call him "I am" and the "Lamb", and they are bringing him to the city; they have made the truth stink in these parts, and truly my dear G.F. bore it so long ... and he sees he suffered it too long now.[88]

Howgill was in Bristol at the time, where Fox still had strong support. By Howgill's account Nayler's sin was that of causing a public scandal within Quaker ranks. Howgill was apparently offended by the public declaration of calling Nayler "I am" (the name of God in the Torah) and the "Lamb" (the name of Christ in John's *Apocalypse*). Nayler's followers were seen to go too far in scandalizing Quakers by using exalted language before a public that was unable to accept what appeared to the orthodox as blasphemy. Privately, as has been shown, Quakers including Howgill were not beyond using exalted

---

[88]"Howgill to Fell", *Etting MSS.*, p. 33. Nayler was accused of immorality during this journey and these charges also found their way into the court records. Specifically, the night before Nayler entered Bristol he took a chamber in Bedminster where he was accused of staying alone with three women of his company. He was apparently found the next morning in bed with one of them. While the insinuations of immorality were no more than pernicious slander Nayler's intimacy with his group did not make it difficult to imagine that such things were occurring. While awaiting trial before Parliament he was seen sitting breast to breast with Martha Simmonds and she was heard to ask him "to go with her" to which he replied "he was not free" (Cobbett, *State Trials*, 5, p. 803 and Burton, *Diary*, pp. 10-11). Because of these scenes, which were all too common throughout this time, Nayler was vulnerable to charges of immorality and ranterism. The 'enthusiasm' of Nayler's followers was one of the untrained forces at work in early Quakerism. He constantly allowed his followers to touch him, kiss him, lie prostrate before him, and worship him. Certainly, elements of ranterism cannot be ruled out among Nayler's followers but Nayler himself categorically denied all charges of immorality. "I am clear before God," he said, "God is my record" (Nayler, *Glory to God Almighty Who Ruleth in the Heavens*, p. 3). Concerning the charges of immorality against Nayler *see* John Deacon, *An Exact History of the Life of James Nayler*, p. 32 and Richard Blome, *The Fanatick History: or, an Exact Relation and Account of the Old Anabaptists and New Quakers* (London, 1660), p. 108. Nayler answered Blome in *A Short Answer to a Book Called The Fanatick History* (London, 1660), p. 4.

162

language towards Fox. Fox was called "Son of God", "god of life and power", "the first and the last" and "the second appearance of him who is blessed forever". Were these statements any less excessive that those used towards Nayler? Had these private statements been public knowledge at the time they, too, would have scandalized Friends.

By October 23 a definite sign was taking shape within the Nayler group. Nayler rode on a horse and the women went before him, sometimes spreading their garments in his path. They approached Bristol in particularly foul weather. One witness, George Witherly, said they walked along a horse and cart path up to their knees in mud. Some walked ahead, some alongside and some behind Nayler singing, "Holy, holy, holy, Lord God of Israel". At times their singing was a "buzzing melodious noise" that was not readily understandable, possibly a form of singing in other tongues. They continued in this fashion through the streets of Bristol until they were stopped and arrested by the authorities.[89]

The entire group (which consisted of Martha Simmonds, Hannah Stranger and possibly her husband John Stranger, Timothy Wedlock, Robert Crabb, Samuel Cater and Dorcas Erbury - the latter three being Nayler's fellow prisoners at Exeter)[90] was committed to Newgate Prison, despite a

---

[89]Deacon, *The Grand Imposter*, p. 426. Other reports of this event may be found in Cobbett, *State Trials*, 5, p. 806; *A Brief Account of James Nayler, The Quaker*, pp. 1489-90; "George Bishop to Margaret Fell" (October 22, 1656), *Swarth. MSS.*, 1, No. 188; George Bishop, *Throne of Truth Exalted*, pp. 4-5 and Grigge, *The Quakers Jesus: or, the Unswaddling of that Child James Nailor* (London, 1658), pp. 3-4. By Fox's directions not one of the thousand Bristol Friends was to participate in the affair. Bristol Friends were to remain aloof from the whole affair. According to Bishop's report only one Friend was on hand to protest (*See also DNB*, pp. 131-32). Fogelklou's interpretation of this was that "the whole sign passed off like a farce". She portrayed Nayler as a helpless pawn who "lacked the power to put a resolute stop to the whole performance. He could not help himself. He was far away in some strange land" (*James Nayler*, p. 186). Furthermore, there was no precedent for this in Nayler's life. Never before had he performed a sign. It was totally out of character for him. The interpretation given in the body of this study suggests the opposite. Nayler knew what he was doing and consented to be used as a sign in this manner to achieve his own goals.

[90]George Bishop's report of the incident included John Stranger although he was not included in Deacon's report. Timothy Wedlock is the Thomas Woodcock referred to in Cobbett, *State Trials*, 5, p. 806. There was also a June Woodcock who was accused of calling Nayler the "Prophet of the most High" (*Ibid.*, p. 809).

pass they had allegedly received from Oliver Cromwell.[91]   Their imprisonment was based on the content of certain letters found on the person of Nayler - letters which contained sufficient evidence to detain the group on charges of blasphemy. Fox could be grateful that Margaret Fell's letter to Nayler in which she refered to Fox as "him to whom all nations should bow" was not found in Nayler's personal effects. The reason it was not found was that George Bishop intercepted it, opened it, and because of its contents, withheld it and kept it private "lest it should be taken".[92] This was sufficient evidence that as early as 1656 Quakers were concealing incriminating evidence about their leader.

The day following their apprehension the group was examined by a committee consisting of the Bristol Magistracy and certain clergy led by John Deacon, William Grigge and Ralph Farmer.[93]   Nayler was asked several times throughout the examination whether he was the Son of God. Each time he replied affirmatively.   When asked if his name was Jesus he remained silent. When asked if he considered himself 'sent' by God to a measure greater than others he replied "I have nothing at present given me of my Father to answer." When the letters from his followers were produced he did not deny the names that had been attributed to him - "fairest of ten thousand", "Prophet of the most High", "King of Israel",[94] "Everlasting Son of Righteousness", "Prince of Peace", "Son of God", "Holy One of Israel", "Son of Righteousnes", and "Jesus" - but he denied that this was blasphemy because

---

[91]"Bishop to Fell", *Swarth. MSS.*, 1, No. 188.

[92]*Ibid.*, p. 188. One of the letters found on Nayler was a letter written to him by Fox while he was imprisoned at Exeter. Nayler, after reading it had wept and declared that in several things he was wrong (*Etting MSS.*, p. 30).

[93]Deacon, Farmer and Grigge later wrote their versions of this examination and the later trial before Parliament. Quaker versions come from sundry letters contained in Quaker manuscript collections.

[94]Martha Simmonds said that Nayler had been annointed "King of Israel" by a prophet whom she refused to identify (Farmer, *Satan Enthroned*, p. 16). For an extensive list of these titles see Cobbett, *State Trials*, 5, pp. 808-13 and *A Brief Account of James Nayler, the Quaker*, pp. 1489-90.

"what is received of the Lord is truth" and the Spirit of the Lord moved and commanded them.[95]

Martha Simmonds, John and Hannah Stranger, Timothy Wedlock and Dorcas Erbury all testified that they believed Nayler was the 'Son of God'. Simmonds went as far as to say that "James Nayler ... is buried in me, and hath promised to come again."[96] Cater and Crabb testified that they did not believe Nayler was the 'Prince of Peace' but that Christ was ruler in him. On the basis of their testimony Cater and Crabb were released.

Dorcas Erbury's testimony was the most damaging. She said that Nayler was the "Holy One of Israel" and added that she would seal it with her blood. She confirmed that she believed he was the "only begotten Son of God" and "I know of no other Saviour" but Nayler. The questioning then proceeded as follows:

Q. Dost thou believe in James Nayler?
A. Yea, in him whom thou callest so, I do.
Q. By what dost thou use to call him?
A. The Son of God: but I am to serve him,
 and to call him Lord and Master.
Q. Jesus was crucified; but this man,
 you call the Son of God, is alive.
A. He hath shook off his carnal body.
Q. Why, what body hath he then?
A. Say not the Scriptures, thy natural body
 I will change, and it shall be spiritual?

---

[95]Deacon, *The Grand Imposter*, pp. 428-30.

[96]*Ibid.*, p. 431. In this revealing statement Simmonds appeared to be combining Fox's theology of immanence (Nayler who was Christ was in her) while at the same time he was being revealed externally as a sign of the imminent Kingdom. In a sense Martha Simmonds and Nayler were on very different tracks, theologically. Simmonds and her group believed that Nayler was Jesus reincarnate. Nayler never believed that of himself, always making the distinction between James Nayler the creature and the Christ within him. This was very well explained by Nayler in his pamphlet, *Satan's Design Discovered* (London, 1655). While he never altered his belief in that distinction (one that was adhered to by Fox as well) he did nothing to deter his followers from worshipping him as the Messiah, falling down before him, kissing his feet, attributing to him the attributes and titles of Christ - which all strongly suggested that he allowed their actions in order to enhance his claim to leadership. While under guard in Bristol, for example, he had visits from one of his followers, Sarah Blackberry, who repeatedly knelt before him. Many of the women whom Nayler attracted were from the lower orders, while many of the women whom Fox attracted (ie. while in prison at Carlisle and Derby) were aristocratic.

Q. Hath a spirit flesh and bones?
A. His flesh and bones are new.

Notice the intimation of celestial flesh in this last line. Erbury had captured the real essence of their belief - there was a distinction between the creature and Christ but somehow Nayler's natural, carnal body had been transformed into a new, transfigured body - the body of Jesus and Nayler's followers even believed that it looked identical to Jesus.[97] This was a real gloss on Fox. Fox, too, claimed to be the Son of God and even a new revelation of the inner Christ, but he never claimed to be Jesus. Jesus had died while the pre-existent Christ who dwelt in him and empowered him for his special mission had lived on in his saints. Nayler's followers adapted Fox's theology to suit their own purposes. Martha Simmonds' "external" eschatology was admirably suited to the new claim that Nayler was more than a new mode of revelation of the pre-existent Christ - he was the historical messiah come again, a radical alteration of Fox's eschatology which emphasized the celestial presence of the pre-existent body of Christ.

Armed with this evidence the Bristol Magistracy put together the most damning case possible against Nayler. They concluded that "James Nayler did assume the gesture, words, honour, worship and miracles of our blessed Saviour, [and] the names and incommunicable attributes and titles of our blessed Saviour."[98] Nayler now became an effective tool in the city's ongoing battle against Quakers. The Bristol Magistracy had long tried to suppress Quakers but failed due to a lack of Commonwealth laws governing the suppression of sectarianism. They had been challenged on this very point by John and Hannah Stranger. They did not believe that they had broken any law of the land. Now the city decided to capitalize on the Nayler case by

---

[97]Deacon, *The Grand Imposter*, p. 433. Another version is in Grigge, *The Quakers Jesus*, pp. 10-11. All this evidence prompted Farmer to write, "if those high testimonies of those infallible saints ... be true, James is as good, yea, better than ... [George Fox]" (*Satan Enthroned*, p. 31). This was precisely the point of the whole dispute.

[98]Cobbett, *State Trials*, 5, p. 805 and *A Brief Account of James Nayler, the Quaker*, p. 1490 which stated that "this deceiver had so far gained upon his followers by his impostures, that they ascribed to him divine honours, and gave him in Scripture phrase the same titles which are applicable to none but Christ himself." The judgment was later adopted by the Parliamentary Committee (*Memoirs*, p. 20).

passing responsibility for sentencing on to the Second Protectorate Parliament in the hope that Parliament would be provoked into action, not only against Nayler but against all religious dissent.[99]   Nayler, Martha Simmonds, John and Hannah Stranger and Dorcas Erbury were then sent to London.[100]

At this point, as Bittle described, Nayler became part of a larger political struggle over which he had no control. His case became a political and religious *cause célèbre* - a showcase trial that defined the powers of Protector and Parliament as well as the extent of religious liberty contained in the *Instrument of Government*. The case did not belong in Parliament, it belonged in a court of law but circumstance dictated that Nayler was a useful stalling tactic for Parliament in its struggle with Cromwell.[101] Parliament was also in the unique position of being able to enact new and specific legislation to convict a Quaker of blasphemy and opponents of Quakerism, already having failed at Lancaster, may have pressed hard to get the matter into Parliament with the hope that newer and tougher legislation would be enacted against sectarianism.   Nayler, without a powerful protector like Judge Fell became a victim of larger forces who used him and crushed him to achieve their own goals.

On Nov. 16, 1656, a Parliamentary Committee sat in the Painted Chamber[102] and began to prepare the case focusing primarily on the blasphemy charge. The Committee reached a number of resolutions which in every part agreed with the findings of the Bristol examiners.[103] That is,

---

[99]It may have been that the Bristol magistracy believed that Nayler was the Quaker kingpin and by "crushing Nayler they were suppressing Quakerism" (*DNB*, p. 133).

[100]On the way they sang in the towns through which they passed ["George Taylor and Thomas Willan to Margaret Fell" (October 6, 1656), *Swarth. MSS.*, 1, No. 294].

[101]Bittle, *James Nayler*, pp. 111-12, and his excellent discussion, pp. 151-67.

[102]A chamber in the old palace of Westminster, in which in early times Parliament often assembled, and in which the Sovereign sometimes met with the two houses. The walls were painted with a series of battle scenes.

[103]*See Memoires of the Life, Ministry, Trial, and Sufferings of that Very Emminent Person James Nailor, The Quakers Great Apostle* (London, 1719) and Grigge, *The Quakers*

Nayler had accepted from his followers the worship and titles reserved only for Christ. Nayler was asked if he had ever reproved his followers for their actions to which he replied "I never understood that they gave that honour but to God."[104] He denied that worship and honour should be given to him, James Nayler, "but if any were moved to give such things to the appearance of God in him as to a sign of Christ's second coming being revealed in his saints ... he did not judge them for it."[105] No honour was to be given to James Nayler the creature but Nayler did allow his followers to pay homage

---

Jesus, pp. 6-14 for the most complete accounts of the proceedings of this examination and trial. Other full accounts are contained in Burton, *Diary*; Cobbett, *State Trials*; Cobbett, *Parliamentary History of England*; Deacon, *An Exact History of the Life of James Nayler*; Deacon, *The Grand Imposter*; *A True Narrative of the Examination, Trial, and Sufferings of James Naylor* (London, 1657) and Farmer, *Satan Enthroned*. Sundry Quaker letters and pamphlets also refer to the trial although most references to Nayler in Quaker sources were simply left out of the record. C.V. Wedgwood said that the trial was part of a Parliamentary game. In the Fall of 1656 Cromwell had been forced to open his second Parliament in order to secure funding and supplies for his war against Spain. Parliament had its own designs least of which were to attend to Cromwell's needs. The Nayler trial, in Dec., 1656, interrupted business for a full week. As it was the case never should have gone to Parliament but should have remained in the hands of the civil courts where precedent for charging Quakers under the *Blasphemy Act* had already been established. Still, it was a convenient stalling tactic, a message to Cromwell that parliament did not treat his agenda with urgency [C.V. Wedgwood, *Oliver Cromwell* (London: Corgi, 1973), pp. 104-5]. The editor of Neale's *History of the Puritans* also said that the House of Commons was "no court of judicature" and it was illegal for them to pass sentence on Nayler (*History of the Puritans*, 4, p. 143).

[104]Cobbett, *State Trials*, p. 814. During the parliamentary trial it was again mentioned that Nayler failed to rebuke his followers for worshipping him (Burton, *Diary*, 1, pp. 73, 129).

[105]Anthony Pearson and Gervase Benson, *Copies of Nayler's Trial Before Parliament, with George Fox's Exhortation* (1656), in *Swarth. MSS.*, 3, p. 78. While the group was in custody in London Richard Hubberthorne visited Nayler and reported that the women were continuing to act "in imitations and singing" and kneel down before Nayler. Nayler, he said, justified their actions saying that they acted "in innocency" ("Hubberthorne to Fell", *Caton MSS.*, 3, p. 370). The same type of incident was recorded in Cobbett. While in custody Nayler's usual posture was to sit in a chair and his followers would sit or kneel in front of him, singing "Holy, holy to the Almighty" all day long. Martha Simmonds would sing "Behold the King of Righteousness is come". Jesus had come as promised to occupy the throne of David. It was reported and confirmed by Nayler that Sarah Blackberry (who later became a close friend of Richard Hubberthorne) came up to him and said "Rise up, my love, my dove, my fair-one, and come away: Why sittest thou on the pots?" If he was Jesus why would he continue to languish in custody when he could rise up and demonstrate his power to the world? (*State Trials*, 5, pp. 814-15). Nayler said he understood these words to be spoken as they were in the Canticles - of Christ's Church (Burton, *Diary*, 1, p. 48).

to the high measure of Christ in him, as a sign of Christ's second coming in the saints,[106] a position he had consistently maintained. Fox, too, privately allowed exalted language he did not allow his followers to perform the sort of street drama which impersonated Jesus, even though he was not shy about using street drama of his own.

The Committee concluded its examination by asking Nayler if he had anything further to say. He replied,

> I do abhor that any of the honour which is due to God should be given to me, as I am a creature: But it pleased the Lord to set me up as a sign of the coming of the righteous one; and what hath been done in the passing through the towns, I was commanded by the power of the Lord to suffer such things to be done to the outward as a sign. I abhor any honour as a creature.[107]

Here again appeared the notion, by this time an integral part of Quaker dogma, of the distinction between the carnal flesh that was in this instance James Nayler and the heavenly flesh of Christ who inhabited and transformed the believer. Personally, Nayler's views were in line with Fox's own notions of celestial inhabitation. In fact, Nayler had originally helped Fox clarify his views. It is worth repeating that Fox never disputed with Nayler over the celestially-fleshed inner Christ. They seemed to be in agreement here. What abhorred Fox was Nayler's scandalous public conduct and the tendency of his followers to identify him with Jesus. As for Nayler, his idea that his actions were a sign of the coming of Christ recalled what he had written to Margaret Fell that he had seen his suffering long before it came. Nayler knew that he was going to be called to enact some sign that would attract the world to the second appearance of Christ and it was on the

---

[106]In a letter to Margaret Fell reporting on the examination before the committee of Parliament Richard Hubberthorne understood Nayler to deny saying that he (the creature James Nayler) was Christ, but that Christ was in him. This was wholly in keeping with Fox's teaching on celestial inhabitation which led to so many blasphemy trials and in fact made the language of the dispute possible and understandable. Hubberthorne blamed Nayler's situation on "That power of darkness in the women" which sought dominion over him ["Richard Hubberthorne to Margaret Fell" (November, 11, 1656) in Barclay, *Letters*, pp. 45-46].

[107]Cobbett, *State Trials*, p. 815.

basis of this worthy calling that he defended himself before Parliament. The choreography of the sign with all its dramatic posturing and exalted language was to serve this ultimate purpose - to rivet the attention of the world on Christ's appearance.

The Parliamentary Committee prepared reports (which contained the unsubstantiated story of adultery with Mrs. Roper)[108] to present before the House on December 5. The case was then debated over the course of three weeks. Nayler again told the House that the Lord set him up as a sign to the nation of the coming of Christ. He denied his followers worshipped the creature, James Nayler, only the Christ within him.[109] Some in the House felt that Nayler should be tried for blasphemy since they believed Nayler said his outward flesh was God. To make the flesh God, they argued, was to make God visible which was tantamount to "ungodding God" - blasphemy according to the *Act* since it deposed the majesty of God.[110] Others disagreed, saying that Nayler never claimed to be Christ, only that Christ was in him in the highest measure. At one point Lord President Lawrence said,

> I wonder why any man should be so amazed at this. Is not God in every horse, in every stone, in every creature ... Imprudent persons run away with notions, and not being able to distinguish, sad consequences arise ... If you hang every man that says, Christ in you the hope of glory, you will hang a good many ... I do not believe that James Nayler thinks himself to be the only Christ; but that Christ is in him in the highest measure ... It is hard to define what is blasphemy ... but this is to themselves, about the notion of God. This is not to us.[111]

Colonel Sydenham understood well enough that Nayler's position was in fact representative of the Quaker position generally when he said, "If Nayler be a blasphemer, all the generations of them are so, and he and all the rest must

[108] *See Memoires*, p. 18.

[109] Burton, *Diary*, 1, p. 11.

[110] *Ibid.*, 1, pp. 27, 59, 67-68. Some believed that Nayler implied God "came down in the flesh at Exeter, in James Nayler ... [and if so] ... we ought all to go and worship James Nayler" (*Ibid.*, 1, 60, 67-68).

[111] *Ibid.*, 1, pp. 62-63.

undergo the same punishment. The opinions they hold, do border so near a glorious truth, that I cannot pass any judgment that it is blasphemy."[112] Fox himself wrote to Parliament at this time. Did not the Apostles say to the saints that Christ was in them, he asked? This was not a matter to be tried as blasphemy before Parliament. He then gave an overview of Jesus' entry into Jerusalem and his subsequent trial for blasphemy, leaving Parliament to complete the analogy.[113] Fox never denounced Nayler publicly or challenged Nayler's theology. His sign itself was in keeping with Quaker practice and apart from consenting to be called by the name of Jesus - which was the historical name of Christ - his claims were identical with those of Fox, who claimed in his own way, full equality with God. Nayler's actions neither contravened Quaker doctrine nor, by a *strict* interpretation, existing law. Thus, Fox's letter to Parliament appeared to defend Nayler's actions but only to the extent that he was in fact defending himself and his own movement from the charge of blasphemy by extension. Had not Fox himself been similarly charged for blasphemy (calling himself by the name of Christ) and had he not attained leadership of the movement on the basis of similar claims to divine sonship? He was fortunate that Judge Fell succeeded in discrediting all but one of the witnesses against him at Lancaster (whereas Nayler's street drama had many witnesses) and that he was not the one who had to appear before Parliament for his claims, in addition to the adoration from his followers, would almost certainly have been condemned again as they were at Derby in 1650.

---

[112]*Ibid.*, 1, p. 86. As bizarre as Nayler's actions were they were not unique, even outside Quaker ranks. Ranters, Levellers and Diggers were but a few of the many groups and individuals who held to the idea of the indwelling God in some form or other. Even if Nayler purported to be the Messiah he had good company in William Hackett and Lodowick Muggleton. Mary Vanlop also purported to follow a man whom she claimed was the Messiah. In 1561 John Moore said he was Christ and William Jeffery worshipped him for which he was sent to Bedlam (Burton, *Diary*, 1, pp. 72-73).

[113]Robert Rich, William Tomlinson and George Fox, *Copies of Some Few of the Papers Given into the House of Parliament in the Time of James Nayler's Trial There* (London, 1657), p. 6.

Many others petitioned Parliament on behalf of Nayler and religious toleration.[114] They encouraged Parliament not to tamper with the religious freedoms guaranteed in the recent constitution, the *Instrument of Government*. But despite these earnest pleas from tolerant and enlightened people Nayler was found guilty of blasphemy. He was not sentenced to death[115] but his penalty was extremely harsh.[116] During the first part of his

---

[114]Grigge, *The Quakers Jesus*, pp. 15-18.

[115]The argument for punishing Nayler by death for being a blasphemer was abstract and complex, and the subject was debated for a full week in Parliament. As Lord Commissioner Whitelocke pointed out in his 'Opinion' to Parliament there was no law in England to justify Nayler's execution for blasphemy. The *Ordinance* against blasphemy, passed by the Long Parliament "is not now in force" having been superseded by the more moderate *Blasphemy Act*. Some wanted to prove that blasphemy was a heresy and, they said, heresy was punishable by death under the common law. But even that law, said Whitelocke, was open to question. The law referred to was a writ passed by Arundel, Archbishop of Canterbury in the time of Henry IV - *De Haeretico Comburendo*. It was passed specifically for the suppression of the Lollards, whom we now think "were good Christians" said Whitelocke. He argued that this writ was not to be found in the most ancient manuscript registers which were a "true part and demonstration of the common law", and being of a later date and more specific intent it could not be used to condemn Nayler to death. Furthermore, even if heresy was punishable by death under the common law, *lex terrae*, it could not be proved that blasphemy was heresy since "they are offences of a different nature". Heresy was *Crimen Judicii*, an erroneous opinion belonging to the judgement of the courts (ie. refusing to pay tithes). Blasphemy was *Crimen malitiae*, a malicious opinion, this time against God, but which nonetheless, opinion did not belong to the courts. Heresy, Whitelocke continued, was defined by the first four general Councils of the Church and the authority of these Councils was legally established by Justinian. Note the recourse to Roman Law again. There was nothing in these Councils reckoning blasphemy as heresy. For these reasons, he warned, Parliament should be careful in its proceedings against Nayler. Nayler's accusers then tried to prove heresy on Nayler's view of Christ. This done Nayler could be executed if not under common law then under a new bill of Attainder passed by Parliament. Whitelocke warned that such a move would not serve the country well. Why repeat similar questionable judgments made in the days of Edward II and Richard II, or when quick executions of dissidents occurred unnecessarily when Henry issued the *Constitutions of Clarendon* in his dispute with the Pope. Furthermore, why should England imitate other countries where blasphemers were put to death as heretics. And did not Lutherans hold the Ubiquity of Christ (the omnipresence of Christ's body) in such sort that news of Nayler's death would not be pleasing to them? In addition Parliament would do well to learn from the the cases of Wolsey and the Earl of Strafford. To punish by death through subsequent law was a dangerous precedent. Others said a Bill of Attainder would appease the nations that mocked England as the "great nursery of blasphemies and heresies." In the end Nayler barely escaped death by the narrowest margin of 14 votes (*See* Cobbett, *State Trials*, 5, pp. 817, 821-28; Burton, *Diary*, 1, pp. 86 and 128-31).

[116]The full sentence, given on December 17, 1656, may be found in Cobbett, *State Trials*, 5, pp. 817-18; Cobbett, *Cobbett's Parliamentary History of England*, 3, p. 1488 and

172

sentence Nayler was pilloried, brutally whipped and imprisoned. He refused to recant.[117] Cromwell intervened on humanitarian grounds but Parliament stood firm on its initial decision to continue the punishment.[118]

During the second part of Nayler's sentence, he was again pilloried, his tongue was bored with a red-hot iron and his forehead was branded with a 'B'. While at the pillory Robert Rich placed a placard over Nayler reading "This is the King of the Jews."[119] This was promptly torn down by the presiding officer. Rich remained by Nayler, crying, stroking his hair and face, kissing his hands and licking the wound on his forehead. His women followers also gathered around the pillory, one behind and two at his feet, just as the three Mary's had gathered around Jesus at his crucifixion (John 19:25).[120] The epiphany continued and his followers continued to exalt him. Proclaiming Nayler to be the external Jesus come again was not what Fox (and perhaps Margaret Fell) claimed for himself, but the exalted claims of Nayler, Milner and Toldervy[121] were a product of Fox's notion of celestial

---

Memoirs, pp. 46-47. For a detailed discussion of the legality of the punishment *see* Burton, *Diary*, 1, pp. 96ff., 104-49, 153-58.

[117]*Memoires*, pp. 65-66.

[118]Cromwell's letter may be found in Barclay, *Letters*, pp. 47-48. *See also* Grigge, *The Quakers Jesus*, p. 18. Cromwell was still showing interest in Nayler a year later.

[119]*Memoires*, p. 53.

[120]Deacon, *An Exact History of the Life of James Nayler*, pp. 35-45; *A True Narrative of the Examination, Trial, and Sufferings of James Nayler*, pp. 40-41; Cobbett, *State Trials*, 5, p. 820.

[121]John Toldervy was so taken with the idea that Christ inhabited him that he wrote: "I was really possessed with a confident belief, that Christ Jesus that died at Jerusalem was a figure of me, and that I was the true Christ" (J. Toldervy, *The Foot Out of the Snare*, p. 21). Toldervy even engaged in a metaphoric action of reenacting Christ's crucifixion (*Ibid.*, p. 38). John Gilpin, another erstwhile Quaker, spoke and acted in a similar manner in 1653 (Gilpin, *The Quakers Shaken*, pp. 6-7), as did James Milner. George Whitehead disclaimed these actions as "strange whimsey's" that were not part of Quaker principles [*An Antidote Against the Venome of the Snake in the Grass* (London, 1697), p. 6]. Such a view could only be maintained if mention of celestial inhabitation and exalted language was selectively edited from the record, and to do that would be to cut the theological heart out of early Quakerism and leave future generations with little grounds to explain the exalted language that remained, in addition to the proliferation of indecorous and charismatic activity that focused on the apocalyptic return

inhabitation. To believe that one was literally inhabited by the flesh and bone of Christ - was Christ in some sense - could create an impression that one was the external Jesus. The protean nature of celestial inhabitation makes any exalted claim coming from the Quaker community of that time seem less excessive.

On January 17, 1657 the next part of the sentence was carried out in Bristol. Nayler was made to ride a horse backwards through the streets, a cruel reversal of his triumphant entry only two months earlier. Robert Rich was again present, riding in front of Nayler and singing "Holy, holy". On January 23 Nayler was committed to Bridewell Prison where he was to remain until September, 1659.[122]

Politically, Nayler had been an instrument in the hands of a Parliament that was making extensive claims for itself, especially as they affected liberty of conscience. In addition, Parliament got, in Nayler, a man who symbolized the fears of many toward religious enthusiasm. They used Nayler to turn back the clock of religious toleration. They made their point - "that a liberty which produced Nayler was a liberty extended too far."[123]

Nayler's trial and conviction were as a reaction against the extensive religious freedoms guaranteed under the *Instrument* which Cromwell regarded as the permanent guarantee of the country's rights and freedoms.

---

of Christ. To understand that apocalyptic return of Christ in figurative terms alone is to miss the galvanizing truth of those early years.

[122]The editor of Neale's *History of the Puritans* said that even Neale's censure of the judgement as "much too severe for such a wrongheaded obstinate creature" was too gentle. "It was repugnant to humanity, equity and wisdom. For though the religious extravagances of Nayler might reasonably shock pious and sober minds, his criminality ought to have been estimated not by the sound of the titles and claims which he assumed, or which were given to him; but by the delusion and frenzy which seized his brain: and on this ground he was an object of pity, not indignation, and he should have been assigned to a physician for a cure of his madness, and not to the the executioner of public justice" (*History of the Puritans*, 4, p. 142). This was a common carricature of Nayler - that he was an object of pity, he was mad. It was, possibly, the only reasonable interpretation of the time. When the choreography of the dispute is rendered as messianic, however, Nayler is cast in a very different light. Nonetheless, the comment from Neale's *History* illustrated how disgusted many of Nayler's contemporaries, or near contemporaries, were by the sentence in an age that was shedding its 'inquisitorial' mentality in favour of toleration and freedom of conscience.

[123]Bittle, *James Nayler*, p. 161.

Parliament defied the *Instrument* and all it stood for as a stepping stone to sovereignty.[124] Eventually, Cromwell dissolved Parliament, fearing among other things, its propensity to tamper with the *Instrument*. Nayler's case may have had some effect on Cromwell's decision.

With the help of powerful friends like Judge Fell Fox had been acquitted of blasphemy at Lancaster in 1652, while Nayler was cruelly punished by Parliament in 1656. Bittle found some reason for this discrepancy in the changing political winds (specifically the struggle between Protector and Parliament) and I'm sure he is right. But the politicization of the Nayler case only explained his victimization, not the reasons behind the incident itself and for that we must look to the messianic struggle between Fox and Nayler.

Both Fox and Nayler had something to gain from this affair and a great deal to lose. Behind the incident, with its sincere rhetoric about seeking a sign for Christ's return, was Nayler's bid to seize the reigns of power and become the leader of the saints of the new age. Fogelklou's reading of Nayler was that he was "exceedingly proud, unconsciously ambitious, and, above all, intent upon preserving temporal and spiritual independence,"[125] in a movement that was autocratically ruled by Fox. The "inner Christ" in him, "his regal type of gentleness and his kingdom of peace"[126] was to be demonstrated before all men, including Fox! But Fogelklou didn't take her interpretation far enough. It was not only his regal type of gentleness that was to be demonstrated before all men - it was the fact that, according to his followers, he was the very person of Jesus and an avatar in his own right. And this was the exalted language that was used, indeed was necessary, to seize the reigns of power. Fox's claims for himself dictated the choreography of the dispute. The discourse could not have proceeded in any other way. Thus, when Martha Simmonds confronted Fox in Launceston she attempted to undermine his claim to divine sonship. It

---

[124]*Ibid.*, p. 163.

[125]Fogelklou, *James Nayler*, p. 149.

[126]*Ibid.*, p. 148.

was all a very self-conscious debate. The dispute had a design, even if the chosen means of dramatization appear to a modern to be farcical. The choreography of the dispute reveals the inadequacy and the patent anachronisms of those interpretations which portray Nayler as mad or deluded and his followers as simple and credulous. Indeed the word "choreography" with its overtones of theatricality may give a misleading impression if one regards theatre (erroneously) as frivolous. The substantive process of the dispute was deadly serious.

Since this struggle for control was fought under the early Quaker rubrics of the principle of the indwelling Christ and his return it should neither be hidden from view nor pushed to the fringes of the movement. From its inception only a fine line separated God and creature in Quakerism and the whole struggle between Fox and Nayler demonstrated the ambiguity inherent in the doctrine of immanence. It was never properly defined. Fox learned early to cloak the doctrine in theologically ambiguous terms while early Quaker apologists tended to ignore facing its consequences or simply denied what Fox's opponents charged - that he claimed equality with God. The whole issue was begging for a Nayler incident and what was surprising was that it took nearly half a decade to emerge, a testament to the power and success of Fox's own avatarial claims.

The incident was an important event in early Quaker history because it exposed certain ambiguities in Fox's theology of the celestial inhabitation. Nayler was not acting out of character with the general tone of Fox's own dramatic life and message. Signs and wonders and exalted claims to divine sonship were normative in early Quakerism. They were even common knowledge among Fox's opponents and were rigorously defended from within the movement. The apocalyptic return of Christ to dwell in his saints was the first principle of Quakerism - it was possible for the saints to be divinized. It was, however, not possible for every saint to be the leader of the saints of the new age, nor was it possible for every saint to be a sign of the final revelation of Christ in human history - that is, to have a higher measure of Christ in them than all others. In very practical terms the logic of this meant that any leader must be the Son of God and more - he had to be the highest revelation of Christ. It was suggested above that Martha Simmonds had a different and more disturbing eschatology in mind when she supported Nayler as an "external" Jesus come again. She created or choreographed the whole sign event into a pitch for an imminent, external eschatology. She and her followers were able to outbid Fox, or at least they tried to, by proclaiming Nayler to be the "external" Jesus, the second appearance of the promised Messiah. He looked, so it was claimed, identical to Jesus. He behaved as Jesus behaved. He had the same "regal spirit of gentleness" Jesus had. And so, really, it had to be if he were to snatch the leadership from Fox. Nayler's behaviour tells us, among other things, just how large Fox's claims were and had to be if he was to claim and sustain his prophetic position.

6

RETREAT

Karl von Clausewitz, the Prussian military strategist, argued that retreat was harder to organize than attack. Certainly it is more difficult to do well. One has the feeling that Fox did not 'organize' his retreat. Rather it 'happened' as a result of the bitter dispute with Nayler, an equally bitter dispute with persistent critics and the threat of a restored Monarchy. But nevertheless, it was well done. It was, as we will see in this chapter, not a wholesale change (that only came in the 1670's when Fox's doctrine of celestial inhabitation was transformed) but it was a deft response that partly disarmed the worst criticisms and yet retained the substance of Fox's charisma and his doctrine of celestial inhabitation. In general terms, then, this chapter is about the retreat from Fox's language of avatarship and about Fox's retreat or backing away from his own exalted claims while still clinging to the idea of the celestial inhabitation.[1]

---

[1]The periodization of Quakerism in the historical literature has generally divided the movement into a first and second period with the break occurring in 1660 with the Restoration of the monarchy. What is argued here, as a sub-plot to the unmaking of a God theme is that the transformation of Quakerism began immediately after the Nayler incident. Braithwaite also saw that Quakers entered a post-Nayler retreat. But his judgement was that the Nayler incident had a good effect on Quakers "for it effectually warned Quaker leaders of the perils attending the over-emphasis they had laid on the infallibility of the life possessed by the Spirit of Christ" (*Beginnings*, p. 271). Braithwaite's conclusion was tainted by anachronistic assessments. The flouting of decorum and the "high language" that was a part of early Quaker style was abhorrent to Braithwaite even if he was able, barely, to accept the quaking in meetings as the exuberance that accompanied "the first manifestations of such experience"

Following the harrowing trauma of the Nayler incident Fox became more circumspect.[2] He retreated from his bold pre-Nayler Sonship claims, although he did not renounce them.[3] The pace of miracles and 'appearances' slowed but never completely stopped. Similarly, going naked as a sign receded. Fox's own rhetoric was lowered and the crusading apocalyptic of Quakers in general was severely muted. There was, as well, a notable absence of blasphemy trials. Nayler allegedly recanted for the sake of peace and unity and many of his followers eventually rejoined the movement after the initial rush of post-Nayler charismatic excitement died down. The first signs of church discipline and formal organization began to appear as early as 1656, an attempt to reign in the divisive influences unleashed by Nayler. Friends even began to censure their own writings.[4]

---

meetings as the exuberance that accompanied "the first manifestations of such experience" (*Ibid.*, p. 276). But along with Janney, Jones and Cadbury he simply could not accept the rest. The "extravagances of language," he said, nearly cost Quakerism everything, not least throwing "doubt on the validity of the great experience of the Inner Light" (*Ibid.*, p. 276). Braithwaite was party to the ideas that emerged after Penn and Barclay transformed the Inner Light - ideas that bore little resemblance to Fox's original message. "High language" did not emerge from a faulty mental environment as Quaker interpreters would have us believe. We need neither justify or excuse it; praise it or blame it. Fox's doctrine of the Christ who dwelt within had its own integrity - an integrity which strikes the twentieth century reader as 'otherness' or even incomprehensible strangeness.

[2]That is, he became more circumspect in some ways, for example, by slowing the pace of his miracles and not applying exalted language to his own person. In other respects his boundless energies and ceaseless round of activity continued. He continued to travel widely throughout England, Scotland and Wales. In Wales, where he was made aware of the disruption caused by some of Nayler's followers, he let it be known "that the day of their visitation was over" (Braithwaite, *Beginnings*, p. 347), after which he held great meetings in Cardiff and Radnorshire, the latter being attended by thousands. By travelling widely he was able to keep one step ahead of the authorities. He may also have found an openness to his charismatic ministry in areas where his reputation as a religious megalomaniac hadn't yet preceded him. In Wales, for example, his visit occurred during a drought. He said: "It was a noted thing generally amongst people that when I came still I brought rain ... and as far as Truth spread in the North and South there was rain enough" (*Cambridge Journal*, 1, p. 273). The tradition continues in America that rain will accompany a Yearly Meeting (Braithwaite, *Beginnings*, p. 349 n.2).

[3]Some Quakers continued to use exalted language in their private correspondence until it was finally edited or cut out of the record.

[4]As early as 1656. Friends even omitted reports of inner dissension whenever public letters were addressed to Friends. Oliver suggested that this was an attempt to allay persecution (P. Oliver, "Quaker Testimony and the Lamb's War," p. 82). It was equally a

The absence of blasphemy trials (Nayler's was the last such trial) and the ceasing of Son of God talk was the most obvious sign of retreat. Fox continued to make exalted claims for the saints but he was more cautious and circumspect about himself. It is worth pondering his ideas about celestial inhabitation once again in order to set the context for the discussion about retreat. In his book, *The Great Mystery of the Great Whore* (1659) it would seem Fox had conceded nothing. The saints were the sons of God. They were partakers of the divine nature. They knew the bodily presence of Christ. They assumed the glorified body of Christ. They were not distinct from Christ. Fox used all these phrases to express his continuing belief in the deification of the saints.[5] He had changed nothing as it pertained to his belief in the unity of the celestial flesh. But he had rendered down his own exalted claims. He still believed that Christ was *in* the saints. This could be given a spiritual reading (ie. that Christ was far away in heaven and spiritually dwelt *in* the saints) but that is not what Fox meant, even in 1659. He meant that the glorified Christ was literally *in* the saints and he provided a catalogue of Scripture verses to prove that point - verses that had been corrupted by the translators.[6] There was no Christ far away in heaven. Heaven was within. God's essence, heaven, the New Jerusalem, the glorified body of Christ - they were all within. The saints were the incarnation of Christ on earth. The saints were resurrected, glorified, perfected and deified. There was, however, no more bold Son of God talk as it applied only to Fox.

The doctrine of celestial inhabitation enabled both Fox and Nayler to further their own claims in the leadership dispute. The nature and authority of the person had been at issue in disputes over supremacy. The world had watched this pitched battle of Messiahs and was aghast at what it saw. As a result Fox was forced to render down his own personal, exalted claims and change his emphasis to the deification of the saints in general. To soft-pedal

---

to be united at all costs and thus the censoring of any controversial, extravagant or unseemly material (*See A Testimony From the Brethren ... in ... 1666* in Barclay, *Letters*, pp. 322-23).

[5]Fox, *Great Mystery of the Great Whore*, 3, pp. 57, 59, 180-83, 206, 221, 235, 243-44, 291-92, 340, 344-45, 358, 400, 457, 509.

[6]*Ibid.*, 3, pp. 581-83. Fox is preoccupied with the preposition 'ε υ' and in most cases his corrections are accurate. In fact he missed Galatians 1:16.

change his emphasis to the deification of the saints in general. To soft-pedal his claims was one way to remove a divisive issue as well as to avoid, after Nayler, what was clearly general contempt and abhorrence. Fox never referred to himself as the Son of God between 1657 and 1659. Even though he continued to assert the divinity of the saints and the unity of the celestial flesh,[7] his caution was, properly speaking, a retreat. Only once thereafter did he risk applying the title to himself and that was in a very orthodox and metaphorical way in a 1660 letter to Charles II.[8]

The letter is also worth a brief assessment, given its circumstances and its relation to other, earlier Son of God statements. Norman Penney, to mitigate the "extravagance" and "outrageousness" of early Quakerism, regarded all Fox's Son of God statements as extentions of the 'sons of God' passage in Romans 8:14. But closer examination of these passages show that very rarely did Fox specifically associate his 'sonship' to the Romans 8 text and once was in his letter to Charles II. The letter was deliberately cautious and a mark of retreat, in spite of the fact that it appeared at a time when Quaker signs and wonders and apocalyptic hopes had reemerged amidst the tumult of political change. A letter to a monarch is risky business, so it is understandable that the letter should be more cautious and circumspect than his earlier, bolder pre-Nayler statements. Those statements did not carry the same sense of metaphor. They were not couched in the language of Romans 8, or Galatians 3:26. They did not suggest that Fox was, in a Pauline sense, part of Christ's family of faith as a child of God. This reference indicated a new carefulness and a more temperate tone in Fox, and this new tone appeared much later in different form in a 1671 letter to the Governor of Barbados. At the same time the well chosen biblical citation here implies no retraction of earlier claims by Fox. It was not a recantation. It was cleverly done, and left Fox defensible should he come to any further blasphemy trouble. Even so, Fox's letter to Charles II still claimed, radically, that he was in a pre-Fall state of perfection, so he was still not as cautious as he

---

[7]"And the saint are not distinct from him [Christ]", (*Ibid.*, p. 291).

[8]*Cambridge Journal*, 1, p. 381. *See* ch. 4 p. 119 for the text of the letter.

might have been. On the other hand, he was trying to make it crystal clear that he was no rebel, no incendiary. How could he have been, he implied, if he was in a state of innocence - a pre-carnal state that was beyond war and violence and carnal weapons.

This was the only recorded time Fox specifically described himself as the Son of God after the Nayler incident. That alone was very telling. No more bold Son of God talk in the retreat years suggested that he was very badly burned by Nayler, badly enough to back off from his avatar claims and even sacrifice his pre-eminence in the movement, at least temporarily. The 1660 letter was a withdrawal into more innocuous language even if he had not changed his own exalted views about himself.

The retreat into careful language occurred again in 1671. The aforementioned letter to the Governor of Barbados was the closest Fox ever came to a statement of faith and it looked fairly conservative except for some slight but significant reservations.[9] For example, he was at pains to describe Scripture as the "words" rather than the "word" of God[10] intimating that he did not acknowledge Scripture's finality. They were not a source of fixed doctrinal certainty about God's work, but words. This implied further revelation which was the point Fox made in that passage. But it also implied that the words had to be coded "in the power of God". They were a cluster of symbols that could be perverted by the ministers. They only made up truth if you had been admitted to the power and if you were visited and imbued and inhabited by the celestial Christ in the flesh. In the interests of brevity, circumspection and caution Fox did not spell it out, but the celestial flesh idea was lurking in the background.

In the actual letter Fox made no claim to sonship, yet the local Baptists in Barbados rekindled the blasphemy charges against him. Again Fox refrained from using dangerous terminology to defend himself. Instead he claimed to have the same spirit as the Apostles. A new tack on an old

---

[9]Quakers have generally accepted this letter as an orthodox statement of faith from Fox and a modification of his earlier views [see David Holden, *Friends Divided: Conflict and Division in the Society of Friends* (Richmond, Indiana: Friends United Press, 1988), p. 2].

[10]*Cambridge Journal*, 2, p. 200.

course for that spirit, to him, was Christ's glorified flesh. His language implied inflated claims while he prudently desisted from the old avatarial language.[11]

The background to this unruly incident was described by John Stubbs, who was present with Fox at the time. Stubbs wrote a letter to Margaret Fell about the incident. He informed her that the Baptists had attacked Fox at a general meeting on the basis of a letter the erstwhile Quaker John Pennyman[12] had sent to them from England. In that letter Pennyman related some contentious statements Solomon Eccles had made about Fox in 1668 in his Broadside *The Quakers Challenge*.[13] Those statements, intimated that Eccles believed Fox was the creator of the world and therefore Christ. Stubbs wrote: "and so a Baptist speaker when thy husband stood up to speak asked him if his name were Mr. Fox ... and asked him if he owned such and (such) titles as were given him by Solomon Eccles in a certain paragraph

[11]There is also a lack of eschatological discussion in the letter, or, is eschatology implied in the wily acceptance of Scripture as the "words" of God rather than the "word" of God, with its denial of completeness and finality?

[12]Quakers disowned John Pennyman in 1670 since he had become an opponent of their movement.

[13]Pennyman's letter was written on August 21, 1671 and taken by Pennyman to Devonshire House where he gave it to John Bolton to read in the meeting then in progress. But no-one would read it and Pennyman was barred from entering the meeting. He then decided to make the letter public and he sent it to a printer. The printed version, which contained the letter and other sundry comments may be found at FRL, London, *Tract Volume N/22b*, a folio which makes up various of his papers and books written between 1670 and 1680, the period after his disownment. This is the version that was sent to Barbados. The letter specifically referred to Eccles' exalted language about Fox which Pennyman called blasphemous. Even Paul, he said, had rebuked people for using exalted language towards him. What then of Fox who seemed to encourage it? He was unable to find any Quaker willing to explain the words and since Fox and Eccles had departed for Barbados they, too, were unavailable to defend themselves against the accusations. Since Fox had not publicly denounced Eccles and had instead taken him along on the journey, Pennyman took this as general approval rather than disapproval of Eccles' exalted language. Pennyman closed his letter with an appeal to Quakers to answer his charges against Fox and Eccles. Since this general appeal received no response Pennyman saw to it that his letter followed Fox and Eccles to Barbados where it created no small stir and a serious threat to Fox and Eccles whose lives were briefly endangered. Apparently the letter was read at an open meeting before hundreds of people, after which a Baptist preacher named Thomas Hatchman mounted a vicious attack against Fox [J. Pennyman, *This Following Being a Copy of a Letter I Carried to Devonshire-House* (London, 1671); Eccles, *Testimony* in Penn, *Judas and the Jews*, pp. 75ff.].

contained in a paper of John Pennymans [sic] ... and a great bawling they made ..."[14] Eccles, who was also present with Fox on the trip called them "bloodthirsty men, who sought my life there."[15] We have no record that described exactly how Fox explained Eccles' language about him but we do know that Fox was forced to admit that he believed he had the same spirit as the Apostles: "they asked me whether I had the same spirit as the apostles had and I said I had ..."[16] His language was not as inflated and therefore could not be used to imply inflated claims but what was most significant about this whole exchange in Barbados was a self-conscious shift he had made from avatar to apostle. From an avatar he seems to have become resigned to a self-designation as apostle. Even that, for some, would seem almost blasphemous, though not in a statutory sense. The fact that he was goaded into this admission is good evidence of his restraint. By the same token, that he was goaded does not invalidate - perhaps strengthens - his statement as a true version of his new self-vision. It is difficult to measure the extent of this retreat objectively or subjectively for Fox himself - how can we measure the qualitative difference between an avatar and an apostle? What could such a shift in self-perception mean from within? Throughout

[14]*Cambridge Journal*, 2, p. 196. One of the copies of Eccles' Broadside now in Friends Reference Library in London has had certain key words of the exalted language marked out in such a way that suggests the one-time owner of the tract disapproved of the exalted language (*Tract volume 103* - FRL). Fox's reputation as a religious megalomaniac continued to follow him wherever he went. Years after the Nayler incident and years after Fox had dropped his exalted claims people hounded him with charges that implied blasphemy. The persistence of the charge was a continuing worry to Quakers and this may have been the reason why Stubbs reported it to Margaret Fell. His opponents had a bit between their teeth and they refused to let it go.

[15]*See* Eccles *Testimony* in Penn, *Judas and the Jews*, p. 74.

[16]*Cambridge Journal*, 2, p. 252. While this was not a novel idea (Fox and other Quakers had said it earlier) Fox's answer suggested little change apart from phraseology adapted within the fires of legal testing and heated controversy. As early as 1655 George Whitehead claimed to have the same spirit as the Apostles, though in lesser degree. Upon making such a claim an opponent challenged him to perform a miracle or speak in tongues [George Whitehead, *The Christian Progress of ... George Whitehead* (London, 1725), pp. 55-56]. *See* Henry Barrow's statement, quoted in Paul Christianson, *Reformers and Babylon: English apocalyptic visions from the reformation to the eve of the civil war* (Toronto: University of Toronto Press, 1978), p. 91.

184

his writings Fox made it clear that he regarded the New Testament phrases about Christ being in the Apostles to be the exalted Christ within. Christ inhabited the Apostles in exactly the same way he inhabited the saints. Thus, to admit that he had the same spirit (this was not the disembodied spirit of later interpreters) as the Apostles was a reaffirmation of his doctrine of celestial inhabitation. To have the Apostles' spirit was to have the celestial flesh of Christ. The change of wording was disarming but essentially cosmetic. For the movement it seemed necessary. Certainly the reaction of Fox's acolytes after he repulsed the attack of the Baptist critics in Barbados was one of relief that he had trounced and confounded his noisy critics. John Stubbs wrote to Margaret Fell "thy [husband] answered things so in the pure wisdom of God ... that the professors lost by their coming and so when they had wearied themselves with bellowing they went away and thy husband continued the meeting."[17] Part of their pleasure must have been that Fox gave no occasion for scandal by making "blasphemous" claims in the debate. A sense of deep relief shines through the reports of the incident to Margaret Fell.

In what may be called the "Barbados Formula" Fox made a confession of faith wrung from him under the fire of vicious critics. This then became a useful formula to be mouthed when he was pressed. It continued to guarantee his special powers and charisma while avoiding the pitfalls of avatarship. At the same time he continued to believe, for all the saints, in the graphic corporeal celestial presence, with no fancy qualifications or refinements: for example, by traditional eucharistic doctrines of transubstantiation.

A closer look at Fox's admission that he had the spirit of the Apostles' suggests that while he was in retreat from his earlier exalted language he was still conceding little to his critics. Fox may have taken a page from the book of Nayler's supporters here. They also claimed the spirit of the Apostles and a spirit even greater than the Apostles'.[18] But long after that claim was dead

---

[17]*Cambridge Journal*, 2, p. 196.

[18]See footnote 69 of this chapter.

for Nayler's people Fox took it up for himself, with the consent of his followers who were content, it seemed, to let Fox alone make such a bold claim. They in turn were no longer gods, sons of God or even apostles.

This formula - that Fox was equal to the Apostles - may well have been Fox's key to survival and a moment of new self-direction and self-definition for him. It was not a 'flash in the pan' idea. As we saw earlier, the origins of the formula can be traced as far back as 1652. By 1671 it had become part of his post-Nayler retreat position and a coded affirmation of celestial inhabitation. When he returned home from America over a year later, in 1672, he began to perform more miracles than at any other time in his career since the early 1650's. Had Fox not arrived at this new self-conception his history may well have been a sad story, beginning with affirmation to end in self-abnegation. Fox was fortunate enough to find a formula that enabled his optimism and his energies to survive amidst retreat and change. It helped him to escape the pitfalls of avatarship while retaining his sense of charisma, mission and uniqueness. He remained inhabited by Christ's flesh and bone. He could still dream dreams, see visions and perform miracles as an Apostle.

The Barbados Formula not only provided Fox with a new personal beginning but it contained all the elements of his earlier equalitarian emphases. Fox, and all the saints, were spiritual successors of the Apostles, possessed the same "Christ in them" and had the same power and spirit.[19] In 1675 Fox said that any preacher who succeeded the Apostles had to demonstrate the same power and spirit they had. Those that had this spirit had revelations, those that were out of it belonged to Babylon. This position was reaffirmed in 1680 and again in 1690 just before his death.[20]

---

[19]This theme was repeated throughout Fox's later writings. *See Doctrinal Books*, 5, pp. 47, 56, 175, 180, 231, 309; 6, p. 104 and *Epistles*, 8, p. 189.

[20]George Fox, *The Protestant Christian Quaker* (1680), in *Doctrinal Books*, 6, p. 104 and *The Inward and Spiritual Warfare* (1690), p. 5. Until the end of his life Fox pursued the theme that the night of apostasy was ending, the last day had come, the seed of the woman was bruising the serpent's head and all this was confirmed by dreams and visions in accordance with Joel's prophecy. If it was not in evidence then it was because the people had strayed from the spirit and power of the Apostles.

Fox's renewed emphasis on the spirit of the Apostles may have appeared to be a retreat into a purely pneumatic theology but in fact it was not. It was his more cautious way of reconfirming that he, like the Apostles, continued to experience the spirit of Pentecost. As we will see in the following chapter he did not alter or refine his belief in the graphic corporeal presence of the celestial flesh of Christ even though he made a necessary retreat from using exalted language, if only to allay persecution and get the hounds off his back.

There is another note to add to this part of the commentary. Following his trip to America and a gruelling imprisonment in Worcester between 1673 and 1675 Fox retired to Swarthmoor Hall in 1675/6 to recover his strength. While there he went through correspondence to himself and others and altered it systematically. Much of this correspondence is now contained in the *Swarthmore Manuscripts*. The manuscripts show evidence that Fox personally tampered with the sources.[21] He made deletions with broad ink strokes. He made corrections that are indisputably in his own hand. He struck out extravagant phrases of adoration and substituted more moderate phrases. In places whole patches were ripped from the sheets (possibly by Margaret Fell who later re-edited the same letters), the jagged edges still revealing the broad ink crossings-out. Richard Sale's 1655 letter to Fox contained some "extreme pseudo-messianic language"[22] which was systematically altered. The alterations are shown here in brackets: "G.F. dear and precious brother in the measure of thy life made manifest in me do I clearly salute thee glory glory to thy name [stroked out by Fox who inserted

---

[21] I am grateful to H. Larry Ingle for drawing my attention to some of these selectively edited letters at Friends' House Library in London. This tampering with the sources did not escape the earlier notice of W.C. Braithwaite but he neither recognized in it Fox's deliberate attempt to rewrite early Quaker history nor drew out its implications regarding the adoration and worship of Fox. He simply reported it (*Beginnings*, p. 105 n.1). Nor did it escape the notice of Geoffrey Nuttall, *Early Quaker Letters From the Swarthmore MSS. to 1660. Calendared, Indexed and Annotated* (Typescript in London. FRL, 1952) and Hugh Barbour, *Quakers in Puritan England*, p. 148. Altering excessive or indecorous language was a widespread practice in late seventeenth century England when loyalties were carefully chosen depending upon who was on the throne.

[22] Nuttall, *Early Quaker Letters*, p. 193.

"be to the Lord"] ... for by thy [stroked out and "his" is inserted] power ..."
Later in the letter Sale again wrote "glory glory to thy name" and "thy name"
is crossed out and "God" inserted.[23] Thomas Curtis wrote to Fox in 1658 and
the whole first paragraph of the letter was devoted to exalted language
towards Fox. The whole first paragraph was stroked out.[24] While Mary
Howgill was in Lancaster prison in 1656 she wrote a letter to Fox in which
she interchanged the word "life" for Fox throughout. In each case Fox
crossed out "life" and put in "friend".[25] Evidence of widespread tampering
occurred in letters sent to Fox by Thomas Holme. Again the tampering is
indicated in brackets. In 1654 Holme wrote to Fox: "G.F. Dear brother ... I
salute thee, who owns the world [crossed out and "art glory" added] for
evermore, to thee [final "e" stroked out and "power" added to read "the
power"] shall all nations bow and bend, thou mighty man of [the heavenly]
war."[26] In 1654 Holme wrote another such letter to Fox only this time all the
opening lines have been torn out along the line marked by Fox's broad black
pen stroke. Some phrases remain just above the ragged tear: "all things stand
by thee" and "thou art the same as ever was ... and among us the beginning ...
the first and last ..."[27] In the winter of 1654 Holme wrote to Fox again to say
that he was being charged with blasphemy and was imprisoned in Chester.
Again the first paragraph of this letter has been torn away and no evidence of
what it said remains, apart from the broad black ink line. This selective[28]
purging by Fox, and later by Margaret Fell, was a deliberate effort to rewrite

---

[23]"Richard Sale to George Fox" (October 25, 1655), *Swarth. MSS.* 4, No. 211.

[24]"Thomas Curtis to George Fox" (1658), *Swarth. MSS.*, 3, No. 87.

[25]"Mary Howgill to George Fox" (1656), *Barclay MSS.*, No. 41.

[26]"Thomas Holme to George Fox" (June 6, 1654), *Swarth. MSS.* 4, No. 244.

[27]"Thomas Holme to George Fox" (September, 1654), *Swarth. MSS.*, 4, No. 249.

[28]Instances of the use of exalted language that went unaltered are: "Ann Burden to George Fox", *Swarth. MSS.*, 3, No. 102; "Richard Hubberthorne to George Fox" (March 16, 1658), *Swarth. MSS.*, 4, No. 13; "Mary Prince to George Fox" (1656), *Swarth. MSS.*, 3, No. 116. Similarly, William Dewsbury's exalted language towards Margaret Fell went unaltered ["William Dewsbury to Margaret Fell" (March, 1660), *Swarth. MSS.*, 4, No. 134].

certain parts of early Quaker history and it tended to be a response to the kind of hounding he suffered in Barbados and the cruel imprisonment he suffered in Worcester. Fox himself instituted the cleansings of the record that were later followed by his editors. Purging exalted language from the record was all part of the retreat.

Fox's retreat was prudent for his movement and in a perverse sense the Nayler affair was providential for him. To have maintained his exalted claims after Nayler would have made him a laughing stock, especially in an age that was growing more skeptical.[29] As it was the old blasphemy charges and Fox's reputation as a megalomaniac followed him to Barbados in 1671, long after he had changed his tune as the 1660 letter to Charles II showed. Fox's concern was to distance himself and all Quakers from any further public humiliation. It was for this and not judicial reasons that Fox backed away from his earlier exalted claims and instead reached a compromise that he could accept - the Barbados Formula in which he believed himself to be equal with the Apostles - a title and status that still carried with it the idea of celestial inhabitation. Nonetheless, this was a formula that enabled Fox to escape the 'bawling and railing' of his opponents (witnessed by his jubilant victory over his vicious critics at Barbados) while at the same time leaving undimmed, at least in his mind, his pre-eminence and mission. He was able to retain the power and vision of his original calling. It was important as a solution and a new beginning for him in the midst of caution and retreat, even if his followers did not follow the fashion of his court as they had done earlier. His claim to be on a par with the Apostles suggested that his star as an avatar had faded and apostleship became the new formula through which he could reassert his dominance and charisma. The Apostles had Christ in them and one of the great signs of apostleship was miracle-working. Fox used this formula often enough between 1671 and 1691 to suggest that it had prevented a failure of nerve, brought him out of an unsettled state and enabled him to meet the challenge of a changing leadership.

---

[29]Following the Restoration the Interregnum Acts and Ordinances were abolished and although most were reinstated by the end of the century Fox was never in danger of being charged with blasphemy after 1660. The real problem with Son of God talk was no longer judicial but a matter of public humiliation, contempt and abhorrence.

After the Restoration another aspect of the retreat was introduced. During the Protectorate and especially between the fall of the Protectorate and the Restoration Quakers could expect friendly treatment from some magistrates and toleration from many others. As a result hope in imminent universal transformation tended to predominate in their writings, along with a tendency to use crusading rhetoric, especially after the fall of the Protectorate. After the Restoration the regime was severely hostile and persecuting. Crusading apocalyptic slowly yielded to pacifism and the idea of transformation through the suffering and patience of the saints. That, in addition to the abandonment of all hope that God would judge and transform the world through an external agent, was the beginning of a major shift in ideology. The Restoration temporarily brightened the hopes of some as changing external events continued to act like a motor that drove the ambivalence of Quaker expectations. But Quaker hopes in Charles were shattered when the *Book of Common Prayer* and the episcopacy were re-authorized and when the Church of England was re-established. To some the apostasy was being set up all over again. To others God was purging his sanctuary.[30] Many Quakers began to distance themselves from their role in the final apocalyptic drama.[31] God alone would supernaturally complete the task of universal transformation, though still within the time frame of their own generation.

A pacifist element was introduced into their writings. Edward Burrough, in a pamphlet directed to the King, said that Quakers had served Parliament in the wars against him and his father but it was in the interests of opposing oppression and in the name of reform. It was not a personal blood feud with the King. Now, said Burrough, the Quakers were "better informed than once we were" and they no longer fought oppression through "outward warring and fighting with carnal weapons". The King was asked to

---

[30]William Dewsbury, *The Breathings of Life* (London, 1662), p. 5 and George Bishop, *An Epistle of Love to all the Saints* (London, 1661), pp. 5, 8, 11-14. Fox said that a further falling away was necessary before the final defeat of the 'son of perdition' (*Concerning the Inward and Spiritual Warfare,* pp. 28-29).

[31]William Bayly, *The Life of Enoch Again Revived*, pp. 15-16.

distinguish between past and present and realize that Quakers had changed.[32] But the question remained - if in the time of retreat and change they could not take up earthly weapons then how and when would the great apocalyptic act of judgement and deliverance occur?   What would be the Quakers role?   Some Quakers, even in the cautious years of retreat, tried to recover the old charismatic power.   In 1662 William Bayly asked, "Oh my God! How long shall it be, ere the seed be gathered into the garner of salvation?   How long shall it be ere wickedness hath an end, and transgression be finished? ... How long shall the enemy prevail ... canst not thou destroy at thy pleasure ... Rouse up thyself, thou Lion of the Tribe of Judah, and let all nations feel thy terrible power."[33]   Quakers generally continued to believe in the imminence of the universal transformation.   The Lord was still expected to come suddenly and miraculously complete his work. A sense of urgency still remained.[34] What might appear at first glance is that Quakers had not renounced their expectation of an imminent universal transformation but instead had distanced themselves from a role in the final apocalyptic drama.

While crusading rhetoric was generally curtailed and a pacifist element was introduced into their writings, Burrough's appeal did little, in the long run, to appease the Royalists and lift the persecution.   There is evidence that Quakers had not really changed all that much, apart from their retreat from contentious language.   Margaret Fell, John Philly, Thomas Taylor, William Gibson and Ellis Hookes all continued to announce the day of the Lord in bold apocalyptic terms until the 1680's[35] and they showed

---

[32]Edward Burrough, *A Visitation of Love* (London, 1660), pp. 10-11.

[33]William Bayly, *The Life of Enoch Again Revived*, pp. 15-16. As late as 1672 Thomas Taylor made a similar appeal for God to arise and judge his enemies: "break the jaws of the wicked ... consume that antichrist spirit in all people that will not have Christ ... arise, arise, and plead the cause of thy covenant" [*A Testimony for Christ* Jesus (1672)].

[34]Edward Burrough, *To the Parliament of the Commonwealth of England* (London, 1659), p. 2 and *A General Epistle to all the Saints* (London, 1660), pp. 12-13; Bishop, *Mene Tekel*, p. 49; Gibson, *Universal Love*, pp. 8-11.

[35]Margaret Fell, *An Evident Demonstration to God's Elect* (London, 1660), p. 7. John Philly called out woes upon Babylon and said "the horseman draweth near to lift up the brut

none of the caution of Quakers in retreat although what they implied was that God and not the saints wielded the sword. There was little comfort in this kind of language for Royalists and opponents of Quakerism in general. A fine line existed between spiritualized crusading rhetoric and actual insurrection. A muted radical apocalyptic strain remained in their thinking and it was linked to Fox's doctrine of celestial inhabitation.

After 1660/61 Quakers may have been committed to abstaining from using earthly weapons but that did not mean that they were not committed to global revolution in which they would be the instruments of a dramatic apocalyptic act. When William Bayly and Thomas Taylor appealed to God to arise and judge his enemies quickly were they not appealing to Quakers? Nowhere was this revolutionary spirit (as it was linked to the doctrine of celestial inhabitation) better exemplified than in Francis Ellington's *Christian Information Concerning These Last Times* (1664). Ellington wanted to demonstrate that in spite of a number of discouraging setbacks Quakers were still to be equated with Christ's saving work on earth.[36] Quakers were the dry bones spoken of by Ezekiel. They were coming together again - "bone to his bone"[37] - a revealing phrase that indicated that some Quakers continued to accept Fox's contentious endogenetic notion of the formation of Christ within the believer well after the Nayler incident. The reconstituting of the dry bones was itself an apocalyptic act that was equated with the Quakers (a new and divine collective being that had been resurrected and fully restored

---

sword and the glittering spear, and a multitude of carcasses shall fall". At another point he said: "The dreadful and most terrible battle-axe of the most just, righteous, powerful Lord God of vengeance is now laid to thy root ... the Lord God [will] now hew down, root up and utterly destroy, yea, his most just and righteous wrath ... and vengeance, is already broke forth upon thee, and shall daily more [*The Arraignment of Christendom* (1664), pp. 85, 91]. *See also* William Gibson, *Universal Love* (London, 1671), pp. 8-11; Thomas Taylor, *A Testimony for Christ Jesus* (1672) and Ellis Hookes, *The Spirit of the Martyrs Revived* (London, 1683).

[36]The notion that Christ's saving work was identified with Quakers was not new with Ellington. It was a familiar charge against Quakers that the work of Christ was being accomplished through them because he had personally appeared in their bodies and this premise led them to believe that Christ was working in and through Quakers to restore the world to its pre-Fall paradisiacal state [*see* Thomas Moore's charges against Nayler in *A Defence Against the Poison of Satan's Design* (London, 1656), pp. 2, 61-62, 65-66, 69-70].

[37]Ellington, *Christian Information*, p. 7.

to the pre-Fall, pre-carnal, paradisiacal state). Quakers were portrayed by Ellington as an army going forth to battle only now they did not handle earthly swords and spears.[38] Ellington resolved the enigma between apocalyptic activism and pacifism by saying that God would supernaturally protect his people and their victory would be sudden, supernatural and imminent.[39] The militancy of earlier years might appear to be tempered in retreat with appeals to wait patiently, unarmed, in humility and love.[40] Or so we might think.

When Ellington turned to discuss Daniel's prophecy of the "Stone" about to smite the image (break the kingdom of Anti-Christ and fill the whole earth with his new kingdom) he specifically equated Christ's saving work on earth with the Quakers: "And the Lord hath by his power cut *us* out of the mountain"(italics mine).[41] Here it would seem that Quakers, heretofore characterized as pacifist, were about to engage in a militant act. What appears to be an inconsistency may be explained by the Quakers' persistent belief in the unity and equality between saint and Christ well after the Nayler incident and into the 1660's. Saint, inward Christ, God, stone, mountain - all were one and the same. The Quakers would not fight with the carnal sword but as the personification of Christ on earth they would suddenly and supernaturally overthrow their enemies. We see again the central, guiding importance of Fox's doctrine of celestial inhabitation as it continued to inform Quaker thinking even in retreat. The identification with the stone (which was to perform a violent apocalyptic act without carnal weapons) is another example of how Quaker language was coded and could only be understood "in the power of God". The opacity and evasiveness of Quaker symbolism was used to escape charges of heresy and heavy persecution. The identification of Quakers with the supernatural work of

---

[38]*Ibid.*, p. 8.

[39]*Ibid.*, p. 8.

[40]Edward Burrough, *A Standard Lifted Up, and an Ensign Held Forth to all Nations* (London, 1658); Gibson, *Universal Love*, pp. 8-11.

[41]Ellington, *Christian Information*, p. 8.

God was a subtle one that continued to brace them through the valley of doubt and despair in the face of dashed apocalyptic hopes and heavy persecution. Much of the militant rhetoric was tempered in the heat of battle, in the way of a disarming pacifism and calls to keep still and patiently wait upon God. But the real source of their radicalism, of their perceived danger to social, religious and political cohesiveness remained. The doctrine of celestial inhabitation rewarded the believer with immense authority and power - power far greater and more dangerous (according to some) than a casual reading of Ellington might first reveal. The source of this radicalism was eventually excised from Quakerism by leading divines in the 1670's but in the years of retreat immediately following the Nayler incident and the Restoration the early, primitivistic vision of celestial inhabitation continued to inform most Quakers.

Ellington's *Christian Information* was the last clear statement of primitive Quaker apocalyptic to make use of Fox's endogenetic ideas. For amidst continuity signs of discontinuity were also beginning to appear. Immediate inspiration was beginning to give way to the "words" of other prophets, ancient and modern. Ellington, for example, used the words of prophets (including Jacob Boehme) to convince Quakers that they were the descendants of Israel "rising up out of the North country".[42] The words of others were used to prove the truth of one's own views and this recourse to external prophecy was novel in Quaker ranks. It was symptomatic of a general devolution of the prophetic spirit within the movement which was part of a general retreat from immediacy after the Nayler incident. The loss of Fox's avatarial status and charismatic authority also forced Quakers to search back beyond Fox for vindication and re-confirmation of their deliverance as the true seed of Christ in the last days. Certainly the loss of charisma precipitated by Nayler led to a search for new forms of authentication, like Boehme's prophecies. It showed how beleaguered Quakers were by the hostility of their opponents and the effects of the

---

[42]*Ibid.*, pp. 9-13.

Clarendon Code. It showed how desperate they were for new forms of authentication, especially when hundreds were dying horrifying deaths in prisons across England.

The Nayler incident dealt Quakers a blow from which they never really fully recovered. They lost their stride. The crusading rhetoric that had the saints, sword in hand, fighting alongside Christ for the overthrow of Babylon never fully returned. The sense of urgency died a slow death in the face of dashed hopes and by the end of the 1670's it was replaced by the idea of a slow, prolonged period of restoration. Quakers never really emerged from the post-Nayler retreat. It became, instead, a catalyst or starting point for a transformation that was a necessary answer to the change imposed on them by retreat. The Nayler incident was obviously not the only reason for the demise of Quaker eschatological hopes but it was a major factor in the retreat from legally and religiously dangerous terminology. The retreat itself then created a new set of questions and problems that eventually led to the transformation we will discuss in the next chapter.

The Nayler incident also caused an immediate retreat from the multitude of miracles, 'appearances' and signs that characterized the earliest years of the movement. This part of the retreat can be clearly charted from the sources. The jump in signs and wonders in 1659 and again in the 1670's may be attributed to changes in the political climate. In 1659 the *Interregnum* ended and this rekindled new hopes for the imminent recovery of the Kingdom. In 1672 the Quakers were temporarily relieved of heavy persecution by James II's *Declaration of Indulgence* and his *Great Pardon of Friends.*

Little is known about the early years, when Quakers were known as 'Children of the Light', except that a multitude of miracles occurred in the days before Fox ever knew about Margaret Fell and Swarthmoor. Between 1652 and 1655 documentation improved and numerous miracles were

TABLE I[43]

DATE	MIRACLES (mainly Fox)	VISIONS (mainly Fox)	GOING NAKED (excluding Fox)
Late 1640's	Numerous	Numerous	
1650 - 1655	17	Numerous	7
1656	0	0	Simpson active
1657 - 1658	2	4	0
1659 - 1660	Numerous	2	Numerous
1661 - 1669	7	6	Briggs/Eccles active
1670 - 1679	24 (all Fox)	13	0
1680 - 1689	11	1	0

[43]The chart analyzes and summarizes data based on a general survey of the sources. It is designed to be an inferential indicator of where the heightened and lessened miracles and sign activity occurred. Sometimes the word 'numerous' was used to refer to a multitude of miracles or signs. I have counted only the specific, individual cases that are recorded or I have used the word "numerous" if it appeared in the sources. There were also recorded, at other times and places, 'miraculous' deliverances on land and sea, especially on the journeys to other countries. These were counted as miracles by some Quakers but they are not counted as such here. The late 1640's, 1652, 1659 and 1661 were times when reports of numerous miracles and signs went out.

recorded.[44]   In 1656, the year of the Nayler incident, all this changed dramatically.   There was not one recorded miracle for that year and in 1657 there was but one report, of a painless child delivery, that was believed to be a miracle.   No miracles were attributed to Fox in 1656 or 1657.   In 1658 there was only one recorded miracle and that was Fox's healing of Cromwell's daughter Lady Claypole through a letter.[45]   The modest nature of this miracle (she was healed of a severe depression), performed through a letter, itself implied that Fox was in retreat and careful not to fuel the attacks of his adversaries who had already called his miracles counterfeit and a certain sign that he was an imposter.   Not only was Fox more circumspect in his use of Son of God talk but he was more cautious in his miracle - working activity as well.

The pattern of retreat began to change in 1659, if only for a brief time. Oliver Cromwell had died and the Protectorate of Richard Cromwell had failed.   The Generals restored the Rump of the Long Parliament and apocalyptic hopes were again raised, among Fifth Monarchy Men, Puritans and Quakers alike.   During this time (May - October, 1659) Fox and the Quakers emerged from their retreat, sensing that the changes in the political

---

[44]"Richard Farnworth to James Nayler" (July 6, 1652), *Swarth. MSS.*, 1, p. 372 (Farnworth healed a woman in Derbyshire); Cadbury, *George Fox's 'Book of Miracles'*, pp. 48-49 and Nos. 21b, 35b, 44d, 49b, 53d and 60b; Francis Higginson, *A Brief Relation*, p. 29, for an unsuccessful healing of a cripple near Kendal.   Sixteen miracles can be specifically dated to this time, most by Fox, but since most of the miracles in the *Book of Miracles* remained undated the number could be substantially greater.

[45]Cadbury, *George Fox's 'Book of Miracles'*, No. 17.   Lady Claypole was apparently healed of an affliction of the mind, probably depression.   Part of the letter reads: "Be still and cool in thy own mind and spirit from thy own thoughts, and then thou wilt feel the principle of God to turn thy mind to Lord God ...   For all distractions, distempers, unruliness, confusion, is in the transgression, which transgression must be brought down, before the principle that hath been transgressed be lifted up, whereby the mind may be seasoned and stilled ...   the light doth make manifest and discover temptations, confusion, distractions, distempers.   Do not look at the temptations, confusions, corruptions, but at the Light ...   For looking down at sin and corruption and distraction, you are swallowed up in it, but looking at the Light that discovers them you will see over them.   That will give victory, and you will find grace and strength, and there is the first step of peace ..." Lady Claypole may have been suffering under the condition of despair that many Puritans of her age suffered and Fox succeeded in drawing her attention away from a preoccupation with sin.   Whatever, her spirits were raised and this was considered to be a miracle by Fox.

climate signalled the miraculous resumption of the growth of the Stone (Christ) into universal proportions. Fox stepped out of the shadows and resumed his public ministry as a miracle - worker. This was probably the time Fox spoke about in his *Epistle Concerning the First Spreading of the Truth* written in 1676:

> For I was sent for to many sick people; and at one time I was sent for to White Chapel, about the third hour in the morning, to a woman that was dying, and her child; and the people were weeping about her. And after a while I was moved, (in the name and power of Christ Jesus), to speak to the woman; and she and her child were raised up, to the astonishment of the people, (when they came in, in the morning) and her child was also healed.[46]

This bold public miracle, almost a raising from the dead, and itself a kind of biblical epiphany, was the first recorded public miracle by Fox since 1655 and it precipitated the setting up of a Women's Meeting (previously discussed in chapter three) which itself became the focus of an outpouring of miraculous phenomena during and subsequent to this time. The exact dating of this miracle continues to elude us, as does the exact dating of the founding of the Women's Meeting, but both may be attributed to the year 1659,[47] and therefore it represents a temporary 'coming out' of Fox and Quakers into a time when it was deemed safer to resume this kind of activity; a time when the preaching of the everlasting gospel and its accompanying miraculous power was seen to coincide with the moving of the 'stone'.

---

[46]*Epistles* (1698), p. 6. The original *MS.* did not contain the words "in the name and power of Christ Jesus" nor "when they came in, in the morning". These were later additions inserted to detract any exalted claims away from Fox to Christ (compare with the *Cambridge Journal*, 2, p. 342. George Whitehead typified the attempt to deflect attention away from Fox. In *Truth Prevalent* he asked what miracles Fox boasted of. In Fox's *Journal*, he said, they were all done by the power of God. This was an impression sometimes falsely left after editorial tampering. In the same work Whitehead tried to shift emphasis away from the importance of the outward miracles to the "spiritual" miracle of conversion [*Truth Prevalent* (London, 1701), pp. 81-82].

[47]*See* chapter three, footnote 26.

Fox's great miracle at White-Chapel was very significant for several reasons. It was his first recorded public miracle since 1655 and it carried much of the bold rhetoric and biblical symbolism that recalled Christ's own miracles and Fox's earlier exalted claims. It also signified that Fox was prepared to emerge from his retreat and restore some of his lost momentum and power by seizing, through the performance of a mighty miracle, his former role of avatar. He was willing to take the risk for various reasons. Nayler was about to be released from prison and this alone would have caused Fox enough anxiety to risk reconfirming his leadership through miracles and exalted claims.[48] The political climate had also changed, temporarily, and every indication was that the 'stone' had begun to move again. Fox was astute enough to seize the moment and it may be that his great miracle at White-Chapel was meant to have this effect. It certainly set a powerful precedent for the Women's Meeting that was formed the next day.

The renewed outpouring of charismata was only temporary, at least in terms of numbers. The rapid devolution of the Commonwealth into bitter factionalism, followed by the Restoration in 1660 forced Fox back into his earlier circumspect and cautious ways. There were no more recorded miracles by Fox until 1662. John Taylor healed a child on the island of Nevis in that same year and Samuel Hooten performed miracles in America between 1664 and 1671. Quakers other than Fox were still performing miracles, albeit outside of England. In England miracles were recorded for the years 1664, 1666, 1667 and 1669, all by Fox except for Mary Atkins' remarkable healing of a Presbyterian woman in 1669. That was the second last recorded cure by a Quaker other than Fox.[49] The slow pace of Fox's miracle-working through the 1660's suddenly increased dramatically throughout the 1670's and 1680's when Fox performed more miracles than at

---

[48]Nayler was released Sept. 8, 1659 as part of a limited amnesty granted to Friends by the restored Rump Parliament (Braithwaite, *Beginnings*, p. 458). Nayler may have had temporary 'leaves' from prison before Sept. 8, 1659.

[49]The last datable miracle in the *Book of Miracles* was by an unnamed Quaker who healed the newborn child of Prince George of Denmark (Cadbury, *George Fox's 'Book of Miracles'*, No. 77a).

any other time in his ministry since the Nayler incident. Temporary changes in the political winds certainly made it safer to promote miracles and visions but Fox's self-designation as an Apostle in 1671 was what gave him a renewed sense of apostolic authority. Apostles were, after all, miracle-workers too! They saw visions and dreamed dreams. There was nothing new, or odd, about the miracles performed during this time - the healings were of various illnesses, for distraction, paralysis and even the King's Evil. Fox's encounter in Barbados seemed to distill him with a new self-understanding which led to the revival of signs and wonders. His first trips abroad occurred in the 1670's and this may have been a way of escaping imprisonment or keeping out of trouble.[50] He performed miracles in America (1672-3) and in Holland (1677)[51] where he became particularly attached to the Collegiants he met, probably because they were so receptive to his message with its emphasis on signs and wonders.[52] The trips abroad seemed to release him from stiffling pressures and daily routine at home and they renewed his self-confidence and enabled him to catch a 'second wind'.

Lessening Son of God talk, loss of eschatological urgency and a dissipation of miracles were not the only indicators of a general retreat. All Quaker sign activity receded. For example, between 1652 and 1655 there were reports that numerous Quakers were going naked as a sign. In addition to these reports twenty-one specific instances were recorded for this period. Then, between 1656 and 1658 there were no recorded cases of going naked as a sign, although William Simpson was probably active in this regard for at least part of 1656, before Nayler's sign enactment. This lack of sign activity

[50]He was imprisoned in 1670, 1673, 1674 and in 1675 he was brought before the King's Bench but was released.

[51]See Cadbury, George Fox's 'Book of Miracles', pp. 30-31, 36-37, 61-62, 110; "Calendar of the Contents of a Volume Known as "Bristol MSS. V", " JFHS, (1912), p. 191 for a vision of Fox while in Barbados and Brayshaw, Personality of George Fox, pp. 173-74.

[52]Edward Haistwell, The Haistwell Diary: A Short Journal of G.F.'s Travels ... 1677 in The Short Journal and Itinerary Journals of George Fox, pp. 239-40; Cadbury, George Fox's 'Book of Miracles', pp., xi, 30-31. Other Quakers, namely George Keith, William Penn and Robert Barclay who accompanied Fox on his Holland trip were more cautious in their views about the use of signs and wonders to confirm the veracity of the Christian faith (Cadbury, George Fox's 'Book of Miracles', pp. 29-30).

200

immediately following the Nayler incident led Kenneth Carroll to the conclusion that Nayler "must have been one of the major reasons for what appears to be a sudden (but temporary) halt to going naked as a sign."[53] Sign activity resumed again in 1659 at the same time that miracles began to reappear. In 1659 Solomon Eccles began his career of going naked as a sign and Thomas Briggs, who went naked as a sign throughout the 1660's, commenced his activity shortly thereafter. What was evident here, again, was that Quakers felt that the political climate had sufficiently changed to the extent that they were able to resume going naked as a sign. They were obviously ready to resume their role as God's threshing instruments in the overthrow of Babylon. But the second burst of sign behaviour was also temporary. After 1661 going naked as sign receded altogether. Eccles, Briggs and Thomas Brown periodically appeared naked throughout the 1660's and there were only two recorded cases in the 1670's, the last one being 1677. This corresponded with a general receding of signs and wonders through the 1660's, 1670's and 1680's. Other kinds of sign activity infrequently occurred as well even through the period of retreat. But these kinds of signs, like blackening one's face with soot, were more moderate, less scandalous, and therefore less prone to bringing the movement into disrepute.

What is clear from *Table I* is that all Quakers tended to shy away from signs and wonders during the post-Nayler and Restoration retreat. Quakers eventually left it exclusively to Fox to perform miracles, see visions and generally embody the charisma of the pre-Nayler years.[54] It is evident that Nayler embarrassed the Quakers and the disruptive tactics of his followers threatened to tear the movement apart. Quakers were forced to retreat, to rescind their controversial behaviour and language in an effort not only to

---

[53]Carroll, "Early Quakers and Going Naked as a Sign," p. 84.

[54]Fox himself never went naked or performed any other controversial sign, although he endorsed these things in others. So as signs like this receded, without Fox to carry them on they eventually died out as a part of the Quaker preaching of the everlasting gospel. There was a general movement away from signs and wonders and prophecies after the Restoration. Antonia Fraser pointed out that after 1660 little was heard, for example, from prophetesses (*The Weaker Vessel*, p. 263).

silence critics but to reassess their situation and their apocalyptic timetable and, at the same time, find new ways of dealing with dissent in the future. The task before Quakers in retreat, then, was one of disassociating themselves from what they and the world perceived was a 'ranter' spirit in their midst. To this end their own exalted language and signs and wonders had to be curtailed and even terminated. Most of all Fox's Son of God talk had to stop. It was prudent to desist from anything that could further tarnish the image and reputation of Quakers in the eyes of the world. Fox, in a sense, had to dethrone himself to save his movement.

The retreat was also fostered by the continuing disruptive activities of Nayler's followers. Everywhere, it seemed, a divisive and disorderly spirit[55] had emerged that caused Quakers to flee from public embarrassment and the excesses of Nayler's followers. After Nayler's imprisonment his followers continued to disrupt meetings and publically embarrass Quakers at a time when it was important to Quakers to be seen as quiet and contrary to the rebellious, enthusiastic, "ranter" spirit (Fox's words) that had arisen in their midst. This is not to say that Quakers themselves had not been characterized by such a spirit, at least before the Nayler incident. But now, what had once been normative had to be restrained in an attempt to dissociate from Nayler's group.

Involved in this retreat was a clear attempt to limit the individualized prophetic spirit by "deferring criticism until after a meeting and voicing it in private".[56] It also involved placing leadership under local elders and

---

[55]Nayler and his group were not the first nor the last to create a stir in Quaker ranks, although their challenge to Fox and Quakerism in general had the most devastating effects. As early as 1654 Richard Farnworth referred to the disorderly conduct of three women prophetesses - Nanny Speck, Bessie Gilburne and Jane Holmes (*Samuel Watson MSS.*, p. 36), and recommended they be spoken to for "causing the truth to suffer". In March, 1656, there were reported cases of jealousy between itinerant ministers (Braithwaite, *Beginnings*, p. 344). Internal difficulties, not necessarily linked to Nayler, were reported in Yeovil in Sept., 1656 ["Francis Howgill to George Fox" (July 21, 1656), in *Barclay MSS.*, No. 33]. And in an undated letter Nayler wrote to a Friend in Scalehouse about divisions there that were occasioned through an exalted spirit (*Caton MSS.*, 2, p. 39. Formerly *Boswell Middleton MSS*). Francis Howgills' sister Mary and Ann Blaykling were also cited for causing "confusion" and trouble among Friends at various times after the Nayler incident.

[56]Bauman, *Let Your Words Be Few*, p. 142.

ultimately "fathers" who were able to discern who spoke "in" and "out" of the Light.[57] This was an option forced upon Quakers largely, though not solely, by the events surrounding the Nayler incident. Many Friends were discouraged by the whole affair[58] and letters of instruction advising appropriate church discipline were largely addressed to these Friends. Quakers were also aware that outsiders were left with "a deep impression of the dangerous tendencies of Quaker principles"[59] and Quakers were pressed to redeem this situation by becoming more cautious and circumspect and by putting tighter controls on the expression of the individual prophetic spirit.[60] There is also evidence that the tendency to control immediacy in the meetings was a major bone of contention between Quakers and Nayler's group. In a letter to Margaret Fell, penned in 1657, Richard Hubberthorne reported that differing interpretations about immediate revelation caused Nayler's followers to continue their disruptive activity in Quaker meetings. At one meeting in London, where hundreds were gathered, Martha Simmonds and six or seven others,

> began to sing and make a noise ... and Martha took a Bible and read a psalm, and they sang it after her, as they do in the steeplehouses, but I [Hubberthorne] keeping clear in innocency, and ministering in the power of the truth as I was moved to the people their singing was confounded. And after that she took a chapter in Ezekiel: which speak [sic] to the rebellious children. And she said the Lord had sent that chapter to be read unto us, and commanded me to be silent and hear it read, but when she saw the truth prevailed over all their deceit ... then she cried out to the people, that we denied the Scriptures; And after that she said, who would have thought that the Quakers would tell people that there is a

---

[57]This was included in the 'minute of advice' drawn up by Quaker elders in Balby, Yorkshire in Nov., 1656. Portions of this document may be found in Braithwaite, *Beginnings*, pp. 310-12. An imperfect copy, incorrectly attributed, is in Barclay, *Letters*, p. 278.

[58]Braithwaite, *Beginnings*, pp. 267-68.

[59]*Ibid.*, p. 268.

[60]*Ibid.*, p. 268.

teacher within them and thou [R.H.] hast taught this three hours.[61]

These tensions and divisions were brought about due to differing opinions about immediate revelation in the ministry and a sense, among Nayler's followers, that Quakers had forsaken their prime mandate of following the inner Christ. There was a good deal of truth to Martha Simmonds claims for in retreat Quakers had begun to deliberately resist the individual spirit of prophecy in their meetings in favour of a more controlled teaching ministry from the elders and "fathers" of the movement, like Richard Hubberthorne.

Martha Simmonds knew Quakerism and its first principles well enough to charge Quakers with backing off from their belief in immediate revelation. No person, she claimed, could usurp the role of Christ, the inner teacher, and for Hubberthorne to speak and control the meeting for three hours was not only contrary to Quaker practice but it overruled the promptings of the inner Christ in each person. By strictly defining who was "in the Light" and who could speak in a meeting Quakers clearly showed signs of retreat. The routinization of the ministry was, however, considered a necessary adjustment in the wake of the Nayler incident.

Nayler and his followers had forced this conservative reaction by using the principle of immediate revelation to achieve their own goals and refashion Quakerism in their own image. What was to define the prophetic word truly spoken under the prompting of the inner Christ and the prophetic word spoken to disrupt and manipulate? Was it failure to obey the designated authority? Were those deemed to be disobedient therefore designated 'out of the light'? It was a fundamental question that Nayler and his followers forced Quakers to answer and Quakers responded by setting strict limits on the individualized prophetic ministry.

---

[61]"Richard Hubberthorne to Margaret Fell", *Caton MSS.* 3, pp. 373-74. In this same letter Hubberthorne reported that Nayler's followers continued to seek him out even after his imprisonment in Bridewell Prison in Jan., 1657. He said that when they were refused entry into the prison they would kneel at the prison walls or create such a stir that they would be admitted to the prison as prisoners, thus achieving their goal of being with their leader (*Ibid.*, p. 375).

Martha Simmonds used her prerogative to freely speak under the prompting of the inner Christ to refashion Quakerism so that it would approximate orthodoxy. The singing of Psalms and even her attempt to introduce a communion meal at one meeting[62] attested to this. Her intentions may or may not have had the best interests of Quakerism in mind, but certain of her actions lead us to wonder just where her loyalties lay. For example, on Feb. 22, 1657, shortly after Hubberthorne recorded the above incident, she, the Strangers and Dorcas Erbury were seen attending an Independent worship service held in part of Westminster Abbey. They were apparently reserved and attentive at both the morning and afternoon services (a contrast to their disruptive tactics in Quaker meetings) and they indicated a desire to hear the preacher, Mr. John Rowe, again.[63] These are puzzling actions from Nayler's most loyal and charismatic followers. The questionable loyalties of Nayler's followers may have justified the strict controls imposed upon them by their Quaker adversaries but such controls were still a retreat.

In spite of their tame performance at Westminter Abbey, Simmonds and her group continued to disrupt Quaker meetings through 1657 and 1658. On April 10, 1657 at a major gathering of Quaker leaders in London (including George Fox, Edward Burrough, John Perrot, Humphrey Norton and William Shaw) it was reported that "The agents of James Nayler come creeping on their bellies to be owned yea Martha their miserable mother, this day hath come to us, with her witchery and filthy enchantments, is set at naught, they are left for miserable examples".[64] Meetings as far away as Wales and Amsterdam were not immune to this kind of disruptive activity. Anne Cargill's constant disruption of meetings in Holland during 1657 and

---

[62]*Ibid.*, 3, p. 376. *See also* Burton, *Diary*, 1, p. 377 note.

[63]Burton, *Diary*, 1, p. 377. Simmonds had always exhibited a more orthodox religious attitude. Even her eschatology, though extreme, was 'orthodox' in the sense that it was an external rather than an internal and realized eschatology. Certainly a huge rift existed between Martha Simmonds and Quakers on many fundamental issues including Christology and eschatology. Much more work needs to be done on Simmonds and her theology and religious loyalties.

[64]"John Perrot, Humphrey Norton and William Shaw" (1657), *Swarth. MSS.*, 5, No. 22.

1658, coupled with the disrepute Nayler's messianic pretentions brought to the movement, eventually led to the disintegration of the Quaker mission in Amsterdam.[65] In this same month, April, 1657, Thomas Holme reported that there were people there who sought to silence his preaching in the Welsh Quaker meetings:

> I covered their nakedness so long as I could, till they manifested their envy in public meetings and after they had so done I would have healed up the breach but nothing would satisfy them but the stopping of my mouth forever ... The honest-hearted is preserved in truth, some is drawn aside which never came to see: they come into our meetings and tumble upon the floor, and when they can no else stop me from speaking one falls a singing, and they sit in meetings in haircloth and ashes, and is acted in all manner of deceit and imagination being full of confusion in their words. My endeavour is to keep Friends cool and quiet, and the other will die of itself.[66]

Quakers themselves had once acted in this way. In 1653 Francis Higginson reported that a typical Quaker meeting involved quaking fits and a "chaos" of different people speaking. Some would fall to the ground, others' lips would quiver, their bellies would swell up and some would foam at the mouth. This would go on for one or two hours after which they would let out a horrible roar "greater sometimes than any bull can make". The speaker at these meetings would say to those who were astounded at the sight, "let them alone, trouble them not, the spirit is now struggling with the flesh, if the spirit overcome they will quickly come out of it again, though it be sorrow now it will be joy in the morning, etc. And when they have said a few words to this effect, they go on with their speaking."[67] Following the Nayler incident Quakers retreated from this kind of ecstatic behaviour. Indeed, this kind of behaviour, including speaking in other tongues, came to be associated strictly with Nayler's group. Quakers, careful to disassociate themselves from Nayler

---

[65]*See* Popkin, "Spinoza's Relations with the Quakers," pp. 19-20, 22.

[66]"Thomas Holme to Margaret Fell" (April 16, 1657), *Swarth. MSS.*, 1, No. 196.

[67]Higginson, *Brief Relation*, p. 15.

began to disassociate themselves from their own charismatic heritage which Nayler's followers kept and faithfully carried on.

In August, 1657, Martha Simmonds' company was back at work disrupting meetings in the Salisbury area[68] and in London two Friends known only as Mildred and Judy disrupted meetings as late as March, 1658. One of them even "said she was above the apostles".[69] The idea that at least some of Nayler's followers were 'above the apostles' was very revealing. It was a common idea among some pre-Nayler Quakers - that they were living in a time that superseded the ministry of Jesus and the apostles, a time that was the final revelation of Christ in history.[70] Even after the Nayler incident Fox maintained his belief that he was at least equal with the Apostles and some of his followers privately continued, recklessly, to claim that he was Christ. But during the years of retreat it was only Nayler's followers who risked using this kind of exalted language openly. Even if Fox and other Quakers continued to believe these things privately they deplored the public display of exalted language and the unfortunate association it had with Nayler's group. In order to distance themselves from Nayler they had to distance themselves from public expression of exalted language.

---

[68]"John Braithwaite to Margaret Fell" (June 3, 1657), *Swarth. MSS.*, 3, No. 129. Braithwaite informed Fell that he had "received some hurt by some of Martha Simmonds company which came there to dwell."

[69]"Richard Hubberthorne to George Fox" (February 16, 1658), *Swarth. MSS.*, 4, No. 15; also "Richard Hubberthorne to George Fox" (March, 1658), *Swarth. MSS.*, 4, No. 12 and "Richard Hubberthorne to George Fox" (March 16, 1658), *Swarth. MSS.*, 4, No. 13 where Hubberthorne relates to Fox that at a meeting in March Mildred tried to keep him from speaking and said she had a vision that the Lord had come to her saying Francis Howgill would be struck dumb. Fox's denunciation of Mildred and Judy is in "George Fox to Anthony Wright", *Swarth. MSS.*, 2, No. 42.

[70]A notion prefigured in Thomas Edwards' list of sectarian errors: "That many Christians in these days have more knowledge than the Apostles, and when the time is come that there shall be true Churches and ministry erected, they shall have greater gifts, and do greater miracles than the Apostles ever did, because the Christian Church was but then in infancy" (*Gangraena*, first edition, p. 28). Edwards may have been referring to Seeker ideas here. John Toldervy wrote of his conversion to Quakerism: "I was persuaded there was a greater revelation to be manifested in me, than there was in Christ, or the Apostles" (The *Foot Out of the Snare*, p. 22).

As late as 1659 Edward Burrough was counselling London Friends to not heed "those rebellious ... spirits amongst you, which may trouble you, as they have formerly done to the great dishonour of the Lord, I wish they were cut off as for Truth's sake, yet I exhort you to bear them with patience."[71] George Whitehead, too, referred to the continued "ranting, bawling and reproaching us, crying out "you have lost the power, you have lost the power"."[72] This sense, on the part of some Quakers, that their brethren had "lost the power" was evidence enough that some kind of post-Nayler retreat had occurred. These same people, continued Whitehead, denounced Fox, and "said a higher was come out, and in standing against it the Quakers were as bad as the priests."[73] It is not unreasonable to suggest that Nayler's very charismatic followers were continuators of the original vision of Fox and the 'spirit' of early Quakerism. That is, they believed they were the chosen saints of the new age and their continuing charismatic behaviour was representative of the greatest and final post-apostolic outpouring of the spirit in accordance with Joel 2. They went as far as to proclaim Nayler a higher revelation of Christ than Fox. He was their Messiah. On the other hand, Fox and the bulk of Quakers who remained loyal to him, let their exalted claims slowly slip away, rather than compete with Nayler's exalted claims with newer and bolder claims of their own. In this sense Nayler cost Fox a great deal (the Barbados Formula at least allowed him to retain something), for he and his followers were forced to publicly disassociate themselves from their earlier fundamental postulates of immediate revelation, perfection, deification and apocalyptic urgency.[74]

---

[71]Quoted in Braithwaite, *Beginnings*, p. 381.

[72]Nayler, *Works*, p. xvi.

[73]*See* Braithwaite, *Beginnings*, p. 270.

[74]In the *Epistle From Friends of the General Meeting Held in London, the 31st of 3rd Month, 1672* ministers were advised "not to teach the highest doctrines like perfection until people's minds were ready for it was a stumbling block to minds biased against Truth". They were also advised to "avoid all imagined, unseasonable and untimely prophesyings" (Barclay, *Letters*, pp. 330-32).

In retreat Quakers appeared to have lost their power and charisma and while they made valiant efforts to redeem some of that lost power and momentum in 1659/60 they never fully recovered it. There was a kind of 'release' after years of retreat. But the ecstasy and demonstrations of charismatic power occasioned by the experience of the Christ who dwelt within never returned. After Nayler it was never a normative part of the Quaker experience in their meetings for worship, although it intermittently appeared from time to time as it did in the case of Prudence Wilson's vision in 1698 or the curious "children's revival" at Waltham Abbey in 1679.[75] The threshing meetings continued and they continued to attract thousands but they were quieter and more controlled.[76] The original widespread demonstration of charismatic power was forever lost to Quakers after Nayler.

By mid-July, 1657 even Nayler appeared to be in retreat. He wrote a letter from prison denouncing the spirit of disorder that had arisen among some of his followers, whom he later called ranters. Other letters from this time suggest that he was also retreating from his exalted claims and was ready for reconciliation with Fox.[77] He was even considering a public

---

[75]For Prudence Wilson's vision see *Reynolds MSS.*, pp. 111-16. The children's revival was mentioned by George Keith in *The Magic of Quakerism* (London, 1707), p. 51 and by the Quaker schoolmaster John Matern in *A Testimony to the Lord's Power and Blessed Appearance In and Amongst Children* (London, 1679). According to Matern a Quaker meeting was held in Waltham Abbey, a town in Essex, on June 4, 1679. Forty or fifty boys and girls, all eight to ten years old, were present and several experienced the "melting of heart" and broke into tears - a phenomenon not unlike the reaction to outbursts of charismatic power in the earliest Quaker meetings. Soon all the children had fallen under the charismatic power which soon reached the adults as well. This continued through the remainder of the meeting and according to Matern continued thereafter in meetings for some time (*Ibid.*, p. 7). Matern, a German who was headmaster of the Quaker school at Waltham Abbey, said that he was so overcome by the same power that he shook and trembled (*Ibid.*, p. 17 - a revisiting of the power of old?). Not long after this incident the children's school was moved out of Waltham Abbey and transferred to Edmonton.

[76]Braithwaite, *Beginnings*, p. 384.

[77]Martha Simmonds herself had cooled off by the autumn of 1657 for Hubberthorne reported that "Martha Simmonds and her company is quiet". He even admitted that "there is something of God stirring in her" ["Richard Hubberthorne to Margaret Fell" (1657), *Caton MSS.*, 3, p. 391]. This is the final reference to Martha Simmonds in Quaker literature even though she lived for another eight years, until April, 1665. There is one other reference to her in the anti-Quaker literature but it is a general comment on her past activities and says nothing

recantation.[78] In late 1657 or early 1658 (before the dissolution of
Parliament) Nayler also wrote a letter to Parliament admitting that it was

---

about her present whereabouts. She may have returned to the Quaker fold, or, more
probably, returned to some kind of 'orthodox' worship. Hannah Stranger condemned her part
in the affair much later, in 1669, and in 1670 she was actively petitioning the King on behalf of
Margaret Fell (Braithwaite, *Beginnings*, p. 269). Robert Rich, who continued to herald
Nayler's cause and attack Fox in writing went to Barbados where he disrupted Quaker
meetings there with his singing. Following his return to England the London clothier resumed
attending Quaker meetings, even though he had long since been disowned by them.
Braithwaite wrote that he "used to come to meetings and walk up and down in a stately
manner, having a long white beard, and being dressed in a black velvet coat with a loose cloth
[worn?] over it. When he heard anything that pleased him he would cry "Amen, amen, amen""
(*Ibid.*, pp. 270-71). Even Rich had finally mellowed, if not retreated. He hadn't lost his
charismatic zeal completely but it was sufficiently muted to be acceptable to Friends. He
remained loyal to Nayler to the end and his curious reference in his Epistles to the "Church of
the First-Born" may have been a reference to the true church of the saints of which he
considered Nayler the founder [Robert Rich, *The Epistles of (Mr. Robert Rich) to the Seven
Churches* (London, 1680, Preface]. Rather than being an organized church it seems to have
been a loose knit collection of diverse individuals who had as their common denominator a tie
to Nayler. These would have included Robert Bacon (who signed a petition for Nayler's
release in 1656), William Rawlinson (son of Thomas Rawlinson, Nayler's fellow prisoner at
Exeter), and William Blackborrow (husband of Sarah Blackborrow [Blackberry] who had
kneeled before Nayler at Bristol along with William Erbury's daughter and Martha Simmonds
(the sister of the well known Quaker printer Giles Calvert). They each received from Rich a
sum of money designated for the Church of the First-Born (*Ibid.*, Preface). Rich and the
enigmatic 'Church of the First-Born' embodied Nayler's cause until well into the 1680's [*See* G.
Nuttall, "The Last of James Nayler: Robert Rich and the Church of the First-Born," *Friends
Quarterly*, (July, 1985), p. 532]. The other six churches were the Roman Catholic, Episcopal,
Presbyterian, Independent, Anabaptist and Quaker and they, too, each received a sum of
money from Rich. Rich was one of the last Quakers, if not the last, to adhere to the original
Quaker notion of celestial inhabitation (Rich, *A Testimony to Truth*, pp. 8-9).

[78]"Alexander Parker to Margaret Fell" (April 15, 1658), Barclay, *Letters*, p. 57. Also
"James Nayler to Margaret Fell" (1656), *Swarth. MSS.*, 3, No. 83; "James Nayler to Margaret
Fell" (1658), *Swarth. MSS.*, 3, No. 84; "John Stubbs and William Caton to Margaret Fell"
(June 10, 1657), *Swarth. MSS.*, 3, No. 152; An Epistle From Francis Howgill, *Swarth. MSS.*,
5, No. 11; "William Dewsbury to James Nayler", *Swarth. MSS.*, 5, No. 50; "Richard
Hubberthorne to James Nayler", *Swarth. MSS.*, 5, No. 51 and Nayler, *Works*, pp. xxv-xxx.
Nayler's recantation requires more careful analysis. What was the extent of his recantation?
Did he ever recant or simply reconcile with Fox and his fellow Quakers? While he was in
prison a paper was reportedly published which purported to be his recantation [*James Naylor's
Recantation*, (London, 1656)]. George Whitehead treated the document as authentic [George
Whitehead, *An Antidote Against the Venome of the Snake in the Grass* (London, 1697), p. 5].
Naylor denied ever writing the document, although it was a reprint of his *To all the People of
the Lord Gathered and Scattered* (1659), under a different title. He never clearly repudiated
his exalted claims and celestial flesh notions but like Fox he retreated from using exalted
language. His repentant spirit was seen by some accusers as a recovery "to a sound state of
mind" (Neale, *History of the Puritans*, 4, p. 143).

210

idolatry for him, as James Nayler the creature, to be exalted and worshipped. The spirit of Christ in him condemned this practice.[79] This was no change from his position at his trial. But the fact that he thought it was necessary to clarify his position with Parliament suggested that he was trying to appear more moderate than his reputation as a heretic and blasphemer implied. Nayler was a person in retreat, a person concerned to redeem lost credibility, and like Fox a person concerned to declare innocence on the basis that he was in the pre-Fall, pre-carnal state in which he could not sin. His clarification before Parliament was necessary both for his restoration to the Quaker fold (which he longed for) and for Quakerism in general. If Nayler was to be restored then all taint of public scandal and blasphemy had to be obliterated. This was the 'psychology' of Quakerism in retreat. Somehow all taint of scandal had to be removed while being seen to remain faithful to the fundamental ideas of immanence, immediate revelation and perfection. Nayler's deep need to reconcile with his brethren forced him to comply. His correspondence from mid-July onward was characteristic of a man in retreat.

By the summer of 1658 Nayler was openly longing for reconciliation with Fox. Alexander Parker, who had visited Nayler in prison, reported to Margaret Fell that Nayler wished her to intercede before Fox on his behalf.[80] Nayler himself wrote to Fell expressing his desire for reconciliation.[81] He was not admitting to guilt in the affair, only that he was prepared to forgive and reconcile for the sake of unity. He still felt that he was the one who had been wronged and maligned. Fox, however, did not share Nayler's concern for reconciliation:

> James thou canst not come to me, who hath the wrong measure and judgment, but my own is my own: thou suffered thy disciples to blaspheme, but life and glory stands over all; and thy disciples ... [take] my words, and [turn] them into a lie; my soul hath suffered, and travailed for you, but I stamp upon the contrary ... I would have compassed your weaknesses, and have gathered you as a hen her chickens ... and you would not;

[79]James Nayler, *A Testimony to Christ Jesus Delivered to the Parliament* (London, 1659). This is a one page Broadside.

[80]"Alexander Parker to Margaret Fell", Barclay, *Letters*, p. 57.

> And James I must not let in any wickedness, nor a lying spirit;
> but it is judged with the spirit of god and my judgment shall
> stand forever, though by thee judged false, and not see thee.
> There is no pardon for thee in this, but judgment, and hast
> denied me before men, and wrote that I judged thee with
> jealousy; from him who is unknown to thee, and you, and the
> world; thee denyst the power of god and calls it deceipt, that is
> the false Christ [Nayler] which is risen after the true Christ
> [Fox], thou hast acted against the truth.[82]

The charge of blasphemy and an unforgiving spirit is indeed a cruel cudgel of power. Fox went on to accuse Nayler of acting contrary to the power of God and of refusing to bow to that power at Exeter. Instead Nayler had made himself a false Christ. He concluded by saying that if Nayler was to be redeemed he would have to bow before that power again - ie. bow before Fox. There is powerful and profound symbolism in this letter which proves that while Fox had publicly retreated from his exalted claims he still privately believed that he was an avatar. Words like 'god', 'power of god', 'Christ' and 'truth' were all used by Fox to personify his divine status and authority. When Nayler set himself "against the truth" (ie. against Fox, or really Christ) he committed an unpardonable sin. At the time Fox wanted to be benevolent. Fox wanted to redeem Nayler from his "weakness" but Nayler would not come so Fox stamped on the spirit of contrariness and wickedness (as the truth personified he could not "let in any wickedness") and he and Margaret Fell literally buried Nayler's name forever.

When the Rump of the Long Parliament resumed in September, 1659, Nayler was released from prison and given into the custody of Francis Howgill and a prominent London Quaker, Edward Byllinge. This, understandably, created grave new anxieties for Fox. The spectre of a free Nayler may even have contributed to his severe psychic or catatonic state which occurred while he was in prison at Reading. A concerned Nayler, now free, went to visit Fox "in tenderness of love"[83] but he was rebuffed, either by

---

[81]"James Nayler to Margaret Fell", *Swarth. MSS.*, 3, No. 84.

[82]"George Fox to James Nayler", *Markey MSS.*, pp. 121-22.

[83]"James Nayler to Margaret Fell" (1658), in Barclay, *Letters*, p. 58.

Fox or the prison authorities, it is not certain. Nayler wrote, "I was not permitted to come where he was".[84] Nayler resumed attending Quaker meetings in London. By October, 1659 he was preaching and was well on his way to assuming his pre-1656 influence and popularity. As Nayler's popularity grew an uneasy Fox, haunted by memories of the great embarrassment, wrote to Hubberthorne suggesting that Nayler be moved to Bishoprick. Fox had done the same thing in 1656. It was his way of removing Nayler from a position of influence.[85] But Hubberthorne and other Quakers were sufficiently reconciled with Nayler that they did not share Fox's distrust - they did not hold the same hostility towards him, but then they had had less to lose. Hubberthorne responded to Fox that Nayler, for the present, belonged in London for "here is a great service for him".[86] This was a certain sign of a post-Nayler democratization of leadership and a certain sign that in retreat Fox had lost some of his authority and divine stature as an avatar. Hubberthorne was able to overrule Fox in a way that had not been possible in 1656 when Nayler was forced to leave London for Yorkshire against his will.

Nayler's retreat was completed after his release from prison and his return to the Quaker fold in London. During this time (the autumn of 1659 and early 1660) he wrote several pamphlets answering those who had written against him while he was in prison[87] and condemning the disruptive activities and wild actions of some of his followers.[88] He also confessed that during the Bristol incident he was "wholly led by others, whose work was to divide

---

[84]*Ibid.*, p. 58.

[85]"Richard Hubberthorne to George Fox" (May 24, 1660), in Barclay, *Letters*, p. 83 and Nayler, *Works*, p. xxi.

[86]*Ibid.*, p. 83.

[87]Scandalous and unfounded charges even appeared in caricatures of Nayler on the Continent (Bittle, *James Nayler*, p. 232 n. 38).

[88]James Nayler, *Having Heard that Some Have Wronged my Words* (London, 1659), p. 3.

[him] from the children of light."[89] He again condemned any and all worship of his person, the idolizing of his person and "all the rest of those wild actions" during his dark night of the soul. He wholly blamed himself for what happened.[90] All this paved the way for his final, public reconciliation (or confession?) before Fox.

The reconciliation occurred in February, 1660. Nayler was the leading Quaker preacher in London at the time and Fox, now freed from prison, had just resumed his public miracle-working and more circumspect Son of God talk. Fox may have thought it necessary to resume these 'proofs' of his authority to meet the Nayler threat. Nor was it unusual that Fox made every effort to avoid Nayler when he visited London in February, 1660. But Dewsbury pressed for and got a meeting between the two. The differing

---

[89]Quakers never abandoned their conviction that Nayler, manipulated by Martha Simmonds, was responsible for the crisis that beset their movement in 1656. This view is the one that has come to dominate the interpretation of these events to the present. Martha Simmonds was responsible for the plague of ranterism that was let loose on the movement. When Fox and other Quakers used the term 'ranter' in this way they intended to use it in a thoroughly derisive way, in a sense that explained what happened. Fox and his theology of celestial adoption were never implicated - all that part of the story was covered up, edited from the sources or simply disappeared after the de-divinization of the inner light. This study has sought to revise the one-sided attribution of blame by pointing out that Fox set the ideological and behavioural precedent for the so-called devolution toward ranterism. Martha Simmonds became a convenient scapegoat for the troublesome and embarrassing events between 1656 and 1659. Fox denounced those who followed Nayler as "loose persons" (*Cambridge Journal*, 2, p. 314). Dewsbury said that Nayler was much wronged at the hands of Martha Simmonds and encouraged Nayler to overcome and judge the spirit of strife and disorder that caused his "downfall" ("William Dewsbury to James Nayler", *Swarth. MSS.*, 5, No. 50). And George Bishop specifically referred to her as "that woman through whom this hour came" adding that the "spirit which darkened [Nayler]" entered him through her "and the other two with her, and all their filth" (*Throne of Truth Exalted*, pp. 4, 5, 9). As Simmonds and her company continued to disrupt meetings William Caton, writing about disturbances of meetings in London, said that "those that adhere after James Nayler" had grown impudent ["William Caton to Margaret Fell" (January 17, 1657), *Swarth. MSS.*, 1, No. 136. For other reactions *see* "Richard Waller and Richard Roper to Margaret Fell" (July 4, 1657), *Barclay MSS.*, No. 24 and "Edward Burrough to George Fox" (December 12, 1656), *Barclay MSS.*, No. 36]. Others said they were an offence ["Richard Hubberthorne to Margaret Fell" (December 10, 1656), in Barclay, *Letters*, p. 48]. Fox called them "rude people and apostates" (Nickalls, *Journal*, p. 289). What else could he and other Quakers have said? To explain, excuse and justify the incident blame was put squarely onto Martha Simmonds and her company ("George Fox to James Nayler", *Markey MSS.*, 5, p. 122).

[90]James Nayler, *To the Life of God in All* (London, 1659), pp. 1-8 and *Glory to God Almighty Who Ruleth in the Heavens*, p. 2.

reports of this meeting reflect what the differing parties wanted to convey about it, Fox and Quakerism in general. For example, Dewsbury said this of the meeting:

> Mighty was His majesty amongst His people in the day He healed up the breach which had been so long to the sadness of the hearts of many. The Lord clothed my dear brethren G[eorge] F[ox], E[dward] B[urrough], F[rancis] H[owgill], with a precious wisdom. A healing spirit did abound within them, with the rest of the Lord's people there that day ... And dear J[ames] N[ayler] the Lord was with him.[91]

It was in Dewsbury's interests to clearly convey the idea that reconciliation had occurred and peace had been made. Quakerism was once again united. What he did not mention was how Fox received Nayler. He had Nayler bow before him and kiss his hands and feet. This was confirmed in a long letter a disgusted Robert Rich sent to Fox. He said that Fox gave Nayler his hand and then his foot to kiss (one recalls the aborted foot kissing episode at Exeter Prison in 1656) after which Nayler (and several others) fell down before Fox and confessed.[92] Fox had stated in his letter to Nayler that this was the only way a reconciliation between the two could have happened. Nayler had to bow before the "truth". This version sounds less like a reconciliation than a public humiliation dramatically staged not only to reassert Fox's dominion and exalted position in his movement but to give Fox a forum to say, through powerful symbolism, that he was still an avatar in firm control of the movement and he demanded the respect and the worship that came with that position.

As Bittle pointed out, while Fox was alive "no edition of Nayler's works appeared in print."[93] There was no evidence that Fox's attitudes about himself had changed in retreat. What had changed, and this was a significant

---

[91]"William Dewsbury to Margaret Fell" (March, 1660), *Swarth. MSS.*, 4, No. 134.

[92]Rich, *Hidden Things Brought To Light*, p. 40.

[93]Bittle, *James Nayler*, p. 174. When George Whitehead's edition did appear it was heavily censored. All the controversial 1656 works were left out. Margaret Fell also struck Nayler from memory. She never mentioned him in her memoirs even though he had been with Fox at Swarthmoor at the beginning in 1652.

change, was that now leading Quakers like Dewsbury played a greater role in orchestrating the internal affairs of the movement and even Fox's own life. But at the actual meeting between Fox and Nayler Fox upstaged everyone by soliciting homage and worship from Nayler and several others who also bowed before him. Fox used the occasion of his alleged reconciliation with Nayler to dramatize his precedence as a living theophany in the movement. The whole exercise was less a reconciliation than an acknowledgment of who Fox was.

Shortly after this incident Nayler travelled to Bristol where he "confessed his offence in a way which tendered and broke the meeting into tears."[94] His "offence" consisted of inflicting upon Quakerism a spirit of division and disorder which brought great suffering upon his peers and disrepute to the movement in general. For this all Quakers, possibly excepting Fox and Fell, were willing to, and indeed did, personally forgive Nayler. His public confession in Bristol indicated that his personal retreat was now complete. He, too, had finally sacrificed his earlier exalted language and charismatic authority to help save the movement.

Retreat did not mean that signs and wonders stopped completely, or that dangerous language ceased altogether. But it was slowed, controlled and kept secretive. The Nayler incident forced all Quakers to consciously guard their language and actions and if at all possible drop dangerous terminology, even if in retreat their principal views remained unchanged. As a result Quakers lost their stride, not in terms of growth but in terms of charismatic power. In the years of retreat it was not uncommon to have General Meetings where thousands of Friends attended.[95] Nonetheless, there was a loss of charismatic power. Nayler's followers sensed this and specifically charged Quakers with having "lost the power". Quakers made the inevitable compromise for control and discipline within the ranks by routinizing the ministry and suppressing damaging material, so that no Quaker should give the world any reason to scorn Quakerism or see it in a

---

[94]Braithwaite, *Beginnings*, p. 274.

[95]This is all well documented by Braithwaite in his chapter on the growth of Quakerism between 1656 and 1660 (*Beginnings*, pp. 368-400).

state of disunity. The concern with public image and unity was a major catalyst in the post-Nayler and Restoration retreat from the dangerous language incited by Fox's theology of celestial inhabitation.

During the retreat it was difficult to recognize any substantive change in the theology itself. Celestial inhabitation remained as did some sense of eschatological urgency and this reappeared in 1659/60, only to slowly fade away for good through the 1660's and 1670's. Fox showed signs of theological retreat, but only in the sense that some of his own exalted claims to divine sonship were omitted or rephrased along the lines of apostleship. *The Great Mystery of the Great Whore* (1659) was a fresh and bold attempt to seize the moment and regain lost momentum. Fox even boldly restated his belief that the saints were equal with God and that Christ was in them in flesh and bone. It was an attempt to recapture lost avatarial power and to get his movement back on track. But in trying to recapture it there was a sad realization that he had lost the moment. His arguments in *The Great Mystery* were worn and repetitious. They had a strangely dated air. They were reminders of the fierce battles fought in the pre-Nayler years. Fox (and Burrough in his *Epistle to the Reader* that introduced the book) was trying to seize the initiative again but the Nayler incident and the subsequent retreat into secretive silence on so many things that mattered had left its mark. The 'enthusiasm' simply waned, not after 1660, as most interpreters of this era of Quaker history suggest,[96] but immediately after the Nayler affair.

Fox's *Great Mystery* suggested two things about the retreat. It was initially uneven and halting, though decisive in its general direction over the decades.[97] It also suggested that nothing had changed (and maybe Fox hoped it hadn't) but in fact the biggest change had already occurred before 1660 and Nayler's followers hadn't missed it. The power was lost due to a

---

[96]*See* Reay, *Quakers and the English Revolution*, p. 112, for example.

[97]Fox's reassertion of his belief in celestial unity in 1659 doesn't negate the idea of retreat. If one is to argue from meticulous analysis and prudent consideration of the sources then Fox's ongoing exalted claims cannot be overlooked. And this would not be the last time Fox would try to seize the moment or re-establish his claim to leadership based on exalted claims. But there was still a tendency toward more circumspect and moderate language, even with Fox, and this was a mark of retreat.

routinization of ministry that stiffled the spontaneity of the prophetic utterance of the inner Christ in every believer. It only remained to bring theology into line with these institutional changes.

Fox emerged from the post-Nayler retreat in firm control of Quakerism. But he was no longer the widely accepted avatar that he once was. The retreat was Fox's unmaking as a 'god'. It cost him time, momentum, power, prestige and divinity. He worked hard to regain all this, and to an extent he succeeded, but one cannot help notice the marked changes in language and attitudes, the falling off of signs and wonders, the readiness to sacrifice 'enthusiasm' for respectability and the willingness on the part of some Quaker leaders to challenge Fox's decisions. There was a time when all that was different, when Fox was the undisputed leader of his movement and an undisputed avatar in his own right.

The retreat (which slowly developed into a full fledged transformation) is a crucial part of the narrative of early Quaker history and it is one that has been generally ignored in the historiography. Quakers were recoiling from Nayler long before the Restoration. They were groping for new ways to deal with the problem of schism and dissent from within. In retreat Quakers were not yet ready for wholesale change, largely because they still hoped for some imminent universal transformation. They still believed in and expected signs and wonders and some continued to think of Fox in highly exalted terms. Quakers were not ready, in retreat, to leave all that behind - at least not yet. In retreat they were in a state of waiting for something, anything to happen. And it did, temporarily, during the last months of the Commonwealth. But even then, when Quaker signs and wonders and apocalyptic hopes resurfaced, it became evident that in retreat they had lost so much momentum and so much of their early prodigious power that they were never able to fully recover it. Fox was a living example of Kant's idea that "prophetic history is possible only if the prophet himself occasions and produces the events he predicts." That was possible when Fox was the undisputed leader and avatar of his movement. But his unmaking as a 'god' had a neutralizing effect on his charismatic ministry and the great hopes for imminent eschatological change that seemed to be interwoven with it. Quakers looked elsewhere, to the prophetic pronouncements of past prophets, to authenticate their claims. Fox lost the power to occasion and produce the events he predicted and his treatment of Nayler at their February, 1660 meeting needs to be interpreted in this light. Nayler forced Fox into retreat and in so doing cost Fox dearly. Apostleship was the most and the best that could be claimed thereafter. Best in the functional sense that it still allowed Fox freedom and authority to promote new revelations without danger: radical eschatology, radical atonement and radical ethics. But it was a recession for him. He was large enough or politic enough a man to see that his recessional was the movement's processional (though church hymns were not his style). His withdrawal allowed the movement to flourish in a changed social, political and cultural context. Radicalism was tamed by retreat and by the need for respectability in a hostile world.

7

TRANSFORMATION

In the last chapter we saw how the seeds of transformation were already sown in the post-Nayler retreat. Immediate revelation was subjected to the control of the elders. The proselytizing spirit and perfectionist language were muted. There was a falling off of signs and wonders and above all Quakers backed away from Fox's language of avatarship. After the Restoration a full scale transformation of certain aspects of Quakerism was under way - the routinization of the ministry, the growth of a formal organization, the deferring of the Kingdom of God, the slow development of pacifism and the development of a distinctive "plain culture" or style. All this change was part of a long process as old ideas continued to exist alongside the new. Since these latter aspects of change have been well documented in the historical literature there is no need to expand on them here.[1]

What has not yet been said, and could well be treated in a larger study beyond the scope of this chapter, is that the most important transformation

---

[1]Detailed accounts of these aspects of the transformation may be found in Reay, *Quakers and the English Revolution*; Bauman, *Let Your Words Be Few*; Cope, "Seventeenth Century Quaker Style"; Oliver, "Quaker Testimony and the Lamb's War"; Cole, "Quakers and the English Revolution"; MacLear, "Quakerism at the End of the Interregnum"; Barbour, *Quakers in Puritan England*; Braithwaite, *Second Period*, pp. 251-89.

of Quakerism involved the de-divinization of the movement in the 1670's.[2]
With de-divinization came a general loss of charismatic power, a loss of
radicalism and a loss of the chosenness and exclusivity that came with the
knowledge that one was deified and specially empowered to work signs and
wonders and actively participate in the 'threshing' process that precipitated
the universal appearance of the Kingdom of God. This important theological
realignment was necessary not only because Quakers were so close to
modernity (faith in Reason and Science)[3] but because it was necessary to put
a stop to the persistent hounding of critics and address the institutional and
ideological changes that had been brought about both by the Nayler incident
and the Restoration. De-divinization is not used in an absolute sense but in a
relative sense here. The emphasis is not on betrayal or villainy, much less on
the notion of some kind of rise and fall. Rather it is thought of as Gilbert
Murray thought of a similar transformation in Greek religion - "as a sort of
failure of nerve".[4]

To interpret the fundamental catalyst of change within early
Quakerism as an act of de-divinization suggests that the traditional
periodization of Quaker history is slightly out of kilter. The political change
brought about by the Restoration cannot be the singular reason for the
transformation of Quakerism that some interpreters suggest. To say that the
adjustments within Quakerism were a reaction to political pressures brought
to bear upon Quakers during the Restoration may be accurate, but it is not

---

[2]Strictly speaking the spiritualizing of the inner light should not diminish the divinity
of the influence involved, for in orthodox trinitarian theory the Spirit is quite as divine as the
pre-existent Son. In fact, the Son carries more kudos. John Reeve, the Muggletonian
opponent of early Quakerism provided a more esoteric word, a word more agreeable to
seventeenth century metaphysics, suggesting that Quakers falsely allowed an immaterial
substance independent of the body. We could coin the word 'de-substantiate', then, to make
the point, gaining accuracy at the expense of being arcane. The word 'de-divinize' seems less
archane.

[3]As for the notion of Enlightenment and the revisions to the idea that belief in magic
remained only at the level of popular culture *see* Margaret Jacobs, "Science and Social Passion:
The Case of Seventeenth Century England," *Journal of the History of Ideas*, 43 (1982), pp. 331-
39 and Robert Darnton, *The Literary Underground of the Old Regime* (Cambridge: Harvard
University Press, 1982).

[4]Murray, *Five Stages of Greek Religion*, (Oxford: Clarendon, 1925), pp. 155-207.

the whole picture. To hang changes in the Quaker movement on political pegs, however convenient, is to miss the inner, spiritual life of the movement. It fails, in a fundamental way, to explain the dynamics behind such a total transformation in such a short time. If political pressure explains the *why* of transformation the redefinition of the inner light explains the *how*. Only this explains how such a wholesale transformation could occur. The forces unleashed by Nayler forever etched on the Quaker mind a fear of chaos and ridicule brought about directly by the uncontrolled, unchecked individual prophetic spirit. Quakers were never quite the same after Nayler.

The transformation of Quakerism began well before the Restoration and continued until well after Fox's death when blasphemy became an issue of blatant denial - denial that Fox ever was what opponents said he was and denial that Fox ever taught that Christ (and therefore God) literally dwelt in the creature and thus deified the creature. It is true that some of Fox's loyal followers were of the mind that he was a 'god' as late as 1675 at the peak of the theological realignment. It was a reminder that not all Quakers had shed their belief in celestial inhabitation. But this kind of thing was rare after the Nayler incident and most Quakers tended to keep contentious views private, apart from the battles fought later in the century and into the next, when hoary old charges of blasphemy were dredged up for new consumption. Quakers were beset by opponents who had a bit between their teeth and would not let it go, but at the same time enough evidence remained for the critic to continue well-founded charges of blasphemy. These charges were a continuing worry to Quakers and were one of the major reasons why some leading Quakers tried to improve their public image (especially after the Restoration) by transforming the doctrine of the inner Christ into a more innocuous and less offensive doctrine. This was achieved through a certain amount of legerdemain on the part of some well-educated Quaker theologians in the 1670's, and the Second Day Morning Meeting that

222

censored Quaker writings and sanctioned the selective editing of the sources in the name of Respectability.[5]

The goal of this chapter is to determine how Quaker apologists proceeded in their arguments against the blasphemy charges of their opponents and specifically to determine how they transformed Fox's doctrine of the inner Christ. Consistently they denied the charges of their opponents and they were able to do this only after they had established that what they thought Fox *intended* with his exalted language was not what his opponents thought. That is, the only way that Quaker apologists could lay the persistent charge of blasphemy to rest was to undercut their opponents charges with a clarified (redefined) concept of the inner Christ. They provided the sophisticated epistemological tool necessary for the eventual success of the transformation toward a respectable, mystical religion. The two tools that made such a transformation possible were restatements leading to a new ideology and tight corporate control that censored Quaker writings and allowed, in the self-interests of the group, bowdlerization. Without the redefinition of the inner Christ Quakerism would have remained an 'enthusiast' sect and it would not have survived the disdain of an increasingly rationalist and scientific seventeenth century.

It is generally believed that the inner light was the one 'constant' that never changed in Quakerism. Upon closer examination, however, it is apparent that this cherished doctrine underwent a massive transformation which subsequently enabled Quakers to embrace wide-ranging change. Political pressure produced a reaction but it fails to explain satisfactorily why Quakers, in ever increasing numbers, were willing to sacrifice the very bedrock of their early experience. There was a time when no amount of political pressure would have persuaded Quakers to alter their conviction about celestial inhabitation. They would have been slaughtered as lambs, one and all, for their beliefs and for the cause of the Lamb's War. Augustine

---

[5]On self-censorship *see* Anabelle Patterson, *Censorship and Interpretation: The Conditions of Writing and Reading in Early Modern England* (Madison, Wisc.: University of Wisconsin Press, 1984).

said "that it is not the penalty which makes true martyrs, but the cause".[6] The Quakers had a cause (a Good Old Cause made over into a Lamb's War) and no penalty was too severe to deter them from pursuing that cause to the end. There must be more to explain the transformation, then, than mere political change. And there is. The blasphemy trials, the Nayler incident and the constant hounding of antagonists who ridiculed Fox's exalted claims were all too vivid reminders to Quaker leaders that there was a kind of chaos at work in their ranks that had to be brought under control. And that chaos spun out of a volatile centre - Fox's doctrine of celestial inhabitation and the ensuing belief in the divinization of the saints and the supremacy of the individual prophetic spirit. By disembodying and de-divinizing the inner Christ, radicalism and enthusiasm could be exorcized, the exorbitant claims minimized, perfection muted, eschatological urgency dropped and an 'in the meantime' ecclesiology adopted. Indeed, by redefining the inner Christ it became possible for the whole movement to be transformed into the respectable and mystical religion that it became.

The de-divinization of Quakerism through re-defining the inner Christ was not Fox's work, and although he never publicly disputed with Penn or Barclay about their erroneous 'clarifications' of his intentions, he personally refused to back away from his belief in celestial inhabitation. When Fox wrote his *Great Mystery of the Great Whore* in 1659 he powerfully restated all his beliefs. Most importantly the celestial flesh of Christ was not distinct from the body of the saints: "And are these not three that bear record in heaven, the Father, the word, and the 'spirit', and are they not all one? How then are they distinct?" "Is not Christ in man? And doth not Christ say they must eat his flesh? And how can any eat Christ's flesh, if his flesh be not in them?" "*And the saints are not distinct from him,* for they sit with him in heavenly places, and he is in them, and they in him" (italics mine).[7] The Godhead was not divided. Christ and therefore the undivided Godhead

---

[6]D.A.B. Caillou, *Sancti Aurelii Augustini Hippoensis Episcopi Operum. Pars VII. Epistolae. In Collectio Selecta SS. Ecclesiae Patrum, Complectens Exquisitissima Opera,* vol. 146 (Paris, 1835), pp. 151-52.

[7]Fox, *Great Mystery of the Great Whore,* 3, pp. 180, 134, 291.

224

resided in the saints. The saints were not distinct from Christ. Herein lies the central, profound truth that led Fox to found a new religion and it was later literally ripped from the record in the name of Respectability.

Fox did not interpret spiritual experience through the accepted mediating symbols and theological distinctions (which is not to say that he did not have his own). In another part of *The Great Mystery* he wrote "Christ's body is a glorified body" which was also "the power of God".[8] He also said that the Spirit or "infallible Spirit"[9] was the power of God which Christ, the prophets and the Apostles had. Fox's concept of "Spirit" was not that of a disembodied Spirit. Light, celestial "glorified" flesh of Christ, Spirit, Spirit of God and power of God were essentially identical.[10] He also used the New Testament phrase "sons of God led by the Spirit of God" just as it occurred shortly thereafter in the letter to Charles II. This means that Fox's Charles II letter, while quoting Scripture and seeming circumspect should still be read in the context of Spirit equalling Christ equalling glorified, celestial flesh of Christ. He was only explicitly more cautious. As we will see, Quaker theologians like Penn and Barclay disembodied the Spirit and turned the literal presence of the glorified body of Christ in the believer into a strictly figurative presence.[11] Fox's frequent use of "flesh and bone" suggests that he had something more palpable in mind. He explicitly associated 'spirit' with a celestial flesh and bone Christ formed within, who was also the power of God, the power of the Apostles and the power of Scriptures[12] - the same endogenetic principle already discussed in chapter four.

Fox's unchanged position with respect to the inner light as celestial ('glorified') flesh is of interest to us here for it is necessary to establish his

[8]*Ibid.*, p. 138.

[9]*Ibid.*, p. 139.

[10]*Ibid.*, p. 66, 154-55, 180, 443, 463-64, 468, 482, 487.

[11]*See* Penn, *The New Athenians* in *Works*, 2, p. 801. Both Penn and Barclay worked with a more orthodox christology. Christ's body existed separate and distinct from the saints.

[12]*GMGW*,3, pp. 464, 505; *GTD*, 5, p. 154; 4, p. 397.

position before moving on to discuss Penn and Barclay. Fox was the mirror which reflected what early Quakerism was and his immutability enables us to assess what Quakerism became. In 1671 he wrote a pamphlet entitled *The Heathen's Divinity*. In that pamphlet he said that it was not necessary for the Scriptures to declare that there was a God for one to know there was a God. That was conveyed through a "divine principle" within. Whether or not one knew to call it Christ did not detract from the fact that that principle was in everyone. This may appear, at first glance, to be a change in his terminology but as the pamphlet proceeded it became increasingly clear that the divine principle was Christ.[13] Fox's language was more subdued but he had not forsaken his longstanding belief. Sometimes he refrained from making the obvious link as, for example, in 1673 when he wrote *To all Professors in the Christian World*. Here he said that "Christ has given to every man a measure according to his ability".[14] Christ, the "seedsman", had sown a light and a seed in the field [heart]. The Spirit of God was within. Notice what appeared to be a subtle change in emphasis. Christ was the giver of light but it was the Spirit that was within. But, in this same work, Fox equated Christ and Spirit. That is, when Christ returned he returned as spiritual flesh.[15] There was a celestial unity in Fox's mind and that meant, unequivocally, that deity was within.

In *A Testimony of What We Believe of Christ*, written in 1675, we discover the same tendency to equate Spirit with the glorified, celestial flesh of Christ. The "spirit is the speaker" who is the pre-existent glorified Christ and that Christ is "immediate".[16] Fox's references to the inner light are also to the celestial flesh of Christ who is also the power of God and Scriptures. Likewise, Fox's references to the Spirit are to the celestial flesh of Christ who was also the power of God. The Spirit was not disembodied.

---

[13]*Gospel Truth Demonstrated*, 4, pp. 392, 399, 405.

[14]*Ibid.*, 4, pp. 410-12.

[15]*Ibid.*, 4, pp. 413-14.

[16]Fox, *A Testimony of What We Believe of Christ* (1675), in *Gospel Truth Demonstrated*, 5, pp. 128-29.

226

Later on Fox spoke of the Spirit as if it was Christ's voice and will. The Christ in this case may be the bestowed Christ. The Spirit is still an extension of Christ, the power of "an extraordinary spirit".[17] Immediately following this seeming separation of Christ and Spirit the identification of Christ, light and power of God are again made clear.[18] So if at times Spirit means will, power and "speakings" of Christ, and is sometimes talked of separately, in Fox's mind spirit is always the outreach of this glorified, flesh and bone celestial Christ. If the reader is at all unclear about Fox's case for the cohabitation of the celestial Christ in the believer the point is made abundantly clear later in the treatise where Fox returns to the endogenetic theme of the saints eating Christ (ie. the glorified Christ).[19]

It is important to notice, as well, how Fox used Scripture in the treatise. It may have given an appearance of orthodoxy but Fox only used Scripture to prove his point: "Christ is formed within" (Galatians), Christ appears a second time to those who will look (Hebrews), the saints assume his body and actually become partakers of the divine nature (I Jn. 17, Ephesians 5:30; John 14). Fox used Scriptures - often ignored by others - that proved that the celestial flesh of Christ dwelt in the saints. What was implied in Fox's doctrine of further revelation was that the "words" of Scripture had to be coded "in the power" of God; they only made up truth, as suggested earlier, if the reader of the words was in the power of God (ie. was inhabited by the celestial flesh of Christ).

In 1679 Fox published the contents of his 1672 debate with Roger Williams in America. Again, he reaffirmed, from Scripture, his belief that Christ was within. The saints were of his flesh and bone and were "partakers of the divine nature", a resounding affirmation of his original belief in the divinization of the saints.[20] He repeated the same theme in 1685 and finally

---

[17]*Ibid.*, 5, p.6 140-41.

[18]*Ibid.*, 5, p. 142.

[19]*Ibid.*, 5, p. 145.

[20]Fox, *A New-England Firebrand Quenched* (1679), p. 42.

in 1688.[21] To the very end he maintained that the inner light was Christ in his celestial flesh; the saints assumed his incorruptible, heavenly body in this life and the saints were equal with God. There was no transformation on this fundamental idea, only a retreat into the more cautious mode of biblical metaphor.

Fox's immutability on these fundamental issues was not generally characteristic of Quakers after the Nayler incident. The best point of departure for understanding what happened to Quakerism in this respect is the response of various Quaker theologians to Fox's bold statement in the *Great Mystery of the Great Whore* that the soul was part of God. The clarification of Quaker theologians on this point was an essential step toward the redefinition of the inner light. Fox's statement in the *Great Mystery* was occasioned by a book written by Jonathan Clapham and William Jenkin, in which they denied that the soul was part of God. It was a created, earthly thing. To this Fox replied that there was a soul in death under transgression and a soul living in the Covenant of God. "Christ brings the soul to God, whereby they come to be one soul".[22] Fox's post-1659 doctrinal books and *Epistles*, written up to the time of his death, reveal no change with respect to the celestial flesh doctrine. He repeatedly affirmed that the inner light was the celestially fleshed Christ and that the saints consequently shared His divinity.[23] There was no evidence of refinement or redefinition on this theme. The glorified soul was divinized. What came out of God was of him and part of him. The saints were consequently partakers of the divine nature.[24] The glorified soul was not human but a part of the divine

---

[21]*Gospel Truth Demonstrated*, 6, pp. 303, 305, 339, 389, 394, 400, 405, 407.

[22]*See* Whitehead's defence of Fox's statement in *The Nature of Christianity* (London, 1671), p. 15.

[23]For example: *Gospel Truth Demonstrated*, 4, pp. 74-75; 5, p. 123; 6, pp. 22, 67, 301, 400; *Epistles*, 7, pp. 39, 290; 8, p. 283.

[24]This idea was foreshadowed in Thomas Edwards' catalogue of sectaries errors: "That man had life before God breathed into him, and that which God breathed into him was part of the divine essence, and shall return into God again" (*Gangraena*, first edition), pp. 21 and 22.

228

essence.[25] This is an important distinction when we come to see that it was the glorified soul that Quaker theologians de-divinized.

Fox's accusers did not miss this occasion to charge blasphemy over his view of the divinity of the soul. It was to one such accuser, Thomas Hicks, that William Penn responded in his book *Reason Against Railing* (1673). Penn's learned answer is a profound example of the re-interpretation process at work. But first, what did Fox really say in the passage exegeted by Penn?

> God breathed into man the breath of life, and he became a living soul ... And is not this [breath of life] that cometh out from God, which is in God's hand, part of God, of God, from God, and goes to God again? Which soul Christ is the bishop of. And dost not thou [Clapham and Jenkin] speak of a human soul, an earthly soul, and is earthly immortal? Cannot it die nor be killed? And is not that which came out from God, which God hath in his hand, taken up into God again, which Christ the power of God is bishop of, is not this of God's being? And dost not the Scripture say, 'God is all in all'?[26]

By way of review of chapter four we know that Fox meant exactly what he said - the soul was part of the divine essence. It was a separate entity, by virtue of which it came out from God and *shared* the divine essence to the extent that it was equal with God. As Howgill once wrote: "There is equality in nature, tho' not in stature". The saints were equal with God in nature but not the sum total of what or who God was.

How did Penn interpret Fox's words? In his answer to Hicks he did some linguistic juggling that clearly altered the sense that the believer shared anything with the divine nature. He said that when Fox said the soul was part of God he "intends" to mean "the divine life, power and virtue, by which

---

[25]In his 1677 treatise *The Spirit of Man the Candle of the Lord* Fox identified the spirit, body, mind, soul and conscience with natural, created man. The spirit was the candle (natural and created) which, when lit by Christ enabled the believer to be grafted into Christ and perfected (Gospel Truth Demonstrated, 5, pp. 341-81, 346). The soul was divinized at the birth of Christ within. Fox's inner light never changed. It always remained the presence of the celestial Christ.

[26]Fox, *The Great Mystery of the Great Whore*, 3, p. 181.

Adam in soul and body came to live in God".[27] Penn uses the preposition "to" rather than "from" and the soul was now a "power" or a "virtue" divinely bestowed which enabled one to move "to" God and live in Him. This was a huge, albeit subtle, shift in emphasis. By definition "to" "expresses motion directed towards and reaching ... denoting the place, thing, or person approached and reached".[28] This is the opposite of "from". Fox's soul "came out *from* God" but Penn brilliantly and formatively (as far as future generations were concerned) re-interpreted it as a divine power that directed the person *to* God.[29] The soul was divested of its divine nature. It was a divinely bestowed life within, quite separate from God. Even after regeneration, when it was restored to its "primitive perfection" the soul was not of the same substance as God.[30] This was an absolute reversal of Fox's "intent" in the *Great Mystery*, yet Penn's became the definitive interpretation of Fox. Penn showed here all the brilliance of Schillebeeckx reinterpreting St. Thomas on the sacrament, or Barth reinterpreting Luther. It was masterly.[31]

---

[27]William Penn, *Reason Against Railing, and Truth Against Fiction Being an Answer to ... Thomas Hicks, an Anabaptist Teacher*, in *Works*, 2, p. 521.

[28]*The Compact Edition of the Oxford English Dictionary*, 2, p. 84.

[29]Even if Penn had continued to speak of the inner light as "of" or "from" God, Endy states that Penn still separated God and man. The "Christ within" was a "distinct being". The spirit was the instrument or vehicle through which encounter with the divine occurred (Endy, *William Penn*, pp. 153-54, 169-70, 197-98, 271). Endy discussed Penn's christology in the context of his concern for the historical Christ. Penn avoided, said Endy, speculation on the heavenly flesh of Christ largely because his radical dualism, his separation of the eternal Christ and the human garment, rendered heavenly flesh no workable solution (*Ibid.*, p. 291). On the other hand, said Endy, Penn was confused by what Fox meant by the "spiritual body" of Christ. He did not believe Fox ever said the "spiritual body" of Christ was an "immaterial substance" but the eating of Christ's heavenly flesh was "a metaphor for the regenerating communion with Christ within" [*Ibid.*, p. 291. *See also* Penn, *The New Athenians* (1692) in *Works*, 2, pp. 801-5].

[30]Endy, *William Penn*, p. 192.

[31]Edward Schillebeeckx, *The Eucharist* (London: Sheed and Ward, 1968) and Karl Barth, *The Epistle to the Romans* (London: Oxford University Press, 1933), pp. 141, 324, 411. Schillebeeckx is a Thomist but in fact reinterprets St. Thomas radically. Contra the Tridentine formula of transubstantiation he tends to reinterpret the presence of Christ in the sacrament in the way of symbolic action. Barth, in his commentary on Romans, may "return" to Luther

Penn went on to accuse Thomas Hicks of being the one who misinterpreted Fox, of committing a "monstrous blasphemy against God, and horrid injustice to us".[32] Finally, and definitively, he concluded that in no sense "can we be thought so to believe of the soul, as by him [Hicks] represented."[33] That is, Quakers did not believe the soul was part of God. What are we to think, then, of Fox's statement in the *The Great Mystery* to the contrary: "it is not horrid blasphemy to say the soul is part of God, for it came out of him, and that which came out of him is of him".[34] Fox's very words reveal that Penn was wrong about this aspect of Fox's teaching and this needs to be heard because it had and continues to have wide-ranging implications on interpretations of Fox. To read Fox through the exegesis of Quaker theologians like William Penn may serve a useful purpose in vindicating Fox from charges of blasphemy but it also leads to historical inaccuracies. Involved in this great reversal of Fox's teaching was a denial (made possible by the de-divinization of the inner light) that Fox was who he said he was. And the denial became so successfully entrenched in later Quaker dogma that certain crucial aspects of Fox's teaching were kept hidden from the inquisitive mind for many centuries.

Penn's sophisticated reinterpretation of Fox went even further. He technically interpreted the word "breathed" as used by Fox. Fox wrote, "God breathed into man the breath of life, and he became a living soul". In English, said Penn, "breathed" means "inspired" as drawn from the Latin *inspirare* and the Greek *emphusao*. God breathed into, enlivened, inspired, quickened or as the Hebrew *neshamah* suggested, God blew into man the breath of life and thus inspired man. Penn used a commentary by Rabbi Nachmanni (Nehamanides?) to support his view. When God breathed into man he:

---

but his return is a radical reinterpretation of the key doctrines of knowledge, faith, predestination and the resurrrection.

[32]Penn, *Reason Against Railing*, in *Works*, 2, p. 522.

[33]*Ibid.*, p. 522.

[34]Fox, *Great Mystery of the Great Whore*, 3, pp. 434-35.

> inspired man with something of his own substance ... he
> contributed something to him, and bestowed something of his
> own divinity on him, and that God did inspire man with the
> Holy Ghost ... which is as much as can be collected or justly
> concluded from what George Fox hath said concerning men.[35]

By using authorities like Rabbi Nachmanni, Penn was able to redefine what Fox meant when he said that God "breathed into man". The soul did not come out from God (as Fox originally intended) but was, rather, a separate entity that was the recipient of a divine empowering or enlivening (ie. by the Holy Ghost) which enabled it to seek out and come to God. The soul was given something of God in order to return to God, but the idea was not blasphemous and far less dangerous than Fox had intended. Penn's soul was no extension of the divine essence. In the *Great Mystery* Fox repeatedly said that it was.[36]

In *The New Athenians* Penn went a step further. He said Fox never intended to say, as he said in the *Great Mystery*, that Christ and the saints were not distinct:

> You will have us confound God and his saints, from a passage
> in G.F.'s. *Mystery*: "He is deceived, that saith, Christ is distinct
> from his saints." The page is not quoted, but we know the
> place: We suppose it is a mis-printing gives you that
> apprehension; distinct for divided; they are distinct, but not
> divided. And this is that which was intended.[37]

This was the old argument that unity did not imply equality. But again Fox's meanings were being systematically altered. Fox and other early Quakers cited in chapter four explicitly said that Christ and the saints were not distinct and these could not all have been misprints. The misprint argument is difficult to accept given the contrary views in a wider body of evidence that supports Fox's literalist view.

------

[35]Penn, *Reason Against Railing*, pp. 521-22. *See also* Penn, *The Invalidity of John Faldo's Vindication, Works*, 2, pp. 435-36.

[36]Fox, *The Great Mystery of the Great Whore*, 3, pp. 134, 181, 434.

[37]Penn, *The New Athenians* in *Works*, 2, p. 802. *See* Fox, *The Great Mystery of the Great Whore*, 3, pp. 180, 291 for similar statements.

The interpretations of Penn, and as we shall see, Barclay, were part of a great reversal and a massive re-interpretation of Fox that reshaped Quakerism over time and waylaid subsequent interpretations of Fox and early Quakerism. The reinterpretation of Fox, in the name of respectability enabled Quakers to theologically distance themselves from the blasphemy charges and unchecked enthusiasm. Fox and the early Quakers were not what their critics said they were - or so went the argument. They misunderstood Fox's inner Christ who was then presented through the murky lens of Penn, Barclay, George Whitehead, Thomas Ellwood and other later Quaker theologians. It is now time to let Fox speak for himself again, especially with regard to his views on the inner Christ. Croese and Macauley understood that Penn and Barclay did something to bring Quakers into the 'orthodox' fold but they did not know what because their knowledge of Fox was largely formed from bowdlerized sources and the myth that Fox was a respectable mystic (albeit with some crude, anarchical tendencies) and not the avatar and thaumaturge that he really was.[38]

Penn was not the first Quaker to de-divinize the inner light by articulating a more 'orthodox' and commonplace concept of the soul[39] but his

---

[38]With the increased emphasis on reason as the foundation of Christian faith came the minimizing and even outright denial of Fox's miracles. They were reinterpreted as being in the spiritual sphere, rather than the physical. A good example of this change in attitude would be the selective editing of the often quoted account of Katharine Evans and Sarah Cheevers, that thousands were healed at Quaker meetings. A later editor of this statement added "mystically" (Compare *This is a Short Relation of Some Cruel Sufferings (for Truth's Sake) of Katharine Evans and Sarah Cheevers* (1662), p. 9 with the revised edition, *A Brief History of the Voyage of Katharine Evans and Sarah Cheevers to the Island of Malta* (London, 1715), pp. 22-23. Gerard Croese noticed this change in attitude and mentioned it in his general history of Quakers, written in 1696: "The Quakers who succeeded these first beginners do not make so much noise either of miracles or visions, nor do they willingly write or speak of those of their sect that preceded them, unless very cautiously and warily ... they do not make their religion depend on [miracles] ... but ... take care lest if these signs be not clear and manifest to all, they should come to be despised and laughed at (Croese, *General History,* pp. 28ff.).

[39]In 1661 Samuel Fisher (who wrote in Latin and was fluent in Greek philosophy) wrote a book entitled *Apocrypta Apocalypta.* There he carefully delineated the classical tripartite view of man as body, soul and spirit which he presented as being very Quaker. The soul was the 'life of the body'. It was every part of the body. It was man's "self". It was higher than the earthly body. But both were created - one was outward and the other was inward. It was the spirit of man which constituted, "man in his primitive perfection, it is that breath of life

reinterpretation of Fox was the first major assault on the thorny and contentious early Quaker doctrine of celestial inhabitation. Soon to follow would be Robert Barclay's great codification of Quaker doctrine which eventually came to be regarded as official (or should we say 'correct') Quaker teaching on the inner light. According to Barclay the soul, or the spirit (he made no distinction) was the inward person. Its chief function was to wait upon God, but it could be incapacitated by self-will.[40] However, when the "seed" was planted the soul could be inclined toward God. By nourishing the "seed" in the soul the spiritual birth occurred which enabled the believer to partake of the spiritual Christ.[41] What did Barclay mean by all this? When he spoke of the soul, seed or light he did not mean what Fox meant. He was always careful to keep the distinction between creator and creature. To the end of his life Fox said that the "seed" and "light" were the inner Christ - literally the body of the glorified Christ within. This was never metaphorical. The Spirit of the heavenly Christ was never disembodied. Here, in contrast, is what Barclay said, and now we move closer to the heart of the great reversal as the discussion moves away from the concept of the "soul" to the more significant definition of the "light":

> When we speak of the seed, grace, word of God or the light and say that everyone possesses a measure of it, we do not refer to the proper nature and essence of God ... The seed or light in man may be quenched, bruised,

---

which God breathed into his soul after he had formed him ... whereby he came to be a living soul; a soul that did partake of something of God's own life ... this is that living principle of the divine nature, which man had before his degeneration, and shall again after his resurrection, partake of' [Samuel Fisher, *Apocrypta Apocalypta* (London, 1661), pp. 10-11]. Fisher appeared to be agreeing with Fox, but what was it that man partook of after his glorification? It was "man in his primitive perfection", enlivened by the breath of God, the spark of life, that "principle of the divine nature" within that gave life and perfection. But that principle of divine nature neither suggested that the soul was part of God's essence nor that the distinction between the creator and the creature was lost, as Fox believed to the end of his life. We hear nothing from Fisher that would link it to the inner light. The spark of life within the saints simply enabled them to become men of God, doers of his will. There was no intimation that they were equal with God. Fisher kept a strict distinction between creator and creature. His fine-tuning of Fox via the medium of Greek philosophy enabled him to keep God and man separate while still acknowledging that the spirit of man had a divine enabling to lead people back to the primitive state.

[40]Barclay, *Apology*, p. 265.

> wounded ... but this is not so of God's own nature ...
> When we speak of the seed or light we understand a
> spiritual, celestial, and invisible principle, a principle in
> which God dwells as Father, Son and Spirit. A measure
> of this glorious and divine principle exists as a seed in
> all men which by its nature draws, invites, and inclines
> the individual toward God. Some call this the
> *vehiculum Dei*, or the spiritual body of Christ, the flesh
> and blood of Christ, which came down from heaven ...[42]

The light was a spiritual principle in which the godhead dwelt. It was not
part of man's nature and was quite distinct from his soul. It was not Reason
(a natural, created light); it was a divine presence. Nor was it conscience
which "arises from the natural faculties of man's soul which may be defiled
and corrupted."[43] The light was incorruptible. It informed conscience. It
was supernatural and sufficient for salvation. It was inward and spiritual. It
was the "seed" planted within but distinct from the creature. But it was not
part of the literal body of Christ or of the divine essence. It was a divine
presence. This tiny, incorruptible "seed" contained life and salvation and
given the right conditions could grow into the Kingdom of God within. *It
contained the power to save*, but it was not in any way a residual part of God's
image that somehow remained after the Fall, nor was it a natural power of
the will.[44] The "light" or "seed" was a divine *presence* infused into the soul, a
"law written on the heart", by which salvation was known to everyone. This,
said Barclay, was the "universal evangelical principle".[45] In a sense it was the
formation of Christ within for as the "seed" grew the way was prepared for
spiritual union with Christ. Christ spiritually inhabited the "seed" without

---

[41]*Ibid.*, pp. 332, 339.

[42]*Ibid.*, p. 85. Barclay derived his notion of *vehiculum Dei* from Keith who developed
his notion about the pre-existent heavenly humanity of Christ from the esoteric circle that
gathered around Anne, Vicountess Conway.

[43]*Ibid.*, p. 92. Barclay also distinguished between "conscience" and "mind". The latter
could be blinded or contaminated while the former would still trouble it. The "mind" was the
thinking part of man.

[44]*Ibid.*, p. 109.

[45]*Ibid.*, pp. 123, 163.

sharing anything of his essence with the believer. The believer did not become Christ.[46] Thus, the "seed", "light", "divine principle" or *vehiculum Dei* were all the same thing, a kind of tabernacle which contained the divine presence. In every case the divine presence was distinct from the soul even after the new birth had occurred. Contrary to Fox it was never the pre-existent Christ inhabiting and divinizing the believer.[47] Fox's literalism was lost.

Barclay, too, openly spoke of the Christ within, resurrected and taking shape as the new man. But the larger question is who, exactly, was Barclay's inner Christ? Who, or what, inhabited the inner spaces of the believer - the tabernacle or "seed"? Barclay believed that the seed, light, divine principle or *vehiculum Dei* was spiritually inhabited by the divine presence. It was not Christ nor was Christ's "flesh and bone" glorified body in it. It was only a vehicle created and used by God to draw people back to himself. By refashioning Fox's concept of the "seed" or "light" Barclay was able to break off the renewed creature from God and yet say that Christ dwelt within and the believer became one with him, metaphorically. Christ was only within in the larger sense that there was a divine principle within, which was

---

[46]*Ibid.*, pp. 145, 85, 329, 330. Lief Eeg-Olofsson also reached the conclusion that "according to Barclay the inner light is not a part of man's soul", but "Christ is always in man through the inner light". The union between man and Christ is a purely spiritual one. Christ is in man but there is no merging of essences [L. Eeg-Olofsson, *The Conception of the Inner light in Robert Barclay's Theology* (Lund: CWK Gleerup, 1954), pp. 72, 75, 220, 258]. Olofsson failed to represent Barclay as a major paradigm shift away from early Quaker concepts of the inner light.

[47]Barclay's "seed" was a spiritual substance in which the Godhead dwelt but it was separate and distinct from man. Keith once described the "seed" or *vehiculum Dei* as not "the Godhead itself, but a certain middle nature, substance or being, between the Godhead and mankind" [George Keith, *The Way to the City of God* (London, 1678), p. 130]. As Braithwaite explained, "It was a divine influence, outside man's proper nature, which, if not resisted, would beget in him new life" (*Second Period*, p. 391). Although Barclay's inner light was de-divinized it was still a divine principle within which was sufficient for salvation. This left the historical atonement wanting and ultimately led to the Keith dispute later in the century. As long as the inner light was Christ there was never any question that atonement was guaranteed. Salvation, justification and sanctification (as Fox said repeatedly) were within the believer, personified in the person of the indwelling Christ. There was no question of external mediation. When the inner light was de-divinized the basis of salvation remained within but the door was opened to reposition Christ as saviour and mediator in an orthodox sense and this was what the Keith controversy was all about.

synonymous with the light which was "sometimes called Christ".[48] The Christ within was no more than a spiritual presence. This was a spiritualizing of the inner Christ that had nothing in common with Fox's doctrine of celestial inhabitation. And yet Barclay's view informed later interpretations of Fox and shaped the dominant view of Fox and early Quakerism for over three centuries.

In Barclay's view of things there was no hint of a literal presence of the heavenly body of Christ in the believer, as it had inhabited Jesus. In no sense was the divine principle within "part of man's nature or a relic of the good that Adam lost by his fall. It was something separate and distinct from man's soul and from all the soul's faculties."[49] The soul was created and distinct from God. It was enlightened by the divine principle within which directed man toward God. The soul, or reason, on its own was incapable of doing this because it had been affected by the Fall to the point that it was ruled by the rational principle (antichrist) that ruled the natural world. The divine principle (seed, light) was the *vehiculum Dei*, the mediator of Christ to mankind. And Barclay was careful to point out that neither the soul nor the divine principle were technically of the "proper nature and essence of God".[50] What Barclay was saying was that when Quakers affirmed that Christ dwelt in them, they meant he was mediated as a divine principle in the *vehiculum Dei*. It was not literally the celestial Christ who dwelt in the saints, as Fox believed to the end of his life. The very idea of mediation removed the hint of blasphemy and any hint that the saints assumed the incorruptible body of the pre-existent Christ and thus became indistinguishable from God.[51] Now Quakers were presented as being very orthodox for they were not equated in any way with the celestial Christ or the historical Jesus who was the only one

---

[48]Barclay, *Apology*, p. 89. Which came to be the view of Quaker interpreters through the ages. Edward Grubb, for example, said that to be a Son of God or a "partaker of the divine nature" was no more than God's purpose or will at work within [*Thoughts on the Divine in Man* (London: Friends' Book Centre, 1931), p. 9].

[49]Barclay, *Apology*, p. 91.

[50]*Ibid.*, p. 85.

[51]*Ibid.*, p. 86.

who could be said to be fully God and fully man. Without the corporeal sense of the indwelling Christ Fox's optimisim about the potential to be restored to perfection and to the pre-Fall state of glory was severely damaged.[52]

The position put forth in the 1670's, that Fox never intended to mean that the soul was a part of the divine essence, may have served the purpose of proving that there was no ranterism in the Quaker fold (a big concern for George Whitehead) but it was light years away from the Fox who declared himself to be the Son of God, the final revelation of God in apocalyptic history and the one who said "that which is in him [Christ], and is not distinct from him."[53] Fox's inner Christ was not Barclay's or Penn's inner Christ.

Furthermore, Fox's doctrine of immanence was an eschatological corollary of his views on the inner Christ. This was not so with Penn and Barclay. The immanent Kingdom as Fox envisioned it withered away in Barclay and Penn - eschatology died altogether. Penn's and Barclay's inner Christ was a triumph of sorts over the imminent eschatology that had preoccupied Quakers in the late 1650's and early 1660's. The idea of being in the vanguard of some collective salvation-process, some rectification of history (the Lamb's War no less), was given up as Fox's inner Christ as

---

[52]This had an effect on the Quaker view of man. Because Christ did not literally dwell in the believer there was reversion back to the Augustinian view. There was less optimism about the goodness of man. The Calvinism of Barclay's Scottish heritage was always close to the surface and his conviction of the innate depravity of human nature was one of the fundamental principles in his *Apology*. In this sense he also reshaped Quakerism to fit a more Augustinian mould. Barclay was not necessarily out of step with Fox on this point for Fox also believed in the depravity of human nature. But Fox had an incomparably more optimistic view of man's capacity to be fully perfected and restored to the pre-Fall state in this life. This optimism was severely curtailed when the inner light was de-divinized. Said Barclay: "Even though a man may reach the state where he is capable of resisting sin but sins anyhow, nevertheless a state can be attained in this life in which it becomes so natural to act righteously that a condition of stability is achieved in which sin is impossible. Perhaps there are those who can say with certainty that they have attained this state. Personally, I have to be modest and merely say that it is attainable, because I confess ingenuously that I have not yet attained it" (*Ibid.*, p. 157). Without the presence of the indwelling Christ to transform the person perfection became an immense struggle of the will to habitually live in accordance with the divine inner principle so that the gifted spiritual athlete might possibly attain perfection. How far this was from Fox!

[53]Fox, *The Great Mystery of the Great Whore*, 3, p. 464.

celestial flesh was given up, over time, without even a struggle. Even Fox finally accepted the fact that the Lamb's War would not be brought to a quick conclusion but a reading of his last epistles and doctrinal works gives no indication that he had given up the Lamb's War. He spoke less of the Lamb and the saints having the victory and there was a distinct impression of a solitary soldier marching on valiantly, knowing that his troops had lost the will to fight in the same war. He repeated over and over again the basic tenets of his message (as we reviewed them in earlier chapters) not to the world now but to his own followers. Fox was well aware of a substantial weakening of his original doctrine of celestial inhabitation. He tirelessly encouraged them to seek the Christ within, to be perfect, to possess the New Jerusalem that had come and to recognize that signs and wonders were a true sign of the Kingdom. To the very end he spoke of the necessity of preaching the everlasting gospel over the head of the great whore of Babylon. To the very end he spoke of Christ the stone cut from the mountain without hands and filling the whole earth in his day. By the logic of Fox's theology of immanence the Lamb's War would never stop until Babylon had been crushed.

But the process of de-divinizing the inner light had already begun to erode Fox's teaching and change the character of the Lamb's War. Everything that Fox and early Quakers fought so hard to establish was in danger of being lost when the saint ceased to be literally inhabited by the celestial Christ. When the inner light was transformed and the historic, transfigured Christ was re-located back in heaven and far away from the immediate affairs of the world the Lamb's War necessarily ceased. It was replaced by another secular, tamer, and very human war against violence and injustice. Quakers became types of mystics whose highly regarded benevolence toward humankind was an act of divinely inspired conscience. They ceased to be god-filled or divinized saints on the vanguard of the final apocalyptic event of history which would witness once and for all time the crushing of Babylon and the final establishment of the Kingdom of God - the Kingdom in which they would rule as God's nobility.

Barclay codified for succeeding generations the transformation that had been occurring in Quakerism since the Nayler incident.[54] The fundamental principle upon which Fox founded his movement was that the literal presence of the inner light transformed the saints into gods - that is they became one with God and indistinguishable God. They were literally the flesh and bone body of Christ on earth. By the time Barclay wrote his *Apology* in 1676 the groundwork for a complete reversal of this position was laid. Slowly Quakerism was de-divinized and slowly it began to re-enter the pale of respectable orthodox non-conformity. Fox's inner light (continue to use that term if you like said Barclay) was now no more than an impersonal, mediating *vehiculum Dei* which helped direct fallen man back *to* God.

Part of this change involved a new focus on the work of the Spirit rather than Christ. Throughout Barclay's *Apology* it was the disembodied Spirit that was the main token of the Christian, not the inner light. The disembodied Spirit was the infallible teacher within, the one who spoke to and through the saint, who revealed God's will, who was the source of truth and the final rule of faith. Contrary to Fox the infallible Spirit was not equated with the pre-existent celestial Christ.[55]

Thus, after the Nayler incident we begin to hear less and less about the inward Christ as a celestial inhabitation and more and more about "Reason" and "conscience" as a vehicle for the leading of the Holy Spirit which directed people toward God and a morally good life (ie. to live in

---

[54]Not all Quaker authors were of the view that Barclay transformed Fox's view of the inner light. Others, like Rufus Jones, believed that Barclay misrepresented Fox's experimental and immediate experience of Christ as an inner teacher. Jones, however, was no closer to the real Fox than Barclay. Jones' view of Fox's inner light was that of a mystical experience of a high order, akin to *raptus* (Jones, *Introduction* to Braithwaite, *Second Period*). When H.G. Wood reviewed Leif Eeg-Olofsson's book *The Conception of the Inner light in Robert Barclay's Theology* he said that "an experienced, inner, spiritual apprehension of a historic revelation ... was what George Fox was really after," and Barclay obscured Fox's idea of Christ as an inward teacher and turned the doctrine of the inner light into "an intellectualistic-moralistic mysticism" [*Theology*, 57 (Aug., 1954), pp. 350-51]. Each of these authors and reviewers have missed what Fox's celestial inhabitation theology was all about. Until we understand exactly what Fox himself believed about the inner light (or as long as the view that Fox was a respectable mystic and tame dissenter is perpetuated) we are not in a position to determine how his vision was transformed.

[55]Barclay, *Apology*, pp. 31-43.

God's will and according to his law).[56] Conscience began to usurp the place that Fox had specifically reserved for the inner light. Ultimately we may call the inner light what we will, "conscience", "Reason", "nature", "light", "divine principle" or *vehiculum Dei* and it does not matter. The literal and personal presence of the pre-existent celestial Christ was transformed into an impersonal principle, a moral power, that was only guided by what had become the disembodied Holy Spirit. Quaker theology was transformed from the literalistic christopresentism of Fox (a traditionally more dangerous kind of theology in Christian history) to a disembodied Spirit religion in which eternal truths were mediated and interpreted through the guidance of the disembodied Spirit (traditionally more orthodox and less extravagant in its claims). The inner light, though bestowed by God, was not part of God's nature. Penn and Barclay were the first to systematically render down the heady celestial inhabitation ethics that lacked definition in favor of an ethical platform based on appeals to Reason. Reason was the inner light, a moral power of judgment enabling one to navigate the pitfalls of life.[57]

The great reversal, the replacing of the inner light with impersonal "Reason" or "conscience", was the most fundamental and significant

---

[56]Barbour, *Quakers in Puritan England*, pp. 240-41. According to Barbour Quakers found that instead of using extravagant language about the inner light and thus offending the world they could make "conscientious appeals to ... any sensitive man ... [to] bring about new political and social reforms" (*Ibid.*, p. 241). Penn appealed to Reason because, in his words, the understanding could only be convinced by arguments that were rational. Penn's "Reason" (which was synonymous with soul, light and divine principle) was a moral power and the cohesive force behind his whole world of thought. It was natural and created and divinely empowered without taking upon itself anything of the divine essence. Actually, Penn was really the beginning of a well defined ethical platform in Quakerism, one that was based not on the inner light, but on Reason or conscience [This was in no sense equated with the "shallow humanism" that Nuttall equated with a post-1660 devolution of Quakerism. Nor was Fox party to Barclay's ethical platform as Nuttall suggested (*See* Nuttall, *James Nayler: A Fresh Approach*, p. 20].

[57]The Cambridge Platonists believed that through Reason perfection and union with God could be pursued. Nor was human nature totally depraved. Their idea of perfection was similar to Penn's but very different from Fox's. Perfection was an aspiration toward an Ideal which classic Unitarians like William Ellery Channing said "we express by the word perfection". But the Cambridge Platonists had none of Fox's eschatology, none of his exalted language, none of his view of totally depraved human nature, none of his idea of man being restored to pre-Fall perfection and none of his ideas about the deification of the saints.

transformation in early Quakerism. It was of far more consequence than the social changes that have been well documented by others. It gave Quakers the epistemological tool with which they could exorcize the entire edifice of exalted language and enthusiasm that was a product of Fox's doctrine of the celestial inhabitation and the consequent deification of the saint. The stain of blasphemy and heresy could be and was removed. Quakers were not blasphemers and heretics and Penn and Barclay provided the exegetical edifice which freed them to carry on in the world and take their place alongside their less radical non-conformist kin.

Penn's and Barclay's reconstructed Quakerism was the beginning of a very gradual but dramatic transformation of Quaker perceptions of the inner light. In time (certainly by the second decade of the eighteenth century) it had wholly displaced the early, primitivistic notion of celestial inhabitation. The chronology of Henry More's statements about Quakerism provides us with one of the best accounts for interpreting the progress of this transformation, as well as for determining that Quaker theological positions were not fixed but were still fluid and amorphous at least until the end of the seventeenth century.

In 1656, More, who may have been reacting to the Nayler incident, charged that Quakerism was diabolic because its heavy reliance on the inner light led to extremes.[58] In mid-1660, when his book *An Explanation of the Grand Mystery of Godliness* appeared, he explained for the first time what he meant by undue reliance on the inner light. Quakers, he said, were to be identified with "the worst of all heresies", Familism, because they disregarded the life and work of the historical Christ.[59] Quakers were depicted as a total apostasy of Christianity and the logical result of their notion of unity between Christ and saint was that they would become gods and be deserving of divine adoration.[60] He affirmed that the inner light was the fundamental premise

[58]Powicke, *The Cambridge Platonists*, p. 168.

[59]As Nigel Smith points out, he may have used the term as a slur, to show his general disdain for all such expanded allegorical systems (*Perfection Proclaimed*), pp. 180-81.

[60]More, *Grand Mystery of Godliness*, Book 1, chapter 6, p. 146; Powicke, *The Cambridge Platonists*, p. 168.

242

of his own religion,[61] but by failing to balance the inward light with a proper doctrine of the outward or historical Christ the Quakers had been led into all manner of excesses. He also held forth, for the first time, an idea that was to inform his view of Quakerism from beginning to end - that there were two kinds of Quakers, "silly-minded" Quakers and "well-meaning" or "better-minded" Quakers.[62] He failed to explain what he meant by well-meaning Quakers but he clearly identified the silly-minded with those, the majority by implication, whom he linked to Familists - those who held excessive notions about identity with Christ, denied immortality after this life, denied dependence on the outward Christ and denied that the soul was mortal. Perhaps the fault was More's, to consider some Quaker ideas about the inner light as silly-minded or "nebulous and confused" as he would write in 1667. But if not, if he was right, then it is an indicator that Fox's celestial flesh notion was being opposed from within his movement as early as the 1660's. That is, the notion of the inner light as a divine enabling or inspiration quite separate and distinct from the believer was being represented by some Quakers as early as 1661 and More saw this as characteristic of a newer, emergent Quakerism that was set in contradistinction to the nebulous and confused ideas of earlier Quakerism (and still maintained by Fox) that equated the inner light with the celestial flesh of Christ.

In 1667, when the first edition of his *Divine Dialogues* appeared, More continued to rail against Quakers as the offspring of Familism. Yet, he said, despite their "inconsistencies and absurdities" their idea of "keeping to the light within them was fundamentally right".[63] The problem with Quakerism, as he saw it, was the tenacious tendency of the majority of Quakers to hold "nebulous and confused" views on the inner light and this was a fault that they

---

[61]More, *Grand Mystery of Godliness*, Book 8, chapter 12, p. 408. The idea of the inner light as a divine principle, Reason or conscience was common to the body of ideas generally associated with the Cambridge Platonists among whom Henry More was an important figure.

[62]*Ibid.*, Book 10, chapter 13, pp. 530-34.

[63]More, *Divine Dialogues* (first edition), p. 569.

had still not rectified in 1668.[64]   Robert Rich's inclusion of some Quakers, including George Fox the Younger, in his late 1660's list of those who belonged to the cryptic "Church of the First-Born" is a leading indicator that some Quakers had not fully abandoned the original profession as it pertained to celestial inhabitation.   A characteristic of this non-institutional, highly spiritualized church was the belief that Christ appeared *in* the saints "face to face, as bone of their bone, and flesh of their flesh".[65]

A very important development began to take place in More's views in the early to mid-1670's.   He came into correspondence with some well-meaning Quakers who encouraged him in his hope that Quakers were leaving behind their Familism and adopting a more orthodox position regarding the historical Christ, a position that hopefully would restore them to the Christian fold.   More became linked to a select group of more sophisticated and aristocratic Quakers whom he met during his regular visits to Ragley Hall.   His former student and close friend, Lady Ann Conway had become a Quaker and her home at Ragley, in Warwickshire, became a new centre of Quaker activity.   It was not the kind of charismatic, missionary oriented activity generally associated with Margaret Fell and Swarthmoor Hall.   The activity took the form of a more sophisticated theological discussion group which, according to the correspondence of the period, focused on the nature of the inner light.   The loose agenda of this select group of educated Quakers (which included George Keith, William Penn,

---

[64]In 1669 John Owen was still unclear about where Quakers stood on central doctrines like christology. Owen called on them to cease their "confused noise and humming" and "to speak intelligibly and according to the usage of other men, or the pattern of Scripture" (quoted in Endy, *William Penn*, p. 274).

[65]Robert Rich, *Love Without Dissimulation* (late 1660's), p. 6. Rich was the only person to mention the Church of the First-Born. It was considered to be the true church, invisible through the ages. Included in its ranks were the Familists, Jacob Boehme, Nayler and other Quakers, though not all. Its position in Rich's list of seven churches suggested that it was the church of highest revelation. It was a general view of things in England at that time that England was the scene of post-Reformation revelatory progress from Catholicism to Episcopal to Presbyterian to Independent to Baptist to Quaker (as Quakers saw it) to the Church of the First-Born (as Rich saw it). Penn provided a similar list of spiritual progression (*See* "William Penn to Lady Conway", August 20, 1675 in Nicolson, *Conway Letters*, p. 402). A similar list may also be found in Fox (*Epistles* 7, p. 314).

Robert Barclay, George Whitehead, Lady Conway and Mercury van Helmont) was to improve the image of Quakers by 'clarifying' the notion of the inner light and soliciting the approval of Henry More.

By 1674 both Keith and Penn were in regular correspondence with More. He, in turn, was becoming increasingly favourable to their writings, especially Keith's *Immediate Revelation* and Penn's writings against John Faldo. During this time they and George Whitehead also visited More at his lodgings in London and Cambridge and encouraged, even begged him to lend his weighty support to their cause. Fox was never party to this.

In May, 1675 More wrote an important letter to Penn in which he said the writings of Keith and Penn gave him reason to hope that Quakers were now emerging from "that low beginning of an heartless and hopeless Familism".[66] "I must confess", he said, "that I have ever an invincible suspicion (so far as I can see) that this was the first state of the Quakers".[67] He then added that "being of this persuasion you cannot imagine how much pleased I was with my converse with George Keith".[68] Keith had apparently re-assured More that all Quakers believed in the historicity of the Gospels and Keith was undoubtedly correct. What he apparently did not say was that Quakers, at the same time, believed that the new revelation imparted by Fox superseded the historical revelation in the Gospels.

Based upon re-assurances from Keith and the substance of Penn's writings More said that he was encouraged Quakers had two such able guides and if all Quakers were of the same mind then he was sure they were free of the Familism from which they had sprung. But More was far from convinced that all Quakers were of the same mind. He only hoped that they would follow the example of Keith and Penn and "disencumber those exalted things they profess ... from such things as make them seem uncouth and ridiculous".[69] If Quakers continued to disregard the outward Christ and the

[66]Nicolson, *Conway Letters*, p. 69.

[67]*Ibid.*, p. 69.

[68]*Ibid.*, p. 69.

[69]*Ibid.*, p. 71.

external sacraments then vestiges of Familism would remain among them, a disturbing thought since they had shown signs of emerging to a sounder faith.[70]

More's cautious attitude towards Quakers continued through 1675. In December of that year he advised Lady Conway that Quakers were "an errant sect". There were good and bad among them. He explained to Lady Conway that he had told George Whitehead he was open to discussion with Quakers but his purpose was to lead them out of their errors.[71] More told Lady Conway that William Penn and some others (including George Keith) had asked him to give a better report of Quakers.[72] This tells us a great deal about the attitudes of certain key Quakers in the 1670's - about their need to distance themselves from the slur of blasphemy and enthusism. More's response was that he had and would continue to give a good report of those few Quakers in whom he found a better testimony but he would not make pronouncements on behalf of the whole sect since it generally continued to adhere to Familist principles.[73] In January, 1676 More consequently warned Lady Conway not to be oversure that Quakers had nothing to do with

---

[70]The same letter in R. Ward, *The Life of the Learned and Pious Dr. Henry More* (London, 1701), pp. 328-29.

[71]"Henry More to Lady Conway" (December 7, 1675), in Nicolson, *Conway Letters*, pp. 414-15. In the same month he wrote to Lady Conway again, this time out of concern for George Keith who had adopted the notion that the soul of Christ extended out of his body into all creation (Keith may have reached his views about the transmigration of souls and the extension of Christ's soul through the universe via the influence of Van Helmont). This, said More, was another example of the Quaker tendency to listen only to the inner light (the great Familist error) without heeding the historical Christ, "so one error begets another" (*Ibid.*, p. 415). Not only did More's suspicions about the Familist tendency of Quakerism continued to be confirmed but he was concerned to point out to Lady Conway the dangers in a theology that placed too much emphasis on the inner light. Keith, he said, was a man of good report but he was "liable to over headstrong enthusiasm" - a general tendency of all Quakers - and it would be best if he kept his ideas quiet, so as not to "disparage the honest principles of Quakers". More's concern was not in the extravagance of the notions (he himself wasn't free of extravagant notions) but how they impinged on and weakened the doctrine of the historic Christ.

[72]*Ibid.*, p. 416.

[73]*Ibid.*, p. 416.

Familism.[74] He reminded her that James Nayler "who was at least equal with George Fox is to me a demonstration how much at least many of them were tinctured with Familism".[75] Old and well-formed opinions and images die hard even for the honest and discerning critic like Henry More. Association with Familism, ranterism and blasphemous language was precisely the image of Quakerism that Penn, Keith and others were so desperate to excise from the movement but More, ever the discerning critic, was not convinced, even by their arguments, that Quakerism had made the requisite adjustments away from Familism.

The friendship within the group grew during 1676. In March Keith asked Robert Barclay to visit Lady Conway since he would be helpful to her and van Helmont. He also asked Barclay to pass his greetings on to Henry More.[76] We see even from this terse comment how closely knit the group was, even though More was never really a part of it. The visits and correspondence continued through 1677 and 1678. In late 1677 Lady Conway asked More to meet with the "best and chiefest of the Quakers" (Penn, Keith, Barclay and Fox "their great leader"). One is immediately struck with the designation "best and chiefest of the Quakers". Apart from Fox's inclusion because of his stature in the movement, there is a clear indication in this statement that a leadership shift had occurred and with it had come a greater currency for the more sophisticated views of Penn and Barclay. Primitivistic Quakerism as it was focused in the North and specifically at Swarthmoor Hall seemed distant and remote.

Lady Conway's stated concern was to clear Quakers and Fox of the charge of Familism.[77] Fox was an interesting inclusion for his presence at the meeting represented, for More, everything distasteful about Quakerism.

---

[74]"Henry More to Lady Conway" (Jan. 10, 1676), in Nicolson, *Conway Letters*, p. 417.

[75]*Ibid.*, p. 417.

[76]"George Keith to Robert Barclay" (March 12, 1676), in *Reliquiae Barclaianae* (London, 1870), ix-x.

[77]Powicke, *The Cambridge Platonists*, pp. 166-67. *See also The Short Journal and Itinerary Journals of George Fox*, p. 233.

247

Fox repelled More perhaps because he would not be swayed by More, having an alien cast of mind! The event confirms for us the sharp division not only in More's mind but in the Quaker leadership itself. Quaker leaders like Penn and Barclay were in step with More. Fox was not.

More's general attitude remained unchanged over the remaining years of his correspondence with Quakers. The Quaker group at Ragley Hall was dispersed following Lady Conway's untimely death in February, 1679. Francis Mercury van Helmont returned to the Continent and became a self-proclaimed "Seeker". More, who continued to correspond with Penn in Pennsylvania, had a powerful influence on the new generation of Quaker leadership that gathered at Ragley Hall in the 1670's. Powicke, for example, pointed out links between More's *anima mundi* and Barclay's *vehiculum Dei*.[78] On the other hand his final impressions remained as he had first formed them. Quakers, he said in 1678, came very "near a glorious truth of Christ's nearness as an intercessor"[79] but the majority continued to cling to Familist notions. When the second edition of More's *Divine Dialogues* were written in 1678 he continued to express his contempt for the appendages of Familism that remained in Quakerism. He again cited Nayler as an example of this "dangerous madness", a product of total disregard for the historical Christ. More was convinced, as late as 1678 that Quakers had not yet shed their Familist mask.[80] Quaker theology was still in a fluid state. It had not yet entered the pale of respectable orthodoxy.

More's greatest source of encouragement (and greatest influence) lay with the new generation of Quaker leaders whom he perceived were well advanced in shaking their Familist origins. He was particularly impressed with Barclay's *Apology* for the way in which it related the historical and inward Christ. He was encouraged that his earlier views about the "better-minded" Quakers were still being confirmed and his hope continued that they

---

[78]Powicke, "Henry More, Cambridge Platonist; and Lady Conway, of Ragley", p. 219.

[79]More, *Scholia to Dialogue 5, Divine Dialogues* (London, 1713), p. 575.

[80]*Ibid.*, p. 575.

would all "carefully wipe off the last vestiges of Familism" by following the lead of Penn and Barclay.

More played a role in their transformation and thus in the transformation of Quakerism into a respectable mystical religion. More, and all Cambridge Platonists, believed that through Reason (as a natural organ within) the individual truth was conveyed. Through Reason God spoke. And at all times the leading of the inner light (Reason) was tied to the outward, historical Word. Penn and Barclay worked hard to bring Quakers into line with this way of thinking and in time their views prevailed. Fox on the other hand remained firm in his views until his death, like a solitary soldier (a former General) who was increasingly out of step with the rest of his troops. If we turn now to look at the great controversies of the 1690's we will see that More's interpretive sense of things (as it pertained to the division between Quakers who continued to hold to Fox's celestial inhabitation notions and the new generation of Quaker leaders who de-divinized the inner light) is a useful model in interpreting later developments as they reflect on the progress of the transformation.

The debates over the inner light and the implications of that doctrine were not restricted only to Quaker debates with outsiders. Debates raged in their own ranks, most notably between George Keith and Public Friends on both sides of the Atlantic. What was notable about these debates was that they focused on christology and only tangentially on blasphemy. Yet, old beliefs were revived rather than repudiated. The heart of the Keith dispute (which raged from the early 1690's until 1695 when Keith was disowned) was Keith's impatience with Quaker insistence on the inner at the expense of the outer Christ. Note, however, that Keith was attacking the very Quaker leaders who had been influenced by Henry More - William Penn, Robert Barclay and George Whitehead. The battle lines were reset along the lines of a transformed Quakerism that had shed its lingering notion of celestial inhabitation but had, as More had already noted about Penn and Barclay, retained its overemphasis on the inner light - the inner light not as a celestial presence but as Reason or conscience - a de-divinized inner light - but still an inner light that was the source of authority and revealer of truth. According to Keith Quakers had not gone far enough in their transformation. They still showed disregard for the historical Christ and thus for the important role of the Gospels and the external sacraments in the salvatory process and the life of faith.

Keith, under the influence of Henry More, had his own personal struggles (especially during his time at Ragley Hall), about how to relate the idea of the inward Christ with the outward, historical Christ. The fullest treatment of Keith's christology is found in his 1677 book *The Way Cast Up*. There he developed his distinctive notions about the pre-existent humanity of Christ. It shows how far some Quakers had moved from Fox's literalistic notions of celestial inhabitation. According to Keith, before Christ came outwardly in the flesh as the "son of Mary" he was pre-existent and had a body of heavenly (spiritual) flesh and blood. He was the Heavenly Man.[81] This Heavenly Man assumed human flesh (becoming known as the 'Word') and he subsequently ascended into Heaven to sit at the right hand of the Father and assume a life in the godhead which the pre-existent Christ had always shared and of which no person could partake.[82] Christ and saint were separate and distinct. There was no unity nor equality. The 'Word' was a part of the godhead, part of deity, in a way that no person ever could be. Keith was absolutely clear that Christ could not literally inhabit the believer: "the saints cannot be Christ, even as Man; they only partake of some measure or ray ... they have not the centre or spring of his soul and life in them".[83] By 1677, then, Keith had clearly departed from Fox's notions of celestial inhabitation and followed Penn and Barclay by redefining the inner light.

Nevertheless the saints were in some way, both before and after the Incarnation, inhabited by Christ the Heavenly Man and it was upon his flesh and blood that they fed.[84] In order to explain how Christ dwelt in the saint while at the same time remaining separate and distinct Keith developed, to More's disdain, the notion of the extension of the soul of Christ throughout

[81]George Keith, *The Way Cast Up* (1677), pp. 92 and 103.

[82]*Ibid.*, pp. 83 and 123.

[83]*Ibid.*, p. 103.

[84]*Ibid.*, pp. 95-96.

250

the universe.[85] What inhabited the saints was not Christ's heavenly body but an extension of his life and Spirit. The believer fed upon Christ's heavenly body by way of Christ's "soul that is extended unto us here upon earth".[86] Keith was very careful to explain that he did not mean that the man Christ Jesus inhabited the believer, nor did the pre-existent Christ, nor did the outward person who ascended to the right-hand of the Father: "But when I say, the soul or spirit of Christ as man is extended unto us, I do not understand the Nephesh of his soul [the actual soul of Christ], but the Neschamah [the dignity and excellency of the soul of Christ] ... that divine spirit of life, that God breathed into Adam."[87] What was extended throughout the universe, and upon which the saints of all ages fed, was not the Heavenly Man, nor the actual soul of Christ but the divine life of Christ that was breathed into Adam. Christ was kept wholly in his distant heavenly abode, totally separate and distinct from the saints. This was consistent with Penn's and Barclay's redefinition of the inner light (although Keith, under the influence of van Helmont came to similar conclusions through a different conceptual framework) and it was a radical departure from Fox's and early Quaker notions of celestial inhabitation. We need only recall statements by Fox, Nayler, Howgill and Farnworth about the unity and equality between Christ and saint, how the saint shared the very nature of Christ, the indivisibility of sanctifier and sanctified, how Christ's glorified body (flesh and bone) inhabited every particle of the believer and was not locked up in a

---

[85]Although Penn, Barclay and Keith moved away from Fox's notion of celestial flesh one persistent charge laid squarely at Keith was that Quakers (and the Church in all ages) fed on the flesh of the pre-existent, heavenly man (Christ) and so became like him [See John Robertson, *Rusticus ad Clericum ... in Answer to Venus Patroclus* (1694), p. 274]. Keith and other learned Quakers were in fact attempting to back away from this lingering notion of early Quaker endogenesis. In 1694 John Robertson defended Keith from this charge by directing the critic to read Henry More on the celestial bodies of men. More, he said, was not censored for these strange beliefs, "and so you may allow George Keith some latitude in such metaphysical stuff" (*Ibid.*, p. 276). Robertson defended Keith (as Whitehead defended Eccles) even though he didn't take the idea seriously. Such high-blown notions were, by 1694, clearly in disrepute among Quakers.

[86]Keith, *Way Cast Up*, pp. 123, 133, 142, 145 and 159.

[87]*Ibid.*, p. 143.

distant heaven (it was not divided), not to mention all the exalted language that logically flowed from those very concepts, to see how great a chasm lay between the notion of Fox and primitive Quakerism and the transformed Quakerism of the 1690's that was adopted by some leading Quaker theologians.

Keith was very much a part of the spiritualizing process that had been occurring in Quakerism since the mid-1670's. His dispute with Quakers like Penn, Barclay and Whitehead was not over Fox's notion of celestial inhabitation. He himself had participated in the transformation of that doctrine. He had no quarrel with the attempts to spiritualize Fox's inner light, only with the persistent Quaker tendency to give the inner light primacy over the external work of the historical Christ. Keith tended to follow the criticism of Henry More in his charge that Quakers ignored the historical Christ. The debate, which began in Pennsylvania, focused on the sufficiency of the inner light for salvation and its precedence over Scripture and the historical Christ.[88] The very nature of the debate revealed the extent of the fall away from Fox's celestial flesh notions, at least on the part of some. In a work against William Penn Keith specifically argued for the sufficiency of Christ's work in the past and for the sufficiency as Scripture as a rule of faith. The inner light alone was not sufficient for salvation.[89] The argument over whether the inner light was sufficient for salvation was an issue that could only have arisen after the inner light had been de-divinized. Before de-divinization the question would have been unthinkable. When the inner light was Christ (literally the celestial body of Christ in the saints) then atonement was *ipso facto* guaranteed. By de-divinizing the inner light the door was opened for re-positioning Christ in the role of a mediator between God and person - in the orthodox sense. Since some leading Quakers insisted on retaining the idea that even the de-divinized inner light was sufficient for salvation Keith, it appeared, tried to get Quakers to admit to heresy. Broadly

---

[88]For an excellent introduction to the dispute as it focused on the leadership crisis *see* J. Butler, ""Gospel Order Improved": The Keithian Schism and the Exercise of Ministerial Authority in Pennsylvania," *William and Mary Quarterly*, 31 (July, 1974), pp. 431-52.

[89]George Keith, *The Deism of William Penn* (London, 1699).

speaking he was trying to convict them of claiming identity with God (for that was the only way the inner light could be sufficient for salvation) and at Philadelphia he was partly successful. The point was not to bring judicial penalties down on their heads (since that was no longer possible) but the general abhorrence and opprobrium of "orthodox" Christian society, from high Anglicans to Baptists.

The issue, then, had to do with the sufficiency of the inner light and where salvation lay. While the inner light was literally the celestial Christ inhabiting the believer the full sufficiency of salvation lay within, and this was how Quakers in America were forced to confront Keith. But when the inner light was disembodied it lost the sufficiency and authority of its former status. Penn, Barclay and Whitehead found themselves on shaky ground as they tried to maintain the absolute authority of an inner light that had been relegated to an ethical principle albeit guided by divine empowerment but without the real source of its power - the actual presence of the celestial Christ in the believer. Keith attacked Penn on this very point. The inner light was not absolute. It was, therefore, not a sufficient guide and rule of faith. It had to be supplemented with the outward Christ and the Scriptures as a guide and rule of faith.

Pressed by Keith, who assailed the notion of the inner light as sufficient for salvation, the Philadelphia elders countered with a remarkable declaration entitled *Our Ancient Testimony Renewed*.[90] They made some very bold assertions that had not been heard in quite the same way since the Nayler incident. This included the assertions that Christ and the saints are one, sanctified and sanctifier are one, and the saints are "made partakers of

---

[90]George Keith, *Some Reasons and Causes of the Late Separation* (London, 1693), pp. 8-9. The Quakers responded with *Our Ancient Testimony Renewed* (London, 1695). This latter document, "Given forth by a meeting of public Friends ... at Philadelphia ... in 1695" was printed in London that same year and appended to Gerard Croese's *General History of the Quakers* (1696) at the request of the Second Day Morning Meeting. Apparently they had heard that a letter of G. Keith's was going to be added to the English edition and they requested room for a response to the letter (*see* Joseph Smith, *Catalogue of Friends Books*, 1, pp. 481-82). One wonders why the Second Day Morning Meeting, always concerned to control even the intimation of heresy, would have chosen this statement with its contentious views.

the divine nature".[91] These statements may appear to be anomalies at such a late date - 1695. Clearly, Fox's doctrine of celestial inhabitation had not fallen into total disrepute among Quakers - something Henry More had already noted in the late 1670's. That they came from America and not from England may be significant. But again, American Quakerism was not noted for its 'enthusiasm' or its radical theology. On the contrary it tended to be smug and orthodox. Keith apparently sent the beleaguered Quaker elders scurrying back to their ancient testimony for the theological authority necessary to silence him. And that ancient testimony said the inner light was sufficient for salvation and was an absolute and authoritative guide in matters of faith precisely because the undivided Christ inhabited the saint. The return to contentious language was a risk, especially the claim that sanctified and sanctifier were one. This was the exact language that brought charges of blasphemy raining down on Fox. And it must have been a very controversial claim in Puritan New-England, especially after William King's widely publicized blasphemy trial in Salem (1681) that involved both Quakers and Puritans.[92] Which all goes to show the magnitude and the seriousness of Keith's challenge.[93] It is also a very revealing point that Quakers found it necessary to defer to the most contentious elements in Fox's teaching. The fact that Quakers continued to cite Fox as their authority, including his doctrine of equality between Christ and saint did not escape the notice of anti-Quaker apologists, as we will see shortly.

---

[91]*Our Ancient Testimony Renewed*, pp. 34-36.

[92]C.G. Pestana, "The Social World of Salem: William King's 1681 Blasphemy Trial," *American Quarterly*, 41 (1989), pp. 308-27.

[93]Keith was not beyond charging his fellow Quakers with having a "ranter" spirit and a "notionist" spirit - a product of their heavy emphasis on the inner light. He said that it was heresy to say that Christ was only a spirit. It was also heresy to believe the saints could be perfected this side of the grave. Keith himself once subscribed to these things as a licensed Quaker minister in the 1670's and 1680's but he became increasingly orthodox in the heat of his conflict with the powerful Quaker elders. He was ultimately disowned for tearing "at the heart of Quaker decorum" (Butler, ""Gospel Order Improved": The Keithian Schism," p. 446). Like Nayler his protest had scandalized Quakers and at all costs they were concerned "to protect Quaker order" (*Ibid.*, p. 447). Keith was shunned as a schismatic and powerful Pennsylvania Quaker legislators were able to censure his publishing.

Keith was condemned at the 1692 Yearly Meeting and eventually disowned by the American Quakers. He left America in 1694 and returned to England where he hoped to make a better impression on English Friends. But even there things quickly deteriorated and within five months of his return the Second Day Morning Meeting rebuked him for publishing an attack on their American Quakers without its permission. By September, 1695, English Friends had also disowned him in the interests of unity and harmony.

In 1696 there began a series of debates between Keith and the Quakers at Turner's Hall, London. These debates continued to the end of the century and in each case Keith scored doctrinal points over his Quaker opponents who generally refused to engage him in debate apart from matters of order and decorum: ie. - Keith had been wrong by becoming a schismatic. Now he was a disowned Quaker, a troublemaker and a heretic. Nonetheless, Keith's apostasy revealed the nature of the dispute. He disclaimed Penn for believing that the "seed" was an inner principle of divine light. Christ was in heaven, not within. He disclaimed George Whitehead for saying that the righteousness of the saints was the same in kind and nature with the one who works it, for the saints are partakers of the divine nature. Such a statement confounded creature and creator.[94] Whitehead said this in 1659 and he became much more cautious and orthodox in later years. Once again the attacks related to early, more extravagant claims and this was as close as Keith came to resurrecting the old charge of blasphemy.[95] It is noteworthy that he failed to pick up on the extravagant claims made by the Pennsylvania Quakers in 1695. But then, it was not much use his citing the Quaker statement from far off colonial America in England. To make his point he

---

[94]George Keith, *An Exact Narrative of the Proceedings at Turner's Hall* (London, 1696), pp. 24, 32; George Whitehead, *The Voice of Wisdom Uttered Forth, Against Antichrist's Folly and Deceit* (1659), p. 36.

[95]Keith did accept the Quaker position that everyone had "a principle of natural reason in them" [*The Fundamental Truth of Christianity* (London, 1688), p. 8] but he rejected their idea that that principle had deity in it. His argument appeared to have been over the location of the godhead and he argued for a traditionally orthodox concept of the historical Christ being in heaven with a glorified body and quite apart and separate from the saints.

needed English Quakers to convict themselves of heresy out of their own mouths. But the English Quakers did not rise to the bait nor did they own that heresy. Keith failed in his attempt to make Quakers appear to the world as theological crazies, worthy of contempt and avoidance.

The general response of English Quakers to Keith's charges was best summarized in a letter to Keith from John Humphrey and contained in one of Keith's accounts of the proceedings at Turner's Hall:

> Who is he that dares to make a distinction between Christ's body and his spirit, and to put asunder what God hath joined together? ... Christ in us is the hope of glory, and they that draw us to look for Christ without, we are not to go forth after them ... they relish too much of carnality, a carnal body of Christ in heaven, a carnal election and reprobation, a carnal justification and adoption, a carnal day of judgment and resurrection, beyond the grave.[96]

This was a classic restatement of early Quaker notions on celestial inhabitation. It was in full agreement with the ancient testimony of Nayler and Howgill who criticized their accusers for disembodying and dividing the Spirit. Some Quakers, maybe still a majority as Henry More thought, retained Fox's notions of celestial inhabitation, albeit privately. But they were ready to risk proclamation of these views when necessary, especially when pressed to do so by stubborn adversaries like George Keith. Quakers found Fox's doctrine of celestial inhabitation welcome ammunition to silence opponents like Keith who attacked the doctrine of the inner light as an insufficient guide and rule of faith. The notion of celestial inhabitation was an excellent reply, maybe the only possible reply to seal the defence, even if Quakers by this time were less than enthusiastic about throwing these ideas out into the public arena again. It was a risk and Quakers exposed themselves to fresh charges of blasphemy.

The Keith dispute is relevant to our discussion of the transformation of Quakerism, even though it was only tangentially concerned with blasphemy. It demonstrated, clearly, the divisions that Henry More had already seen in the 1660's and 1670's. Some Quakers like Penn and Barclay

---

[96]Keith, *Exact Narrative of the Proceedings at Turner's Hall* (1696), p. 41.

successfuly redefined Fox's inner light and thus neutralized the inherent danger in confusing creature and creator. They developed an innocuous spiritualized, mystical religion that took its place within the pale of respectable non-conformity. The tension between this internalized, spiritualized religion and an externalized religion that placed more emphasis on the outward Christ, the Scriptures and the external sacraments (Keith) remained submerged and resurfaced periodically through the centuries in the form of bitter disputes and schisms. On the other hand, certain powerful sentiments for the ancient testimony of Fox and the early Quakers lingered among the leadership, especially when it was pressed by one of its own to re-confirm the sufficiency and absolute authority of the inner light.

Anti-Quaker apologists in the late 1690's and the early part of the eigteenth century were not all convinced that Quakers had renounced their ancient notions of celestial inhabitation. And there were enough clues between the 1670's and 1695, when Keith was finally disowned by English Quakers, to suggest that these anti-Quaker apologists may have been at least partially correct in their assessment. Penn had excused one erstwhile Quaker, Robert Norwood, for saying that the soul had more divinity in it than most thought.[97] And there was the *Ancient Testimony* of the Philadelphia Quakers and the testimony of Humphrey Norton in England - both written against the threat of George Keith. These were indicators that Quakers, even leading Quakers, had not completely renounced Fox's notions of celestial inhabitation. Their reconfirmation of the unity and equality of God and saint and their condemnation of the disembodiment of the Spirit was further proof that vestiges of Fox's doctrine of celestial inhabitation remained well into the 1690's and beyond.

On the other hand certain well-meaning Quakers, as More would have called them, not only subscribed to Penn's and Barclay's transformed doctrines of the inner light but they worked hard to deny outright the charges of blasphemy. They were able to do this either through syntactical juggling or by exegeting the exalted language from the past through the lens of transformed notions about the inner light. In 1674, for example, George

---

[97]*Ibid.*, p. 56.

Whitehead responded to Jeremiah Ives charges against Solomon Eccles. In 1668 Eccles made a controversial statement (in answer to a pamphlet written against Fox by Lodowick Muggleton) that suggested he (Eccles) believed Fox was the creator of the world:

> Stand up Muggleton the sorcerer, whose mouth is full of cursing, lies, blasphemy: who calls thy last book, A Looking-Glass for Geo. Fox, whose name thou art not worthy to take into thy mouth, who is a prophet indeed, and hath been faithful in the Lord's business from the beginning. It was said of Christ that he was in the world, and the world was made by Him, and the world knew him not: so it may said of this true prophet (Geo. Fox) whom John [Reeve?] said, he was not: But thou will feel this prophet (Geoe. Fox) one day as a heavy millstone upon thee: and although the world knows him not, yet he is known.[98]

Eccles may have been making a metaphor and not an equivalence but it is not clear. If he was making an equivalence he was not the first Quaker to do so. Eccles later clarified his statement, saying: "I did not say nor did I ever believe that the world was made by George Fox, but by Christ who was in the world and the world knew him not".[99] Whitehead concurred with Eccles' clarification and went on to say that if Eccles did believe that Fox was creator of the world then he was fit for Bedlam.[100] We have already seen, however, that correct early Quaker understanding of celestial inhabitation made a separation between the pre-existent inward Christ and the outer body. The pre-existent Christ who was creator of the world did dwell in George Fox in the bodily form of the fullness of the godhead. Whitehead, however, excused Eccles for a little failure of syntax which gave a wrong impression. For this, he said, some charity must be shown to Eccles. Technically the phrase "the world knew him not" should "only be antecedent to" the phrase "so it may be

---

[98]Solomon Eccles, *The Quakers Challenge* (1668), p. 6. Cited and rejected as blasphemous by Edward Beckham, *A Brief Discovery*, pp. 4-5 and Charles Leslie, *The Snake in the Grass*, p. 113. Eccles, George Whitehead and Joseph Wyeth all responded to the charges.

[99]Eccles' *Testimony* may be found on pages 73-80 of William Penn, *Judas and the Jews* (London, 1673). *See* p. 75.

[100]George Whitehead, *A Serious Search into Jeremiah Ives' Questions to Quakers* (London, 1674), p. 59.

said of this true prophet". That is, Fox was in the world and it did not know him either. The phrase "the world was made by him" is not antecedent to "so it may be said of this true prophet".[101] Eccles' clarification and Whitehead's syntactical juggling it did nothing to dispel the notion that exalted language was directed towards Fox by his followers. Charles Leslie's version of Eccles' words was: "the world was made by him; and the world knew him not: so it may be said of this true prophet (George Fox) whom John said he was not". Who was it whom John said he was not, asked Leslie? Was it not Christ? He then added a new charge - Quakers were deliberately altering the works of Ancient Friends.[102]

Backpedalling became more frequent among defenders of Quakerism as the century wore on. A general attitude of denial had set in and even though Eccles revised statement, if read carefully, still likened Fox to Christ Quakers were in a position to deny charges of blasphemy on the basis of their transformed doctrine of the inner light which was not only more innocuous but more orthodox and acceptable to leading intellectuals of the day like Henry More.

The most interesting battles, from the point of view of this study, and the ones that portrayed a full-blown denial of exalted language, occurred in the 1690's and the opening decades of the eighteenth century when anti-Quaker authors like Charles Leslie, Edward Beckham and Edward Cockson revived old blasphemy charges against Fox.[103] A petition to Government even appeared in 1699, which recalled all the old blasphemy charges,[104] from the 1653 pamphlet *Saul's Errand to Damascus* to Fox's *Great Mystery* and Howgill's *Works*. Leslie accused Fox of claiming to be Christ and equal with

---

[101]*Ibid.*, p. 58. *See also* George Whitehead, *Innocency Against Envy* (London, 1691), p. 18.

[102]Leslie, *A Defence of a Book Entitled A Snake in the Grass*, pp. 40-41, 52-53, 70-72.

[103]Edward Beckham, *A Brief Discovery*, pp. 3-6; Edward Cockson, *Quakerism Dissected and Laid Open* (London, 1708), pp. 1-5; Charles Leslie, *The Snake in the Grass*.

[104]*Some Few of the Quakers Many Horrid Blasphemies ... Destructive to Government* (London, 1699), pp. 6-9.

God[105] and indeed Fox had made that claim. He also said that other Quakers, namely John Audland and Josiah Coale, believed that Fox was Christ and indeed they did believe that the celestial flesh of Christ literally inhabited Fox so completely that to them he was no longer George Fox but the Son of God. They testified to this during numerous examinations.

These were very old charges that should have long since been laid to rest but they betrayed the concern on the part of some that Quakers continued to hold to blasphemous notions. Quaker answers, in turn, betrayed their tendency to continue deny and cover-up rather than finally admit to the real sense and direction of Fox's celestial inhabitation theology. After all, if they had now changed their tune why not try to convince their opponents of that? Certainly Henry More had been convinced that some well-meaning Quakers had changed. Instead, said Leslie, they continued to excuse Fox and his early followers as Penn had excused their exalted language in *Judas and the Jews*,[106] as Quakers denied the authenticity of controversial letters by John Audland and Josiah Coale[107] and as Whitehead excused Eccles' exalted language of Fox.

Leslie and others still had a bit between their teeth and they would not let it go. Quakers, on the other hand continued to deny that Fox and early Quakers had emitted even a whiff of blasphemy, denials made possible by the transformation of the doctrine of the inner light. George Whitehead wrote in 1697 that Quakers neither pretended to nor saw cause to perform miracles to prove their divinity. This was contrary to Quaker beliefs in the 1650's. He said Fox never claimed to be equal with God or Christ since "God's indwelling in people could not render them God", a statement directly

---

[105]Leslie, *Snake in the Grass*, pp. 34, 50, 75, 67 and 109-11.

[106]William Penn, *Judas and the Jews* (1673), p. 74.

[107]"John Audland to George Fox" (Bristol, 1655). See Leslie, *The Snake in the Grass*, p. 112 and Cockson, *Quakers Dissected*, p. 3. John Whiting's response is in *The Rector Corrected*, pp. 9-10. For the charges against Coale see John Faldo, *A Vindication of Quakers No Christianity*, p. 87; Cockson, *Quakerism Dissected*, p. 3 and Leslie, *The Snake in the Grass*, p. 111. The Quaker response may be found in Penn, *Judas and the Jews*, p. 44; Penn, *The Invalidity of John Faldo's Vindication* (1673), *Works*, 2, p. 314 and John Whiting, *The Rector Corrected*, p. 9.

contrary to statements by Fox in *Saul's Errand to Damascus*. He further said that Christ had a glorified, spiritual body separate from believers (contrary to Howgill's and Nayler's claims that the Christ within was not divided); that "we positively deny giving those peculiar titles of Christ to ourselves, or to any other" (contrary to the exalted language used towards Fox and Nayler); that "they do not make their souls of the same person and substance with God. I know no such expression used by Quakers"; that Fox intended to distinguish between the soul of man and God, "for we ever distinguished between the soul of man and that which saves it" and that while saints enjoy the resurrection life in the present there is yet a future appearance of Christ[108] (all contrary to Fox's own statements). This is a remarkably comprehensive catalogue of blatant denials that formed part of the emerging myth about early Quakerism. So many learned Quaker exegetes in the 1670's, 1680's and 1690's found it necessary to unequivocally state that the saint was *separate and distinct* from Christ, in clear contradistinction to Fox's own statements, that the disclaimer itself alerts one to a profound truth: had there not been one whiff of blasphemy (according to the *Act* and orthodoxy) there would have been no necessity to mount such a massive theological shift. Surely not all Fox's opponents were liars and bigots!

Joseph Wyeth answered Leslie in a 1699 book entitled *Anguis Flagellatus*. He admitted that Fox had visions and revelations but he denied that any Quaker claimed to be "as infallible as the Apostles, or Christ himself. I demand an instance".[109] Was this a case of willful blindness? Even a cursory reading of Fox's *Great Mystery* proves to the reader that Fox believed the saints and Christ to be one and equal. And Fox's epistles and doctrinal writings were full of instances where he claimed he and the saints were in the same infallible spirit as the Apostles.[110] Then followed a series of blatant denials to Leslie's charges. Fox's letter to Cromwell was not left out of the 1694 edition of the *Journal* because it gave offence. After all,

---

[108]Whitehead, *Truth Prevalent*, p. 83.

[109]Wyeth, *Anguis Flagellatus*, p. 103.

[110]*See also* Nickall's, *Journal*, p. 606; *Doctrinal Books*, 6, pp. 98, 104, 470.

anyone who belonged to the Kingdom of God was a "King". Curiously, Fox never used the word "King" in that letter. He used the term "Son of God."[111] Wyeth also denied that any Quaker had ever kneeled before Fox and no Quaker would have stood for it.[112] Leslie, he said, gave no firm proof for such allegations. But on this point we know that Wyeth was incorrect. Most notably, Fox had Nayler and several others bow before him at the time of his public reconciliation with Nayler.

In George Whitehead's *Supplement* to Wyeth's *Anguis Flagellatus* he continued to deny that any Quaker was ever called by the name of Christ, or Jesus. Whitehead confessed to believing in an historic Christ who was born of a virgin, lived in Judea, was crucified (no Quaker ever lived that life, he said) and now existed *outside* the saints. There was a sublte reversion to orthodox views of Christ - to a distant "flesh and blood" Christ, distinct in everyway from the saint. There was still a spiritual presence but not in the sense that the believer partook of the divine nature. The early lack of distinction between creature and creator, between literal and symbolic, had been clarified by Penn and Barclay and it became the entrenched position of transformed Quakerism. All that remained was a spiritual presence of an external Christ. It was through the lens of this position that later Quaker writers interpreted Fox and early Quakerism. And it was on this platform that they combated their persistent accusers. No reference was ever made to the fact that Fox's celestial inhabitation theology had been dropped, or the inner light deliberately de-divinized, or Christ adeptly re-positioned as a mediator between God and person. According to this view it was unthinkable to say that any Quaker believed that they were equal with Christ. Instead they argued as if this had always been authentic Quaker theology. How brilliant a transformation! How subtle a withdrawal! Fox's vision was re-made into the vision of transformed Quakerism.

Why all the trouble to deny charges of blasphemy at such a late date? To preserve the emerging myth of Quakerism as a respectable, tame,

---

[111]Wyeth, *Anguis Flagellatus*, p. 175. Compare with *Cambridge Journal*, 1, p. 161.

[112]*Ibid.*, p. 182.

mystical sect for future generations, possibly. The fact that extravagant language was being selectively purged from the sources was a sign that Quakers were rewriting (even covering-up) unseemly parts of their early history. But the issue of blasphemy would not go away. The fact that some Quakers continued to make public declarations that implicitly implied they had not changed did not help. Leslie accused Quaker leaders of a cover-up and proceeded to raise old blasphemy charges for new consumption. The charges were very old and even the severest critics were unable to cite anything more recent than the early 1660's, but their goal, it appears, was to discredit the very source of Quaker authority - George Fox.

As late as 1700 Leslie still was not convinced that Quakers did not continue to worship Fox as a Christ. He responded to George Whitehead's claim that Quakers never worshipped George Fox by saying that Fox's idea of the Christ within could be used to mean anything and Quakers could use it privately to attribute divinity to Fox and to attribute divinity to themselves.[113] But some leading Quakers had changed even though they refused to admit that a change had been necessary. To admit necessary change on the doctrine of the inner light would have been to admit to the correctness of their accusers' charges; to admit to scandalous and blasphemous origins which they were not willing to do. Instead through a brilliant and generally unnoticed transformation of the inner light and a subsequent selective editing of the sources early Quakerism was placed in a protective bubble which left later defenders of the movement little choice but to defend their version of Fox and primitive Quakerism. They refused to change their patent answers.

By the time the opening years of the eighteenth century were reached the denials had become an accepted part of Quaker dogma, an essential ingredient in sustaining the myth of Fox as a tame dissenter. Even the doctrine of celestial inhabitation passed quietly from view, superseded, finally, by Penn's and Barclay's version of the inner light. Nowhere was this shift as obvious as in the writings of Richard Claridge, John Field and John

---

[113]George Whitehead, *Innocency Against Envy*, p. 18 as a response to Francis Bugg, *Some of the Quakers Principles*, section 32.

Whiting. Claridge was a learned Quaker whose treatises reflected the shift away from the inner light. In *Melius Inquirendum* (1706) Christ was clearly presented as separate and distinct from the saints. He was in heaven and apart from the saints. Furthermore, Christ's coming would be a future, external event - a complete reversal of Fox's teachings and all early Quakers.[114] The shift from a fully immanent eschatology to an external and futurist eschatology was completed in Claridge. Even the thousand year reign of Christ with the saints and the Day of Judgment were presented as future, external events.[115] There was no sense of immanence, let alone imminence! It all sounded so orthodox. A thin veneer of Fox's inner light remained in a very abstract and mystical sense. But there was no sense of the heavenly body of Christ being assumed by the saints. The saints were saved by faith in Christ, not, as Fox said, by virtue of the elect "seed" in them. Notably, in this treatise and *Tractatus Hierographicus* (1721) the emphasis was on a disembodied Spirit theology, and any hint of the inner light as the revealer of immediate revelation was nowhere to be found.

When John Field wrote *The True Christ Owned* in 1707 he too portrayed a very orthodox Christ in heaven with a glorified body. He did dwell in the saints in a mystical way, but not with his heavenly body. That remained distinct and separate from the saints: "Tho' the body of Christ that died could not be in any man, yet Christ is in every man".[116] There was no physical, corporeal presence, only a divine empowering already codified by Penn and Barclay as correct Quaker teaching. And in *The Rector Corrected* (1708) John Whiting responded to some very old but not forgotten blasphemy charges against Quakers, contained in Edward Cockson's book *Quakerism Dissected and Laid Open*. Whiting simply dismissed all charges as forgeries. Fox was not guilty of blasphemy since he was acquitted of such charges at Lancaster in 1652. The exalted language used by Fox was not of

---

[114]Richard Claridge, *Melius Inquirendum* (London, 1706), p. 178.

[115]*Ibid.*, pp. 179-80.

[116]John Field, *The True Christ Owned* (London, 1707), p. 13. *See also* pp. 6-7.

himself but of Christ, a Christ distant and distinct from the saints.[117] This was a departure from the standard Quaker defence against the charges that exalted language was addressed to Fox. It was not to Fox as Christ but to the Christ *in* him. George Whitehead, for example, defended Fox against the charges of Francis Bugg in 1693 by saying that the adoration was not to Fox but to the Christ in him.[118] George Bishop had defended Nayler in a similar manner in 1657: those who wrote to Nayler, inscribing christological titles to him, wrote to the Spirit of God that was in him.[119] Generally, the early Quaker "Spirit" was not a disembodied Spirit while the later Quaker "spirit" was disembodied. In early Quakerism the actual heavenly body of Christ inhabited every particle of the believer and divinized the believer. Dorcas Erbury testified to the fact that she believed Nayler had been transformed into Jesus. Fox and Nayler were even seen to have a greater stature than others. The disclaimers to the contrary did little to convince opponents of Quakerism that Fox and Nayler were not the recipients of exalted language. Edward Beckham said, "from such Protestants as these, good Lord deliver us, notwithstanding their now wording the matter otherwise, whilst they mean the same thing; and their principles the same as they ever were."[120] Thus, by the time John Whiting wrote *The Rector Corrected* in 1708 a distinct change had necessarily occurred in Quaker defence statements. The exalted language used by Fox of himself and by others towards him was to Christ but not to the Christ *in* him. This disclaimer represented the final stage of the transformation, the total excising of the inner light from within.

---

[117]John Whiting, *The Rector Corrected* (London, 1708), pp. 7-13.

[118]George Whitehead, *Innocency Triumphant Over Insolency ... In Answer to Francis Bugg's ... New Rome Arraigned* (London, 1693), p. 18.

[119]Bishop, *Throne of Truth Exalted*, p. 31.

[120]Beckham, *A Brief Discovery*, p. 5.

As for the letter to Cromwell, Whiting said that he had no knowledge of it,[121] suggesting that the bowdlerization of the sources had begun to serve its purpose. Any reference Fox made to the 'Son of God' was no more than "all that are led by the Spirit of God", the interpretation accepted by Quaker interpreters to the present. Even the controversial statements by Nayler, Audland and Coale could not be authenticated, prompting Whiting to charge Cockson with basing arguments on speculation: "does not this chapman deal in rare ware?"[122] One wonders who, by this time, was dealing in rare ware.

Finally, the ideological transformation of Quakerism included and maybe imposed upon Fox a personal transformation. We saw in the last chapter that his self-dethronement and theological retreat was limited. The best indicator that Fox had lost control of his movement was that his death caused no stir over succession. Fox must have known of the effort on the part of Quaker divines to reinterpret his inner light into a less dangerous and more innocuous divine principle. If so this would explain certain unexplained events in his life. The first was his momentous 1671 vision of the treasure in the vault in which he (George Fox) spoke of the inward Christ:

And I had a vision about that time that I was in this travail and sufferings that I was walking in the fields and many friends was [sic] with me and I bid them dig in the earth: and they did and I went down: and there was a mighty vault top full of people kept under the earth rocks and stones: and so I bid them break open the earth and let all the people out: and they did and all the people came forth to liberty and it was a mighty place. And when they had done I went on and bid them dig again (they did) and there was a mighty vault full of people and I bid them throw it down and let all the people out and so they did. And I went down again and bid them dig again and friends said unto me George thou findest out all things and so there they digged and I went down: and went along the vault: and there sat a woman in white looking at time how it past away: and there followed me a women down in the vault in which vault was the treasure: and so she laid her hand on the treasure on my left hand and then time wisked on apace: but I calpt my

---

[121]John Whiting, *The Rector Corrected*, p. 8. George Whitehead never denied the authenticity of the letters. He said they were incorrectly cited (*Innocency Against Envy*, p. 18 and *An Antidote Against the Venome of the Snake in the Grass*, p. 250).

[122]Whiting, *The Rector Corrected*, p. 10.

hand upon her: and said touch not the treasure. And then time past not so swift. Them that can read these things must have the earth...stony nature off them.[123]

Such a vision can be interpreted as an effort by Fox to slow down the pace of change in his movement by calling Quakers back to his original message of the celestially-fleshed inner Christ while at the same time reasserting his spiritual authority over his movement. Is this why Ellwood edited the vision out of his edition of Fox's *Journal*: because he represented the views of Penn, Barclay and transformed Quakerism which had an aversion to any hint of a celestially-fleshed inner Christ, which was, after all, the "treasure" Fox warned the Quakers not to touch.[124] Fox used visions and charisma to communicate unexceptionable truth.

The vision of the vault was also accompanied by a new outpouring of miraculous phenomena. Fox's vision occurred in 1671. In 1672 and 1673 he was in America (where he worked several miracles) and returned home in June, 1673. The King's *Declaration of Indulgence* had just been revoked but its effects were still being felt. More importantly the *Great Pardon of Friends* had received Royal assent in September, 1672 and all Friends had been released from prison.[125] There were two recorded miracles for 1673, after

[123]*Cambridge Journal*, 2, p. 175. Just before his death John Camm had a vision of a large mine with precious ore to be dug out and many were needed in this great labour [*The Memory of the Righteous Revived* (London, 1689), Bb-Bf].

[124]*Gospel Truth Demonstrated*, 5, pp. 148, 253; 6, p. 387.

[125]Charles II had good reason to show mercy to Quakers. In Jan. 1669/70 he had been reminded that it was a Friend, Richard Carver, who had been aboard the ship that carried him away from his pursuers after the battle of Worchester and that same Friend carried him ashore in France. Charles II's brother, James II, was also assisted by a Quaker in his flight to France after the battle of the Boyne [*See* H. Cadbury, "Some Light on Charles II and Friends," *JFHS*, 53 (1972), pp. 53-55]. The *Declaration of Indulgence* was issued in March, 1672, on the eve of the war with Holland. The King may have issued the *Declaration* to keep his Kingdom peaceable during the war abroad. The *Declaration* "suspended the execution of all *Penal Laws*, and authorized meetings of Nonconformists, but not of Papists, in allowed places and with approved teachers, if open and free to all persons" (Braithwaite, *Second Period*, pp. 81-82). Quakers took this opportunity to appeal to Charles for the release of imprisoned Friends. They presented the King with a lengthy list of imprisoned Friends (including praemunired persons and those under the sentence of banishment). Charles, showing an unusual spirit of magnanimity, simply said "I'll pardon them", an act that became known as the *Great Pardon of Friends* or the *Charter of Release* in which Charles II granted

Fox's return home. Then eight were recorded for 1674, more than at any other time since the early 1650's. The miracle working dropped off again after 1675, the year the *Penal Laws* were reinstituted, but picked up again in 1685, the year James issued his *Declaration of Indulgence* and 1,500 Quakers (incarcerated after the government crackdown following the *Rye House Plot*) were released from prison.

A series of events converged which enabled Fox to temporarily break out of his shell and discover his old charisma and exalted claims. Fox sensed there was a theological shift away from his message and he used his vision and the miracles to rivet the attention of Friends on his original message - the presence of the celestial Christ in their midst. He reasserted himself as the model and example for them to follow. He personified those things generally associated with Christ. Increased miracles and appearances also corresponded with a time of greater toleration in the country. Fox, always keenly sensitive to new opportunities, used the occasion to attempt a restoration by reasserting his charismatic powers and exalted claims. Fox would never have split ranks over theology (he was too committed to the

---

pardon and release to 491 persons imprisoned for contempt, misdemeanours, not attending Church, refusing the oath of allegiance and supremacy and frequenting seditious conventicles. The lengthy legal document, carefully handwritten to include the names of every Quaker to be liberated, was drawn up and discharged under the Great Seal, signed by Charles. It appeared on Sept. 13, 1672 on 11 skins of vellum. This is still preserved at Friends' Reference Library in London. The restored Great Seal is appended by new cords. The Patent was circulated through the country by Friends who travelled on foot or on horseback from prison to prison. The original was passed through the eastern counties and copies were passed through the rest of England. The original was carried by a Quaker named Edward Man who kept "the bulky Patent tied across the saddle behind him in its leather case, with the tin box for the Great Seal hanging from it" (*Ibid.*, p. 84). By the end of the year all Friends were liberated apart from a few that were not reached due to remote locations or oversight. Some had to pay gaolers for their release and others were retained for up to another six months, at the gaolers' discretion. Although the *Declaration of Indulgence* and the *Great Pardon* were a sign that the fires of heavy persecution meeted out by the Cavalier Parliament were beginning to die down full toleration was nearly two decades away. And even while the *Declaration of Indulgence* was in effect Parliament responded with its own *Test Act* which made life no easier for Catholics and Non-Conformists, especially those who wished to hold public office. *The Declaration of Indulgence* was revoked in March, 1673 and the persecution of Non-Conformists resumed in 1674 following Charles' new alliance with the Church of England. In 1675 the licensing of Non-Conformist ministers was terminated and the suspended *Penal Laws* were re-activated. Terrible persecution still lay ahead for Quakers. The *Toleration Act* of 1689 signalled the end of the disruption of meetings and the imprisonment of Quakers. Fox lived long enough to see all Quakers out of prison and out of any further judicial danger. He died two years later.

principle of unity) but if theological change concerned him then one way to redress it would have been through a new outpouring of signs and wonders. A reappraisal of the sources suggests that he did just this. When miracles and visions had ceased among the rank and file Fox's miracles in the 1670's multiplied fourfold over the previous decade. The number of recorded visions (all by Fox) doubled.[125] Five of those visions occurred in 1673, the year Penn wrote *Reason Against Railing* wherein he redefined the inner light. There was a renaissance of supernatural powers in the 1670's and above all, it was Fox who used them to reassert his original message of the celestially-fleshed inner Christ. Henry More repeatedly referred to this "Familist" (his term) tendency in Fox.

The 1670's were a time of new beginnings for Fox. Cadbury described this decade and the 1650's as the two most prolific decades of Fox's life.[127] He galvanized his talents and his self-confidence. He secured in his own mind and that of his followers, his pre-eminence and his mission while avoiding the former pitfalls of avatarship. He arrived at a new conception of himself as an apostle (on a par with the Apostles of the early church) and this helped him to cope with the loss of absolute leadership. As an apostle with a special calling he remained the first among equals while reconciling himself to changes within his movement. He remained 'above the crowd' and somewhat aloof. He belonged to no Quaker delegated body, not even the Yearly Meeting.[128] This is remarkable and it suggests that in the later years he was aware of some distance between himself and his movement. Those around him saw his influence as that of a revered and powerful personality. Penn said, "He held his place in the church of God with great meekness and a most engaging humility and moderation - his authority was inward and not outward."[129] This characterization demonstrates just how well Fox had carved out his niche within the changing Society. It also demonstrates that

[125]*See* Table I, p. 195.

[127]Cadbury, "George Fox's Later Years," p. 751.

[128]*Ibid.*, p. 740.

[129]*Ibid.*, p. 740. Quoted by Cadbury.

Fox had reached a solution to his personal dilemma that implied continued exalted status, even though others simply revered him as a special person but not as a 'god'. He was revered and not worshipped apart from within his own family. As late as 1675 his stepson-in-law, Thomas Lower still referred to him as "a blessing to nations, the joy of his people, the second appearance of him who is blessed". It would appear that Fox's family continued to worship him as a 'god' long after the rest of his movement had radically altered their views. The comforting and more than advisory devotion of his wife Margaret and her family must have been a continuing source of encouragement and strength for Fox.

According to Braithwaite, "He remained to the last in close touch with affairs, but only as a revered elder among brethren".[130] In England at least, the avatar was dead. He continued his itinerant ministry as long as his health allowed. A 1677 trip to Europe temporarily liberated Fox from the pressures and routine of his life at home and he revived some his old charisma, strength and vigor. There he again spoke of opening the Scriptures to great crowds as in the days of old. Apart from a subsequent revisit to Holland this was his last major journey. The apostle, as he now thought of himself, spent most of his last fifteen years in or near London.[131]

The testimonials given at his burial referred to him as an "ancient, honourable and worthy man", a "good man", a "worthy champion", a "fixed star in the firmament of God's glory" and by Penn, a "prince fallen in Israel".[132] To all, with the possible exception of the immediate Fell family,

---

[130]Braithwaite, *Second Period*, p. 432.

[131]Fox died Jan. 13, 1691 by the Gregorian calendar or, Nov. 13, 1690 by the Julian calendar.

[132]*Cambridge Journal*, 2, pp. 369-71. Also *An Epistle Concerning the Decease of George Fox*, p. 2 in volume 3 of the Francis Bugg collection of Quaker printed sources at Christ Church, Oxford. He was certainly treated as a prince by his own. He was never without a place to lodge. Benjamin and Mary Antrobus, in London, stored his personal effects for him. His library of 335 books was kept at William Meade's house. In addition Friends showered him with gifts and care. They gave him gold, land, money, clothes, interests in merchant ships and even homes. He was never in want. He was personally cared for when he was sick. In later years he had his own *amanuensis*. Critics accused him of having as much plenty as any knight in England. He was legally referred to as "George Fox of London,

he was no more than a mere mortal. There was no more worship and no more "Son of God" talk. He was not even a great apostle or prophet. Hannah Darlington Monaghan even asks whether they were burying a prophet," or was it only dear George who had passed from their sight?"[133] He was no longer a 'god', a prophet or even an apostle. He was a good man and a father who encouraged his children to walk in the light, live in unity; and be mindful of the presence of Christ among them.[134]

Still, at the burial, many were crushed and broken. It is not clear exactly what happened at the Grace Church street meeting that gathered in remembrance of Fox but there was a charismatic outpouring of some sort that prompted one person to liken it to the Apostles meeting after the death of Christ when the power of God fell on them and they prophesied.[135] There is no evidence of any wild behaviour as there was at the early threshing meetings but there was a venting of immense feeling toward Fox so that not one person in the room was not "crushed and broken down by the weight of that glory [so] that for a considerable time, there was nothing but deep sighs, groans and tears and roaring to admiration."[136] To the end lingering comparisons to Christ remained, at least in the minds of some.

After his death a select group of Quaker elders removed any hint of worship towards Fox, or exalted language used by Fox of himself, from his works. The new Fox was created by a new generation of Quaker divines and editors. He was not the charismatic prophet and thaumaturge of old. Some of this transformation occurred in Fox's own lifetime but Fox himself never ceased to consider himself as a special and divinely anointed emissary of God. There was enough evidence of this in the sources - that is, of a man straining to retain his charisma and his power. He was fortunate enough to

---

gentleman" or "gentleman of Swarthmoor" (Cadbury, "George Fox's Later Years", p. 742) a title of respect for one who had once been mocked and ridiculed as a megalomaniac and languished in prison for blasphemy.

[133]Monaghan, *Dear George*, p. 367.

[134]*Cambridge Journal*, 2, p. 369.

[135]*Ibid.*, 2, pp. 371.

[136]*Ibid.*, 2, p. 370.

make the requisite adjustments to his loss of leadership and remain true to his original calling without a loss of zeal or self-esteem. The Barbados Formula helped him to make the necessary transition from avatar to apostle. In the midst of change and transformation he strove to regain the charismatic power that was his at first and it did make one brief pentecostal return at his burial - not so much in the to be expected "sighs and tears" as in the "groans and roarings" and the fleeting sense of reliving Pentecost. Perhaps this was nostalgic hyperbole, or perhaps this was the last echo of Dionysian ecstasy.[137]

---

[137]Maybe Fox's funeral was one final outbreak of indecorous ecstatic 'Dionysian' behaviour. This kind of "possessed" behaviour happened at Dionysian festivals in ancient Greece. In the nineteenth century Nietzsche characterized that culture in terms of Apollonian and Dionysian tendencies. He thought the rational, measured, scientific side (the Apollonian) had become too prevalent in his day and he wanted to promote the more intuitive, inspired and imaginative kind of behaviour and thought [Described in his *The Birth of Tragedy*. *See The Encyclopedia of Philosophy*, 5 (New York: Macmillan, 1967), pp. 506-7]. The "roaring" at Fox's funeral may have been literary hyperbole and the funeral a very tame affair. Still some ecstatic behaviour was involved and some Quakers did rekindle the old charismatic power - was it one final great epiphany, or just a testament to the remarkable spirit and power of one very remarkable man? The report of the meeting in the *Cambridge Journal* was ambivalent - and it was that ambivalence, it seemed, that characterized people's responses to Fox from beginning to end.

CONCLUSION

Christopher Hill has written: "Religious groups should not write their own history: hindsight leads to a too early attribution of characteristics which might have become well-known elements in the later story."[1] This study has been an attempt to reassess the nature of early Quakerism and the teachings of its founder without interpreting it through the lens of the later story. We have seen here how the Quaker conviction of the inner light overturned the world order for the individual in an interior, psychological sense. The revolutionary fact that the common person was able to hold Christ within as flesh and bone - was Christ in some sense - was the *modus operandi* of early Quakerism, their principle of social compensation.

Even today the charges of blasphemy against early Quakers are met with utter (even hysterical) disavowal by Quaker scholars. In a way this gives some semblance of right to early Quaker opponents. In the ordinary sense of irreverence and contempt of God the charge was, and is, nonsense. Early Quaker attitudes toward God were nothing if not reverent and devout. In a theological and, in the 1650's, legal sense the charge was a fearsome weapon used by the established orthodoxy to silence dissent. If Fox claimed equality with God it was in a special sense as a witness to the ongoing redemptive process. What was at stake was another view of God, another view of the divine work of salvation, another view of what human response and

---

[1]Hill, "Quakers and the English Revolution", p. 77.

expectation should be, and another view of the destiny of the world. Blasphemy is the cruellest of all cudgels with which to crush an alternative reverent-minded vision. To deny it absolutely seems to admit that all the grounds of orthodoxy (were they proved) are right. And the attitude of denial prevents one seeing what Fox and early Quakers were really claiming.

New theologies provide new opportunities for social mobility and advancement within new organizations. Fox, for example, became a "Prince of Israel" and even a "King" from humble origins. More importantly, in a psychological sense, the social order was overturned. One was ennobled, glorified and innocent of sin if the celestial Christ was within. One was greater than any lord or gentleman. This was how Fox presented himself before Cromwell and before Charles II. There was here a fundamental source of liberation - liberation being an act of ideology, of self-consciousness. Even later, when the inner light became Reason, at least one remained the equal of the lord and gentleman. Even if revolutionary potential was blunted the reformist potential remained.

Fox promoted a new language (or a new cluster of metaphors) for a new theology. New language is necessary when one sees the world in a different way and necessary, too, if one is to become a different person. Terms like the "Lamb's War", the "Inner Light", the "Flaming Sword", the "Seed" and "in the power" of Scriptures (which emphasized the energizing charisma of the record rather than static truth) captured the essence of this new theology. Some words were interpreted freely as allegories.[2] The stone, for instance, represented Christ and the saving work of Christ. Other texts were taken, strictly literally, as meaning what they said.[3] One such, which got

---

[2]One should add as a *caveat* that not all interpreters of Quakerism would agree on the meanings I attach to Fox's primary symbols.

[3]Others believe that Fox's central metaphors were simultaneously fact and symbol. His metaphors expressed an existential reality. As Cope said, Quakers "had a tendency to break down the boundary between literalness and metaphor, between conceptions and things" (Cope, "Seventeenth Century Quaker Style," p. 202). When Fox was once asked from whence he came, he said "From the Lord". Here "metaphor has transcended its normal function, and instead of merely indicating a point of resemblance between two differentiable entities, it has totally merged them" (*Ibid.*, p. 202). Quakers used language in a way that transcended metaphor. They opened their mouths and God spoke. When Stephen Crisp deplored the

Fox into trouble, was I Corinthians 2:15 and 6:2-3 where the saints were said to judge the world, even the angels. This literal claim seemed to imply parity with God. Fox's interpretive powers ranged from the highly speculative and allegorical to the downright repetitive and mechanical. But the purpose of his de-coding was to weave disparate key words, neglected verse and texts into a wholecloth tapestry depicting the cosmic process.

The choice of primary Quaker symbols like "seed" and "light" was a choice which reflected a selection of icons that had 'true' meaning, of course, but it was also a choice that created habits of mind, of thought and even imprinted personality. Attitudes and actions hang on icons in this way. Christ became the "seed", the immanent crusher of the serpent's head. When Fox signed his correspondence "Yours in the Seed" he was thinking of Christ in less transcendent terms and more in terms of a life of committed endeavour. He was thinking in terms of separation from the world and engagement within it by bruising the serpent's head, that is, fighting the evil therein.

Neo-Platonic Christians and mystics from St. Augustine on have been preoccupied with Light. One even thinks in later times of Goethe's dying words: "Light, more light!"; Shelley's "That Light whose smile kindles the Universe" from *Adonais*; John Henry Newman's "Lead, kindly Light" still sung with such gusto; Rabindranath Tagore's "Light, oh where is the light?" from *Gitanjali* or Holman Hunt's painting "The Light of the World", representing John 8:12. All these lights mean different things but no one (apart possibly from the ancient Zoroastrian religion)[4] has been as preoccupied with Light. No one made it the central icon of their thought in the same sense as the early Quakers - of an immanent, inner, substantial, divine presence. Its meaning as the inward Christ - as the celestial flesh of Christ - was soon changed (Penn's and Barclay's inner light was not Fox's

decline of Quaker language as early as 1666 he was not referring to the loss of Quaker plain-language but to the loss of its power to convince. Quaker plain speech had become a type of "counterfeit plain speech", as Professor Johannessen has suggested. It was no more than the fashionable mark of an introverted sect (*See* Bauman, *Let Your Words Be Few*, p. 153).

[4]Light also had some religious significance for the patriarchal Indo-European tribes who invaded the goddess worshipping tribes of Mesopotamia. They applied it to their male deities.

inward Christ) and the change came too soon, before the earliest icons had time to case harden into set dispositions of mind. On the other hand, had Quakerism not been so open to change and reinterpretation it would (like other 1640's sects) surely have failed. New icons and metaphors were discovered, then, to express new views about human nature, about the purposes of the universe and about human destiny. The images themselves became constituents of a new vision of creation and its purposes even after they changed their hue through the entropic process.

The mystics shared with Quakers a personal and individual approach to God, characterized by immediate revelation, but their vision of spiritual unity (apart, possibly, from the Neo-Platonists and Meister Eckhardt)[5] was generally a struggle from one occasional ecstatic epiphany to another which was only a foretaste of what was to come after death, rather than a permanent state of perfection in this life. Theirs was also a disembodied Spirit theology wherein the Spirit empowered them in their quest. It was not a christopresent theology. Quakerism was transformed into a Spirit theology but it began as a radically christopresent theology. Fox's language may be, by definition, mystical (the language of experience as opposed to the dialectic of the academics) but he was more than a mystic - he was first and foremost a charismatic prophet and an avatar.

Some of Fox's guiding images were partially anticipated by the symbols used by his contemporaries; in the archetypal images of the collective unconscious of his time, or in the "common pool of imagery" of the time.[6] For example "light" was a term used by both the Seekers and the

---

[5] Eckhardt seems to have held out the possibility of reaching a state of permanent ecstasy. As Underhill points out, other mystics like the author of the *Theologia Germanica* also spoke of "deified man". She says, however, "that by deification they intend no arrogant claim to identification with God, but as it were a transfusion of their selves by His Self: an entrance upon a new order of life, so high and so harmonious with Reality that it can only be called divine" [Evelyn Underhill, *Mysticism: A Study in the Nature and Development of Man's Spiritual Consciousness* (London: Methuen, 1949), p. 420. First published in 1911].

[6] The idea of archetypal patterns in literature is Jungian, and has in recent years become an accepted part of literary criticism. "Common pool of imagery" is Owen Watkins' phrase, *The Puritan Experience*, p. 212. M. Graves found five predominant images belonged to this common pool of imagery in 17th century sermons: "light/dark", "voice", "seed", "hunger" and "pilgrimage". Quakers used some of these images but Graves concluded that they "were

Cambridge Platonists. Saltmarsh said that history was a struggle between the two "seeds". "Seed" was used in Winstanley's *Truth Lifting Up its Head* and the phrase "lamb" (as in "lamb against beast") was used in his *Fire in the Bush*. Winstanley especially had a strong sense of the immanence of the Spirit, which animated the "human body" of Christ and united saint with Father, only Winstanley's was a spiritual Christ whereas Fox's was celestial flesh.[7] Ranters, too, had an idea "that God had taken their souls out of their bodies into himself, and he occupied the place in their bodies where their souls had been, so that it was no more they that acted or said any thing ... but God in their bodies."[8] Groups like the Ranters and individuals like Winstanley used many symbols which implied some sort of divine immanence and inward empowering. In 1648 Valentine Weigel's work on the *Life of Christ* was translated into English, thus transmitting radical Anabaptist notions on the celestial flesh of Jesus to a wider English audience. Discussing William Penn's metaphorical interpretation of the idea of celestial flesh, Endy had suspected that Fox's idea was more than metaphorical. His suspicion was confined to heavy theological discussion of the Person of Christ but it is encouraging that Endy found heavenly flesh ideas in Fox, even if he did not extend the notion to its presence in the saints. Whether Fox read Weigel's *Life of Christ* is not known. What is evident is that his view of inhabitation by celestial flesh went way beyond discussions about the person of Christ by the Anabaptists, Winstanley and the Ranters.

Symbols like "light" and "seed" tell us something about the powerful hunger in ordinary folk to find new modes of renewal.[9] Fox may not have

set apart from other Protestant groups by the very words they chose to use and not to use" (Graves, "Functions of Key Metaphors in Early Quaker Sermons, 1671-1700", *Quarterly Journal of Speech*, 69 (1983), p. 56.

[7] Gerard Winstanley, *Truth Lifting Up its Head*, in *The Works of Gerard Winstanley*, edited by G.H. Sabine (New York: Russell and Russell, 1965), p. 113. Winstanley did not put major emphasis on the "Lamb's War" like Fox and the Quakers did. Winthrop Hudson may have put too much emphasis on the similarity between Fox and Winstanley at the expense of the more pronounced similarities between Fox and the Seekers [W.S. Hudson, "Gerrard Winstanley and the Early Quakers", *CH*, 12 (1943), pp. 177-94].

[8] Nuttall, *Studies in Christian Enthusiasm*, p. 77.

[9] Edwards, *Gangraena* (revised edition, 1646), volume 1, p. 10.

met or read Saltmarsh, Everard, Winstanley but he may well have come across their echoes in his travels. He forged a composite of these central images and symbols that were around him adding links that were entirely his own to define a new religious movement that emphasized the divinization of the believer through the inner celestially physical Christ.[10] Winstanley, too, had a vision of overturning Babylon and the Beast but neither he nor any other of his contemporaries pursued the divinization theme within the context of such a total cosmology as Fox did.[11]

Fox's synthesizing of powerful symbols into a cosmology that had christopresentism and divinization as its centrepiece was his original contribution not only to seventeenth century religion in England but to the history of Christian thought in general. Fox was a motivator, a synthesizer, a communicator, a propagator, a proselytizer and a charismatic power. He was the discoverer of an inward Christ others had not thought of. His view may best be expressed in an oxymoron, that Christ was a concrete celestial presence. His *Great Mystery of the Great Whore of Babylon* stressed the flesh and bone cohabitation of the celestial Christ in the saint. And his momentous and timely vision in 1671 (edited from the text of the *Journal* by Ellwood) was a re-assertion of the message of the inward, physically present celestial Christ at a time when others in his movement were transforming that concept into the less dangerous and more innocuous concept of a

---

[10]Fox did not to look directly to Continental writers like Sebastian Franck, Caspar Schwenckfeld and Jacob Boehme for these images. They were on his doorstep. Continental undercurrents were carried in England by the Familists, Seekers, Grindletonians, Ranters and by individuals like John Everard and Winstanley. Everard's and Winstanley's ideas were widely diffused, especially among the Seeker groups that Fox encountered and from whom he drew some of his earliest converts. Like the Collegiants, the Seekers awaited new revelation and they used the Schwenckfeldian phrase "doves without mates" to describe themselves. Ranters, too, drew from this same well of imagery.

[11]A recent and fascinating book by Nigel Smith, *Perfection Proclaimed*, emphasizes (among other things) the tendency in radical literature between 1640 and 1660 to merge the self and the Divine. This emphasis is also made by historians who talk of the "second reformation" in the 17th century. Unfortunately Smith does not delve deeply into Fox's theology. He could have strengthened his point had he done so.

divinely empowered moral principle. He was still advocating his doctrine of celestial inhabitation as late as 1687![12]

Early Quakerism under Fox's authority did not have enough time to distill and clarify the early salient signs and metaphors before they came subject to re-interpretation. They were still in a liquid, malleable state when the Nayler dispute forced changes. The de-divinization of the saints created a place for Quakerism within the pale of respectable religious non-conformity but it must also have made Quaker ideals less appealing to the thousands of nameless, faceless ordinary folk who came to hear Fox at Firbank Fell, or who we know appeared at early Quaker threshing meetings. No one knows who these people were for they would appear to hear Quaker "threshers" and then vanish into obscurity again, possibly strengthened with the new hope that they belonged to God's nobility, that they were, or could be, glorified on earth, and that they were soon to become the rulers of the new Kingdom.[13] The change of view helps to explain the changing social, political and economic complexion of the movement, especially among the more educated class.[14]

---

[12]Believers are "children of the promise and of the food and flesh of Christ, ... flesh of his flesh and bone of his bone" [George Fox, (January, 1687), *Box A, Portfolio 10*, No. 24 at FRL. Note also No. 8].

[13]Fox's notion of celestial inhabitation, even the transformation of the saints into the very person of Christ, is to be distinguished from Peter Brown's idea that the saints of old were exemplars and reflections of Christ. Brown reads saintliness in terms of a continuation of the ancient culture of "paidea" - education in which students perfectly imitate their teacher or become intellectual apprentices of their master. When combined with Christian thinking the student became like the saint who was a representation of Christ [Peter Brown, "The Saint as Exemplar in Late Antiquity," *Representations*, 1 (1983), p. 1-26]. I'm suggesting the early Quaker concept of being transformed into the actual celestial flesh was something quite different, and from the orthodox standpoint, something quite heretical.

[14]Early Friends were drawn from the "hard-pressed sections" of the urban and rural *petite-bourgeoisie*, including husbandmen, weavers, tailors and shoe-makers (Cole, "Social Origins of Early Friends," p. 118) but who were the thousands who attended the *innumerable* threshing meetings? Those who came to hear Fox at Firbank Fell were not all rural *petite-bourgeoisie*. Given the geographic location of Firbank Fell they would have been among England's dispossessed, oppressed and poor. Those who formally joined the ranks of Friends may have been largely urban and rural *petite-bourgeoisie* but the appeal of Fox's vision reached beyond the hard-pressed sections of the "middling order" to the very poor and oppressed and this should not be overlooked. To say that the rank and file of Quakerism had become more

280

The social and mystical views do say something about early Quakerism but to say Fox's and Nayler's persecutors were hysterical fails to understand the real reasons why these people were as they were and that there were very real ideological reasons that prompted their behaviour. Fox the charismatic prophet and avatar rather than Fox the mystic, spiritualist or man of conscience has been the focus of this study. It has emphasized a distinctive and a very radical theology which changed over time. It has shown Fox struggling to adjust to change and in so doing, providing for the continued life of his movement while losing, in a tangible way, his direction of it. It has sketched a theology that both responded to social needs and framed a type of character who responded in particular ways to those social needs (ie. through pacifism, egalitarian speech, etc.). It showed that neither Fox nor Nayler were fools, nor were their persecutors utter bigots who persecuted without grounds. They were defending orthodoxy. That is, they were defending "steeplehouse", external Christianity, led by clergy, bolstered by visible institutions, and sustained by the State. They feared an anarchy of "notionism" which had the potential to unravel Christian society. They all had their own imperatives.

Fox has been portrayed sympathetically, as a most extraordinary theological innovator and genius, but neither a saint nor a huckster. By throwing light on the signs and wonders, the miracles and visions, light has also been thrown on a period of religious revival that rivalled the first century

---

plebeian by 1700 [Richard Vann, *The Social Development of English Quakerism* (Harvard University Press, 1969), p. 120] can be misleading. Vann demonstrated that its sources of power were located in flourishing cities like Bristol, London, Dublin and Philadelphia where a new wealthy Quaker aristocracy had arisen. They became the ruling class of Quakerism - "gentry, professional men, yeomen, and wholesale traders" (Reay, *Quakers and the English Revolution*, p. 114) who knew little of the early experience. Vann concluded: "[the] "bourgeoisification" of the Society of Friends, so much oftener described than proved, does have certain reality in the growth of the powers of the meetings for church affairs, which had a decidedly more "bourgeois" complexion than the membership as a whole" (*Ibid.*, p. 121). This new class of Quaker merchants were respectable and respected men of commerce who would have despised the enthusiasm and excesses spawned by Fox's ideas of the divinization of the saints. The changing social complexion of the movement may therefore be said to reflect the changing ideology of the movement. This is clearly illustrated by the Swarthmoor Hall/Ragley Hall, Margaret Fell/Lady Anne Conway, Primitive/Transformed Quaker contrast. Quakerism at Ragley Hall in the 1670's best characterized the change of class in the movement - the shift away from artisan stock to educated and even aristocratic leadership.

A.D. in its vigour and variety, and that in turn sheds light on the cultural history of the century. Fox's truth was the original cornerstone of the movement and his mode of establishing unexceptionable truth was extraordinary. It was a truth attested by direct revelation, miracles, visions and Son of God (later apostolic) claims. Logic, whether dialectical,[15] Aristotelian or Ramist was by-passed. Hermeneutics of the Reformed type were by-passed. Bacon's New Method (*Novum Organum*), his scientific inductive method, did not enter the picture.[16] Fox shunned these attempts to establish unexceptionable truth and he revived the charismatic mode of 'knowing'. This illustrates the importance of charismatic knowledge and charismatic proof as a neglected form of epistemology. Its emphasis was one of Fox's most remarkable contributions to the seventeenth century.

After the Restoration of the many thousands imprisoned well over four hundred Quakers died in prison as a result of filth, disease and verminous straw.[17] These were slow, publicly invisible, agonizing martyrdoms of fatal disease. What believers needed in their time of persecution, particularly to sustain them through an unlovely martyrdom in a fatal prison, was *unshakeable* conviction which Fox's charismatic claims provided. This fact alone throws light on what Fox's claims were all about. Many elements sustain a conviction but one important one is the right and authority behind it. In this case it was the authority of Fox, his new revelation and his divine sonship, which was needed to make ordinary people

---

[15]The Platonic way of discovering unexceptionable truths.

[16]Fox also used other commonly employed ways of establishing truth: Scriptural allusions, doctrinal assertions and the less common argument that good conversation (conversation was the seventeenth century word for behaviour) proved the truth of Quaker beliefs - fruits and works proved the truth of belief. Their humbleness, meekness, soberness, honesty and serious mindedness proved the test of their faith. None of these modes of proof were unusual and they were also used by the Anabaptists, for example, but they were not as novel as charismatic "proofs". As late as 1781 Elizabeth Webb used this classic Quaker appeal to charismatic proof in her autobiography: "I have no learned method in which to deliver my religious experience, either by word or writing, but plainly and simply as the Spirit of Truth directs" [E. Webb, *A Letter From Elizabeth Webb to Anthony William Boehme: Containing Some Account of Her Religious Experience* (Philadelphia, 1786)].

[17]For the figures *see* C. Horle, *The Quakers and the English Legal System, 1660-1688* (Philadelphia: University of Pennsylvania Press, 1988), p. 102.

faithful unto death. These followers needed to be braced through the valley of the shadow. They especially needed courage to face the appalling repressions of the Cavalier Parliament. The teaching of the inner Christ was a wonderful brace. It was a new vision of human nature and of human destiny. It embraced a vision of cosmic reality in terms as large as any competing religious vision of the day. Fox was testifying to the truth just as the patriarchs, prophets, Christ and the Apostles had done. He was prepared to debate texts of scripture to establish that this was the true doctrine but he went beyond the academic din and strife of text-throwing. His deeds and claims went beyond that, cut through it, and proved what proof-texts could never prove. Convinced of such proof, one could take a lot of ridicule, a lot of harrassment, and even the harrowing, lingering martyrdom of a prison-induced death. Fox's claims as an avatar and later as a divinely commissioned apostle lent themselves to the epistemological certainty of his followers.[18] The miracles, signs, visions, prophecies and exalted claims all authenticated the truth of Fox's religious vision.

Additionally, the measure of truth was in the physical sensation of exhilaration. The more feeling, the more conviction. This heightened sense of elation might rise or fall with circumstance but it was ever present. Life, then, was always lived at some level of ecstasy. This was to be "in the power" of Scriptures. This enabled one to "see" the truth about the inner light. The truth was not merely known and acknowledged but felt. Knowledge incited feeling and feeling confirmed knowledge.

The bedrock of Fox's new religion was his doctrine of the real corporeal presence, in full panoply, of the celestial Christ in the saint. So essential was this idea of the cohabitation of the Christ in the believer to Fox's message and so central is it to our understanding of the charismatic nature of early Quakerism that it is an historiographical calamity that it has

---

[18]Alfred Braithwaite pointed out that the majority of imprisonments arose from refusal to take oaths or pay tithes [A.W. Braithwaite, "Early Tithe Prosecutions: Friends as Outlaws," *JFHS*, 49 (1960), p. 148] but as was said above, the conviction required to sustain Quakers through long agonizing imprisonments and even through the valley of the shadow of death found its source in Fox's charismatic claims both for himself and for ordinary people who thought of themselves as divinely ennobled.

been hidden from view for so long. It is equally an historiographical calamity that contemporary historians have given a spiritualist gloss to Fox's christology by keeping the heavenly flesh and bone of Christ separate and fundamentally alien to human nature and experience - a serious misrepresentation of Fox and an attribution of notions that belong to the later part of the story.

One of the products - perhaps inevitable - of this theme of celestial inhabitation was the lofty claims of Fox and Nayler. The blasphemy charges against Fox and Nayler were neither fanatical nor unjustifiably bigoted. Though hostile, they were an accurate enough recognition of their views. The transcripts we have of Fox's trials provide evidence enough of his exalted claims even when he was on the defensive. What has been argued here is not that where there was smoke there was fire, nor that there was no smoke at all, but that where there was smoke there was hot smoke! The denial of smoke by Fox's now respectable defenders leaves one with a very thin explanation for the behaviour of his opponents. They were merely malicious, vengeful, bigoted and full of hatred. Which begs the question - Why? Why were they full of hatred? One doesn't have to agree with Fox's enemies to see that by their light they had reason! This study has tried to explain both the wild enthusiasm within early Quakerism and the alarm at it from without. Fox *was* claiming divinity in an opaque way, for himself and for his followers. At times, in his own way, he even claimed equality with God and both he and Nayler allowed the God in them to be exalted by their followers. Fox was eventually forced to retreat from this position as it rebounded on his leadership and on the movement.

The Nayler incident scandalized Friends publicly and privately and forced them to find ways to contain the chaotic forces unleashed by Nayler. The first Church discipline appeared. Heady language was toned down. The pace of miracles slowed drastically.[19] The great shakings and quakings of the

---

[19]Quaker attitudes towards signs and wonders also began to slowly change. They did not reject miracles and visions because of their belief in continuing revelation. But they renounced miracles as "the only sign and evidence of inspiration". They did not "prove the verity of the Christian faith" which is maintained by "truth, reason, equity, holiness". The sick may still be healed but miracles no longer had a central role in the maintaining of faith

early years ceased, leaving some Quakers with the feeling that Quakerism had betrayed its original calling.[20] Language and metaphors became more conservative and more biblical, while some contentious phrases and images were simply dropped. For example, Fox ceased using Son of God talk. Perfectionist claims were muted. Crusading rhetoric was dropped and eschatological urgency receded, a reaction as well to dashed hopes and

---

[William Penn and George Whitehead, *A Serious Apology for the Principles and Practices of the People Called Quakers* (1671), in *Works*, 2, pp. 38-39]. In 1677 Penn opposed the Collegiant view that miracles confirmed the calling of a true messenger of God. The Christian religion had already been confirmed by miracles and such things were now needless among Christians (Cadbury, *George Fox's 'Book of Miracles'*, p. 28). Barclay confirmed this view. He always related miracles to Christ and his Apostles and never once mentioned the miracles of Fox and other early Quakers. He affirmed that God could still speak through revelations which he defined as inward leading, not external appearances (*See* Barclay, *Apology*, p. 16). Faith required no external props. The glaring omission, on the part of these Quaker writers in the 1660's and 1670's, of any reference to Fox's miracles strongly suggests that Quakerism was retreating from earlier extravagances and was making a deliberate effort to hide it from the record. Keith and Penington went even further. They saw no necessary continuance for miracles (ie. external appearances) for they only left a dispute in the mind [George Keith, *Immediate Revelation* (1676), pp. 7, 17. *See also* Brayshaw, *Personality of George Fox*, pp. 173 ff.]. Quakers learned that claims to miracles in an age of skepticism only made them subject to abuse and ridicule and given the ruthless attacks upon them in this matter by Charles Leslie, Samuel Newton and Francis Bugg their reactions were understandable. Later editors of Fox's works even went as far as to say that his miracles were of a spiritual nature and not part of the physical sphere (*Cambridge Journal*, 1, p. 195 and accompanying editorial comment by Norman Penney on p. 433). As we have seen earlier both Henry More and Gerard Croese made reference to the cautious attitude Quakers later adopted toward miracles.

[20]This prompted the following remarkable statement from Patrick Livingstone in 1667: "Now those that were with us, and are gone from us, they pretend to own the first coming forth, and they cry, where is the power that was at first? But this power thousands witness, and are established in it ... the mighty motions of the bodies of Friends are ceased, and Friends are still and cool, and quiet; therefore these persons are made to think that the same power is not in meetings ... But O ye foolish ones ... can ye not discern the times, that time and this time? When physick is given to the body ... and when all is purged out, the physick leaves working and the body is still. Were not all the breakings and meltings, and terrible shakings and quaking of Friends bodies, to purge out sin, and to bring to stillness, coolness and calmness of mind?" [Patrick Livingstone, *Plain and Downright Dealing* (London, 1667), p. 10]. Livingstone was speaking as if the great work of purging the saints of sin was completed and thus the need for excessive activity in meetings was no longer necessary. The shakings, breakings and meltings were only for a little time (*Ibid.*, p. 10). It is an interesting thought that intimated that Friends were now perfected. But more important to Livingstone was the idea that Friends should be seen to have retreated from the ecstasies of the early years to a more durable and solid condition of stillness, calmness and coolness of mind. Gone was any sense of eschatological urgency that had accompanied the birth of the Kingdom within. The saints were to be still and quiet and wait patiently as a suffering community until the Kingdom should come.

Restoration persecution. But important events in early Quakerism were not necessarily precipitated by political change. Fox's 1671 vision recovering the inner Christ occurred *before* the *Declaration of Indulgence* and the retreat began *before* the Restoration.

Quakers had to change, or die. The entropic qualities inherent in their enthusiastic religion enabled them to adapt to changes in environment and survive heavy persecution. Quakerism survived when other civil war sects failed, partly because it was able to transform itself under the direction of very able people like William Penn and Robert Barclay and partly because Fox was able to adjust to shared leadership and assume the role of a respected, but unintrusive, father-figure to the movement. Fox was not unchangeable, unmalleable or ineluctable. Unfortunately for Fox the changes outran him. In the interests of unity he never explicitly decried these changes. At the same time he used his authority as a role model and charismatic leader to refocus his movement on his original vision of the inward celestially-fleshed Christ. With his avatarial star fading he was not granted widespread support, at least at home.

In the 1670's Henry More found reason to believe that some Quakers had discarded their original "Familist" notions while other Quakers retained ideas of the inner light that were "nebulous and confused". Fox's doctrine of celestial inhabitation was under siege and perhaps disintegrating even in his own movement. After the Nayler incident it was increasingly Fox alone who embodied the old days of pentecostal fire and power. Fox was not generally prone to solemn, regretful thoughts but he must secretly have longed for the "les neiges d'antan" (the snows of yesteryear), to borrow Villon's late medieval refrain.

The de-divinization of the inner light involved a shift from the idea of the real, corporeal presence of the glorified flesh of Christ in the saint, to a doctrine of the disembodied spiritual presence which was a mere spiritual influence or inspiration.[21] De-divinization provided the epistemological

---

[21]The stages described in this study strangely parallel theories of the divine presence in the elements of the Eucharist in Fox's day - ie. from Catholic to Reformed to Zwinglian. But one could not say that sacramental theory was the fount of Quaker doctrine or change, only that it was an interesting coincidence.

tools to reframe Quakerism in a more innocuous, sometimes mystical, sometimes rational language.[22] Although Fox's imagery and metaphors of light, seed and even inner Christ were retained there was a fundamental shift in the conception of these metaphors which assumed the function of true metaphor and were stripped of Fox's tendency to merge the identities of God and human. This shift enabled later interpreters of Fox to reshape Fox himself into a mythical figure - a Mystic, Quietist, Radical Puritan or Spiritual Reformer. The scope and magnitude of his charismatic ministry was so severely attenuated to avoid embarrassment that the importance of Fox as an avatar and charismatic prophet who originated a new variety of the Christian religion that liberated, sustained, empowered and ennobled people who believed in him by divinizing them so graphically was lost.

Penn, Barclay and Whitehead claimed to accurately interpret Fox's high language as figurative. Fox did have a wide range of interpretation but on the doctrine of celestial inhabitation he was a literalist. Henry More, John Reeve and many other contemporaries, including most early Quakers, understood this. Fox could and did read some Scriptures in terms of the largest and most far-reaching metaphors (ie. the "Stone" as Christ). Other passages he read quite literally (ie. the saints judging even the angels). The literal was suggested by each Scripture text that read "Christ *in* you". The literal reading, in turn, helps to make sense of a whole gamut of behaviour - the quakings, thaumaturgic claims, blasphemy problems and the Nayler incident. Were "flesh and bone" mere figures certain aspects of early Quaker deportment remain unexplainable.

---

[22]The de-divinization of the inner light, when combined with the creation of the Second Day Morning Meeting in 1673 sealed the fate of the early vision. The need to curb extravagances was a pressing one, especially in the climate of Restoration persecution. Fox himself set the example by selectively editing the Swarthmore Letters in the early 1670's. In 1683 he outlined rules by which Friends' books were to be printed [*Box A, Portfolio 10* (November 19, 1683) at FRL]. The Second Day Morning Meeting performed an important function for it became the tool through which Quaker leaders were able to stamp out enthusiasm. Manuscripts were edited with this in mind and anything that smacked of enthusiasm was omitted or altered. Fox's works were posthumously selectively edited with this in mind. Repressed by the Second Day Morning Meeting was excessive language, "apocalyptic papers, and anything chaotic in expression" (Cope, "Seventeenth Century Quaker Style," p. 227). They intervened whenever they could to ensure that the image the world received of Quakerism (especially through the written word) was a respectable and inoffensive one.

Although this study has not been about ethics the shift from the early to the later transformed doctrine of the inner light had far-reaching ethical consequences. The sensation of Christ within in Fox's terms lead to fellow-feeling. But the fellow-feeling was reserved for the saints and specifically for other Quakers. With the rest of the world standing under judgment Quaker charity remained at home, within the community of the faithful. The transformed doctrine universalized divine inspiration and presence - it was differently conceived. The sense of judgment on the external world was mitigated. So Quaker beneficence came to be applied more generally and the Quaker became - as we would say now - less judgmental. This may help to explain why Fox and early Quakers did not oppose slavery (though they demanded decent treatment of slaves) while later Quakerism attacked the institution. The shift to a *universal* divine spark made it possible to regard slaves as worthy of dignity: hence the attack on slavery.[23] This can only happen when one sees the inner light as universal rather than fiercely sectarian. The early doctrine of the inner light as celestial inhabitation, while it may have heightened ethical energy, also circumscribed the application of beneficence while the later doctrine eroded these limits and religious xenophobia generally as it transformed the inner light into a universal property.

By the time of Fox's death in 1691 the great reversal was complete in England and soon to be complete after the 1695 Philadelphia elders' "Ancient Testimony" was published in America. The claims of Fox to divine sonship, the challenge of Nayler as a look-alike re-incarnate Messiah, to Fox's daring assertions - clear blasphemies to antagonists - tell us something of the leadership, the persuasiveness and the uncommon power of the early movement. It was rooted in charismatic, theanthropical and theophanous claims that were more radical than any to come out of the Radical Reformation. Such claims were less fanciful than purposive, designed to serve the didactic ends of the claimant and the claimant's followers. His

---

[23]Officially as early as 1727 [*see* Leonore Loft, "Quakers, Brissot and Eighteenth Century Abolitionists," *JFHS*, 55 (1989), p. 279]. Individual concerns were expressed as early as 1688 [*see* the *Mennonite Historical Bulletin*, 48 (July, 1987), p. 1].

realized eschatology found responsive chords among the oppressed. Signs and wonders made fervent converts.

Yet the revolutionary theology, its blinding originality and its powerful implications all became too much to bear. The imperious summons to be a living member of the the glorified Kingdom and the consciousness of being inhabited by celestial flesh and bone began to slip away and Quakers adopted the more benign witness of egalitarian ethics and social conscience, sustained by the belief that the conscience in all was divinely inspired. The Son of God, the avatar, the magus, was made over into the respectable leader of a spiritual revival, into yet another spiritual reformer. To accept Fox only on these terms is to miss the galvanizing truth and perilous conviction of those early days; to miss how he captured the hunger of ordinary people for renewal, and for a world made decent.

This study is at once a celebration of the outrageous and an acknowledgement of the power of Respectability. Although we have long known of Respectability's power in the shaping and mis-shaping of character, a not-so-recent book like R.D. Laing's *The Politics of the Family* still comes as a shock. Similarly it is surprising to see Respectability at work in the religious sphere. Religious societies, like families, develop coping strategies for protection against the threat of the outside world. Keeping a public and private face, denial and replacement are aspects of these coping strategies. Like a Roman villa, Respectability has many rooms and passages, with annexes and extensions, added over the centuries, but all conforming to the overall style. To be beyond the boundaries was not in those days just to be an outsider, it was to be, at times, quite literally an outlaw. The forces of Respectability were ruthless to persecute and crucify. I had the good fortune to be locked in the dungeon at Lancaster Castle by the keeper. It was the same dungeon where Fox and many other Quakers had been incarcerated. After the heavy dungeon door was shut, plunging one into total darkness, the dropping of the bolt sounded like the clap of doom. Fox was there, without noticeable light, without fresh air, without heat, without furniture, without toilet, and with only a scattering of straw for comfort. I can only begin to imagine how he and his fellow Quakers (men, women and children) survived, and what bruises were left on their minds. The conditions were so appalling that one would, over time, be forced into retreat from the exalted language that lay at the root of such antagonism, such fury and such heavy persecution. Fox bent ever so slightly to the threats of Respectability. He left it to his chief disciples to let go of his central doctrines and bring Quakerism within Respectability's pale. If there is a greatness in Fox's witness there is no less greatness in his adjustment to his witness: changing its tone, holding to its core, without diehard resistance to the restatements of his successors.

This study has taken aspects of Quakerism that many historians have pushed to the periphery and moved them to the middle of things. The enthusiasm, the ecstasies, the indecorum of running naked as a sign or making tumult in a church, the miracles, healings, visions, all these have taken centre stage. As well the blasphemy charges - both those that were legally threatening and those more lasting ones that were polemically damaging - belong to the centre. So does the Nayler affair. The argument, however, has not elevated what some have seen as aberrations into centrepieces to be perverse, or for the sake of mere revisionism. It is the evidence that places these events at the centre. Not only are they important events in their own right, they are inferentially important in that they lead us to a fuller understanding of what Fox and early Quakerism went through. Their meanings are important; their significances matter.

One revises past history in order to understand more fully. Take, for instance, the doctrine of the inner light as celestial flesh. Fox clung to this doctrine consistently on his own and on his believers' behalf. It is difficult to understand the "Christ within" that was so central a theme without an *effort* to understand it. It was an electrifying conception. More largely it seems impossible to comprehend both the triumphs and the power as well as the trials and harrowings of early Quakerism without some grasp of this idea. Yet to this day, and in spite of the devoted work of early twentieth century editors like Henry Cadbury who revered the evidence, you will find no mention at all in studies of early Quaker history. This is truly staggering. We know why some materials were excised from the records by the early editors, and we can understand why certain attitudes to the evidence have been developed by historians sympathetic to Quakerism over the centuries. But sympathy can be served by confronting issues as much as by side-stepping or tip-toeing around them: frankness can evoke sympathy as well as evasion. For if in the short run truth can be scandalous, in the long run, surely, it cannot be disreputable. As for Respectability and its triumph over early Quakerism we can say of it what Sir Walter Raleigh said of Death at the end of his *History of the World*: "Whom none could advise, thou hast persuaded".

BIBLIOGRAPHY

I. REFERENCE WORKS

A Catalogue of Friends Books. London, 1708.

British Museum Catalogue of Friends Books.

Cadbury, H., ed. *Annual Catalogue of George Fox's Papers*. London: Religious Society of Friends, 1939.

Davies, G. *A Bibliography of British History, Stuart Period 1603-1714*. Oxford: Clarendon, 1970.

Dictionary of Quaker Biography. In process of compilation. FRL. London.

Early English Books 1641-1700. Selected from Donald Wing's Short Title Catalogue: A Cross Index of the Microfilm Collection. Ann Arbor: UMI, 1982 and 1987.

Greaves, R.L. and R. Zaller. *A Biographical Dictionary of British Radicals in the Seventeenth Century*, 3 vols. Brighton, Sussex: Harvester Press, 1982-84.

Madan, F. *Oxford Books*. Oxford, 1895-1935.

Nuttall, G.F. *Early Quaker Letters From the Swarthmore MSS. to 1660. Calendared, Indexed and Annotated*. Typescript in London. Friends Reference Library, 1952.

Pollard, A.W. and G.R. Redgrave., eds. *A Short Title Catalogue of Books Printed in England, Scotland, and Ireland and of English Books Printed Abroad, 1475-1640*. London: The Bibliographic Society, 1963. First published in 1926.

Smith, Joseph. *Bibliotheca Quakeristica: A Bibliography of Miscellaneous Literature Relating to the Friends*. London: Joseph Smith, 1887.

Joseph Smith was a nineteenth century Quaker librarian. His catalogue lists over 18,000 entries and is still the most exhaustive Quaker bibliography. Titles missed by Smith can be located in Wing.

_____. *Bibliotheca Anti-Quakeriana, or a Catalogue of Books Adverse to the Society of Friends*. London: Joseph Smith, 1873.

_____. *A Descriptive Catalogue of Friends Books*. 2 Volumes. London: Joseph Smith, 1867.

Stephen, L. and S. Lee (eds.). *The Dictionary of National Biography*, 21 vols. London: Humphrey Milford, From 1917.

Turner, A., *A Bibliography of Quaker Literature*, 1893-1967. Ann Arbour: University Microfilms, 1976.

Wing, D.G. *Short Title Catalogue of Books Printed in England, Ireland, Wales and British America ..., 1641- 1700*, 3 vols. New York: Index Society, 1945-51.

Wood, A. *Athenae Oxonienses*, 3 vols. London, 1817.

II. PRIMARY SOURCES

MANUSCRIPT COLLECTIONS

London. Friends' Reference Library:

A.R. Barclay MSS.

Boswell Middleton MSS. Now called *Caton MSS. II*.

Catalogue of Books and Papers, Belonging to Friends at the Chamber in Whitehart Court, Gracechurch Street, London, taken anno 1741. 5 vols.

Caton MSS. 3 vols.

Children of the Light Papers: Box A - George Fox and Stephen Crisp MSS. and Portfolio 10.

These papers were gathered and prepared for the use of the "Morning Meeting" in 1687 to establish the origin of the name "Children of the Light".

Epistles and Queries of George Fox's (Fox Papers Xx).

Etting MSS.

Extracts From Register Books. Temp. MSS. 750.

Fox papers marked with letters.

Gibson MSS.

Great Pardon of Friends.

Haistwell Diary.

Manuscript Book of Extracts, 1672-1772.

Markey MSS.

Numbered Portfolios. A collection of MSS. in 42 vols.

Original Records of Friends Sufferings.

Reynolds MSS. Box 1.

Spence MSS.

Swarthmore MSS. A collection of about 1400 early Quaker letters in 7 volumes.

> A companion set of Transcript volumes are available at FRL but discrepancies exist when checked against the original. Nuttall's *Early Quaker Letters* indexes and cross-references the letters up to 1660.

Thirnbeck MSS.

This is a Book of Some of the Travels and Passages of George Fox.

Watson MSS.

London. British Library.

Oxford. Christ Church.

> The library contains a collection of over 400 Quaker books and tracts bound in over 40 volumes, acquired for the college from the library of Francis Bugg, a noted seventeenth century opponent of Quakerism.

Oxford. Bodleian Library. Bodleian MSS. MS. AD.A.95: The American Journey of George Fox, 1671-3.

PUBLISHED SOURCES

Works listed in this section which are also listed in Wing include the entry number assigned in that work.

Abbott, W.C. *The Writings and Speeches of Oliver Cromwell.* 4 Volumes. New York: Russell and Russell, 1970. First published 1937-47.

A Brief Account of James Nayler, the Quaker. In W. Cobbett, *Cobbett's Parliamentary History of England*, vol. 3. London: R. Bagshaw, 1808.

A Brief History of the Voyage of Katharine Evans and Sarah Cheevers to the Island of Malta. London, 1715.

Aldham, Thomas, et. al. *A Brief Discovery of the Three-fold Estate of Antichrist ... Whereunto is Added the Trial of One George Fox, in Lancashire.* London, 1653. A894B

A List of Some of the Grand Blasphemers. London, 1654. L2406

Barbour, H. and A.O., Roberts, eds. *Early Quaker Writings, 1650-1700.* Grand Rapids: Eerdmans, 1973.

Barclay, A.R., ed. *Letters of Early Friends.* London: Harvey and Darton, 1841.

Barclay, Robert. *Barclay's Apology in Modern English.* Edited by Dean Freiday. The Hemlock Press, 1980.

Bates, Elisha. *Appeal to the Society of Friends.* London: Hamilton Adams, 1836.

Baxter, Richard. *The Quakers Catechism.* London, 1655. B1361

_____. *A Christian Directory.* London, 1678. B1220

Bayly, William. *A Short Relation or Testimony of the Working of the Light of Christ in Me.* London, 1659. B1537

_____. *The Life of Enoch Again Revived.* London, 1662. B1532

_____. *Deep Calleth Unto Deep.* London, 1663. B1522

_____. *An Arrow Shot Against Babylon.* London, 1663. B1518

_____. *The Great and Dreadful Day of the Lord God.* London, 1664. B1528

_____. *Seven Thunders Uttering Their Voices.* London, 1655. B1535

_____. *The Dreadful and Terrible Day of the Lord God.* No Date. B1523

_____. *The True Christ Owned in a Few Plain Words.* London, 1667. B1542

_____. *A Collection of the Several Writings of that True Prophet ... William Bayly.* London, 1676. B1517

Beckham, Edward. *The Principles of the Quakers Further Shown to be Blasphemous and Seditious.* London, 1700. B1653

_____. *A Brief Discovery of Some of the Blasphemous and Seditious Principles and Practices of the People, Called Quakers.* London, 1699. B1652

Besse, J.A. *A Collection of the Sufferings of the People Called Quakers.* 2 Volumes. London: Meeting of Sufferings, 1753.

> Friends from across England were required to contribute data of all local persecution of Quakers and report this to the Meeting for Sufferings in London. Fuller collections have been compiled in several county studies like Norman Penney's *Record of the Sufferings of Quakers in Cornwall* (1928).

Bishop, George. *Jesus Christ the Same Today, as Yesterday.* London, 1655. B2995

_____. *The Throne of Truth Exalted Over the Powers of Darkness.* 1657. B3008

_____. *Mene Tekel, or, The Council of Officers of the Army.* London, 1659. B3000

_____. *The Warnings of the Lord to the Men of This Generation.* London, 1660. B3016

_____. *An Epistle of Love to all the Saints.* London, 1661. B2992

_____. *The Burden of Babylon, and the Triumph of Sion.* London, 1661. B2989

_____. *The Last Trump, or one More Warning.* London, 1662. B2996

_____. *A Treatise Concerning the Resurrection.* 1662. B3012

_____. *A Looking - Glass for the Times.* London, 1668. B2998

Blome, Richard. *The Fanatick History: or an Exact Account of the Old Anabaptists and the New Quakers.* London, 1660. B3212

Boehme, J. *Mercurius Teutonicus; or, a Christian Information Concerning the Last Times ... Gathered Out of the Mystical Writings of ... Jacob Behmen.* London: M. Simmonds, 1649. Reissued by Lodowick Lloyd in 1656. B3409, B3410

Brockbank, E. "Letter From Richard Hubberthorne Concerning George Fox and James Nayler." *JFHS*, 26 (1929), p. 11.

Bugg, Francis. *Battering Rams Against New Rome*. London, 1690.

_____. *Some of the Quakers Principles and Doctrines*. London, 1693. B5395

_____. *New Rome Arraigned*. London, 1693. B5376

_____. *The Quakers Set in Their True Light*. London, 1696. B5388

_____. *A Modest Defence of My Book, Entitled Quakerism Exposed*. London, 1700. B5375

_____. *The Pilgrim's Progress, from Quakerism to Christianity*. London, 1698. B5382

_____. *News from New Rome*. London, 1701.

_____. *A Finishing Stroke ... Whereby the Great Mystery of the Little Whore is Further Unfolded*. London, 1712.

_____. *A New Frame for the Picture of Quakerism*. London, 1719.

Burrough, Edward. *A Warning From the Lord to the Inhabitants of Underbarrow*. London, 1654. B6057

_____. *To the Camp of the Lord, in England*. In Francis Howgill, *This is Only to Go Amongst Friends*. London, 1656. B6037

_____. *A Trumpet of the Lord*. London, 1656. B6048

_____. *A Measure of the Times*. London, 1657. B6012

_____. *Many Strong Reasons Confounded*. London, 1657. B6011A

_____. *Some of the Principles of the Quakers ... Vindicated*. London, 1658. B6024

_____. *A Standard Lifted Up*. London, 1658. B6029

_____. *Epistle to the Reader*. A Preface to George Fox, *The Great Mystery of the Great Whore Unfolded* (1659). F1832

_____. *A Visitation and Warning Proclaimed*. London, 1659. B6055

_____. *A Discovery of Some Part of the War Between the Kingdom of the Lamb and the Kingdom of Antichrist*. London, 1659. B5999A

_____. *Satans Design Defeated*. London, 1659. B6022

_____. *A General Epistle to all the Saints*. London, 1660. B6005

_____. *A Visitation of Love unto the King, and Those Called Royalists*. London, 1660. B6056

_____. *A Visitation and Presentation*. London, 1660. A supposed reprint of *A Visitation of Love*. B6054

_____. *A Testimony Concerning the Life, Death, Trials, Travels and Labours of Edward Burroughs*. London, 1662.

_____. *The Memorable Works of a Son of Thunder and Consolation ... Edward Burroughs*. 1672.

Burton, Thomas. *The Diary of Thomas Burton, Esq.*, 4 vols. Edited by John T. Rutt. London: Henry Colburn, 1828.

Cadbury, H.J., ed. *George Fox's 'Book of Miracles'*. N.Y.: Octagon Press, 1973. First published in 1948.

_____., ed. *Narrative Papers of George Fox*. Richmond, Indiana: Friends United Press, 1973.

_____. "George Keith to Henry More," *JFHS*, 46 (1954), pp. 59-63.

Camm, Ann. *The Testimony of Ann Camm Concerning John Audland Her Late Husband*. In John Camm and John Audland. *The Memory of the Righteous Revived*. London, 1689. C390

Camm, John and John Audland. *The Memory of the Righteous Revived; Being a Brief Collection of the Books and Written Epistles of John Camm and John Audland*. London, 1689. C390

Casaubon, Meric. *A Treatise Concerning Enthusiasm*. London, 1654. C812-3.

Caton, William. *The Moderate Enquirer Resolved*. 1671. C1515-1516

Charles I. *Eikon Basilike or the King's Book*. Edited by Edward Almack. London: De La More Press, 1904. First printed in Royston, 1662. C2075.

Clapham, J. *A Full Discovery and Confutation of the Damnable and Wicked Doctrines of the Quakers*. London, 1656. C4407

Claridge, Richard. *The Divinity, Universality and Sufficiency of the Light Within*. London, 1701.

_____. *Melius Inquirendum*. London, 1706.

_____. *A Distinction Between the Presence of God, as Our Maker ... and His Presence as Our Redeemer*. London, 1713.

298

_____. *A Plea for Mechanick Preachers*. London, 1727.

Coale, Josiah. *The Books and Diverse Epistles ... of Josiah Coale*. 1671. C4751

_____. *A Vindication of the Light Within*. No Date.

_____. *To All Who Desire to Know the Way to the Kingdom*. No Date.

Cobbett, William. *Cobbett's Complete Collection of State Trials and Proceedings for High Treason and other Crimes and Misdemeanors from the Earliest Period to the Present Time*. Edited by Thomas Bayly Howell. 33 volumes. London: R. Bagshaw, 1810.

_____. *Parliamentary History of England from the Norman Conquest in 1066 to the Year 1803*. 36 volumes. London: R. Bagshaw, 1806-1820.

Cockson, Edward. *Quakerism Dissected and Laid Open*. London, 1708.

Croese, Gerard. *The General History of the Quakers*. London, 1696. C6965

Crouch, W. *Posthuma Christiana*. London: J. Sowle, 1712.

Deacon, John. *The Grand Imposter Examined: or, the Life, Trial, and Examination of James Nayler*. London, 1656. D484

_____. *A Public Discovery of a Secret Deceit*. London, 1656. D487

_____. *An Exact History of the Life of James Naylor*. London, 1657. D482

Dewsbury, William. *Several Letters Written to the Saints*. London, 1654. With James Nayler, George Fox and John Whitehead.D1272

_____. *The Discovery of Man's Return to his First Estate*. London, 1654. D1259

_____. *The Discovery of the Great Enmity of the Serpent Against the Seed of Woman*. London, 1655. D1264

_____. *A True Testimony of What was Done ... at the General Assizes ... at Northampton*. London, 1655.

_____. *A True Prophecie of the Mighty Day of the Lord Which is Coming*. London, 1655. D1279.

_____. *The Mighty Day of the Lord is Coming*. London, 1656. D1271

_____. *The Breathings of Life to God's Spiritual Israel*. London, 1663. D1257

299

_____. *The Faithful Testimony of That Ancient Servant of the Lord and Minister of the Everlasting Gospel, William Dewsbury.* London, 1689. D1267

Divine Light, Manifesting the Love of God Unto the Whole World. 1646. D1722.

Droutman, J.S. "Extracts from a Respectful Petition Made by the Friends of the Christian Society Called Quakers Delivered at the National Assembly in Paris, France on Thursday, 10 February 1791," *Friends World News* (No. 2, 1983), pp. 15-16.

Eccles, Solomon. *Signs are from the Lord ... to Forewarn Them of Some Imminent Judgment Near at Hand.* London, 1663. E130

_____. *The Quaker's Challenge.* 1668.

Edmundson, William. *A Journal.* Dublin, 1715.

Edwards, Thomas. *Gangraena.* 1st edition and revised 2 volume edition. London, 1646. E228-230

Ellington, Francis. *Christian Information Concerning These Last Times.* London, 1664. E541

Elson, Mary. *A True Information of Our Blessed Women's Meeting.* Contained in *An Epistle for True Love, Unity and Order in the Church of Christ.* With Anne Whitehead. 1680. W1882

Faldo, John. *A Vindication of Quakerism No Christianity.* London, 1673.

Farmer, Ralph. *The Great Mysteries of Godliness and Ungodliness ... Discovered from the Writings and Speakings of ... Quakers.* London, 1655. F441

_____. *Satan Enthroned in His Chair of Pestilence ... Being a True Narrative and Relation of the Manner of James Nailer (that Emminent Quaker's) Entrance Into the City of Bristol.* London, 1657. F444

Farnworth, Richard. *Light Risen Out of Darkness.* London, 1653. F490

_____. *A Voice of the First Trumpet.* London, 1653. F512B

_____. *A Brief Discovery of the Kingdom of Antichrist.* 1653. F472A

_____. *Truth Cleared of Scandals.* London, 1654. F512

_____. *Witchcraft Cast out from the Religious Seed.* London, 1655. F513

_____. *The Spiritual Man Judgeth all Things.* London, 1655. With George Fox. F505

_____. *Antichrist's Man of War, Apprehended*. London, 1655. F470

_____. *An Account of Richard Farnworth's Commitment to Prison*. 1655.

_____. *The Pure Language of the Spirit of Truth*. London, 1655. F494

_____. *A Rod to Drive Out Wild Boars*. 1655. F502

_____. *Truth Ascended, or the Annointed and Sealed*. London, 1663. F511

Fell, Margaret. *False prophets, Antichrists, Deceivers Which are in the World ... Also, Some of the Ranters Principles Answered*. London, 1655. F631

_____. *A Testimony of the Touch-Stone*. London, 1656. F636.

_____. *An Evident Demonstration to God's Elect*. London, 1660. F629.

_____. *A Brief Collection of Remarkable Passages and Occurrences Relating to ... Margaret Fell ... Together With Sundry of Her Epistles, Books and Christian Testimonies*. London, 1710.

Field, John. *A Testimony to Christ*. London, 1697. F866

_____. *The Weakness of George Keith's Reasons for Denouncing Quakerism*. London, 1700. F868

_____. *The True Christ Owned as God and Man*. London, 1707.

Firth, C.H. and R.S. Rait, eds. *Acts and Ordinances of the Interregnum, 1642-1660*. 2 volumes. London:Wyman and Sons, 1911.

Fisher, Samuel. *Christianismus Redivivus*. London, 1655. F1049.

_____. *Apocrypta Apocalypta*. London, 1661. F1047

Fox, George. *The Works of George Fox*. 8 volumes. Philadelphia: Gould, 1831.

Vols. 1-2: *Journal* (Ellwood Text). F1854

Vol. 3 : *The Great Mystery of the Great Whore*.

Vols. 4-6: *Gospel Truth Demonstrated*. Doctrinal works.

Vols. 7-8: *Epistles*. Short epistles and letters.

Many of Fox's epistles, letters and short doctrinal treatises were not included in this edition of his works. The original plans for publishing all Fox's writings were abandoned after the first three folio volumes were completed - the *Journal* (1694), *Epistles* (1698) and the *Doctrinal Treatises* (1706). Much of the missing material may be located in the various manuscript collections located at Friends Reference Library, London.

_____. *George Fox: An Autobiography.* Edited by Rufus Jones. 2 vols. Philadelphia: Ferris and Leach, 1903.

_____. *The Journal of George Fox.* Edited by Norman Penney. London: Cambridge University Press, 1911.

This is the *Spence MS.* published *verbatim* and *literatim.* It is also referred to as the *Cambridge Journal.* This edition is most valuable for its biographical notes and cross references of main figures. Another *Journal,* referred to in the *Annual Catalogue* as the *Great Journal,* has been identified by Cadbury as a similar but now lost manuscript.

_____. *The Short Journal and Itinerary Journals of George Fox.* Edited by Norman Penney. London: Cambridge University Press, 1925.

The *Short Journal,* dictated by Fox, is here printed *verbatim* and *literatim* from a *MS.* that is either the original or a contemporary copy. There is another *MS.* at Friends Reference Library, London, that closely follows the *Short Journal* and is referred to as *"A".* It is of seventeenth century vintage and is entitled *This is a Book of the Travels and Passages of George Fox's.*

_____. *The Journal of George Fox.* Edited by J.L. Nickalls. London: Religious Society of Friends, 1952.

This is the most complete contemporary edition of Fox's *Journal* drawing text from four major sources - the *Spence MS.,* the Ellwood text, the *Short Journal* and Fox's *American Diaries.*

_____. *Several Petitions Answered, That Were Put up by the Priests of Westmoreland.* London, 1653. With James Nayler. N316A

_____. *Saul's Errand to Damascus.* London, 1653. F1894

_____. *News Coming Out of the North ... the Terrible Day of the Lord is Appearing.* London, 1654. F1867.

_____. *The Vials of the Wrath of God Upon the Seat of the Man of Sin.* London, 1654. F1975-6.

_____. *A Declaration Against all Professions and Professors.* London, 1655. F1784

_____. *The Teachers of the World Unveiled.* London, 1656. F1924.

_____. *A Declaration of the Difference of the Ministers of the Word from the Ministers of the World.* London. 1656. F1784.

302

_____. *That all Might See Who They Were That had a Command, and did Pay Tithes.* London, 1657. F1931

_____. *The Pearl Found in England.* London, 1658. F1878

_____. *The Great Mystery of the Great Whore.* London, 1659. F1832

_____. *A Primer for Scholars and Doctors of Europe.* London, 1659. F1884

_____. *To the Parliament of the Commonwealth of England, Fifty- Nine Particulars Laid Down For Regulating Things.* London, 1659. F1958.

_____. *An Epistle General to all Those Who are of the Royal Priesthood.* London, 1660. F1802.

_____. *A Distinction Between the Phanatick Spirit and the Spirit of God.* London, 1660. F1796

_____. *A Battledoor for Teachers and Professors to Learn Singular and Plural.* London, 1660. F1751.

_____. *The Sum of Such Particulars as are Charged Against George Fox in the Mittimus by Which He Stands Committed.* London, 1660. F1923.

_____. *An Answer to the Arguments of Jews ... that the Messiah is not Come.* London, 1661. F1745

_____. *The Line of Righteousness and Justice.* London, 1661. F1857

_____. *Concerning Sons and Daughters and Prophetesses, Speaking and Prophesying, in the Law and in the Gospel.* London. No Date. F1771

_____. *A General Epistle to be Read in all the Christian Meetings in the World.* 1662. F1825

_____. *Old Simon the Sorcerer, Who Hath Bewitched the Whole City of Christendom.* London, 1663. F1870

_____. *The Examination of Margaret Fell and George Fox, at the Several Assizes Held at Lancaster (1663-64).* 1664. In *The Harleian Miscellany,* volume 6, pp. 282-299.

_____. *Something in Answer to Lodowick Muggleton's Book, Which he Calls, The Quaker's Neck Broken.* London, 1667. F1914

_____. *Some Principles of the Elect People of God in Scorn Called Quakers.* 1671. F1907

_____. *The Heathen's Divinity.* 1671. F1835

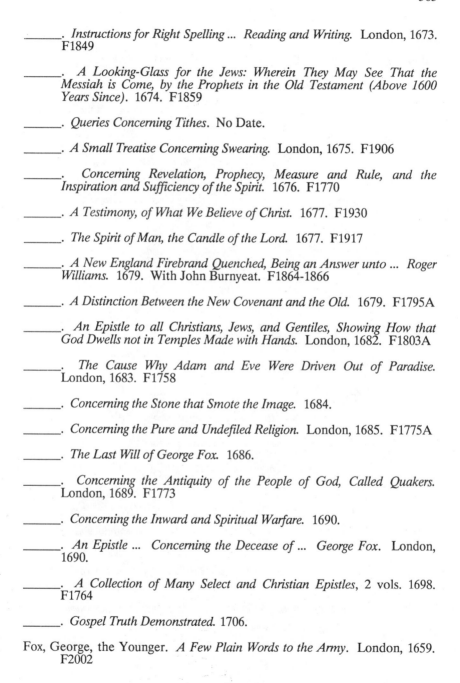

———. *Instructions for Right Spelling ... Reading and Writing.* London, 1673. F1849

———. *A Looking-Glass for the Jews: Wherein They May See That the Messiah is Come, by the Prophets in the Old Testament (Above 1600 Years Since).* 1674. F1859

———. *Queries Concerning Tithes.* No Date.

———. *A Small Treatise Concerning Swearing.* London, 1675. F1906

———. *Concerning Revelation, Prophecy, Measure and Rule, and the Inspiration and Sufficiency of the Spirit.* 1676. F1770

———. *A Testimony, of What We Believe of Christ.* 1677. F1930

———. *The Spirit of Man, the Candle of the Lord.* 1677. F1917

———. *A New England Firebrand Quenched, Being an Answer unto ... Roger Williams.* 1679. With John Burnyeat. F1864-1866

———. *A Distinction Between the New Covenant and the Old.* 1679. F1795A

———. *An Epistle to all Christians, Jews, and Gentiles, Showing How that God Dwells not in Temples Made with Hands.* London, 1682. F1803A

———. *The Cause Why Adam and Eve Were Driven Out of Paradise.* London, 1683. F1758

———. *Concerning the Stone that Smote the Image.* 1684.

———. *Concerning the Pure and Undefiled Religion.* London, 1685. F1775A

———. *The Last Will of George Fox.* 1686.

———. *Concerning the Antiquity of the People of God, Called Quakers.* London, 1689. F1773

———. *Concerning the Inward and Spiritual Warfare.* 1690.

———. *An Epistle ... Concerning the Decease of ... George Fox.* London, 1690.

———. *A Collection of Many Select and Christian Epistles,* 2 vols. 1698. F1764

———. *Gospel Truth Demonstrated.* 1706.

Fox, George, the Younger. *A Few Plain Words to the Army.* London, 1659. F2002

Gibson, William. *Universal Love.* 1671. G688

Glanville, J. *Saducismus Triumphatus.* London, 1681. G822

Gratton, John. *A Journal.* London, 1720.

Green, J.J. "Correspondence of Anne, Vicountess Conway, "Quaker Lady," 1675," *JFHS,* 7 (1910), pp. 7-17; 49-55.

Grigge, William. *The Quaker's Jesus or, the Unswaddling of That Child James Nailor, Which a Wicked Toleration Hath Midwived into the World.* London: M. Simmons, London, 1658. G2023

Harleian Miscellany, or, a Collection of ... Pamphlets and Tracts ... Found in the late Earl of Oxford's Library (1744-6), 10 volumes. London: John White, et. al., 1808ff.

Hicks, Thomas. *A Dialogue Between a Christian and a Quaker.* 1673. H1921

> This was part of the dispute between the Baptist Thomas Hicks and various Friends including George Keith, William Loddington, William Meade and William Penn.

Higginson, Francis. *A Brief Relation of the Irreligion of the Northern Quakers.* London, 1653. H1953

Hookes, Ellis. *The Spirit of the Martyrs Revived.* London, 1682. H2664

Howgill, Francis. *The Standard of the Lord.* London, 1653.

_____. *This was the Word of the Lord.* London, 1654. With John Camm.

_____. *The Fiery Darts of the Devil Quenched.* London, 1654. H3159

_____. *A Woe Against the Magistrates, Priests and People of Kendall.* 1654. H3189

_____. *This is Only to go Amongst Friends.* London, 1654. H3182

_____. *The Inheritance of Jacob Discovered After His Return Out of Egypt.* London, 1656. H3168

_____. *Some of the Mysteries of God's Kingdom Declared.* London, 1658. H3179

_____. *Mystery Babylon the Mother of Harlots Discovered.* London, 1659. H3173

_____. *The Invisible Things of God Brought to Light.* London, 1659. H3169

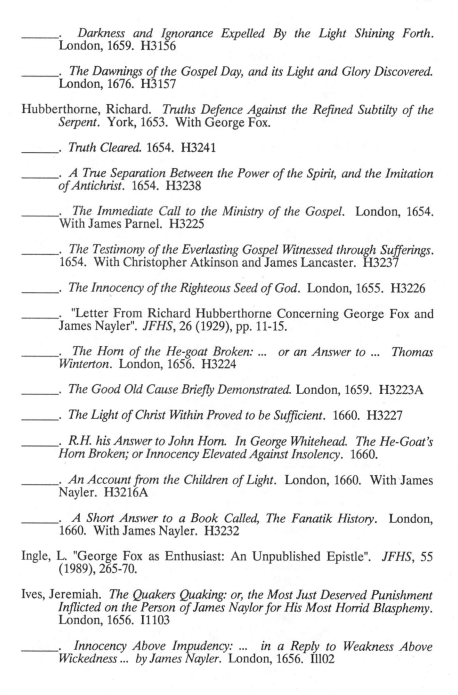

_____. *Darkness and Ignorance Expelled By the Light Shining Forth.* London, 1659. H3156

_____. *The Dawnings of the Gospel Day, and its Light and Glory Discovered.* London, 1676. H3157

Hubberthorne, Richard. *Truths Defence Against the Refined Subtilty of the Serpent.* York, 1653. With George Fox.

_____. *Truth Cleared.* 1654. H3241

_____. *A True Separation Between the Power of the Spirit, and the Imitation of Antichrist.* 1654. H3238

_____. *The Immediate Call to the Ministry of the Gospel.* London, 1654. With James Parnel. H3225

_____. *The Testimony of the Everlasting Gospel Witnessed through Sufferings.* 1654. With Christopher Atkinson and James Lancaster. H3237

_____. *The Innocency of the Righteous Seed of God.* London, 1655. H3226

_____. "Letter From Richard Hubberthorne Concerning George Fox and James Nayler". *JFHS*, 26 (1929), pp. 11-15.

_____. *The Horn of the He-goat Broken: ... or an Answer to ... Thomas Winterton.* London, 1656. H3224

_____. *The Good Old Cause Briefly Demonstrated.* London, 1659. H3223A

_____. *The Light of Christ Within Proved to be Sufficient.* 1660. H3227

_____. *R.H. his Answer to John Horn. In George Whitehead. The He-Goat's Horn Broken; or Innocency Elevated Against Insolency.* 1660.

_____. *An Account from the Children of Light.* London, 1660. With James Nayler. H3216A

_____. *A Short Answer to a Book Called, The Fanatik History.* London, 1660. With James Nayler. H3232

Ingle, L. "George Fox as Enthusiast: An Unpublished Epistle". *JFHS*, 55 (1989), 265-70.

Ives, Jeremiah. *The Quakers Quaking: or, the Most Just Deserved Punishment Inflicted on the Person of James Naylor for His Most Horrid Blasphemy.* London, 1656. I1103

_____. *Innocency Above Impudency: ... in a Reply to Weakness Above Wickedness ... by James Nayler.* London, 1656. I1102

306

_____. *A Sober Request to the Quakers*. London, 1674. I1105

Answered by William Penn and George Whitehead.

Josten, C.H. (ed.). *Elias Ashmole (1617-1692), His Autobiographical and Historical Notes*. Oxford: Clarendon Press, 1966.

Keith, George. *George Keith's Vindication*. 1674. K229

_____. *Immediate Revelation ... Not Ceased.* London, 1675. K175

_____. *The Quaker's Creed Concerning the Man Jesus Christ.* London, 1676. K195

_____. *The Way Cast Up.* Aberdeen, 1677. K231-234

_____. *The Way to the City of God.* Aberdeen, 1678. K235

_____. *The True Christ Owned.* London, 1679. K219

_____. *The Rector Corrected.* London, 1680. K198

_____. *Divine Immediate Revelation and Inspiration Continued in the True Church.* London, 1684. K157A

_____. *The Fundamental Truths of Christianity.* London, 1688. K168

_____. *The Presbyterian and Independent Visible Churches in New England.* Philadelphia, 1689. K190

_____. *A Vision Concerning the Mischieveous Separation Among Friends in Old England.* Philadelphia, 1692. K230

_____. *An Account of the Great Divisions Among Quakers in Pennsylvania.* London, 1692. K136

_____. *Some Reasons and Causes of the Late Separation that hath Come to Pass at Philadelphia Betwixt Us, Called by Some the Separate Meeting and Others that Meet Apart from Us.* Philadelphia, 1692. From the collection of George Keith's papers. K215

_____ and Thomas Budd. *The Plea of the Innocent Against the False Judgment of the Guilty.* Philadelphia, 1692. K189

_____. *The Christian Quaker: or, George Keith's Eyes Opened.* London, 1693. K152

_____. *More Divisions Amongst the Quakers: As Appears by the Following Books of Their own Writing. I. The Chrisitan Faith of New-England Quakers Condemned by a Meeting of Pennsylvania Quakers. II. The*

False Judgment of a Yearly Meeting of Quakers in Maryland, Condemned by George Keith, Thomas Budd, etc. London, 1693. K182

_____. *A Farther Account of the Great Divisions Among the Quakers in Pennsylvania.* London, 1693. K166

_____. *The Pretended Yearly Meeting of the Quakers, Their Nameless Bull of Excommunication Given Forth Against George Keith.* 1695. K193

_____. *An Exact Narrative of the Proceedings at Turners-Hall, the 11th Month Called June, 1696.* London, 1696. K161

_____. *A Second Narrative of the Proceedings at Turners-Hall, the 29th of the Month Called April, 1697.* London, 1697. K204

_____. *A Third Narrative of the Proceedings at Turner's Hall, the 21st Day of April, 1698.* London, 1698. K218

_____. *The Deism of William Penn, and his Brethren.* London, 1699. K156

_____. *George Keith's Fourth Narrative, of his Proceedings at Turner's Hall ... Jan., 1699.* London, 1700.

_____. *George Keith's Fifth Narrative, of His Proceedings at Turner's Hall: Detecting the Quakers Errors. The 4th of June, 1701.* London, 1701. K167

_____. *The Magic of Quakerism or, the Chief Mysteries of Quakerism Laid Open.* London, 1707.

Lawson, Thomas. *Of the False Ministry.* In Thomas Aldham, *A Brief Discovery of the Three-fold Estate of Antichrist.* 1653.

_____. *Dragon's Fall Before the Ark.* 1679. L724

_____. *Babylon's Fall.* No date.

Leslie, Charles. *The Snake in the Grass.* London, 1696. L1156

_____. *Primitive Heresy Revived in the Faith and Practice of the People Called Quakers.* London, 1698. L1140

_____. *A Defence of a Book Entitled The Snake in the Grass. In Reply to George Whitehead, Joseph Wyeth*, etc. London, 1700. L1126

"A Letter From Henry More to William Penn". *BFHA*, 16 (1927), pp. 67-71.

Lilburne, John. *A Work of the Beast.* 1638. 15599

Livingstone, Patrick. *Plain and Downright-Dealing.* London, 1667. L2605

Marshall, Charles. *The Way of Life Revealed*. 1674. M746

_____. *The Trumpet of the Lord Sounded Out of Sion*. 1675. M745

_____. *A Vision of Charles Marshall's Seen in the 6th Month 1676*. 1676.

Matern, J. *The Testimony to the Lord's Power and Blessed Appearance in and Amongst Children*. London, 1679.

Mather, Cotton. *Magnalia Christi Americana; or The Ecclesiastical History of New England*. Cambridge, Mass.: Belknap Press, 1977. First published in 1702.

Mather, Increase. *An Essay for the Recording of Illustrious Providences*. Delmar, New York: Scholars Facsimiles and Reprints, 1977. First published in 1684. I1206

Memoires of the Life, Ministry, Trial, and Sufferings of that Very Emminent Person James Nailer, The Quakers' Great Apostle. London. 1719.

Moore, Thomas. *A Defence Against the Poison of Satan's Design, Cast Out of his Mouth by James Nayler*. London, 1656. M2600

_____. *An Antidote Against the Spreading Infections of the Spirit of Antichrist*. London. 1655. M2597

More, Henry. *An Explanation of The Grand Mystery of Godliness*. London, 1660. M2658

_____. *Divine Dialogues*. London, 1668. 2nd Edition, 1713. M2650.

Mortimer, R.S. "Allegations Against George Fox by Ministers in North Lancashire". *JFHS*, 39 (1947), pp. 15-17.

Muggleton, Lodowick. *The Neck of the Quakers Broken*. Amsterdam, 1663. M3048

_____. *A Looking-Glass for George Fox*. 1668. N3046

Nayler, James. *Sin Kept Out of the Kingdom*. 1653. N317A

_____. *Several Petitions Answered that were put up by the Priests of Westmorland Against James Nayler*. London, 1653. With George Fox. N316A

_____. *The Power and Glory of the Lord Shining Forth Out of the North*. London, 1653. N302

_____. *Saul's Errand to Damascus*. London, 1653. With George Fox. N313

_____. *A Lamentation (by one of England's Prophets) Over the Ruins of this Oppressed Nation.* York, 1653). N292

_____. *A Copy of a Letter to Some Friends Concerning George Fox's Trial.* In Thomas Aldham, *A Brief Discovery of a Threefold Estate of Antichrist.* 1653. A894B

_____. *Several Papers: Some of Them Given Forth by George Fox; Others by James Nayler.* 1653.

_____. *Truth Cleared from Scandals Being James Nayler's Answer and Declaration Touching on Some Things Charged Upon Him in the Lancashire Petition.* 1654. N324

_____. *A Discovery of the Man of Sin.* London, 1654. N274

_____. *The Railer Rebuked.* London, 1654. N306

_____. *A Fool Answered According to His Folly.* London, 1655.

_____. *An Answer to the Book Called, The Perfect Pharisee.* 1655. N261

_____. *An Answer to a Book Called The Quakers Catechism, Put Out by Richard Baxter.* London, 1655. N258

_____. *Satan's Design Discovered ... an Answer to Thomas Moore.* London, 1655. N313

_____. *A Second Answer to Thomas Moore.* London, 1655. N314

_____. *A Discovery of the Beast.* London, 1655. N271

_____. *A Vindication of Truth.* London, 1656. N326

_____. *Love to the Lost.* London, 1656.

_____. *A Public Discovery ... an Answer to a Book Entitled A Public Discovery of a Secret Deciet, [by] John Deacon.* London, 1656. N305

_____. *Weakness above Wickedness, ... an Answer to a Book Called, Quakers Quaking, devised by Jeremiah Ives.* London, 1656. N327

_____. *Wickedness Weighed: in an Answer to a Book, Called The Quaker's Quaking Principle ... by Ellis Bradshaw.* London, 1656. N331

_____. *The Light of Christ.* London, 1656. N293

_____. *Antichrist in Man Christ's Enemy.* London, 1656. N263

_____. *How Sin is Strengthened.* London, 1657. N285

310

_____. *The Lamb's War Against the Man of Sin*. London, 1656. N290

_____. *James Nailor's Recantation Penned and Directed by Himself to all the People of the Lord*. London, 1659. N307

This is a reprint of Nayler's *To all the People of the Lord, Gathered and Scattered*, (1659).

_____. *Having Heard that Some Have Wronged My Words Which I Spoke Before the Committee of Parliament ... Some Have printed Words Which I Spoke Not; and Some Have Printed a Paper, and Calls it James Naylor's Recantation, Unknown to Me*. London, 1659. N284

_____. *A Testimony to Christ Jesus Delivered to the Parliament*. London, 1659.

_____. *Several Papers of Confessions ... Which Begins Thus, "O England Thy Time is Come"*. No Date. N316

_____. *To the Life of God in All*. London, 1659. N321

_____. *Glory to God Almighty*. London. No Date. N282

_____. *A Short Answer to a Book Called The Fanatik History ... by Richard Blome*. London, 1660. With Richard Hubberthorne. H3232 and N317

_____. *A Collection of Sundry Books, Epistles and Papers Written by James Nayler, Some of Which Were Never Before Printed*. Edited by George Whitehead, London, 1716.

Nicolson, M. (ed.). *The Conway Letters: The Correspondence of Anne, Viscountess Conway, Henry More, and their Friends, 1642-1684*. New Haven: Yale University Press, 1930.

Our Ancient Testimony Renewed Concerning Our Lord and Saviour Jesus Christ ... Given Forth by a Meeting of Public Friends ... at Philadelphia ... 1695. Appended to the English edition of Gerard Croese's *The General History of the Quakers*. London, 1696.

Pagitt, Ephraim. *Heresiography*. London, 1662. P174-182

Pantheon Anabaptisticum et Enthusiasticum. Frankfurt am Main, 1701.

Parnell, James. *A Shield of the Truth*. London, 1655. P533

Patrides, C.A.(ed.). *The Cambridge Platonists*, 1969.

Penington, Isaac. *Babylon the Great Described*. London, 1659. P1153

311

_____. *The Axe Laid to the Root of the Old Corrupt Tree*. London, 1659. P1152

_____. *Concerning the Sum or Substance of our Religion*. 1666. P1158

_____. *Life and Immortality Brought to Light by the Gospel*. 1671.

_____. *Divine Essays, or Considerations about Several Things in Religion*. London, 1654. P1162

_____. *The Flesh and Blood of Christ*. London, 1675. P1168

_____. *The Works of ... Isaac Penington*. London, 1681.

_____. *Letters of Isaac Penington*. Edited by J. Barclay. London, 1829.

Penn, William. *A Collection of the Works of William Penn*, 2 volumes. London: J. Sowle, 1726.

_____. *The Great Case of Liberty of Conscience*. London, 1670. P1299

_____. *An Answer to the Seditious and Scandalous Pamphlet, Entitled "The Trial of Penn and Meade ... at the Old Bailey"*. London, 1671.

_____. *A Serious Apology for the Principles and Practices of the People Called Quakers*. 1671. With George Whitehead. W1957

_____. *Judas and the Jews*. London, 1673. P1307

_____. *Reason Against Railing, and Truth Against Fiction Being an Answer to ... Thomas Hicks, an Anabaptist Teacher*. London, 1673. P1351

_____. *The Invalidity of John Faldo's Vindication of his Book, Called, Quakerism No Christianity*. London, 1673. P1305

_____. *Plain Dealing with a Traducing Anabaptist*. London, 1674. P1339

_____. *The Counterfeit Christian Detected*. London, 1674. P1271

_____. *The Christian Quaker*. London, 1674. With George Whitehead. P1266

_____. *Jeremy Ive's Sober Request Proved ... to be False*. London, 1674. P1306

_____. *The New Athenians*. London, 1692. P1325

_____. *The Rise and Progress of the People Called Quakers*. Richmond, Indiana: Friends United Press, 1980. Originally published as the *Introduction* to the Ellwood edition of Fox's *Journal* (1694).

312

_____. *Primitive Christianity Revived*. London: T. Sowle, 1699. P1342

Penney, Norman, ed. *Extracts From State Papers Relating to Friends, 1654-1672*. London: Headley Brothers, 1913.

_____, ed. *First Publishers of Truth: Being Early Records (Now First Printed) of the Introduction of Quakerism into the Counties of England and Wales*. London: Headley Brothers, 1907.

The Yearly Meeting of 1676 asked all local Meetings to report their historical origins and early leadership. Penney has compiled the data from those Meetings that did contribute to this project.

Penneyman, John. *This Following Being a Copy of a Letter I Carried to Devonshire House*. London, 1671. P1421-1422

Pepys, Samuel. *Diary and Correspondence of Samuel Pepys*, 4 volumes. New York: Bigelow, Brown and Co., 1848.

Perrot, John. *The Vision of John Perrot Wherein is Contained the Future of the State of Europe*. London, 1682. P1637.

_____. *Battering Rams Against Rome*. London, 1661. P1612.

Philly, John, *The Arraignment of Christendom*. 1664. P2127

Prynne, William. *The Quakers Unmasked*. London, 1655. P4045

Quacker Greuel. Das ist abschenliche auffrurische verdammliche Ihrtum der neuen Schwermer welche genennet werden Quaker. Hamburg, 1702.

Reliquiae Barclaianae. London, 1870.

Reliquiae Baxterianae, or, Mr. Richard Baxter's Narrative of the Most Memorable Passages of his Life and Times. Edited by M. Sylvester. London: T. Parkhurst, 1696. B1370

Rich, Robert. *The Saints Testimony*. London, 1655.

_____. *Copies of Some Few of the Papers Given into the House of Parliament in the Time of James Nayler's Trial*. London, 1656.

Collected papers of Robert Rich, William Tomlinson and George Fox.

_____. *Love Without Dissimulation*. London, 1667. R1361

_____. *Hidden Things Brought to Light or the Discord of the Grand Quakers Among Themselves. Discovered in Some Letters, Papers, and Passages Written to and from George Fox, James Nayler, and John Perrott; Wherein May be Seen the Cause and Ground of Their Differences, and*

Falling Out: and What Manner of Spirit, Moved and Acted in Each of Them. London, 1678. R1358

_____. *A Testimony to the Truth as it is in Jesus, or, the Spiritual Appearance and In-Dwelling of Jesus Christ in Believers Compared With His Appearance in the Flesh of His Humanity.* 1679.

_____. *The Epistles of (Mr. Robert Rich) to the Seven Churches.* London, 1680. R1356

Rigge, Ambrose. *Of Perfection, the Great Mystery of Antichrist.* London, 1657. R1486

_____. *A Standard of Righteousness Lifted up Unto the Nations.* 1683. R1492

_____. *The Good Old Way and Truth.* London, 1669. R1483

_____. *True Christianity Vindicated.* London, 1679. R1498

_____. *A Treatise Concerning the Internal Word.* London, 1704.

Robertson, John. *Rusticus ad Clericum ... In Answer to Verus Patroclus.* Aberdeen, 1694. R1607

Sabine, G.H., ed. *The Works of Gerard Winstanley.* New York: Russell and Russell, 1965.

Sachse, W.L. *English History in the Making: Readings From the Sources, to 1689,* 2 vols. New York: John Wiley, 1967.

Saltmarsh, John. *The Smoke in the Temple.* London, 1646. S498

Sewel, William. *The History of the Rise, Increase, and Progress of the Christian People Called Quakers.* 2 volumes. London: Darton and Harvey, 1834. First published in Low Dutch in 1717.

Sherlocke, Richard. *The Quakers Wild Questions.* London, 1654. S3254

Simmonds, Martha. *A Lamentation for the Lost Sheep of the House of Israel.* London, 1655. S3793

_____. *When the Lord Jesus Came to Jerusalem.* 1655. Appended to *A Lamentation for the Lost Sheep of the House of Israel.* S3794

_____. *O England, Thy Time is Come.* London, 1656. With James Nayler and Hannah Stranger. S3793

Simpson, William. *From One Who was Moved of the Lord God to go as a Sign Among the Priests and Professors.* London, 1659. S3843

_____. *A Discovery of the Priests and Professors, and Their Nakedness and Shame Which is Coming Upon Them*. London, 1660. S3842

_____. *Going Naked, a Sign*. London, 1660. S3845

Smith, Humphrey. *The Vision of Humphrey Smith Which he Saw Concerning London*. London, 1660. S4084

Some Few of the Quakers Many Horrid Blasphemies ... Destructive to Government. Delivered to Members of Both Houses ... March, 1699. London, 1699. S4506

Steere, D., ed. *Quaker Spirituality: Selected Writings*. N.Y.: Paulist Press, 1984.

Swinton, John (?). *England's Warning*. 1664. See Smith, *Descriptive Catalogue*, 2, p. 689. S6283

Taylor, Thomas. *A Trumpet Sounded from Under the Altar*. 1658. T590

_____. *A Testimony for Christ Jesus*. 1672. T584

_____. *Truth's Innocency and Simplicity*. London, 1697. T591

The collected works of Thomas Taylor.

This is a Short Relation of Some of the Cruel Sufferings (for the Truth's Sake) of Katharine Evans and Sarah Cheevers. London, 1662. T935

Toldervy, John. *The Foot Out of the Snare*. London, 1656. T1767

_____. *The Snare Broken*. London, 1656. T1770

_____. *The Naked Truth*. London, 1656. T1769

Tomlinson, William. *Seven Particulars*. London, 1657. T1851

A True Narrative of the Examination, Trial, and Sufferings of James Nayler. 1657. T2789

Contains *Copies of Some few of the Papers*.

Underhill, Thomas. *Hell Broke Loose, or an History of the Quakers*. London, 1660. U43

Vokins, Joan. *God's Mighty Power Magnified*. London, 1691. V685

Ward, Richard. *The Life of the Learned and Pious Dr. Henry More*. London, 1710.

Weigel, Valentine. *Life of Christ*. London: Giles Calvert, 1648.

Welde, Thomas. *A Further Discovery of that Generation of Men Called Quakers: By Way of a Reply to an Answer of James Nayler to the Perfect Pharisee.* Gateside, 1654. W1268

Whitehead, George. *The Voice of Wisdom ... Against Antichrist's Folly and Deceit.* 1659. W1972

_____. *The He-Goat's Horn Broken.* London, 1660. With Richard Hubberthorne. H1933

_____. *The Light and Life of Christ Within.* London, 1668. W1941

_____. *The Divinity of Christ.* London, 1669. Preface by George Fox and John Stubbs. W1925

_____. *The Nature of Christianity.* 1671. With postscripts by George Keith. W1942

_____. *The Christian Quaker.* 1673. With William Penn. W1908

_____. *A Serious Search into Jeremy Ive's Questions to Quakers.* London, 1674. W1958

_____. *Innocency Against Envy; in a Brief Examination of Francis Bugg's Two Invective Pamphlets ... The Quakers Detected; [and] Battering Rams Against New Rome.* London, 1691. W1934

_____. *The Divine Light of Christ in Man.* London, 1692. W1924

_____. *Innocency Triumphant Over Insolency ... in Answer to Francis Bugg's ... New Rome Arraigned.* London, 1693. W1934

_____. *An Antidote Against the Venome of the Snake in the Grass.* London, 1697. W1889

_____. *A Supplement [to Joseph Wyeth's "Anguis Flagellatus;" or, a Switch for the Snake].* 1699. W3757

_____. *Truth Prevalent.* London, 1701.

_____. *Light and Truth Triumphant; or, George Keith's Imagined Magic of Quakerism Confirmed, Utterly Confounded, and Confronted.* London, 1712.

_____. *The Christian Progress of ... George Whitehead.* London, 1725.

Whitehead, John. *The Enmity Between the Two Seeds.* London, 1655. W1975

_____. *A Small Treatise.* London, 1661. W1981

Whiting, John. *The Rector Corrected ... in Answer to Edward Cockson.* London, 1708.

Wilkinson, J. *Quakerism Examined: in a Reply to the Letter of Samuel Tuke.* London, 1836.

Wilkinson, R. *The Saints Travel to the Land of Canaan.* London, 1648.

Williams, Roger. *George Fox Digged Out of His Burrows.* Boston, 1676. W2764

Winterton, Thomas. *The Quaking Prophets Two Ways Proved False Prophets.* London, 1655. W3093

Wyeth, Joseph. *Anguis Flagellatus: or, a Switch for the Snake.* London, 1699. W3757

Young, Samuel. *The Foxonian Quakers, Dunces, Liars, and Slanderers, Proved out of George Fox's Journal and other Scriblers.* London, 1697. Y80

III. SECONDARY SOURCES

Anderson, A.B. "The Social Origins of the Early Quakers." *QH*, 68 (1979), pp. 33-40.

_____. "A Study in the Sociology of Religious Persecution: The First Quakers." *Journal of Religious History*, 9 (1977).

Andrews, W. "A Glance at New York in 1697: The Travel Diary of Dr. Benjamin Bullivant". *The New York Historical Society Quarterly*, 40 (1956), pp. 55-73.

Aylmer, G.E., ed. *The Interregnum: The Quest for Settlement 1646-1660.* London: Macmillan, 1972.

Ball, B. *A Great Expectation: Eschatological Thought in English Protestantism to 1660.* Leiden: E.J. Brill, 1975.

Barbour, H. and J.W. Frost. *The Quakers.* New York: Greenwood Press, 1988.

Barbour, H. "Quaker Prophetesses and Mothers in Israel." In *Seeking the Light: Essays in Quaker History in Honor of Edwin B. Bronner.* Edited by J.W. Frost and J.M. Moore. Wallingford: Pendle Hill Publications, 1986, pp. 41-60.

_____. "Ranters, Diggers and Quakers Reborn." *QH*, 64 (1975), pp. 60-65.

_____. "Protestant Quakerism." *Quaker Religious Thought*, IX (1969), pp. 2-53.

_____. *The Quakers in Puritan England*. New Haven: Yale University Press, 1964.

Barclay, R. *The Inner Life of the Religious Socities of the Commonwealth*. London: Hodder and Stoughton, 1876.

Bauman, R. *Let Your Words be Few: Symbolism of Speaking and Silence Among Seventeenth Century Quakers*. London: Cambridge University Press, 1983.

Benson, L. *What Did George Fox Teach About Christ?* Gloucester, England: Fellowship Press, 1976.

_____. *Catholic Quakerism*. Gloucester: The Author, 1966.

Bernstein, E. *Cromwell and Communism: Socialism and Democracy in the Great English Revolution*. London: Frank Cass and Co., 1966. First published in 1930.

Bittle, W.G. *James Nayler, 1618-1660: The Quaker Indicted by Parliament*. Richmond: Friends United Press, 1986.

_____. "Religious Toleration and the Trial of James Nayler: A New Interpretation." *QH*, 73 (1984), pp. 29-33.

Bitterman, M.G.F. "Early Quaker Literature of Defence." *CH*, 42 (1973), pp. 203-228.

Blackwood, B.G. "Agrarian Unrest and Early Lancashire Quakers," *JFHS*, 51 (1966), pp. 72-6.

Bossy, J. *Christianity in the West 1400-1700*. Oxford: Oxford University Press, 1985.

Brailsford, M.R. *A Quaker From Cromwell's Army: James Nayler*. London. 1927.

Braithwaite, A.W. "Early Friends Testimony Against Carnal Weapons." *JFHS*, 52 (1969), pp. 101-5.

_____. "George Fox's Last Imprisonment," *JFHS*, 51 (1967), pp. 159-66.

_____. "Early Tithe Prosecutions: Friends as Outlaws," *JFHS*, 49 (1959-61), pp. 148-56.

Braithwaite, W.C. *The Beginnings of Quakerism to 1660*. 2nd edition. York: William Sessions, 1981. First published in 1912.

318

_____. *The Second Period of Quakerism*. 2nd edition. York: William Sessions, 1979. First published in 1919.

_____. "Westmorland and the Swaledale Seekers." *JFHS*, 5 (1908), pp. 3-10.

Brauer, J. "Types of Puritan Piety," *CH*, 56 (1987), pp. 39-58.

Brayshaw, A.N. *The Personality of George Fox*. London: Allenson, 1933.

Brinton, H., ed. *Children of the Light: In Honor of Rufus Jones*. New York: Macmillan, 1938.

Brown, C. *Miracles and the Critical Mind*. Grand Rapids: Eerdmans, 1984.

Brown, P. "The Saint as Exemplar in Late Antiquity". *Representations*, 1 (1983), pp. 1-26.

Butler, E.M. *The Myth of the Magus*. London: Cambridge University Press, 1948.

Butler, J. " "Gospel Order Improved": The Keithian Schism and the Exercise of Quaker Ministerial Authority in Pennsylvania". *William and Mary Quarterly*, 31 (July, 1974), pp. 431-452.

Cadbury, H.J. "The Editio Princeps of Fox's Journal." *JFHS*, 53 (1974), pp. 197-218.

_____. "Some Light on Charles II and Friends." *JFHS*, 53 (1972), pp. 53-60.

_____."Tracing the Influence of Sebastian Franck." *JFHS*, 52(1970), pp. 168-169.

_____. "Glimpses of Quakerism in America in 1697." *QH*, 53 (1964), pp. 37-44.

_____. "Early Use of the Word 'Quaker'." *JFHS*, 49(1959), pp.3-5.

_____. "George Keith to Henry More." *JFHS*, 46 (1954), pp. 59-63.

_____. "Revised Views of Quaker Origins." *The Friend*, 112 (1954), pp. 5-7.

_____. "George Fox's Later Years." Concluding essay in *The Journal of George Fox*, 713-756. Edited by J.L. Nickalls. London: The Religious Society of Friends, 1975. First published in 1952.

_____. "Recording the Rise of Truth." *BFHA*, 41 (1952), pp. 3-11.

_____. "Early Quakerism and Uncanonical Lore." *Harvard Theological Review*, 40 (1947), pp. 177-204.

_____. "An Obscure Chapter in Quaker History." *Journal of Religion*, 24 (1944), pp. 201-213.

_____. "Hebraica and the Jews in Early Quaker Interest." In H. Brinton, ed. *Children of the Light: In Honour of Rufus M. Jones*. New York: Macmillan, 1938), pp. 135-163.

_____. "George Fox's Library Again." *JFHS*, 30 (1933), pp. 9-19.

_____. "George Fox's Library: Further Identifications." *JFHS*, 29 (1932), pp. 63-71.

_____. "George Fox and Sixteenth Century Bibles." *JFHS*, 21 (1924), pp. 1-8.

Capp, B. *The Fifth Monarchy Men: A Study in Seventeenth Century English Millenarianism*. London: Faber and Faber, 1972.

_____. "The Millenium and Eschatology in England." *P&P*, 57 (1972), pp. 156-62.

Carlyle, T. *The Works of Thomas Carlyle*. New York: Charles Scribners Sons, 1903.

Carroll, K. "A Look at James Milner and His 'False Prophecy'." *QH*, 74 (1985), pp. 18-26.

_____. "Early Quakers and Going Naked as a Sign." *QH*, 67 (1978), pp. 69-87.

_____. "Singing in the Spirit in Early Quakerism." *QH*, 73 (1984), pp. 1-13.

_____. "Quaker Attitudes Towards Signs and Wonders." *JFHS*, 54 (1977), pp. 70-84.

_____. "Sackcloth and Ashes and Other Signs and Wonders." *JFHS*, 52 (1975), pp. 314-325.

_____. "Martha Simmonds: A Quaker Enigma." *JFHS*, 53 (1972), pp. 31-52.

Cherry, C.L. "Enthusiasm and Madness: Anti-Quakerism in the Seventeenth Century." *QH*, 74 (1984).

Christianson, P. *Reformers and Babylon: English Apocalyptic Visions from the Reformation to the Eve of the Civil War*. Toronto: University of Toronto Press, 1978.

Chrysostum, K. "The Diggers, the Ranters and the Early Quakers." *The American Benedictine Review*, 25 (1974), pp. 460-475.

320

Cody, E.J. "The Price of Perfection: The Irony of George Keith." *Pennsylvania History*, 39 (1972), pp. 1-19.

Cole, A. "The Social Origins of the Early Friends." *JFHS*, 48 (1957), pp. 99-118.

_____. "The Quakers and the English Revolution." *P&P*, 10 (1956), pp. 39-53.

Collier, H.E. "Miracles and Healings During the First Period of Quakerism." *Friends' Quarterly Examiner*, (1944), pp. 28-35.

_____. "Then and Now: Miracles and Healing." *Friends Quarterly Examiner*, (1945).

Collinson, P. *Godly People: Essays on English Protestantism and Puritanism*. London: Hambledon Press, 1983.

Cope, J.I. "Seventeenth Century Quaker Style." In *Seventeenth Century Prose: Modern Essays in Criticism*. Edited by S. Fish. New York: Oxford University Press, 1971, pp. 200-235.

Creasey, M. *"Inward" and "Outward": A Study in Early Quaker Language*. London: Friends' Historical Society, 1962.

_____. "Early Quaker Christology: With Special Reference to the Teaching and Significance of Isaac Penington, 1616-1679." D.Phil. thesis, University of Leeds, 1956.

Curtis, T.C. "Quarter Sessions Appearances and Their Background: A Seventeenth Century Regional Study." In *Crime in England 1550-1800*. Edited by J.S. Cockburn. Princeton: Princeton University Press, 1977.

Dailey, B.R. "The Husbands of Margaret Fell: An Essay on Religious Metaphor and Social Change." *The Seventeenth Century*, 2 (1987), pp. 55-71.

Darnton, Robert. *The Literary Underground of the Old Regime*. Cambridge: Harvard University Press, 1982.

_____. *Mesmerism and the End of the Enlightenment in France*. Cambridge: Harvard University Press, 1968.

Davis, J.C. *Fear, Myth and History: The Ranters and Their Historians*. Cambridge: Cambridge University Press, 1986.

Doncaster, H. "Foreward." In W.C. Braithwaite, *The Beginnings of Quakerism*, 2nd edition. York, 1981.

_____. "Early Quaker Thought on "That State in Which Adam Was Before He Fell."" *JFHS*, 41 (1949), pp. 13-24.

Dow, F.D. *Radicalism in the English Revolution 1640-1660*. Oxford: Basil Blackwell, 1985.

Durnbaugh, D.F. "Baptists and Quakers - Left-Wing Puritans?" *QH*, 62 (1973), pp. 67-82.

Edwards, G.W. "The London Six Weeks Meeting." *JFHS*, 50 (1962-4), pp. 228-45.

_____. "The Great Fire of London." *JFHS*, 51 (1966), pp. 67-71.

Edwards, I.L. "The Women Friends of London: The Two Weeks and Box Meetings." *JFHS*, 47 (1955), pp. 3-21.

Eeg-Olofsson, L. *The Conception of the Inner Light in Robert Barclay's Theology*. Lund: CWK Gleerup, 1954.

Ellenberger, H.F. *The Discovery of the Unconscious*. New York: Basic Books, 1970.

Endy, M.B. "The Interpretation of Quakerism: Rufus Jones and his Critics." *QH*, 70 (1981), pp. 3-21.

_____. *William Penn and Early Quakerism*. Princeton University Press, 1973.

Evans, E.L. "Morgan Llwyd and the Early Friends." *Friends' Quarterly*, 8 (1954), pp. 48-57.

Festinger, L. *When Prophecy Fails: A Social, Psychological Study of a Modern Group that Predicted the Destruction of the World*. University of Minnesota Press, 1956.

Fix, A. "Radical Reformation and Second Reformation in Holland: The Intellectual Consequences of the Sixteenth-Century Religious Upheaval and the Coming of the Rational World View." *SCJ*, 18 (1987), pp. 63-80.

Fogelklou, Emilia. *James Nayler: The Rebel Saint, 1618-1660*. London: Ernst Benn, 1933.

Fraser, A. *The Weaker Vessel*. New York: Alfred Knopf, 1984.

Frost, J.W. and J.M. Moore, eds. *Seeking the Light: Essays in Quaker History in Honor of Edwin B. Bronner*. Philadelphia: Pendle Hill, 1986.

Frost, J.W. "The Dry Bones of Quaker Theology." *CH*, 39 (1970), pp. 503-523.

Gardiner, S.R. *History of the Commonwealth and Protectorate, 1649-1656.* New York: AMS Press, 1965.

Garrett, C. *Respectable Folly: Millenarians and the French Revolution in France and England.* Baltimore: Johns Hopkins University Press, 1975.

"George Fox's Papers." *JFHS,* 36 (1939), pp. 63-64.

Goad, D.G. "Elisha Bates and the Beaconite Controversy." *QH,* 73 (1984), pp. 34-47.

Graves, M. "Functions of Key Metaphors in Early Quaker Sermons, 1671-1700". *Quarterly Journal of Speech,* 69 (1983), pp. 364-78.

Greaves, R. *Deliver Us From Evil: The Radical Underground in Britain, 1660-1663.* New York: Oxford University Press, 1986.

_____. "The Puritan Non-Conformist Tradition in England, 1560-1700: Historiographical Reflections." *Albion,* 17 (1986), pp. 449-86.

Green, I.M. *The Re-Establishment of the Church of England, 1660-1663.* Oxford, 1978.

Grubb, E. *Thoughts on the Divine in Man.* London: Friends Book Centre, 1931.

_____. "Spiritual Healing Among Early Friends." *Quaker History and Thought.* London, 1925, chapter three, pp. 149-67.

_____. "George Fox and Spiritual Healing." *The Friend,* (1924), pp. 600-601.

_____. *The Historic and Inward Christ.* Bishopsgate: Headley Bros, 1914.

Grubb, M. "The Beacon Separation." *JFHS,* 55 (1988), pp. 190-98.

Gummere, A.M. *Witchcraft and Quakerism.* Philadelphia: The Biddle Press, 1908.

Gwyn, D. *Apocalypse of the Word: The Life and Message of George Fox.* Richmond, Indiana: Friends United Press, 1986.

Hall, F.B. "The Thought of Robert Barclay: An Evaluation." *Quaker Religious Thought,* 7 (1965), pp. 2-31.

Hill, C. *A Turbulent, Seditious and Factious People: John Bunyan and his Church.* Oxford University Press, 1988.

_____. *The Experience of Defeat: Milton and Some Contemporaries.* London: Penguin, 1985.

323

_____."The Quakers and the English Revolution." *Quaker Monthly*, (1984), pp. 77-80.

_____. *Milton and the English Revolution.* New York: Viking, 1977.

_____. *The World Turned Upside Down: Radical Ideas During the English Revolution.* New York: Penguin, 1975.

_____. *Antichrist in Seventeenth Century England.* London: Oxford University Press, 1971.

_____. *The Century of Revolution 1603-1714.* New York: W.W. Norton, 1961.

Hobhouse, S. "Jacob Boehme's Influence in England." *JFHS*, 33 (1936), p. 54.

Hodgkin, T. *Introduction* to *The First Publishers of Truth.* Edited by Norman Penney. London: Headley Bros., 1904.

Holden, D. *Friends Divided.* Richmond, Indiana: Friends United Press, 1988.

Holdsworth, C.J. "Mystics and Heretics in the Middle Ages: Rufus Jones Reconsidered." *JFHS*, 53 (1972), pp. 9-30.

Holland, R.F. "The Miraculous." *American Philosophical Quarterly*, 2 (1965), pp. 43-51.

Horle, C.W. *The Quakers and the English Legal System, 1660-1688.* Philadelphia: University of Pennsylvania Press, 1988.

_____."Quakers and Baptists 1647-1660." *Baptist Quarterly*, 26 (1976), pp. 344-362.

Howe, D.W. "The Cambridge Platonists of Old England and the Cambridge Platonists of New England," *CH*, 57 (Dec., 1988), pp. 470-485.

Hudson, W.S. "A Suppressed Chapter in Quaker History." *Journal of Religion*, 24 (1944), pp. 108-118.

_____. Notes and Communications - Quaker History: Dr. Hudson Replies." *Journal of Religion*, 24 (1944), pp. 279-81.

_____. "Gerrard Winstanley and the Early Quakers." *CH*, 12 (1943), pp. 177-94.

Hull, W.I. "The Mennonites and Quakers of Holland." In *Children of the Light.* Edited by H. Brinton. New York: Macmillan, 1938.

324

_____. *William Sewel of Amsterdam, 1653-1720: The First Historian of Quakerism*. Philadelphia: Swarthmore College Monograph No. 1, 1933.

_____. *The Rise of Quakerism in Amsterdam, 1655-1665*. Philadelphia: Swarthmore College Monograph, No. 4, 1938.

_____. *Benjamin Furly and Quakerism in Rotterdam*. Philadelphia: Swarthmore College Monograph, No. 5, 1941.

Hume, D. *The History of England*. Volume 5. Philadelphia: Porter and Coates, 1776.

Huntington, Jr., F.C. "Quakerism During the Commonwealth: The Experience of the Light." *QH*, 71 (1982), pp. 69-88.

Hurwich, J. "The Social Origins of the Early Quakers." *P&P*, 48 (1970), pp. 156-162.

Hutton, R. *The Restoration: A Political and Religious History of England and Wales, 1658-1667*. Oxford: Clarendon Press, 1985.

Ingle, L. and Jaan Ingle. "The Excommunication of George Fox, 1678." *JFHS*, 56 (1991), pp. 71-75.

_____. "On the the Folly of Seeking the Quaker Holy Grail." *Quaker Religious Thought*, 25 (No. 1, 1991), pp. 17-26.

_____. "From Mysticism to Radicalism: Recent Historiography of Quaker Beginnings." *QH*, 76 (1987), pp. 79-94.

_____. "New Light on Old Quaker History." *Friends Journal*, 32 (May, 1986), pp. 13-14.

Jacobs, Margaret. "Science and Social Passion: The Case of Seventeenth Century England." *Journal of the History of Ideas*, 43 (1982), pp. 331-39.

James, W. *The Varieties of Religious Experience*. London: Longman, Green and Co., 1915.

Janney, S. *History of the Religious Society of Friends*, 4 volumes. Philadelphia: Zell, 1861-1868.

Johnson, G.A. "From Seeker to Finder: A Study in Seventeenth Century English Spiritualism Before the Quakers." *CH*, 17 (1948), pp. 299-315.

Jones, Rufus. *Mysticism and Democracy in the English Commonwealth*. London: Oxford, 1946.

_____. *The Quakers in the American Colonies*. London: Macmillan, 1923.

_____. *The Life of George Fox*. London: Macmillan, 1923.

_____. *Spiritual Reformers in the Sixteenth and Seventeenth Centuries*. Boston: Beacon Press, 1959. First published in 1914.

_____. *Introduction* to W.C. Braithwaite, *The Beginnings of Quakerism to 1660*. 1st edition. London: Macmillan, 1912.

_____. *Studies in Mystical Religion*. N.Y.: Russell and Russell, 1979. First published in 1909.

Jordan, W.K. *The Development of Religious Toleration in England*, 4 vols. Cambridge, Mass.: Harvard University Press, 1932-40.

Keeble, N.H. *The Literary Culture of Non-Conformity in Late Seventeenth Century England*. Leicester University Press, 1987.

Keene, J.C. "Historical Quakerism and Mysticism," *Quaker Religious Thought*, 7 (1963), pp. 2-9.

Kennedy, T.C. "History and Quaker Renaissance: The Vision of John Wilhelm Rountree." *JFHS*, 55 (1986), pp. 35-56.

Kent, S.A. "Psychology and Quaker Mysticism: The Legacy of William James and Rufus Jones." *QH*, 76 (1987), pp. 1- 17.

_____. "The Papist Charges Against the Inter-Regnum Quakers." *JRH*, 12 (1982), pp. 180-190.

King, R. *George Fox and the Light Within, 1650-1660*. Philadelphia, 1940.

Kirby, E.W. *George Keith (1636-1716)*. New York: D. Appleton-Century Co., 1942.

Knight, R. *The Founder of Quakerism: A Psychological Study of the Mysticism of George Fox*. London: The Swarthmore Press, 1922.

Knox, R. *Enthusiasm: A Chapter in the History of Religion*. Oxford University Press, 1950.

Kolakowski, L. *Chrétiens sans Église. La conscience religieuse le lien confessionel au XVIIe siècle*. Paris: Gallimard, 1969.

Kunze, B.Y. "Religious Authority and Social Status in Seventeenth Century England: The Friendship of Margaret Fell, George Fox, and William Penn." *CH*, 57 (1988), pp. 170-86.

Lane Fox, R. *Pagans and Christians in the Mediterranean World from the second centruy A.D. to the conversion of Constantine*. Penguin, 1988. First published in 1986.

326

Larner, C. *Witchcraft and Religion: The Politics of Popular Belief.* Oxford: Basil Blackwell, 1985.

Liu, Tai. *Discord in Zion: The Puritan Divines and the Puritan Revolution, 1640-1660.* The Hague: Nijhoff, 1973.

Lloyd, A. *Quaker Social History, 1669-1738.* London: Longmans, 1950.

Loft, L. "Quakers, Brissot and Eighteenth Century Abolitionists." *JFHS*, 55 (1989), pp. 277-89.

Lovejoy, D.S. *Religious Enthusiasm in the New World: Heresy to Revolution.* Harvard University Press, 1985.

Macauley, T.B. *The History of England.* In *The Works of Lord Macauley.* Philadelphia: The University Library Association.

Macdonald, M. *Mystical Bedlam: Madness, Anxiety and Healing in Seventeenth Century England.* Cambridge University Press, 1981.

Mack, P. "Women as Prophets During the English Civil War." *Feminist Studies*, 8 (1982), pp. 19-45.

_____. "The Prophet and Her Audience: Gender and Knowledge in the World Turned Upside Down." *Revising the English Revolution: Reflections and Elaborations on the Work of Christopher Hill.* Edited by G. Eley and W. Hunt. London: Routledge, Chapman and Hall, 1988.

Maclear, J.F. "Quakerism at the End of the Interregnum: A Chapter in the Domestication of Radical Puritanism." *CH*, 19 (Dec., 1950), pp. 240-270.

Mackey, J.P., ed. *Religious Imagination.* Edinburgh University Press, 1986.

Masson, D. *The Life of John Milton, Narrated in Connextion with the Political, Ecclesiastical and Literary History of the Time.* London: Macmillan, 1877.

McGregor, J.F. and B. Reay, eds. *Radical Religion in the English Revolution.* Oxford University Press, 1984.

McGregor, J.F. "Ranterism and the Development of Early Quakerism." *JRH*, 9 (1977), pp. 349-363.

McLaughlin, R.E. *Caspar Schwenckfeld Reluctant Radical: His Life to 1540.* New Haven: Yale University Press, 1986.

Merli, F.J. "Naylor's Case and the Dilemma of the Protectorate." *University of Birmingham Historical Journal*, 10 (1965), pp. 44-59.

Miller, P. *Orthodoxy in Massachusetts, 1630-1650.* Boston: Beacon Press, 1954.

_____. *The New England Mind: The Seventeenth Century.* Cambridge: Harvard University Press, 1954.

Monaghan, H.D. *Dear George: George Fox, Man and Prophet.* Philadelphia: Franklin, 1970.

Morgan, E.S. *Visible Saints: The History of a Puritan Idea.* New York: New York University Press, 1963.

Morgan, N.J. "The Quakers and the Establishment, 1660-1730, with specific reference to the North-West of England." Ph.D. thesis, University of Lancaster, 1985.

Mortimer, R.S. "The First Century of Quaker Printers." *JFHS*, 40 (1948), pp. 37-49; 41 (1949) pp. 74-84.

Mullett, M. *Radical Religious Movements in Early Modern Europe.* London: George, Allen and Unwin, 1980.

Neale, Daniel. *The History of the Puritans, or Protestant Nonconformists: From the Reformation in 1517, to the Revolution in 1688.* 4 volumes. London: W. Baynes, 1822. First published in 1732.

Nicolson, M.H. "George Keith and the Cambridge Platonists." *Philosophical Review*, 39 (1930), pp. 36-55.

Nickalls, J.L. "George Fox's Library." *JFHS*, 28 (1931), pp. 3-21.

Noble, V. *The Man in Leather Breeches: The Life and Times of George Fox.* New York: Philosophical Library, 1953.

Nuttall, G. "A Letter by James Nayler Appropriated to George Fox." *JFHS*, 55 (1988), pp. 178-79.

_____. "The Last of James Nayler, Robert Rich and the Church of the First-Born." *Friends Quarterly*, 60 (1985), pp. 527-34.

_____. "Nothing Else Would Do: Early Friends and the Bible." *The Friends Quarterly*, 22 (1982), pp. 651-59.

_____. "Puritan and Quaker Mysticism." *Theology*, 78 (1975), pp. 518-31.

_____. *James Nayler: A Fresh Approach. Journal of the Friends Historical Society.* Supplement No. 26 (1954).

_____. "George Fox and His Journal." The *Introduction* to J.L. Nickalls, *The Journal of George Fox* (1952), pp. xix-xxxvii.

_____. *Studies in Christian Enthusiasm: Illustrated from Early Quakerism*. Philadelphia: Pendle Hill, 1948.

_____. "Unity with the Creation: George Fox and the Hermetic Philosophy." *Friends Quarterly*, 1 (1947), pp. 134-143.

_____. *The Holy Spirit in Puritan Faith and Experience*. Oxford: Basil Blackwell, 1947.

Oliver, P.M. "The Problems of Authority, Discipline, and Tradition in the First Century of English Quakerism." *Friends Quarterly*, (July, 1975), pp. 115-125.

Oliver, P.M. "Quaker Testimony and the Lamb's War." Ph.D. thesis, University of Melbourne, 1977.

O'Malley, T.P. "The Press and Quakerism, 1653-1659." *JFHS*, 54 (1979), pp. 169-84.

_____. "Defying the Powers and Tempering the Spirit." *Journal of Ecclesiastical History*, 33 (1982), pp. 72-88.

Ormsby-Lennon, H. "Metaphor and Madness." *ETC: A Review of General Semantics*, 33 (1976), pp. 307-18.

Patterson, A.M. *Censorship and Interpretation: The Conditions of Writing and Reading in Early Modern England*. Madison, Wisc.: University of Wisconsin Press, 1984.

Pestana, C.G. "The Social World of Salem: William King's 1681 Blasphemy Trial." *American Quarterly*, 41 (1989), pp. 308-27.

Pickvance, T.J. *George Fox and the Purefoys: A Study in the Puritan Background in Fenny Drayton in the 16th and 17th Centuries*. London: Friends Historical Society, 1970.

_____. "George Fox's Use of the Word 'Seed'." *JFHS*, 41 (1949), pp. 25-28.

Popkin, R.H. "Spinoza's Relationship With the Quakers in Amsterdam." *QH*, 73 (1984), pp. 14-20.

Powicke, F.J. *The Cambridge Platonists: A Study*. London: J.M. Dent, 1926.

_____. "Henry More, Cambridge Platonist; and Lady Conway of Ragley, Platonist and Quakeress". *Friends Quarterly Examiner*, 55 (1921), pp. 199-220.

Punshon, J. *Portrait in Grey: A Short History of the Quakers*. London: London Yearly Meeting, 1984.

Reay, B. *The Quakers and the English Revolution*. N.Y.: St. Martin's, 1985.

_____. "Quakerism and Society." In *Radical Religion in the English Revolution*. Edited by J.F. McGregor and B. Reay. London, Oxford University Press, 1984.

_____. "The Authorities and Early Restoration Quakerism." *Journal of Ecclesiastical History*, 34 (1983), pp. 69-84.

_____. "The Social Origins of Early Quakerism." *Journal of Interdisciplinary History*, XI (1980), pp. 55-72.

_____. "Quaker Opposition to Tithes, 1652-1660." *P&P*, 86 (1980), pp. 98-118.

_____. "Popular Hostility Towards Quakers in Mid- Seventeenth Century England." *Social History*, 5 (1980), pp. 387-407.

_____. "The Quakers, 1659, and the Restoration of the Monarchy." *History*, 63 (1978), pp. 193-213.

Richardson, R.C. *The Debate on the English Revolution*. London: Methuen, 1977.

Rosen, G. *Madness in Society*. N.Y.: Harper and Row, 1968.

Ross, Isabel. *Margaret Fell: Mother of Quakerism*. London: Longmans, Green and Co., 1949.

Royce, J. "George Fox as a Mystic." *Harvard Theological Review*, 6 (1913), pp. 31-59.

Saxon, B. "Woe to the Bloody City of Lichfield." *JFHS*, 41 (1949), pp. 86-7.

Scott, R.C. "Authority and Experience: John Wilhelm Rountree and the Dilemna of 19th Century British Quakerism." *JFHS*, 49 (1960), pp. 75-95.

Seppänen, A. "The Inner Light in the Journals of George Fox: A Semantic Study." L.Phil. thesis. Helsinki University, 1965.

Shantz, D. "Cognito et Communicato Christi Interna: The Contribution of Valentin Crautwald to Sixteenth Century Schwenckfeldian Spiritualism." Ph.D. thesis, University of Waterloo, 1986.

Sheeran, M.J. *Beyond Majority Rule: Voteless Decisions in the Religious Society of Friends*. Philadelphia Yearly Meeting, 1983.

Simpson, A. *Puritanism in Old and New England*. Chicago: University of Chicago Press, 1955.

Smith, N. *Perfection Proclaimed: Language and Literature in English Radical Religion, 1640-1666.* Oxford: Clarendon Press, 1989.

Smith, E. *The Life of William Dewsbury.* London, 1836.

Stone, L. *Family, Sex and Marriage in England, 1500-1800.* London: Weidenfeld and Nicolson, 1977.

Tallack, W. *George Fox, the Friends, and the Early Baptists.* London: S.W. Partridge, 1868.

Taylor, E.F. *The Valiant Sixty.* York: Sessions Book Trust, 1988. First published in 1947.

_____. "The First Publishers of Truth". *JFHS*, 19 (1922), pp. 61-81.

Thomas, A. *The Quaker Seekers of Wales.* London: Swarthmore, 1924.

Thomas, K. *Man and the Natural World: Changing Attitudes in England, 1500-1800.* London: Allan Lane, 1983.

_____. *Religion and the Decline of Magic.* Penguin University Books, 1973.

_____. "Women and the Civil War Sects." *P&P*, 13 (1958), pp. 42-62.

Tolles, F.B. "1652 in History: Changing Perspectives on the Founding of Quakerism." *BFHA*, 41 (1952), pp. 12-27.

_____. *Introduction* to W.C. Braithwaite. *The Beginnings of Quakerism to 1660*, 2nd Edition. 1955.

Tolmie, M. *The Triumph of the Saints.* Cambridge University Press, 1977.

Toon, P., ed. *Puritans, the Millenium and the Future of Israel: Puritan Eschatology 1600-1660.* London: James Clark and Co., 1970.

Trevor-Roper, H. *The Crisis of the Seventeenth Century: Religion, the Reformation and Social Change.* N.Y.: Harper and Row, 1968.

Troeltsch, E. *The Social Teaching of the Christian Churches*, 2 volumes. University of Chicago Press, Phoenix Edition, 1981. First published in 1904.

Tual, J. "Sexual Equality and Congugal Harmony: The Way to Celestial Bliss. A View of Early Quaker Matrimony." *JFHS*, 55 (1988), pp. 161-73.

Tyacke, N. *The Anti-Calvinists: The Rise of English Armenianism, ca. 1590-1640.* Oxford: Oxford University Press, 1990.

Underhill, E. *Mysticism: A Study in the Nature of Man's Spiritual Consciousness.* London: Methuen, 1949. First published in 1911.

Underwood, T.L. "Early Quaker Eschatology." In *Puritans, The Millenium and the Future of Israel. Puritan Eschatology 1600-1660.* Edited by P. Toon. London: James Clark, 1970.

Vann, R. *The Social Development of English Quakerism.* Harvard University Press, 1969.

_____. "Quakerism and the Social Structure in the Interregnum." *P&P*, 43 (1969), pp. 71-91.

_____. "Rejoinder to Hurwich." *P&P*, 48 (1970), pp. 162-64.

Wagstaff, W.R. *A History of the Society of Friends.* London: Wiley and Putnam, 1845.

Wallace, D. *Puritans and Predestination: Grace in English Protestant Theology, 1525-1695.* Chapel Hill: University of North Carolina Press, 1982.

Walter, J. and K. Wrightson. "Dearth and the Social Order in Early Modern England." *P&P*, 71 (1976).

Washburn, M.F. *Movement and Mental Imagery.* N.Y.: Arno Press, 1966. First published in 1932.

Watkins, O. *The Puritan Experience.* London: Routledge and Kegan Paul, 1972.

_____. "Some Early Quaker Autobiographies." *JFHS*, 45 (1953), pp. 65-74.

Watts, M. *The Dissenters: From the Reformation to the French Revolution.* Oxford: Clarendon, 1978.

Weber, M. *The Protestant Ethic and the Spirit of Capitalism.* New York: Scribner, 1958. First published in 1911.

Wedgwood, C.V. *Oliver Cromwell.* London: Transworld, 1975.

Weidhorn, M. *Dreams in Seventeenth Century English Literature.* The Hague: Martinus Nijhof, 1970.

Wilkinson, John. *Quakerism Examined: in Reply to a Letter of Samuel Tuke.* London: Thomas Ward, 1836.

Woolrych, A. *Commonwealth to Protectorate.* Oxford: Clarendon, 1982.

Worden, B. *The Rump Parliament 1648-1653.* Cambridge University Press, 1974.

Wright, L.M. *The Literary Life of the Early Friends, 1650-1725.* New York: Columbia University Press, 1932.

INDEX

A

Abrams, Galenus, 71n.74
Aldham, Thomas, 118
Ames, William, 88
Amsterdam, 205
Anabaptist, 6, 89, 277
Anglican, 41, 68, 70
Antichrist, 36, 37
Anticlericalism, 4, 20, 21
Appleby, 92, 100, 110
Apocalyptic, 23-45, 189-94
Aristotle, 82, 281
Arius Montanus, 28n.22
Atkins, Mary, 56
Audland, John, 32, 126, 259, 265
Augustine, 222, 275
Avatar, 19, 24, 33-34, 41, 75, 174,
    181, 183, 198, 211, 212, 214,
    217, 232, 269, 276, 280, 282,
    286, 288;
    defined, xi-xii

B

Bacon, Francis, 281
Balby, 133
Baldock, 56
Baptists, 5, 22, 56, 146, 181-82, 252
Barbados, 60, 180-81, 183-85, 188,
    207, 271
Barbour, Hugh, 4
Barclay, Robert, 81, 134-35, 223-
    25, 232-41, 244, 246-52, 255,
    261-63, 266, 275, 285-86;
    redefines the inner light,
    233-37; and perfection,
    237n.52
Barrowe, Henry, xiii
Barth, Karl, 73, 91, 229
Barton, Nathaniel, 99
Bates, Elisha, 118, 134n.149
Baxter, Richard, 3, 84, 88, 97, 134
Bayly, William, 190-91
Beaconite Controversy, 133

Bealand, Hugh, 93, 95
Becket, Thomas, xiiin.3, 31n.28,
    72n.76
Beckham, Edward, 131, 258, 264
Bedlam, 73, 257
Bennet, Gervase, 99
Benson, Gervase, 112
Benson, Lewis, 18
Biddle, John, 104
Bishop, George, 84n.22, 128, 147,
    163, 264
Bishoprick, 212
Bittle, W.G., 156, 166, 174, 214
Blasphemy, 19, 21, 63, 71, 76-78,
    84, 92-93, 97-100, 102, 104-
    113, 117,
    118, 123-124, 132, 161,
    163, 166, 169-71, 174, 178-
    81, 187-88, 210-11, 221-22,
    227, 229-31, 236, 241, 245,
    248, 253-59, 261, 263, 273-
    74, 283
Blasphemy Act, 98, 105-7, 111-
    113, 169, 171n.115
Blasphemy Ordinance, 98
Boehme, Jacob, xiii, 5, 12, 35, 193
Bogomils, 6
Book of Enoch, 33n.34
Boston Common, 72
Bourne, Edward, 65
Braithwaite, W.C., 135, 141, 269
Brauer, Jerald, 17
Brayshaw, A. Neave, 49, 72
Bridewell Prison, 173
Briggins, Peter, 58
Briggs, Thomas, 200
Bristol, 43, 145, 147-48, 159-63,
    165, 166, 173, 212, 215
Brockbank, E., 155
Brown, Thomas, 200
Bugg, Francis, 59, 68, 131, 264
Bull and Mouth Inn, 144
Bunderlin, Hans, 12
Bunyan, John, 5, 84, 88, 97, 124
Burden, Ann, 126, 128

336

DDS

DATE DUE
